ISTANBUL

Also by Thomas F. Madden

Venice
Empires of Trust

ISTANBUL

City of Majesty at the
Crossroads of the World

THOMAS F. MADDEN

VIKING

For Page, Helena, and Melinda
who always come too

CONTENTS

Part III
Ottoman Constantinople (1453–1923)

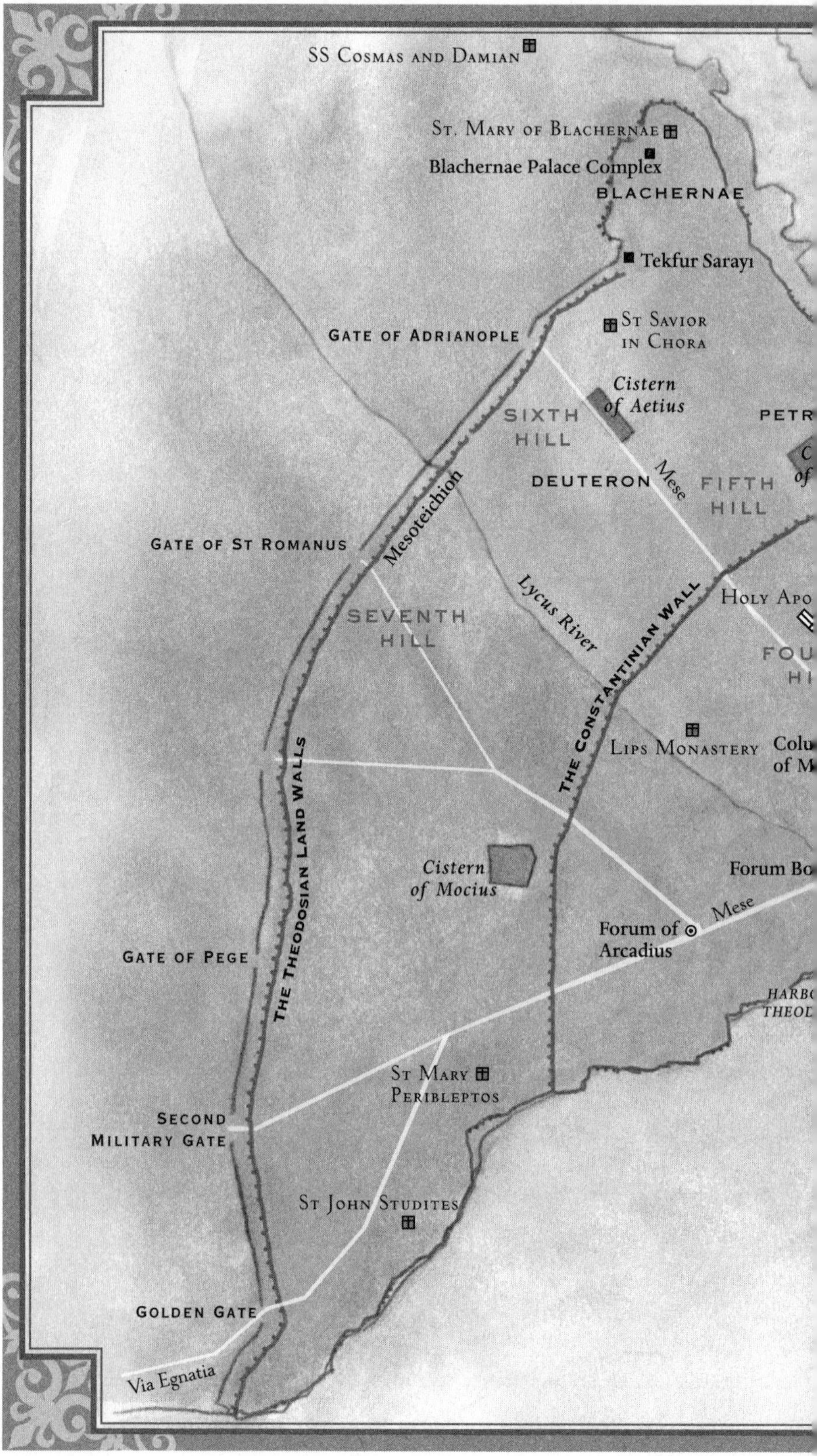

SS COSMAS AND DAMIAN

ST. MARY OF BLACHERNAE

Blachernae Palace Complex

BLACHERNAE

Tekfur Sarayı

GATE OF ADRIANOPLE

ST SAVIOR
IN CHORA

Cistern
of Aetius

PETR

SIXTH
HILL

DEUTERON   *Mese*   FIFTH
HILL

GATE OF ST ROMANUS

Mesoteichion

Lycus River

SEVENTH
HILL

HOLY APO

FOU
HI

LIPS MONASTERY

Colu
of M

THE CONSTANTINIAN WALL

Forum Bo

Cistern
of Mocius

Mese

Forum of
Arcadius

THE THEODOSIAN LAND WALLS

GATE OF PEGE

HARBO
THEOL

ST MARY
PERIBLEPTOS

SECOND
MILITARY GATE

ST JOHN STUDITES

GOLDEN GATE

Via Egnatia

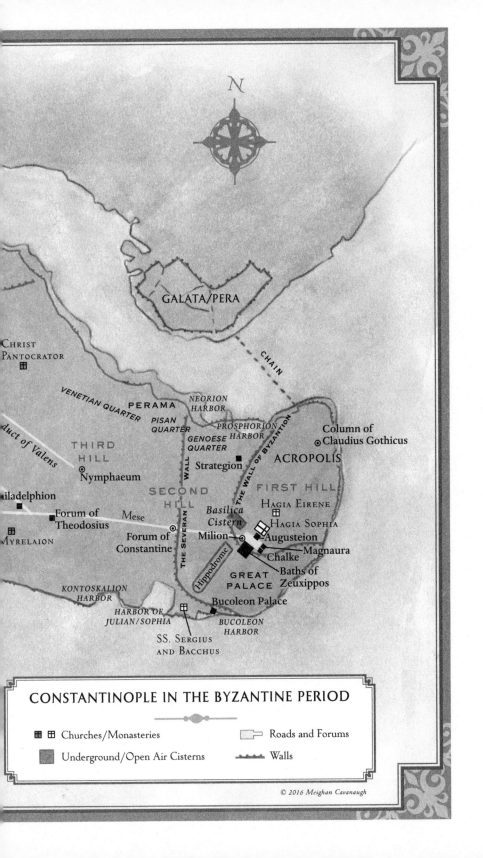

N

CHRIST
PANTOCRATOR

GALATA/PERA

CHAIN

VENETIAN QUARTER   PERAMA   NEORION
                            HARBOR
                   PISAN
                   QUARTER   PROSPHORION
aduct of Valens   THIRD   GENOESE   HARBOR
                  HILL   QUARTER   Column of
                                                  ⊙ Claudius Gothicus
                  ⊙ Nymphaeum   Strategion ▪   ACROPOLIS

iladelphion   SECOND   FIRST HILL
                 HILL   HAGIA EIRENE
▪ Forum of   ⊞
  Theodosius   Mese   Basilica   HAGIA SOPHIA
⊞   ⊙ Forum of   Cistern   Augusteion
MYRELAION   Constantine Milion ⊙   Chalke ── Magnaura
                                            Baths of
                             Hippodrome   Zeuxippos
                 KONTOSKALION   GREAT
                 HARBOR   PALACE
              HARBOR OF   Bucoleon Palace
              JULIAN/SOPHIA ⊞
                             BUCOLEON
                 SS. SERGIUS HARBOR
                 AND BACCHUS

CONSTANTINOPLE IN THE BYZANTINE PERIOD

⊞ ⊞ Churches/Monasteries   Roads and Forums

    Underground/Open Air Cisterns   Walls

© 2016 Meighan Cavanaugh

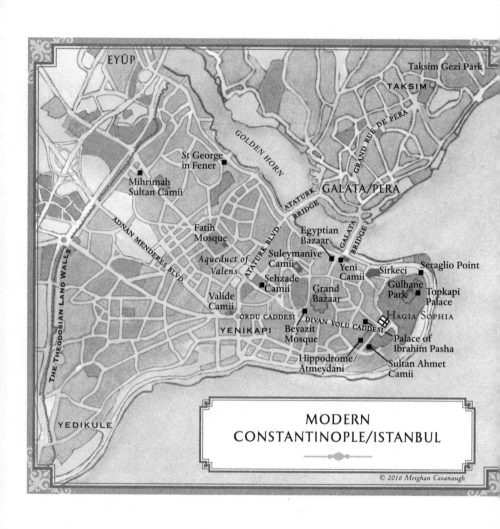

MODERN
CONSTANTINOPLE/ISTANBUL

© 2016 Meighan Cavanaugh

PREFACE

Though all other cities have their periods of government and are subject to the decays of time, Constantinople alone seems to claim a kind of immortality and will continue to be a city as long as humanity shall live either to inhabit it or rebuild it.

Pierre Gilles, *The Antiquities of Constantinople* (1548)

On the waves of the Sea of Marmara bobbed dozens of Greek triremes, sails full of wind, oars slapping noisily against the rowdy waters as they strained against the southern currents. Ahead to the north surged the Bosporus Strait, famed for dashing vessels against the walls of its rocky cliffs. Beyond that was *Pontos Axeinos*, the Inhospitable Sea, where pirates roamed and warlike tribes watched hungrily from the wooded shores. Pressing defiantly northward, the vessels entered the Bosporus. A few miles of hard going later, they shifted their sails and rudders to turn sharply west, toward the opening of a river there. Skirting easily into the placid waters of the natural harbor, the sailors disembarked, hauling their supplies onto shore. To the south rose the green hills of a verdant peninsula, thrusting out against the maw of the Bosporus. A half hour's climb up a nearby hill at the tip of the peninsula rewarded them with a breathtaking panorama of their new home. They stood in Europe, yet just across the strait to the east they could see the shores of Asia. Perched on the Greek frontier, they looked north to the endless Thracian forests and the Bosporus waterway, leading to mythical places unknown. It was here, around the year 667 BC, that these few hundred settlers broke ground on a bold new settlement.

Although in time it would grow in ways those colonists could never imagine, the city would ever remain suspended between worlds: Greeks and Persians, Western Romans and Eastern Romans, Catholics and Orthodox, Europeans and Asians, Christians and Muslims, West and East. In its many incarnations it would by turns become a den of debauchery, a city of saints, a smoldering ruin, and a glistening capital of two empires. It would be hailed as the greatest Christian city in the world before converting to Islam, taking on the mantle of the Muslim caliphate.

Today it is Istanbul. Yet across the centuries it has answered to many names: Byzantion, New Rome, Antoniniana, Constantinople, Queen of Cities, Miklagard, Tsargrad, Stamboul, Islambul, the Gate of Happiness, and perhaps most eloquently of all, "the City."

It remains the City. "Istanbul" is simply a Turkish hearing of the Greek phrase στην Πόλη, meaning "in or to the City." It was an appropriate name, for across the centuries it so dwarfed all other cities that it seemed to stand completely apart. It mattered little whether one was a thousand miles away from its majesty or just across the strait that splashed against its massive walls. "The City" was always the megalopolis on the Bosporus, set like a jewel between two continents and two seas.

It is hard not to stand in awe when considering the extraordinary history of this extraordinary place. Once, it was a magnificent city of rulers, a place in which geography conspired to give it dominion over its horizons. From its sprawling palaces, history's most powerful men sent forth commands to the distant reaches of their vast empires. The empires obeyed, revering their capital, showering it with wealth, adorning it with architectural marvels, and lifting it up to become a city above all others.

Although it has marked the passage of more than twenty-five centuries, Istanbul is no ruin of antiquity. It remains a vibrant, energetic, and exceedingly prosperous place. With nearly fifteen million inhabitants, Istanbul is today Europe's largest city, and the fifth largest in the world. Its financial districts are packed with modern skyscrapers teeming with commercial activity. Rapid increases across all sectors of Istanbul's economy form the engine that drives consistent and impressive growth throughout the entire country. After substantial increases post-2010, Turkey's economy was still growing at twice the rate of that of the European Union in 2014. Istanbul's rising prosperity is evident enough in its revived neighborhoods, beautiful parks, and flourishing art communities. Indeed, Istanbul has become one of the world's premier tourist destinations, touted regularly by the *New York Times* and the *Wall Street Journal* as a place of exotic delights, intriguing history, and a multitude of cultural attractions. Today Istanbul is known as much for its thriving art scene and chic restaurants as for the beauty of the Blue Mosque and the splendor of Topkapi Palace.

The purpose of this book is to bring together the history of this urban marvel into one enjoyable and clear narrative. It is, from the outset, an impossible task. The history of Istanbul is so complex, stretching across so many cultures, events, and lives, that a library of books would not suffice to capture it. Yet if the entire story cannot be told, at least the most important episodes and broadest vistas can be sketched. The overarching goal here is to open up the rich history of Istanbul to any interested reader, while offering guideposts along the way for further exploration. It is well worth the trip. The history of Istanbul is bound tightly to the history of the Western world. All the currents of Mediterranean commerce, thought, religion, and power ran through Istanbul's roads, wharfs, forums, and palaces. It is impossible to study antiquity, the Middle Ages, Christianity, or Islam without sailing past Istanbul's shores, visiting its academies, poking one's head into its churches and mosques. Then as now, it remains "the City."

My own fascination with Istanbul grew out of my study of the Middle Ages. While an undergraduate student, I was astonished to learn that long after the Roman Empire in Europe fell, it held lustily on to life in this city. There the forums remained full, the charioteers raced, and the emperors still ruled amid unrivaled splendor. I first visited Istanbul in 1986, at the beginning of my doctoral studies in history. American tourists were few. Conditions in the city, even in the core areas around the Blue Mosque, were poor. The smells of Istanbul were an unforgettable and inescapable part of the scenery. Some were pleasant, such as the savor of a street döner kebab or a wood-grilled fish on the wharf. But most were not. The worst were the cocktails of diesel exhaust belched from buses, raw sewage, and garbage piled on the streets, garnished with the stifling odor of the polluted Golden Horn waterway. Istanbul's taxis jammed the streets, piloted by men with a hand perpetually on the horn and windows down to bellow at other drivers or unlucky pedestrians. I loved it anyway. For, just beneath the crowded, noisy, malodorous chaos were layers upon layers of historical grandeur. Fourteen-century-old Hagia Sophia could be entered for the equivalent of fifty cents, and there were never lines. Ditto for the nearby Basilica Cistern. A venue for lavish functions and concerts today, the ancient Binbirdirek Cistern was entered through a hole in the ground where an old man rented flashlights to those brave enough to explore the rat-infested cavern.

Since those years, I have spent much time in Istanbul and a good portion of my career researching and writing about it. I have tried to bring the fruits of that work to this history. There is, of course, much to be found in this book on the physical city, its buildings, plazas, roads, and harbors. But above all I have tried to keep the focus on the human stories of those who lived there: the emperors and empresses, craftsmen and architects, sailors and fishermen, street vendors and harem concubines. They are all part of the rich diversity of this most cosmopolitan of cities.

Modern histories often privilege the modern. I have worked hard not to do that here. After all, anything that is twenty-five centuries old deserves our respect. By approaching Istanbul's long lifespan with a more even hand the richness of its earlier centuries is not lost behind the immediacy of contemporary events. Real history requires perspective. The long-lasting effects of the city's Nika Riots in AD 532 are clear enough; the effects of the failed military coup of 2016 are not. One of the difficulties in writing a general history is knowing when to stop. I have cautiously brought this narrative to the time of its writing, but have tried not to exaggerate the importance of current events simply because they are current. The history of Istanbul demonstrates repeatedly that small events scarcely noticed can have profound effects down the centuries. A bit of humility is always advisable when assessing the events of one's own age.

How this city came to dominate its worlds is a story worth the telling.

PART I

BYZANTION

667 BC–AD 330

Byzantion makes all merchant-captains drunk.

Menander, *The Flute Girl*

Chapter 1

———◆———

Across from the City of the Blind

The origins of Istanbul are found in the childhood of Western civilization. Two thousand seven hundred years ago it was common for bands of Greek colonists to board their triremes and roam the shores of the Mediterranean seeking new, profitable homes. Often they were simply groups of men dissatisfied with their current situations and seeking better ones elsewhere. Sometimes they were sent out by their city governments to found new dependent colonies. All these hardy voyagers sought rich, uncivilized lands where they could live securely and conduct trade. To the west, Sicily and southern Italy were already covered with Greek city-states, so many that the early Romans referred to the region as Magna Graecia (Greater Greece).

The Greeks had also begun eyeing lands to their northeast, where they planted new settlements along the coasts of the Sea of Marmara. Set between the Aegean Sea and the Black Sea, the Sea of Marmara was linked to the Greek world by the Hellespont (called today the Dardanelles), a thirty-eight-mile strait separating the continents of Europe and Asia. The islands and coast of the Sea of Marmara were endowed with plentiful resources, including lumber and marble, for which it received its name (*marmara*).

Around 750 BC the Greek city-state of Megara won its independence from nearby Corinth. Megaran merchants did a brisk business shipping textiles, wool, and livestock from their homelands to distant ports for impressive profits. Megaran goods could be found almost everywhere, but increasingly after 700 BC their merchants headed to the Sea of Marmara to sell their wares.

Like their fellow Greeks, the newly independent Megarans sent their first colonists westward to Sicily. Around 725 BC they founded Megara Hyblaea on the eastern shore of the island. Ancient references and modern archaeology testify that Megara Hyblaea was a prosperous port city. Nonetheless, the shift in Megaran trade to the northeast convinced the next group of colonists to settle in Thrace, on the northern shore of the Sea of Marmara. Founded on a steep hill to the east of a natural harbor, Selymbria (modern Silivri) quickly became a wealthy city. Fifteen years later, in 685 BC, the Megarans sent another group of colonists, who settled thirty miles to the west of Selymbria, on the Asian side of the water. Although it faced the Sea of Marmara, Chalcedon (modern Kadıköy) was just west of the Bosporus Strait, the only water link to the Black Sea. The current near Chalcedon was slow, so it must have been founded as a safe harbor for local merchant traffic, as well as a stopping point for those few entrepreneurs risking business along the strait.

In those early years these three Megaran colonies were a risky proposition. Travel from Greece to the Sea of Marmara was time consuming owing to the currents running south out of the Hellespont and to the contrary Etesian (or Meltemi) winds that blew from mid-May to mid-September. Tribes in the forests and plains near the Sea of Marmara were yet another problem. On the European side lived the fierce Thracians, while on the Asian side were the troublesome Bithynians. Yet as more Greek colonies were founded in the area, it slowly became a safer place, and therefore more profitable.

To the north lay the dangerous Black Sea. The Bosporus Strait, which stretches for twenty miles between the Sea of Marmara and the Black Sea and is less than half a mile wide at points, also had a reputation for peril. The popular story of Jason and the Argonauts credited the danger to giant wandering rocks that patrolled the strait in search of unwary vessels to crush. In Apollonius of Rhodes's version, Jason and his men sailed through the Bosporus but were stopped from entering the Black Sea by the Symplegades, massive boulders that slammed violently together when anything passed between them. Determined to defeat the trap, Jason released a dove that darted between the rocks. The giants crashed together with such force that water and steam exploded upward, obscuring the view. The dove made it through, losing only a few tail feathers in the journey. At once Jason ordered his men to row the *Argo* forward, before the rocks were able to strike again. This they did, although the contrary swell of the waters from the Black Sea nearly doomed them. Seeing their danger, the goddess Athena swept them forward—and just in time. The rocks crashed together once again, pulverizing a decoration on the ship's stern but leaving the men unharmed. Jason's victory broke the magic of the Symplegades, and henceforward the way to the Black Sea was open.

As the Greeks settled new colonies closer to the Black Sea it, too, became a less inhospitable place (at least for them). Increasingly they referred to it as simply Pontus, "the Sea." The Sea of Marmara they called Propontis, meaning "before the sea," suggesting that journeys northward were becoming more common. The Black Sea had much to recommend it to the merchants of the Greek world. There one could obtain the rich produce of the Danube and the Crimea, as well as goods that traveled overland from the Asian steppes from as far away as India. The Black Sea might be a difficult place, but the lure of profit was strong.

It was the search for profit that gave birth to the city of Istanbul. In or around 667 BC, ships filled with Megaran colonists sailed into the Bosporus searching for a new home. On the western side of the strait, within view of Chalcedon, arose a lush and hilly peninsula jutting out into the water. Immediately to its north flowed a wide and slow-moving river emptying lazily into the Bosporus. To the west of the peninsula were the dense forests and fertile soils of the Thracian countryside. It seemed in every way a perfect location for a commercial city. The river, which was soon named the Golden Horn (Chrysokeras), provided a natural harbor for vessels, protecting them from the swift currents of the Bosporus running south. It also acted as a fishery, catching with its curved shores confused schools on their way down to the Aegean. The fish in the Golden Horn were so abundant that they could be caught by hand, or by simply throwing rocks into the water. The high hill at the point of the peninsula (modern Seraglio Point) not only allowed one to survey the entire entrance to the mighty Bosporus, but was defended by steep sides and surrounding waters. This was a location from which one could, with sufficient naval strength, command the Bosporus, the link between the Black Sea and the Mediterranean Sea.

The Megaran colonists landed their vessels, performed their rituals of dedication, and began the hard work of building a new city. They named it Byzantion. Those first Greek settlers were engaging in a costly gamble. Chalcedon, just across the Bosporus, had already established itself as the center of commerce in that part of the Sea of Marmara. There was no need for a Greek merchant vessel to fight the Bosporus current to land at Byzantion when Chalcedon was so close and so convenient. Byzantion, though, was focused on a different market, one that remained unproven. For Byzantion to succeed, Greek commerce into the Black Sea needed to flourish.

And it did. Within a century, Greek colonies appeared along the upper Bosporus and even on the southern shores of the Black Sea. Trade through the strait became brisk. Soon Byzantion outstripped the older Chalcedon in every way. Indeed, visitors to the region often assumed that Byzantion was the original settlement and Chalcedon simply a suburb (as it would later become, and remains today). In the early sixth century BC, the Persian general Megabazus was astonished to learn that colonists from Megara had founded Chalcedon seventeen years before the settlement of Byzantion. How could the Chalcedons have missed the rich peninsula just across the Bosporus? He joked that Chalcedon must have been founded by a company of blind men.

Megabazus's jest quickly worked its way into the evolving myths of the city of Byzantion. Early colonists are generally too busy to write histories, leaving it to future generations to compose their own versions of their city's foundation. In Byzantion it was later claimed that the leader of the Megaran colonists was a man named Byzas, the son of the god Poseidon and the nymph Ceroëssa. Bards and poets told rapt audiences that Byzas had led his intrepid band first to the sacred shrines of Delphi, where they sought guidance from the wild prophetess known as the Sibyl. She advised them to found their new home "across from the city of the blind." Byzas was puzzled by the answer but set sail to look for this strange place nonetheless. In time, he and his men came upon the empty slopes of the Bosporus peninsula and stared with disbelief at the existing city across the waves. Surely, they exclaimed, Chalcedon was a city of the blind! That very day they founded Byzantion, named of course for their leader. He became, it was said, its first king.

There is no doubt that later generations of Byzantines believed the story of their heroic founder. Coins struck in Byzantion frequently bore the image of the fabled king Byzas (Illustration 1). The truth, though, is probably less colorful. Modern excavations on the acropolis prove that native Thracians established simple settlements there long before the Greeks of Megara arrived. Recent excavations in the Yenikapı area have also uncovered a Neolithic settlement of huts, graves, and even foot‑ prints dating back to 6000 BC. But there does remain a break in the archaeological record between 1200 BC and the foundation of Byzan‑ tion. So, while the peninsula was settled by Stone Age and Iron Age tribes, it appears to have been vacant when the Megaran colonists ar‑ rived. Were the Chalcedons truly blind? Of course, blindness had nothing to do with any of these choices. The colonists who had settled at Chalce‑ don were simply focused on a different market, one that would later be overshadowed by the growing commercial activity on the Bosporus.

Those first years were undoubtedly difficult for the people of Byzan‑ tion, as they struggled to build shelters and basic defenses against Thra‑ cian raiders. We may assume that they received some assistance and additional settlers from Megara, but others came to join them as well. We hear, for example, of a large number of settlers arriving from Mile‑ tus, on the Aegean coast of Asia Minor. There is no doubt that the city grew steadily during its first century, but how large it became is unclear. As with most Greek cities, its acropolis was the center of government and religious life. Around that, it had land walls that roughly corre‑ sponded to the existing walls around the Topkapi Palace and Gülhane Park. Seawalls were probably unnecessary. The swift current and steep hills along the Bosporus made an armed landing nearly impossible. And the Golden Horn itself could be protected by a thick chain suspended across the river's mouth and fastened to fortified towers on both sides. There must have been an agora, an open area for markets, civic meet‑ ings, and mustering troops. And of course there were shrines and tem‑ ples. Almost certainly there was a temple to Zeuxippus, a local Thracian version of the god Zeus.

Unfortunately, further information about the early history of Byzan‑ tion is scarce. Classical authors mentioned it only when it played a role in larger events. Archaeology is also not much help, given the extraordi‑ nary changes in the city in subsequent centuries. Excavations on the acrop‑ olis in the 1970s revealed a large amount of debris, including weights, figurines, and a vast array of pottery from this period. There is no doubt, then, that Byzantion was a small yet prosperous place.

Byzantion first comes into view on the world stage during the Persian Wars. Theoretically, the natural state of a Greek polis (city-state) was independence—although that did not halt powerful Greeks' bullying their Greek neighbors into submission. In principle, the ancient Greeks believed that civilized life could be found only in the freedom of their own self-governed city-states. Many non-Greeks disagreed. The Greeks, after all, were relative newcomers to civilization. There were far older, wealthier, and more powerful empires to the east. The Persian Empire, based in what is today Iran, had grown rapidly under the rule of Cyrus the Great (559–30 BC). Aside from employing his efficient armies, Cyrus had a novel and surprisingly successful strategy of conquest. When he selected a city, kingdom, or region to add to his empire he would offer the people there a simple choice. They could surrender, in which case their property would be left untouched and their persons unmolested. Leaders and bureaucrats could often keep their positions and even continue to follow their own laws, although they would be responsible to a Persian governor known as a satrap. Aside from that, the conquered were required only to keep the peace, pay a tribute, and provide troops for additional Persian conquests. Cyrus had no interest in changing local languages, religions, or customs. Good members of the Persian Empire could keep them all. Those who refused to surrender or who later rebelled felt the full violence that Cyrus could unleash. And it was awe inspiring. The vanquished had their property taken, their people massacred, and their cities leveled to the ground. Frequently all that remained of Cyrus's enemies were wastelands punctuated by mountains of skulls.

Most people surrendered. Even mighty Babylon gave up with scarcely a fight. When he entered the great Mesopotamian city, Cyrus not only released the captive Jews, but also ordered the rebuilding of their Temple in Jerusalem. This generosity earned Cyrus a prominent place in the Bible, where he is described as a heroic servant of God.

The Greeks did not share the Jews' enthusiasm for Cyrus or his benevolent rule. From their perspective, Cyrus was a barbarian—as were all non-Greeks. Because it was the natural state of Greek men to be free, it was therefore unnatural for them to be subject to non-Greeks. The Greeks closest to the expanding Persian Empire lived in western Asia Minor, where cities such as Troy, Ephesus, and Miletus flourished. In the mid-sixth century BC this region was loosely organized into the Kingdom of Lydia, ruled by Croesus from his capital at Sardis. Like Cyrus, Croesus was interested in expanding his territory, although his methods were less subtle. According to Herodotus, Croesus asked the Oracle at Delphi for advice on a war with Persia. The Oracle responded that Croesus should ally himself with the most powerful Greeks and that his attack would then cause the destruction of a mighty empire.

At some point in the 540s BC, Cyrus moved his forces into Lydia, brushing aside all opposition. Before the Greek allies could arrive to prosecute their invasion of Persia, Cyrus appeared outside the walls of Sardis. In short order, the Persians crushed the Lydian army and captured Croesus himself. The king was probably executed, although Herodotus tells a story in which Cyrus spared his enemy just before he was to be burned alive. In that version, Croesus became one of Cyrus's closest advisers. With or without Croesus, the Lydian kingdom was no more. The Oracle was right: a mighty empire had indeed been destroyed.

In the years after the conquest of Sardis, the Persians in Lydia were kept busy incorporating the various Greek city-states into their empire. As elsewhere, the Greeks were allowed to retain their property, religion, and customs provided they remained loyal. Satraps were appointed to oversee local governments, but even these were almost always chosen among the Greeks. The cities themselves were governed by Greek tyrants appointed by the satraps.

The people of Byzantion no doubt looked on the situation across the Bosporus with trepidation. Having expanded westward to the Aegean Sea, the Persian Empire was prepared to stretch across the strait into Thrace, thereby gaining a foothold in Europe. It is not clear precisely when it did that—certainly before 513 BC, when Byzantion is described within the Persian satrapy of Hellespontine Phrygia. By then, the ruler of the Persian Empire was Darius I (c. 522–486 BC), a man determined to expand his domain deep into Europe. To prepare the way, he was forced to deal with the Scythians, fierce nomads living north and east of the Black Sea. The Scythians had for some time been causing serious trouble for the Persians, conducting border raids, attacking Persian forces, and disrupting the lucrative Black Sea trade. Darius meant to stop it.

Around 513 BC, Darius led a large army to the Bosporus Strait, directly opposite the city of Byzantion. His plan was to cross over, march through Thrace, and then head north to the Danube, scouring the Black Sea coast of all Scythians. There was, though, the problem of the Bosporus, but Darius had a plan for that, too. Mandrocles, a Greek engineer from the island of Samos, had already begun construction on a wide bridge of boats, over which Darius's troops, animals, and wagons could cross. The bridge was built at the narrowest part of the Bosporus, precisely where the Fatih Sultan Mehmet Bridge is today suspended across the waters. Darius was so pleased with this floating marvel that he showered riches upon Mandrocles and placed two marble columns on the opposing shores to mark where he had once conquered the forbidding waves. On the columns, Darius listed the cities that had supported his campaign—in Greek on the western column and in Assyrian on the eastern one. The columns no longer survive, though apparently the Greek one was later sent to Byzantion to adorn a temple of Artemis.

Darius's expedition into Europe was only moderately successful. On the one hand, he never lost a battle. Yet that was only because the Scythians were willing to let their sparsely settled territory do the fighting for them. As the Persian forces marched north toward the Danube, the Scythians simply melted into the forests. With much difficulty Darius and his men crossed the great river, but they were unable to win a decisive victory against their retreating foe. Because there were no cities and little cultivation, there was no way for Darius to convince the Scythians to stand and defend their property. They had none. Finally, he ordered the construction of some fortifications to guard against further disruptions on the Black Sea and returned his army to Thrace. Although Darius himself returned to Sardis, he left one of his generals, Megabazus, to complete the Persian conquest of Thrace. It was this Megabazus who famously proclaimed that Chalcedon had been founded by blind men. Shortly thereafter Macedonia voluntarily allied with the Persian Empire. The territory of free Greeks was rapidly shrinking.

It was perhaps inevitable that the desire of Greeks for self-rule would clash with Persian hegemony. After decades of control by local tyrants and provincial satraps, the Greeks of Asia Minor longed for the idealized days of democracy. In 499 BC the tyrant of Miletus, Aristagoras, summoned the leading citizens of his city to propose a rapid strike against Persian control in the region to free the Ionian cities along the western shore of Asia. They agreed. No sooner did Miletus declare its independence than it was joined by nearly all the other Greek cities in Asia Minor. And from Greece itself came matériel and military support.

Ionian and Athenian forces met in the spring of 498 BC and began their march to the Persian provincial capital at Sardis. Unaware of the danger, the city quickly succumbed. The Greeks set fire to it, burning it to the ground. The core of Persian power in Asia had been destroyed, leading more and more cities to overthrow their satraps. Byzantion, too, declared its independence from Persia.

Darius blamed the Athenians for the rebellion. It was they, he believed, who had stirred up the Ionian Greeks with their talk of freedom and democracy. He swore that he would make them pay. According to Herodotus, Darius ordered a servant to remind him three times daily of his vow of vengeance against Athens. But it was not just Athens that needed taming. Darius also concluded that Greek cities in Asia and Thrace could never be firmly controlled while their cultural brothers remained free in Greece.

The first order of business was to put down the rebellion. The second was to end the Greek problem once and for all.

The Persians brought formidable forces to Asia, yet it still took several years to crush the Ionian revolt. Separate deals were hammered out with various Greek cities, some of which were willing to return to Persian rule in exchange for escaping the usual punishment meted out to rebels. But many cities remained loyal to the Ionian cause, even when clearly lost. The struggle culminated in 494 BC, when the Persians defeated a sizeable Ionian fleet and laid siege to the leading city of the revolt, Miletus. A proud showpiece nestled on the blue shore of the Aegean, Miletus had given the Greek world magnificent poetry, philosophy, art, and even the system of street grids still used by urban planners today. Now it was surrounded by a foreign army with a thirst for vengeance. It did not hold out long. When the walls finally crumbled, the Persian army rounded up the men of the city and put them to the sword. The women and children were sent to the slave markets, and what remained of the city was incinerated. Great Miletus was no more.

The same fate awaited each city in rebellion. After eliminating all opposition in Asia, the Persian armies headed for the Sea of Marmara and the Bosporus. The citizens of Byzantion and Chalcedon knew what fate awaited them. If they made a plea for mercy, it is not recorded. But neither did they stand and fight. Instead, they took everything they could carry and fled north to the Black Sea. There they founded a new city, Mesembria. When the Persians finally arrived at Byzantion they found only the winds of the Bosporus rustling through the empty streets. Like Miletus, Byzantion was eradicated.

True to his plan, Darius followed up his victory over the Greek rebels with campaigns against Greece itself. The naval attack on Athens in 490 BC was a complete disaster for the Persians, who had suffered enormous casualties at the Battle of Marathon. Darius redoubled his efforts, preparing to personally lead a massive invasion of Greece. But he would not live to see that war. In 486 BC the great warlord died in his bed.

Darius's extensive preparations continued uninterrupted under his son, Xerxes I (486–65 BC). The Persians already controlled most of the Aegean shore and many of its islands. In Thrace, provision stations were established to feed the thousands of Persian troops that would soon march across it. It is difficult to tell what part, if any, ruined Byzantion played in all this. Xerxes ordered the construction of two bridges of boats to be constructed at the Hellespont, south of the Sea of Marmara. The Persians' bypassing the Bosporus may suggest that Byzantion was still a field of rubble. There is evidence to suggest that Byzantion was resettled in the 480s, perhaps as a Persian naval base. According to Herodotus, Byzantion contributed one hundred vessels to Xerxes's invasion fleet. Xerxes did not initially enjoy his father's success with long floating bridges. The first attempt to cross the Hellespont was destroyed by storms, causing Xerxes to sentence the strait to be bound in irons and receive three hundred lashings. The sentence was carried out: irons were tossed into the sea, and Persian officials solemnly beat the water with their whips. The Hellespont responded favorably. The subsequent bridges were more successful, allowing Xerxes to march his armies into Greece in 480 BC.

Despite powerful military forces and careful preparations, Xerxes's invasion went poorly from the start. He was delayed, and suffered heavy casualties against the Spartans at the Battle of Thermopylae, although in the end he won the day. Desperate, the Athenians fled Athens, sailing across the water to the Isthmus of Corinth. The Persians burned Athens and then boarded their vessels to hunt down the last of the troublemakers. But at the Battle of Salamis, the Athenian navy defeated the Persians, sending thousands of their soldiers to the bottom of the sea. Most of the Persians were then ordered home to put down a revolt in Babylon, although Xerxes left sufficient forces to continue the war in Greece. The Athenian victory rallied other Greek cities, which banded together to defeat the Persians completely at the Battle of Plataea in 479 BC. Despite extraordinary efforts, the great empire of the East had failed to defeat the rebellious Greeks.

After the victory at Plataea the bronze armor and weapons of the fallen Persians were collected, melted down, and cast into a twenty-foot-tall statue of three serpents, all entwined around one another, with their heads forming the base of a sacred tripod at the top. The magnificent Serpent Column was then given to Delphi as a votive offering of thanks to Apollo for Greece's surprising, seemingly miraculous victory. The warriors of the Dorian Greek state of Sparta placed a pedestal nearby the column, proclaiming that it was a monument in memory of the Spartan contribution to the destruction of the Persians. When pilgrims from other Greek cities objected to Sparta's version of events, the pedestal was removed. In its place, the names of the allied cities were inscribed on the lowest coils of the snakes. That column, which has been on outdoor public display for twenty-five hundred years, is today in Istanbul very near the Blue Mosque. How this fascinating relic came to be there, though, is a story for another chapter.

In the aftermath of the Persian defeat, Greek cities everywhere proclaimed their independence. In some places this required armed action. It was the genius of Persian administration that it relied as much as possible on local citizens. That meant that there were more than a few

Greeks who had profited under Persian rule, and who were now out of a job. Some fled to Persia; others bided their time, hoping for a return of the Persian armies. In Byzantion it appears that Persian interests held on. In 478 BC, Greek forces led by Pausanias, the son of the Spartan king Cleombrotus, liberated Byzantion. The population of the city was probably small, but it may have been augmented by people returning from exile. There is no doubt that Pausanias put considerable effort into securing and refurbishing the city, and as a result gained popularity with the citizens. For all its troubles, Byzantion remained a strategically placed city with a potential for rich profits.

Unfortunately, Pausanias had problems of his own. Back when he was in Sparta he had been charged with conspiring with the Persians to lead a rebellion that would put Sparta in the empire and him as its ty/ rant. He was tried and found not guilty. Now in Byzantion, those sus/ picions arose again. First there were the high/level Persian prisoners in Byzantion who somehow managed to "escape" back to the court of Xerxes. Then there were the whispers of Persian emissaries ushered into the residence of the Spartan general. Some feared that Pausanias would hand over Thrace to the Persians in return for a powerful posi/ tion in conquered Greece. Whether there were any grounds for these fears remains a mystery. There was enough evidence, though, for the Spartan authorities to recall Pausanias to stand trial at home. As before, he was cleared of all charges.

Pausanias returned to Byzantion without an army, but with a well/ spring of goodwill. The citizens of Byzantion proclaimed him leader. He established a government and legal code, modeled unsurprisingly on Sparta. He began building projects and restored ports and markets. The city was once again a center for fishing and trade. Coins began to be minted in Byzantion, and hoard finds suggest that they circulated widely.

Close to royal power in Sparta, Pausanias may have hoped to use Byzantion as a foundation for forming his own kingdom in Thrace. In another age, that might have happened. But in the aftermath of the Persian Wars, Athens was determined to organize the Greek city/states into a defensive alliance to ward off any further invasions. Byzantion was crucial to that effort. Not only could the city resist a Persian cross/ ing of the Bosporus, but more immediately, it could ensure the free flow of grain from the Black Sea. This was important to Athens and other Greek coastal towns without access to large agricultural regions. No enemy, Persian or Greek, could be allowed to close off that strait.

Pausanias's plans for Byzantion, whatever they were, did not agree with those of the Athenian commander of forces, Cimon, who expelled him from the city. Pausanias went to Colophon, in Asia, but a few years later he was again accused of conspiring with the Persians and returned to Sparta. Once again he was cleared of all charges, but his enemies continued to search for evidence. It appears they found something, for Pausanias fled to Sparta's Temple of Athena for sanctuary. The building was sealed, and he starved to death.

Byzantion had paid dearly for the cause of Greek independence. Now, as the city regained its population and restored its properties, it faced a new challenge to its freedom—not from the Persians, but from its Greek defenders.

Chapter 2

Bread for Athens

With the defeat of the Persian Empire the people of Byzantion faced a new era. The fierce wars that had so long raged across Asia Minor and Greece were over. Without the Persian threat, the Greeks were free to pursue their own interests, choose their own governments, and make war on their Greek neighbors at will. This was their way. The Spartans' return home after the liberation of Byzantion was a bold statement that they would no longer prosecute a war once it had met all its objectives.

The Athenians disagreed. Athens had been the Persians' prime target, and its citizens paid for their defiance with blood, treasure, and a home reduced to ashes. They were determined not only to neutralize the threat but also to make certain it never rose again. They would not abandon the Ionian cities of Asia Minor still under Persian rule. So, when the Spartans withdrew from the city of Byzantion, the Athenians arrived in force.

The Athenian idea was big, though deceptively simple. They proposed an alliance of free Greek city-states working together to drive the Persian Empire completely out of the Aegean Sea and Greek Asia Minor. The interested cities held a meeting on the centrally located Aegean island of Delos. There, they forged a pact to work together to neutralize the Persians, exact retribution for their attacks on the Greeks, and see to the continued defense of the allied members. To that end, all the cities would contribute men, ships, and materiel, which would be stockpiled on Delos. Thus was the Delian League formed—and of course Byzantion was a prominent member.

At first all went as planned. The league defeated the Persians, ejecting them completely from the Greek world. But success brought its own problems. With the threat diminished, the Athenians offered to league members the option of contributing money rather than troops and ships.

Since it was cumbersome to keep armies active in a time of peace, most of the cities availed themselves of that option. It is a testament to the healthy economy of Byzantion that its assessed contribution was one of the largest in the league. As before, all funds were stored at Delos, although increasingly the governance of the league was falling to Athens.

Athens's dominance did not go unnoticed. League assessments were not small. Indeed, they had to be sufficient to hire the troops and build the ships that a city would otherwise have contributed. As a result, member cities were largely drained of the funds necessary to muster their own troops or prosecute their own wars. It was not long before some of the members expressed a desire to depart the league. Secession, they would learn, was not an option. When Naxos announced its departure around 471 BC, the league declared war. Naxos's fortifications were destroyed, and it was forced back into the alliance, now without a vote. A similar fate awaited subsequent rebels. The Delian League was a strong but indivisible union.

No doubt many in Byzantion resented the high costs of league membership. But they were in no position to object. Much of the food on Athenian tables made its way from the rich lands of the Ukraine and Crimea, across the Black Sea and through the straits of the Bosporus and the Hellespont. It was absolutely vital that the Athenians maintain control over these strategic waterways. An inscription found in Athens, dating probably to the 420s BC, refers to "Hellespontine Guards" based at Byzantion. The job of these officials was to inspect all grain shipments moving south through the Bosporus and to direct them either toward Athens or to other Aegean allies. This was not something the Athenians were willing to leave to the whims of local merchants. It meant a permanent Athenian presence in Byzantion.

By the mid-fifth century BC the Delian League had become the most powerful military force in Greek history—and a de facto Athenian Empire. In 454 BC the leader of Athens, Pericles, ordered the Delian League treasury relocated from Delos to Athens and began using the league's money to beautify Athens, constructing monumental buildings such as the famous Parthenon. Athens had become the capital city for millions of Greeks who had fought for independence from Persia. In the end, they had traded one overlord for another.

Sparta was strong enough to remain out of the Delian League, and to defend its friends should the league try to bully them into joining. In practice, that meant that the Greek world quickly divided itself into two armed camps. After years of skirmishing, the Peloponnesian War between Athens and Sparta began in 431 BC. The people of Byzantion probably took no active role in the war, but their financial contributions and defense of the Bosporus were essential for Athenian efforts. Almost immediately the Spartan armies destroyed the farmlands around Athens and surrounded its walls. Since Athens relied principally on its powerful navy and access to commercial shipping, the Spartan attack had little effect. As long as the grain barges sailed past the city of Byzantion bound for Athens, all was well.

Yet passive support did not mean active love for Athens. Many in Byzantion likely remembered, perhaps inaccurately, the old days of Pausanias when Sparta built up their city. There is no doubt that a sizeable portion of the population in Byzantion looked to Sparta to free them from the Athenian yoke. This was demonstrated vividly in 413 BC, when news of a stunning defeat for Athens buzzed through the busy ports of Byzantion. Two years earlier, the Athenians had sent a fleet of more than one hundred vessels under the command of Alcibiades to defeat the Greek city of Syracuse. They had been responding to an Ionian request for aid, but it was also an opportunity to wage war on Spartan colonies on the wealthy island of Sicily. Had Athens been successful, the Athenian Empire would have become a truly Mediterranean-wide power. But the Athenian forces were not just defeated, they were completely wiped out. For the first time since the Persian Wars, Athens lay prostrate.

The response to Athens's defeat was the same in Byzantion as in dozens of cities across Ionia and the Aegean. The leaders of the city ejected the Athenian officials, renounced their membership in the Delian League, and offered to support Sparta's new Peloponnesian League. Persia even offered to send money and troops to support Sparta against its old rival. Athens was torn apart by factionalism. In so much chaos, Byzantion was once again free and independent.

But the Peloponnesian War was not yet over. The Athenian commander Alcibiades went east and gained control over a fleet of one

hundred Athenian vessels stored at Samos in case of extreme emergency. That emergency, he reasoned, had come. He refused to recognize an oligarchic revolution in Athens that had been organized to seek
peace from Sparta. He did not attack Athens, but he put sufficient pressure on the city to bring it back to its customary democracy. Then he
turned his fleet northward, heading directly for the straits. At the Hellespont, Alcibiades came upon a Spartan fleet supporting the nearby
rebel cities and cutting off grain shipments to Athens. At the Battle of
Cyzicus in 410 BC, he destroyed the Spartans and restored the region
to Athenian control. He then moved north into the Sea of Marmara
and sailed directly for the mouth of the Bosporus, toward Byzantion.

For those citizens of Byzantion who looked out that day from the
acropolis to see the billowing sails of a hundred Athenian vessels below,
it must have seemed like a recurring bad dream. How could Athenians
be in these waters again, and in such force? Still, Byzantion was prepared to defend itself with a respectable fleet and army, and the Spartans sent a small force under the command of Clearchus. They would
not so easily surrender.

Unfortunately for the Byzantines, this firm resolution was not shared
by other rebel cities. With a measured dose of threats and mercy, Alcibiades had already restored to Athenian obedience most of the cities
along the Hellespont and the shores of the Sea of Marmara. The nearby
city of Selymbria had surrendered almost immediately, accepting an
Athenian garrison in exchange for complete forgiveness. When Byzantion refused a similar deal, Alcibiades set up a naval blockade and laid
siege to the land walls to starve out the defenders. To ensure that traffic
continued to flow on the Bosporus in the meantime, he built a fortified
naval base just across the Bosporus, at the city of Chrysopolis (modern
Üsküdar) and began charging tolls. Alcibiades had come to stay.

Perched on the tip of the peninsula, ancient Byzantion was vulnerable to encirclement. Since Alcibiades ruled the waves, food and other
supplies became increasingly scarce. It was also impossible to do business, which meant the money dried up. Unless something were done
soon, Byzantion would fall. Faced with this grim calculus, Clearchus left
the city to seek additional support and funds from Sparta. It was up to
the Byzantines to hold out until he returned.

Yet no sooner had Clearchus departed than a party arose in Byzantion favoring surrender. Its members were tired of suffering depredation while their neighbors lived comfortably after making peace with Athens. They insisted that envoys be sent to Alcibiades to request a similar arrangement for Byzantion. The surrender party was opposed by a pro-Sparta party, which likely included Spartan members of the city garrison. They swore that they would never give up the fortified area of the acropolis, making any surrender negotiations futile. The people should be patient: wait for Clearchus and the help he would bring. No amount of debate could close the gap between these two positions. Only action could decide the issue. One day, those who favored surrender simply laid down their arms and walked out of the city, claiming to be loyal partisans of Athens. The defending garrison remained firm, but that was largely because the pro-Spartans refused to allow any of the soldiers to leave the fortifications. Sensing that the resistance was unraveling, Alcibiades sent a decree to the garrison in which he personally guaranteed the security of all those who surrendered. That was enough. Most of the garrison switched sides, killing the pro-Spartans and securing the entire city, which they promptly handed over to Alcibiades. The Athenian was as good as his word. Byzantion was left unmolested, although the city was once again firmly under control of the Delian League.

Alcibiades's triumphs saved Athens from military defeat, but could do nothing about its political ills. Rife with factionalism and unforgiving of any defeat, the democracy did not reelect Alcibiades in 406 BC. Subsequent naval defeats led to the trial and execution of many of Athens's top commanders. All this happened while a Spartan general, Lysander, seized the initiative in the ongoing war. In 404 he led a powerful navy back to the Hellespont to cut off Athens's grain. Athens responded by sending an equally powerful fleet to clear the straits. Yet at the Battle of Aegospotami, Lysander crushed the Athenian forces. Securing the Hellespont, Lysander then sailed to Byzantion. Another Athenian fleet attempted to cut him off, but that, too, was quickly dispatched. Once again the seas that surrounded Byzantion were covered in sails, yet this time the vessels were Spartan. With no hope for support from Athens, Byzantion and Chalcedon surrendered, expelling the Athenian officials who had so recently been restored.

The loss of Byzantion was cataclysmic for the Athenians. It was the strategic cornerstone of their empire. Without it, they simply could not continue. They surrendered to Sparta that very year. The Peloponnesian War had at last come to an end.

Byzantion had long chafed under the Athenian Empire. Yet if the Byzantines believed that its demise would bring them greater freedom, they were deceived. Sparta knew well that Byzantion was the leash by which they could hold, or choke, Athens. They would not let it out of their grasp so easily again. The council in Sparta sent to Byzantion a garrison under the command of Clearchus, the same commander who had defended the city against Alcibiades in 409 BC. Needless to say, he was troubled by the events of Byzantion's late defection to the Athenians. Spartan blood and that of Sparta's friends had been spilled in Byzantion by simpering cowards unwilling to abide by their oaths or await aid from their allies. Clearchus would make them pay. He ordered the arrest and execution of all members of the prosurrender party, including many of great wealth and high position. He then established a tyranny that was characterized by a reign of terror so cruel that even the government in Sparta objected. Eventually they recalled Clearchus to stand trial for his crimes against Byzantion. Found guilty and sentenced to death, he fled Sparta, taking up a position in the court of the Persian emperor, Cyrus the Younger.

Since the days of the Delian League, the form of a city's government was often chosen by the nature of its alliances. Athens, the inventor and champion of democracy, looked favorably on those cities that adopted its government. Likewise, Sparta, which was ruled by an oligarchy, promoted that system. With the defeat of Athens, democracy had lost its main proponent. Athens had become an oligarchy under the control of Sparta known as the Thirty Tyrants. Byzantion, too, adopted an oligarchy. Like Athens, Byzantion's government was answerable to Sparta. And given Byzantion's economic and strategic value, Spartan officials remained in the city. Conditions had improved since the bloodbath of Clearchus, yet it appears there remained a good deal of opposition to Sparta's hold on the city. Once again, the fog of memory made Byzantion's days in the defunct Athenian alliance seem preferable to their current Spartan masters.

Fortunately for the Byzantines, the Peloponnesian War had so exhausted Sparta and Athens that neither was in a position to exert the sort of crushing power they had once wielded. Sparta's Thirty Tyrants in Athens did not last long before a former Athenian general, Thrasybulus, cobbled together an army of exiles and toppled them. A lifelong proponent of Athenian democracy, Thrasybulus later began his own campaign of spreading Athenian values and influence across the remnants of Athens's former empire. Where democracies struggled against Spartan tyrannies, Thrasybulus took notice—and in many cases he could offer material and military aid. Around 390 BC, he was sailing through the Aegean seeking just such opportunities. Recognizing a chance to evict the Spartans, the leaders of Byzantion formed a democracy and requested his aid. It was swiftly given. Thrasybulus brought his Athenian fleet into Byzantion's port and ordered the remaining Spartans out. Without support from home, they had no choice but to comply.

A democracy in Byzantion signaled a friendship with Athens, and for the next decade or so, Byzantion was largely left to govern itself for the first time since the Persians crossed the strait more than a century earlier. In 377 BC, Athens formed a second league, this one aimed against an increasingly belligerent Sparta. The Athenians made clear in the new charter (which survives) that the member cities were to remain autonomous, with one vote each. No decision could be made in Athens without the approval of the league. More important, there were to be no tribute payments, and therefore no money to tempt Athenian tyrants to construct new empires. Byzantion joined the league, although it is not precisely clear what if anything the city contributed to the ensuing wars. By 371 the second league had defeated the Spartans, who would never again be in a position to build an empire. With the threat gone, there was no longer any reason to maintain the alliance. But once again the Athenians were reluctant to let it go. Finally, in 357 BC, Byzantion, Chios, Rhodes, and Cos overthrew their democratic governments and withdrew from the league. An Athenian fleet was sent to Chios but failed to take the island. It then made its way to Byzantion, where it was defeated as much by the weather as by the rebels. It was a pitiful little war, fought halfheartedly by a twilight power. The age of the Ionians was coming to an end.

What came to take its place, no one could have foreseen. It came from Macedon, a rough, hilly territory in what is today the central and western parts of the province of Macedonia in Greece. The people who lived there were Greeks—at least they claimed to be. Many of the Greeks in the sophisticated south had their doubts. The Macedonians spoke a Greek dialect, but they had a low, primitive culture. Mainstream Greeks had long since banished despotism and royal dynasties, insisting on their more refined oligarchies or democracies, punctuated periodically by tyrannies when necessary. The Macedonians, on the other hand, had a dynastic monarchy, practiced polygamy, and had little or no exposure to Greek philosophy. They were a boorish, warlike people who lived without a polis. They were not barbarians—most Greeks would give them that. But they were uncomfortably close, an embarrassment to the refined culture of classical Greece.

The Kingdom of Macedon came most dramatically to Greek attention during the 350s BC, when its king, Philip II, began waging vigorous wars to consolidate his power at home and expand his kingdom to the north and south. During those years, Philip often came into conflict with Athens, which attempted to rally its defenses against this latest threat to Greek liberty. When Philip captured Thessaly he became the most powerful leader in the region. Fearful of conquest, many of the Greek city-states began to submit to him. Athens and Sparta did not.

One of Philip's major initiatives in the 340s was to expand his kingdom to include Thrace. He sent his armies against the Scythians, just as the Persians had done in their day. Flush with victories, Philip and his forces arrived in the vicinity of Byzantion. In 340 BC he laid siege to Byzantion and the nearby Greek city of Perinthos, about sixty miles to the west. The conquest of Byzantion would pave the way for a planned campaign eastward against the Persians, and also give Philip solid control over the lucrative traffic that sailed through the Bosporus. Byzantion remained the key to starving proud Athens, and Philip was determined to make use of it.

Yet the Byzantion of 340 BC was better fortified and more energetically defiant than the Byzantion of a decade earlier. The land walls of the city had been rebuilt on such a massive scale that they were considered among the best in the Greek world. Later authors describe the fortifications as having been made from giant, perfectly cut stones forged together so closely with iron bands that they appeared to be solid rocks defending the city. Philip kept up the siege for the better part of a year, during which he burned the crops in the fields and ravaged much of the surrounding countryside. The people of Byzantion sent word to Athens of their plight, and the Athenians eventually responded. Just as things looked the darkest for Byzantion, a fleet of Athenian vessels was spied on the horizon of the Sea of Marmara. The Athenians brought with them soldiers, supplies, and arms. Philip at last relented, dismantled his siege, and returned to Mace, don. It was an uncharacteristic, almost unheard of, defeat for the king, one that damaged his reputation in the Greek world. In Byzantion the people rejoiced and credited the victory to the divine assistance of Hecate, the Greek goddess of crossroads, a favorite in this city of passages. Shortly af, ter Philip's defeat, the Byzantine coins would be minted with the image of a moon and star, the symbol of Hecate. By pure coincidence, it is the same symbol that appears on flags across modern Istanbul.

According to Demosthenes, who worked with now,lost city records, the Assembly in Byzantion met to honor Athens for its support. Demos, thenes quotes a decree produced "in the recordership of Bosporichus," in which a Byzantine assemblyman named Damagetus made a sweeping proposal. After commending the Athenians for saving Byzantion and Perinthos, the proposal stated that henceforth Athenians should have in Byzantion and Perinthos the right of intermarriage, the right to become citizens, the right to own property in the cities, the right to petition the Assembly, and the right to prime seating at the city's games. Further, more, it ordered the creation of a monument that would consist of three colossal statues twenty,four feet in height, representing the cities of By, zantion and Perinthos jointly crowning Athens. It was to be placed in "the Bosporeum," which was likely in the acropolis area. For those unable to see the monument, delegates were to be sent to all the pan,Hellenic games to describe the honor so that "the Greeks may know the merits of the Athenians and the gratitude of the Byzantines and the Perinthians."

Philip, of course, held quite a different view of Athenian meddling in his Thracian campaigns. Indeed, he considered it a direct violation of his treaties with Athens. During the next several years he and his teen, age son, Alexander, waged repeated wars in the south to pacify the Greek city,states, Athens in particular. In the end, they were successful. In 338 BC, Philip organized the Greek cities into a league, which histo,

rians refer to as the League of Corinth. It had one purpose: to launch a
Greek invasion of Persia. The tables were about to be turned.

Yet not by Philip. Less than two years later the king was assassinated
by a member of his own bodyguard. At the age of twenty, Alexander
(soon to be "the Great") took the throne. Since this was Greece, Athens
and most of the other city-states instantly rebelled, but Alexander
moved decisively to bring them to heel. He also waged war in Thrace to
further stabilize that wild region. With his position in Greece secure,
Alexander took up his father's project: he began mustering troops to
invade what remained of the Persian Empire.

We can only assume that the people of Byzantion greeted the news
of Philip's death with some relief. Outside of Sparta, there were few
places in Greece that had successfully defied Philip. There seemed little
doubt that Philip would have eventually returned to Byzantion to claim
the strait. And he would be angry. With Athens subdued, there was no
longer anyone to come to Byzantion's aid. Of course, there remained
the danger of Alexander. Yet amazingly that dissolved, too. It may be
that the young king was more eager than his father to begin a campaign
in the East, and therefore did not want the delay of a long siege on the
Bosporus. Or perhaps he simply considered Byzantion a moot point
with Athens firmly in hand. Whatever the reason, Alexander completely bypassed Byzantion, crossing his formidable armies into Asia at
the Hellespont. Much to their delight, the Byzantines became bystand-
ers to the Macedonian conquests.

The departure of Alexander's forces from Greece would change the
world. Under his command, the Greek and Macedonian armies conquered Asia Minor, Syria, Palestine, Egypt, Assyria, Babylonia, and all
of Persia in a stunning, truly unprecedented campaign. Alexander then
continued east into India before his armies finally revolted and refused
to go farther. Alexander at last returned to Babylon, where he died,
perhaps poisoned, at the age of thirty-two.

Alexander's conquests fundamentally reshaped the culture of antiquity
and ensured the Greek cultural dominance of the West. Greek language
would henceforth become that of the elites throughout the eastern Mediterranean. Greek potentates would rule in Asia, in Africa, and in Europe.
This new age, referred to by historians as the Hellenistic period, would see

a marked increase in Greek commerce, wealth, and cultural output. Byzantion, which was now a free democracy, took full advantage of those changes. As the city grew in population and affluence, it expanded its control over nearby regions. The city of Chalcedon, on the opposite shore of the Bosporus, had merged into Byzantion sometime after Philip's siege. By the time of Alexander's death in 323 BC, Byzantion's influence stretched far into Thrace to the West and into Bithynia in the East. The Byzantines, therefore, had a firm hold on the northern Sea of Marmara as well as both sides of the southern Bosporus Strait. This was an attractive position indeed.

As coins poured into its coffers and a rich diversity of merchants appeared on its docks, Byzantion began to acquire a reputation as a cosmopolitan, albeit hedonistic city. Theopompus of Chios, writing around the 320s BC, explained that since the Byzantines were free members of a democracy and living at a commercial hub, "their entire population spends their days in the marketplaces and near the waterside; hence they have become accustomed to sexual debauchery and drinking deeply in the taverns." Theopompus lamented that the Chalcedons had once been sober and honest, yet after they joined their city to Byzantion, "they descended into corrupt luxury" and soon became "drunks and big spenders."

There must have been something to this assessment, for Theopompus was not alone in making it. Athenaeus of Naucratis, writing in the second century AD, but using ancient poets as his source, described the people of Byzantion as "all drunk with wine and indeed virtually living in the wine shops." He continued: "They rent out their bedrooms along with their wives to any customers. They cannot stand to hear the trumpets of war, even in a dream. In fact, once when a war was declared on them their general Leonides ordered the city's wine dealers to set up shops on the walls, which at last convinced the Byzantine defenders to stop leaving their posts." The Greek playwright Menander, who wrote around 300 BC, took advantage of this well-established stereotype in his works. In *The Flute Girl*, he has an Athenian merchant exclaim, "Byzantion makes all merchant-captains drunk. We drank for you—and good strong stuff too. And now that we have finished, I will tell you, I have four heads instead of just the one."

With wealth and wine came, naturally, song and poetry. Surely Byzantion had an active culture before 300 BC, but we know nothing of it. That is the fault of the papyrus on which the poems, songs, histories, and official records were penned. Papyrus scrolls were durable and cheap, but depending on the climate, they generally survived for only a few centuries. That means, of course, that almost all the words entrusted to writing in the ancient world have been lost. All that survive are some fragments preserved in desert caves and burials, carved inscriptions, and a handful of works that were thought important enough for medieval monks to copy onto parchment many centuries later. Artfully designed pottery fragments found in excavations in Byzantion's acropolis (near the modern Archaeological Museums) testify to growing wealth and imply a flowering of culture in the bustling and sprawling city of the new Hellenistic Age.

During this period, Byzantion was home to Moero, one of ancient Greece's finest female poets. At an early age she produced accomplished heroic poetry. Later she penned epic poems, including one called *Memory*, which told a story of Zeus's childhood. She also wrote a hymn to Poseidon, a narrative poem called *The Curse*, and a variety of short epigrams, including one on the death of a grasshopper. Meleager of Gadara, the ancient collector of epigrams, described Moero's poems as "lilies" woven into his garland of poetry. Barest snippets of her extensive body of work have come down to us today—and those are florid little things. One, for example, is an epigram on a bunch of grapes, which may have accompanied a sculpture or painting.

> Cluster, full of the juice of Dionysus,
> Thou restest under the roof of Aphrodite's golden chamber;
> No longer shall the vine, thy mother, cast her lovely branch
> around thee,
> And put forth above thy head her sweet leaves.

While this is hardly genius, it is unfair to judge Moero's skill on so little evidence. There is no doubt that her contemporaries thought highly of her. The famous Greek sculptor Cephisodotus, son of Praxiteles, is said to have produced a statue of her, which perhaps was displayed in Byzantion.

Moero was either the mother or daughter of another great poet, Homerus of Byzantion. A grammarian and tragic poet, Homerus saw his celebrated work win him a place in the lavish court of King Ptolemy II

Philadelphus, the Greek ruler of Egypt. Ptolemy and his family were generous patrons of science and the arts. Indeed, he is credited with patronizing the Septuagint translation of the Hebrew Bible into Greek. Like the other poets in rich Alexandria, Homerus probably wrote works extolling the monarch. Yet his real talent lay in his more than forty tragic plays, many of which were presumably written and performed in his native Byzantion. All are lost.

The names of only a few other Byzantines from the third century BC survive. Philo of Byzantion, like Homerus before him, was drawn to the wealth of Hellenistic Alexandria. Philo, though, was an accomplished engineer and the author of the *Compendium of Mechanics*, which had chapters on buildings, artillery, mechanical toys, and pneumatics. Among his many inventions, Philo is credited with the first plans for a working water mill. Epigenes of Byzantion was also a mathematician, although with a spiritual bent. He was an astrologer, a branch of fortune-telling that Greek intellectuals generally considered disreputable. He appears to have kept careful astronomical records, including precise observations on the movement of Saturn. Although his work does not survive, his name has ascended into the heavens. A crater thirty miles in diameter on the northern region of the moon is named for him.

The remainder of the third century was a golden age for Byzantion. Just as Alexander the Great had passed it by, so, too, did the great wars and tribulations of the times. In 279 BC the deadly armies of the Gauls pressed into Thrace from the north, determined to loot, pillage, and conquer the now-famed riches of Greece. Since their primary targets were to the south, the Gauls left Byzantion in peace in exchange for a nominal tribute payment. A large contingent of the Gauls that broke from the main armies crossed the Bosporus near Byzantion on their way to join a civil war in nearby Bithynia. These would later settle in northern Anatolia, becoming better known as the Galatians.

Byzantion was threatened again in the 220s BC, but this seems to have been a symptom of its increasing wealth and tighter control over the Bosporus. The navy of Rhodes and the king of Bithynia attacked Byzantion over a toll dispute. Apparently the Byzantines had begun overcharging some merchant vessels to use the strait. Byzantion itself was unharmed for, true to type, the Byzantines agreed to terms rather than hear the trumpets of war.

The people of Byzantion had suffered mightily during the Greek wars largely because they commanded the straits crucial to Athens's survival. With relative peace in the wake of Alexander's conquest, Byzantion found its element. As the ancient poets and writers make abundantly clear, Byzantion was a place of commerce, hedonism, and a strong aversion to war. The Hellenistic Age satisfied these desires in full measure.

Chapter 3

———◆———

Romans Bearing Gifts

To imagine Byzantion in the Hellenistic Age, one must banish any hint of the image of modern Istanbul. The forests of concrete and plains of asphalt that now stretch to the horizon were once thick with towering trees and rich carpets of grass. In the third century BC most of what is today known as the "old city" was uninhabited. The Greek polis of Byzantion was a compact community perched at the very tip of the peninsula, its streets flowing downward from an acropolis set on the rocks that are today under Topkapi Palace. The entire city was only as large as the modern palace grounds, Gülhane Park, and Hagia Sophia. Altogether approximately twenty thousand people lived inside the walls, making it a moderate-size city for its age. Still more dwelled across the Bosporus in the town of Chalcedon, which had politically merged with Byzantion around this time.

Most cities that thrived during antiquity were later abandoned, providing ample opportunities for modern archaeologists to sift through their ruins. Not so with Byzantion, which has been continually occupied throughout its long history. Layer upon layer of civilization has been built up, torn down, and built again on what is today Istanbul, thoroughly obscuring the Hellenic city. As a result, ancient Byzantion is visible only in scattered chance finds and vague literary references across the centuries.

Like any Greek acropolis, Byzantion's city center had a fortification and a government complex. It hosted a number of temples, including one to Dionysius and others to Athena, Artemis, and Aphrodite. A temple to Poseidon was built, appropriately enough, down the hill very near to the sea. Byzantion's commercial traffic was sufficiently brisk to warrant two ports, both nestled on the gentle waters of the Golden Horn. The first, Prosphorion, was within the land walls, probably on the spot of the modern train station (Sirkeçi). The second, Neorion, stood outside the walls, close to what is now the Galata Bridge, on land now occupied by Yeni Cami, or New Mosque. Both were busy places, bustling with merchants and sailors loading and unloading their vessels with the rich commodities of the region.

Farther west, beyond the Neorion, along the shore of the Golden Horn, stretched six of the seven hills that would one day comprise the city of Constantinople. In the third century BC these hills were lush with vegetation and crisscrossed with walkways and trails for the Byzantines to enjoy the views of the harbor. The coastline was dotted with shrines and temples, as well as numerous warehouses. Unfortunately, we heard of these outlying structures only when they were destroyed. The Persians demolished a temple to Hera. Philip II burned a temple to Pluto. These structures suggest that many of the citizens of Byzantion did not live in the walled city, but instead spread out northward along the banks of the Golden Horn, returning to the safety of the fortifications only in times of danger.

Within the walls could be found all the amenities of a civilized Greek city-state. In the northern portion, not far from the Prosphorion Harbor, was the Strategion, an open area used for mustering troops during war and, at all other times, holding public events. It was surrounded by additional shrines and temples, including those to Eleusis, Achilles, and Ajax. Nearby, a round amphitheater faced northward out to the sea, allowing spectators to enjoy the amusements of the theater with the stunning backdrop of the Bosporus.

The southern walls of Byzantion cut sharply to the southeast from roughly modern-day Sultanahmet Park to the shores of the Bosporus. The main land gate was found near the modern ruins of the Milion monument, not far from today's tourist entrance to the Basilica Cistern. Just within that gate was the Tetrastoon, a wide market square surrounded by four decorated porticoes. Remarkably, it remains a square today, just to the southwest of Hagia Sophia. Undoubtedly the commercial life of the Tetrastoon was as active then as now, although the items and services for sale have obviously changed. Like all good marketplaces in the Greek world, it had plenty of religious buildings, including shrines to Tyche and Rhea and a temple to Zeus, renamed Zeuxippus, perhaps in deference to a Thracian version of the god.

Walking outside the main city gate, one would find the start of a long road stretching westward to Thrace and the other Greek city-states along the European shores of the Sea of Marmara. Near the gate, perhaps on the land now occupied by the Blue Mosque, was a temple of Hecate. Anyone making his way down the modern-day street of Divan Yolu follows this ancient road, which has connected the city to the outside world for millennia. Indeed, walking along this street for just twenty minutes will bring one to the Bayezid Camii and the University of Istanbul, where the ancient Byzantines buried their dead.

There was much more to classical Byzantion, but it is all lost, buried beneath a thick overgrowth of concrete and history. There certainly would have been public fountains, gymnasia, and baths. We hear of a Bath of Achilles but, beyond its name, know nothing of it. If the many references in ancient literature can be believed, Byzantion also had more than its share of taverns and wine shops.

As the third century BC came to a close, fresh changes were brewing that would have a profound effect on Byzantion, and the entire Greek world. They came from a most unexpected place: the West. If one takes a map of the Mediterranean Sea and its surrounding lands and draws a line across it, dividing it equally between east and west, one will go a long way toward understanding the history of ancient civilization. Everything to the east of that line was the old world. Civilization began in Mesopotamia and spread east, and west toward the Mediterranean. Eastern Mediterranean areas such as Asia Minor, Syria, and Egypt had ancient, highly sophisticated cultures. Their lands were rich, and the populations prosperous. Greece, at the westernmost portion of the eastern Mediterranean, was a relative newcomer to the practice of civilization, which made it all the more remarkable when its armies managed to conquer so much.

As for the western half of the map, it constituted the outskirts of the ancient world, where civilization was newly or lightly planted, populations were scarce, and wealth scarcer. Most of western Europe was heavily forested and inhabited by primitive tribes. It was known best for the Gauls, a wild people who preyed on the cities they could sack. There were, of course, outposts of civilization in the West. In Sicily and southern Italy, the Greeks had founded urban centers such as Syracuse,

Neapolis (Naples), and Tarentum, which compared favorably to their sisters in the east. There were various non-Greek states in the west. A Phoenician colony at Carthage prospered in North Africa, while a people known as the Etruscans could be found across north Italy. None of these had anything to compare with the might and sophistication of the eastern Hellenistic kingdoms. Scarcely worthy of attention, western non-Greeks were almost invisible in Greek literature.

But that would soon change. A small group of tribes in central Italy, squeezed between the Etruscans to the north and the Greeks to the south, eventually founded their own, struggling city. Its name was Rome.

The Greeks could hardly be blamed for failing to notice an event as seemingly inconsequential as the foundation of Rome. From the Greek perspective, the Romans were barbarians. They had strange customs, based largely on Etruscan practices. They were no more warlike than any Italian people, but they were more successful in the endeavor. Sheltered in their own plain of Latium, they spoke their own language, Latin, although they used adaptations of Greek letters to write it. In those early centuries, the Romans were busy overthrowing Etruscan rule and then persuading, bribing, and bullying other northern Italians into an alliance aimed at defending the region from the Gauls. The Romans were not intrinsically expansionistic, but they were obsessed with defending themselves and their allies. This obsession led to their expansion. Having overthrown their kings, the Romans deeply distrusted concentrated power, fashioning a republic designed to thwart those seeking despotic rule. For the Greeks, the word *tyrant* was merely descriptive. For the Romans, it was an insult.

Although they were not Greeks themselves, the Romans greatly admired and often imitated Greek ways. They embraced Greek gods, mapping them conveniently onto their own local household gods. By 431 BC the city of Rome had temples to the Greek goddess Demeter and the god Apollo. These were primitive terra-cotta affairs, but in time Rome's position and prosperity would grow, allowing the Romans to replace the humble structures with larger versions of stone and marble. By 200 BC, Greek had become the language of high culture among Rome's elites. Indeed, the first history of Rome was penned in Greek, by the Roman author Fabius Pictor. The Romans read Herodotus and

Thucydides, Plato and Aristotle, and they formed a strong cultural bond with these faraway giants. The Greeks did not know about the Romans, but the Romans knew all about the Greeks.

The two groups did not come into close contact until the third century BC, when Rome had consolidated its control over northern Italy and was beginning to take a more active role in the Greek south. By this time, the Romans had established a solid reputation for holding treaties and alliances as sacred trusts. In fact, these agreements were blessed by Roman priests, and it was illegal and sacrilegious for any Roman to break them. Since Greek cities in southern Italy often attacked their weaker Greek neighbors, some of the latter began requesting Roman assistance against the former. Thanks to its victories in northern Italy, Rome became known as a power willing to help the victims of bullies.

The biggest bully in southern Italy was the Greek city-state of Tarentum. Tired of the barbarian Romans meddling in Greek affairs, they summoned to Italy the famous Greek general and ruler Pyrrhus. He arrived with twenty-five thousand professional soldiers and twenty elephants. His mission was a simple one: to champion the cause of Greek freedom by crushing those who would threaten it. The Romans, who still used citizen militias to fight their wars, had never encountered armies like those that now appeared on their shores. In the eponymous "Pyrrhic" victory of 280 BC, Pyrrhus defeated the Roman forces but failed to shake the Roman alliances. A few years later the Romans rebounded, and in 275 they defeated Pyrrhus, removing him completely from Italy.

Rome's astonishing victory over Pyrrhus brought it for the first time to the attention of the larger Greek world. Almost immediately the various Greek cities in southern Italy made their own arrangements to enter alliances with Rome. The Romans represented a genuinely new sort of empire, one that the Greeks found at first difficult to understand. It was based not on outright conquest, but on mutual trust. Romans disliked the concept of empire, and would have strongly denounced the idea that they were building one. Instead, they forged defensive alliances. The problem was that the more allies Rome had, the more wars the Romans were forced to enter into to defend them all. Defeated powers were not annexed, but rather transformed into allies. Rome was the head of the alliance, but unlike Athens during the days of the Delian League, it did not abuse the position. Indeed, the Romans were careful to treat all allies, and especially Greeks, as equals.

This principle was strained in Greek Sicily. In 264 BC, Rome went to war against Carthage over the island. It was a long and difficult struggle, one that forced the Romans not only to create a navy but also to learn how to use it. By 241 BC, the war was over and the Carthaginians driven out of Sicily. The Roman plan was for the Greek city-states there to govern themselves while becoming part of the larger alliance structure. Yet by this time the prosperous and refined Greek cities of Sicily were largely reliant on mercenaries to fight their wars. They had no desire to contribute men and arms to support a citizen militia, preferring to pay for their defense. So Rome obliged, making Sicily the first Roman province. The city-states there remained autonomous, yet they were responsible for paying tributes and working with Roman generals stationed on the island. As members of the Roman alliance, they could no longer wage war against their neighbors, or anyone else, without the approval of Rome. In practice that meant that peace descended on this turbulent region.

Unsurprisingly, events in Sicily made the Romans a topic of conversation across the Mediterranean. Eratosthenes, a Greek mathematician writing around 230 BC, referred to the Romans as "refined barbarians," presumably because they continued to mimic Greek culture and were eager for Greek approval. The Greek historian Timaeus of Tauromenium predicted that the victor of the struggle between Rome and Carthage would go on to take control of the West. Yet this was a matter of real importance only to the small minority of Greeks who found themselves in the West. Most Greeks lived happily in the wealthy and sophisticated East, with little care for Rome.

The struggle between Rome and Carthage came closer to its conclusion during the Second Punic War, fought across Italy, Spain, and Africa between 218 and 201 BC. Timaeus's prediction proved correct: Rome defeated the Carthaginians and won control over the entire western Mediterranean. Although they had not sought it, the Romans had become a power that could rival the Hellenistic kingdoms in Greece, Syria, and Egypt.

Back in Macedon, King Philip V was dreaming of conquering Greece, just as Philip II had done a century earlier. During Rome's struggle with Carthage, Philip V allied himself with the Carthaginian leader Hannibal, in the hope of carving out part of Illyria or the Aegean islands while Rome was preoccupied. Philip had recently built up a navy, and a burning desire to use it. In 202 BC he partnered with various pirates to raid the Greek cities of the Aegean and the Bosporus. Byzantion was among his targets. Although the city was not damaged, commerce along the strait was gravely harmed. Joining together with the Greek kingdom of Pergamum, in Asia Minor, and with the island of Rhodes, Byzantion prosecuted a war against Philip to drive him from the seas. Unfortunately for them, Philip was receiving help from the Seleucid ruler of Syria, Antiochus. Macedon, it seemed, was once again on the rise. The Byzantines and other free Greeks naturally feared a return of Macedonian subjugation.

Philip V was powerful, indeed more powerful than, Philip II, who had tamed Greece easily. Yet just to the west was a new barbarian state, one that had an almost childlike admiration for the Greeks and their culture. Could the Romans be convinced to defend the Greeks against Macedon? It would be a hard sell. The Romans had only just finished their own long and exhausting war against Hannibal. Still, it was worth a try. Ambassadors from Rhodes, Pergamum, and Byzantion sailed to Rome to speak to the Senate.

We can imagine that the arriving Byzantine and other Greek ambassadors were treated with every honor and deference. In the wake of the victory over Carthage, the city of Rome had become a place of affluence. The Roman senators could speak Greek and were well versed in Greek literature, art, and science. They were a receptive audience to the ambassadors' tales of wanton violence and greedy mayhem. The senators could scarcely have avoided remembering the abolition of Greek liberty under the heel of Alexander's father. Now the Romans had an opportunity to defend that liberty by coming to the aid of their cultural ancestors. They quickly dispatched Roman ambassadors to the court of Philip, demanding that he cease his unjust war and make reparations for the harm he had caused the Greeks. The king of Macedon haughtily refused. Rome declared war.

The Second Macedonian War, as historians call it, was waged between 200 and 196 BC. The outcome was never in doubt. Rome had significant naval superiority, numerous and powerful legions, and a group of strong Greek allies, including Byzantion. The Roman commander Flamininus led his legions from victory to victory, ultimately sending Philip back to Macedon and leaving in Roman hands all the cities Philip had captured.

Having expelled the aggressor from Greece, the Romans were left to deal with the fiercely proud and independent Greek city-states. Without the Macedonian threat, the Romans' presence in the Greek homeland became odious for those who lived there. Yet what would happen should the Romans withdraw their forces? There remained the problem of Antiochus of Syria, whose massive empire lay just to the east and who would very much like to claim what Philip could not. If the Romans returned home, who would protect the Greek cities from him? Just as important, who would protect them from one another?

When Greeks congregated in their squares and markets to discuss current events, they pondered what Rome would do with all the Greek cities currently under its control. Given that those cities had fought against Rome, most agreed that the Romans were justified in holding on to them. Some suggested that the Romans establish military bases at strategic locations in Greece, while removing their troops from more famous and high-profile cities such as Thessalonica and Corinth. With each new dispatch from Rome, the rumors grew more heated and more bizarre.

In the spring of 196 BC, all Greeks were invited to the Isthmian Games, an event that always drew large crowds. Flamininus himself would appear, and it was understood that he would have something important to say. The games were opened with great fanfare to a packed stadium. Then, to the surprise of the people, a single herald walked out into the middle of the arena accompanied only by a lone trumpeter. A loud blast brought the thousands in the stands to a complete silence. This was it, the announcement they had been waiting for. No one wanted to miss a word.

The herald took one step forward, opened a scroll, and read the following in a loud voice:

The Senate of Rome and Titus Quinctius [Flamininus] their general, having conquered King Philip and the Macedonians decree that the [Greek] city-states shall be free and released from the payment of tribute, and shall live under their own laws.

The herald then proceeded to list every Greek city-state not already free, including those that had fought against Rome. Having finished his announcement, the herald rolled up his scroll and, with the trumpeter, walked out of the silent arena. For a moment nothing happened. Stunned, the Greeks began to turn to one another, not certain if what they had heard was a bad joke or a horrible mistake. Then, like a thunderclap, a roar of surprise exploded from the crowd. According to Plutarch, the noise was so great that crows flying overhead were knocked unconscious and fell out of the sky. Suddenly no one cared about the games. They demanded that the herald return and read his scroll again. After a few minutes, the herald reappeared and reread the scroll. It was true. Rome was freeing the Greeks—all the Greeks.

The games were then held, although no one paid much attention to them. As soon as the prizes were handed out and the festivities formally concluded, the crowds rushed out of the stands, mobbing Flamininus's box. They showered him with accolades, tossing garlands and ribbons at him and pressing in so tightly that for a moment he began to fear for his life. The Greeks were grateful—grateful that the Romans had come so far to free them and had asked nothing at all in return. This was something unheard of in history. It seemed impossible to believe. As the news spread across Greece, Roman officials and soldiers were stopped in the streets and warmly thanked. According to Livy, Greeks everywhere were saying:

There was one people in the world which would fight for others' liberties at its own cost, to its own peril and with its own toil, not limiting its guaranties of freedom to its neighbors, to men of the immediate vicinity, or to countries that lay close at hand, but ready to cross the sea that there might be no unjust empire anywhere and that everywhere justice, right, and law might prevail.

And with the withdrawal of the last Roman soldier came the Roman Senate's guarantee of Greek independence. Should any power seek to enslave the Greeks again, Rome would respond.

Yet when it came to the Greeks, matters were never that simple. As time went on, many of them soured on the Romans, who had after all been helpful enough, but really should know their place. Some, particularly in Aetolia, in central Greece, began to favor union with the Greek Antiochus, whose great empire included much in the East that Alexander had conquered.

For Byzantion, the situation was even more complex. By right, Antiochus's dominion included most of Asia Minor and Thrace. Byzantion had managed to maintain its independence, but with the defeat of Philip and the departure of the Romans, it was increasingly drawn into Antiochus's orbit. Two powerful states, Rome and Antiochus's Syria, were approaching each other, and Byzantion was right in the middle.

Antiochus did not underestimate the Romans, but he did insist that they respect his rights. He pointed out that he would never think to meddle in Italy. Why, then, did Rome feel the need to bother with Greece? The Romans may well have asked themselves the same question, since their efforts at maintaining order in Greece were becoming increasingly troublesome. Anti-Romanism spread across Greece, largely because the proud Greeks were unaccustomed to barbarian protection. Finally, in 192 BC the Aetolians publicly defied Rome and asked Antiochus to send forces to liberate his fellow Greeks. Antiochus complied, sending a smallish force of about ten thousand men and a few hundred elephants. Other of his armies went to capture independent Greek cities and kingdoms in Asia Minor, such as Pergamum. He may also have sent men to Byzantion. Based on his subsequent discussions with Rome, Antiochus clearly believed that Byzantion belonged to him.

The Roman Senate responded to Antiochus's aggression with a declaration of war. More than forty thousand troops were sent to Greece under the command of Scipio Africanus (the hero of the Second Punic War) and his brother. They made quick work of Antiochus's armies in Greece, and then moved north to Thrace, to cross over into Asia very near Byzantion. The Byzantines offered the Romans every assistance and, according to Livy, even sent their own forces against Antiochus.

The Romans delivered a clear ultimatum to Antiochus: either withdraw from all Greek cities in Asia Minor or face the consequences. He chose the consequences. After his defeat, Antiochus was forced to give up all his claims to Greece, Thrace, and Asia Minor. In 189 BC the Romans declared all Greek cities in these regions to be free and independent, and again withdrew their armies back to Italy.

It appears that Byzantion during these tumultuous years was able to use its position on the borders of Roman and Syrian power to maintain its own practical independence. After 189 BC, however, it not only was legally independent but, like all the Greek cities, had its independence guaranteed by the Roman people. If anyone in Byzantion opposed this situation, it is left unrecorded. Indeed, commercial Byzantion seems to have flourished during an enforced peace that kept trade flowing. Byzantine attitudes toward the Romans during the second century BC mirrored those of other Greek cities in Asia Minor, such as Ephesus and Smyrna. All things considered, they were strongly pro-Roman.

In mainland Greece, however, anti-Roman parties dominated. Roman officials were routinely jeered, even by children in the streets. The Romans remained enamored of Greek culture and proud of their role as the protector of Greek liberty, but they were becoming very tired of the Greeks themselves. Twice in the second century BC, Roman forces had to be deployed to crush Macedonian attempts to conquer Greece and form it into one Greek state. Byzantion supported Rome during both those wars, although most of the Greeks in the south backed the Macedonians. The Senate in Rome became a regular venue for Greek appeals for aid against belligerent Greek neighbors, forcing Rome to act as referee to countless quarrels, and earning the hatred of both sides in the bargain.

In 147 BC, Sparta announced that it was leaving a coalition of Greek cities known as the Achaean League. Since resignation was not an option, the league attacked Sparta, requiring Roman forces in Macedonia to rush southward to put a stop to the fighting. In an attempt to bring peace, Rome sent a blue-ribbon delegation of senators to Corinth to meet with the members of the Achaean Assembly. They were not welcome. Anti-Roman activists led the Corinthians in a mass demonstration that violently turned on the visiting senators, overwhelming their bodyguards. To save themselves, the toga-clad senators ran through the streets of Corinth, while the locals opened their second-story windows and joyfully emptied their chamber pots on Rome's most revered men. The senators barely escaped with their lives.

The laughter and exultation among the Greeks had scarcely died down before the Romans responded. A squadron of warships arrived off the Greek coast in 146 BC. Their commander, Mummius, led four Roman legions against the armies of the Achaean League. After easily defeating them, he went on to capture Corinth. The Greeks had long ago become accustomed to seeing Roman soldiers marching into their cities. Yet this time the Romans had not come as liberators. The citizens of Corinth had gleefully violated the sanctity of Rome's ambassadors. More than a provocation, that was an act of war. And it was only the latest in decades of anti-Roman activities. The Romans had come to the reluctant conclusion that they simply could not afford to pay the extraordinary cost of a Greek liberty that the Greeks themselves valued so little.

When the fighting stopped and the dust had settled, Mummius announced that the citizens of Corinth should assemble to hear the decree of the Senate. No doubt many Greeks expected the Romans to read yet another scroll that confirmed Greek liberty and announced the complete withdrawal of Roman forces. Yet Mummius read a very different decree. The people of the city of Corinth were ordered to evacuate. After its precious art objects were relocated to Rome, Corinth was to be leveled. The assembled Greeks were thunderstruck. This was not at all what they had come to expect. This was not how the Romans had responded in the past. It had taken half a century, but the Greeks had finally exhausted the patience of the Roman people. After the destruction of Corinth, Greece was reorganized into various administrative regions supported by Roman military installations. Theoretically, the Greeks remained free. However, the close proximity of Roman forces told a different story. The Greeks would never again be allowed to wage war against one another or against the Roman people.

The peace imposed upon the Greeks would last for the next four hundred years—an unprecedented achievement. For the Byzantines, the Roman pacification of Greece not only was good news, but brought with it monumental changes for the city on the Bosporus. As a steadfast ally, Byzantion was formally proclaimed by the Roman Senate as completely independent. It was furthermore given sole rights to collect tolls and duties from shipping through the strait.

The year after the destruction of Corinth, a Roman senator, Gnaeus Egnatius, arrived in Macedonia as its new proconsular governor. Almost immediately he ordered the construction of a Roman road, one that would provide easy east–west transportation across Greece and onward toward Asia. Then as now the Romans had a well-deserved reputation as expert road builders. Roman roads snaked across Italy and out into the wider world as the Roman Empire expanded. At its peak, the Roman system consisted of nearly two hundred fifty thousand miles of road. Like modern American interstate highways, the Roman roads had two principal purposes. First and foremost, they provided secure and rapid transportation for armies and military supplies. Second, they were avenues of transportation and commerce for the people and allies of Rome.

The Via Egnatia (as it came to be called) was an extension eastward of the famous Via Appia, which stretched south from Rome, ending at the ports of Brindisi on the boot heel of Italy. Directly across the Adriatic Sea was Dyrrachium (Durrës), which is precisely where the Via Egnatia began. From there the road made a difficult and crooked path through the mountains of Macedonia, finally coming down to the plains at Pella and meeting the Aegean Sea at Thessalonica. Heading east, the new road then linked major Greek coastal cities until it arrived at Kypsela, in Thrace. Because of the length and the difficulty of the terrain, the Via Egnatia took around twenty-five years to complete, and even then it was not finished. We know little about how Romans chose the paths of their roads. Minor changes were probably left to the constructing engineers. Yet the beginning, end, and principal cities along the route must have been decided in Rome. In any case, since there was no compelling reason for the Via Egnatia to end in Kypsela, it may be that there was some indecision about whether to point the road toward the crossing to Asia, along the Hellespont to the south, or at Byzantion to the northeast. Eventually, they decided on the latter.

The arrival of the Via Egnatia at Byzantion's gate must have been an occasion of great celebration in the city. This seven-hundred-mile, twenty-foot-wide highway linked Byzantion directly to Rome. For the merchants of the city, the Via Egnatia provided a safe and free avenue to transport goods overland across Greece and into Italy and the West. A new Roman road begun just across the Bosporus provided the same easy transportation to Asia and points east. The Via Egnatia was, and would remain, an extremely busy road. The harbors of Byzantion had always done a brisk business ferrying travelers and residents across the Bosporus. Now that became an industry. The Byzantines already controlled the waterway linking the Black Sea with the Mediterranean Sea. Now they commanded the only overland route between Europe and Asia, between the western half of the map and the eastern. No city, not even Rome, was so strategically, so powerfully situated.

Byzantion had become a city at the crossroads of the world.

Chapter 4

Ruin and Survival

In the dead of a winter night in AD 195, thousands of fearful, sobbing citizens of Byzantion rushed to their harbor on the Golden Horn and frantically pressed onto the vessels docked there. Quickly the rowers pushed the ships back from the wharf and headed straight for the harbor chain, which was noisily lowered to let them pass out into the dark, swift current of the Bosporus. This was no night to be on the seas. Gale-force winds tore at the vessels' sails and stirred the waters of the strait and the Sea of Marmara into a boiling cauldron of mayhem lit only by the flash of lightning. No one with a choice would have put out onto those treacherous waters. Yet the tearful refugees who prayed that night for deliverance had no choice: for the Romans were angry, and they had come to Byzantion. And they were far worse than any storm.

The events that caused such desperation could not have been foreseen. Relations between Byzantion and the Romans had been excellent for generations. The rise of Roman hegemony over the Mediterranean was in every way good news for the city on the Bosporus. Rome's armies kept the peace across the region, and her navies scoured the waters for pirates and raiders. *Pax Romana* was descending on the world, and the merchants and sailors of Byzantion welcomed it with zeal. What turned Rome against Byzantion had nothing to do with the Byzantines, but with the profound changes affecting the Romans and their empire.

Under the Roman system, cities had different statuses depending on how they had entered the empire. Byzantion, which had always been pro-Roman, enjoyed the most favorable position, known as *civitas libera et foederata* (free and allied city). As such, Byzantion governed itself and its territories without interference from Rome, provided it did not act against the interests of the Roman people. The Byzantines were bound to Rome by treaty, which guaranteed Rome's defense of Byzantion in

return for military support and (later) tribute payments. This arrangement and thousands like it had brought an unprecedented period of
peace and prosperity to the Mediterranean. Byzantion's markets and
ports churned with activity, filled as they were with people from all
corners of the known world. Its growing affluence further enhanced its
dominance in the region. By the first century BC, Byzantion controlled
much of Thrace, including its neighbor Selymbria. Across the Bosporus, it governed Chalcedon, Chrysopolis, and a good portion of Bithynia.
Times were good.

As Rome spread across the eastern Mediterranean, the staggering
size of its holdings eventually strained the political fabric of the Republic, which had been designed to govern a city, not an empire. The Romans tried to patch the holes, but in the end the government broke
apart, which led to destructive civil wars. By the first century BC the
Republic was fading, replaced by various Roman senator/generals able
to control the legions. Byzantion offered its assistance to whichever general came out on top, sending military aid, for example, to contenders
such as Sulla and Pompey. An entirely new government began in 27 BC,
when Augustus Caesar became sole ruler of Rome and its empire. The
Republic was dead in all but name. Henceforth, Rome would be a city
of emperors.

The changes in Rome were bad for its senators, but the provinces
and allies rejoiced at the renewed stability. According to the Roman
historian Tacitus, Byzantion offered many services to Augustus and his
successors, "services possible because [the Byzantines] occupied a district conveniently placed for the transit of generals and armies by land
and sea, and equally so for the transport of supplies." When the quasi-
independent kingdom of Thrace revolted against the Romans in AD 46,
the Byzantines sent troops to help them crush the uprising. Thrace was
then transformed into a Roman province, while Byzantion remained
free. So grateful was Emperor Claudius that he suspended the city's
tribute payments for the next five years.

The next century was one of continued prosperity for the people of
Byzantion. Nonetheless, consolidation of Roman authority meant the
loss of some of Byzantion's far-flung holdings. At some point, perhaps
under Augustus, Bithynia was made a Roman province. Around AD 100

the emperor Trajan placed Byzantion into that province, although the city itself remained free. This was the golden age of the Roman Empire, a massive state stretching from Scotland to the Persian Gulf. Rome's wealth allowed it to establish minimum living standards for the cities in its domain. They received temples, gardens, and other amenities as gifts of the Roman people. Byzantion was no exception. Emperor Hadrian, who may have resided there in AD 118, ordered the construction of a large aqueduct to bring in fresh water for the city's growing population. It was a big project, one that required a massive water bridge to span Byzantion's third and fourth hills. With subsequent modifications and repairs, this structure is the same "Aqueduct of Valens" that towers over modern-day Istanbul. Civilized Roman life required a great deal of freshwater: the fountains that beautified and cooled the city, the public baths that cleansed the citizens and provided opulent meeting places. Byzantion had at this time at least two baths, one of Achilles and the other of Zeuxippus. Both were likely expanded and beautified by Hadrian.

Prolonged peace and stability led cities in the Roman Empire either to neglect their fortifications or, indeed, to have none at all. Not so with Byzantion. Because of their strategic location, the Byzantines paid close attention to their walls. In fact, it was almost an obsession for them. Their land fortifications were legendary, built with massive cut rocks and bound together by iron bands so perfectly that they seemed to be all one. According to Dionysius of Byzantion, the walls stretched three and a half miles across the land and then all along the shores of the peninsula. A mighty chain stretched across the Golden Horn kept invading fleets at bay. The walls were studded by twenty-seven towers, from which defenders could fire at assailants. On the land, we are told, the walls made a zigzag path that had the effect of flanking attackers with deadly towers, making a general assault by land almost impossible. Between the city's main gate, which opened to the Via Egnatia, and the sea there were seven towers. According to Dio Cassius, they could "talk."

If a person approached any of these [towers] except the first, it was silent. But if he shouted anything at the first tower or threw a rock at it, it not only echoed and "spoke," but it also caused the second tower to do the same, and in this way the sound continued from one tower to another through the whole seven. And they did not interrupt one another, but all in their proper turn received the sound from the one before it, took it up and passed it on.

The Byzantines were justifiably proud of their fortifications, behind which they believed they could withstand any attack.

That proposition was put to the test in the late second century. By then, the Roman Empire had begun its long slide into decay. Rome prospered while it had strong emperors with a firm hand on the military and central government. When that was lacking, when control over the empire was uncertain, the system broke down. Every general was a potential emperor. All that stood between him and imperial power was the current emperor. Any weakness in Rome, therefore, immediately led to civil wars as imperial contenders sprouted across the provinces.

Byzantion had always managed to sidestep these power struggles. It was, after all, better to let the Romans work out such matters on their own. Undoubtedly that was the Byzantine plan in 192, when the mentally unstable emperor Commodus was assassinated by his elite bodyguard, the Praetorian Guard. Although the purpose of the Guard was to defend the emperor, the unit had become increasingly corrupt. The leaders fancied themselves kingmakers, and indeed they were. Shortly after the assassination of Commodus, the Guard elevated the urban prefect of Rome, Pertinax, to the throne. He immediately launched a series of reforms, some of which threatened the Guard's lucrative position. When they demanded the customary tribute (i.e., bribe) for supporting his elevation to the throne, Pertinax refused. They assassinated him. Casting away all pretense, the leaders of the Guard then auctioned off the emperorship to the highest bidder. One Didius Julianus promised the most, so he became the next caesar.

Didius Julianus was hated in Rome, and almost everywhere else. So, in 193, the people took to the streets of Rome demanding that the Senate recall the popular governor of Syria, Pescennius Niger, to take the throne. From his headquarters in Antioch, Niger accepted the Roman people's nomination. He began traveling across the eastern portion of the empire, securing the support of the Roman governors and major cities there. When that was finished, he planned to sail to Rome, reunite with his wife and children there, and become the new emperor.

But another Roman general, this one on the Danube frontier, inter-vened. Septimius Severus, the governor of Pannonia Superior, had been watching events in the capital for some time. Didius Julianus's unpopu-larity was an opportunity for Severus to claim the imperial title for himself, but Niger's quick acceptance in the east threatened to close that door. Severus would have to be quicker. With a little prodding and many promises, his Danubian legions proclaimed Severus emperor. Al-ready in the West, Severus marched on Rome before Niger could set sail. Without a fight, Rome accepted Severus as emperor. Severus's re-form agenda was a bit more pointed than Pertinax's. After removing Didius Julianus, he ordered the execution of all members of the Praeto-rian Guard who had had a hand in Pertinax's assassination; the rest he fired. Then he arrested Niger's family and sent word to the would-be emperor that he should relinquish his claim.

Like everyone else in the East, the Byzantines had a preference for Niger. Little is known about the man, although his cognomen "the Just" suggests why he inspired such broad approval. Unfortunately for Niger, he did not command as many legions as Septimius Severus. If he were to be successful in his bid, he would need to move swiftly, winning quick and decisive battles against Severus's European forces in the hope that the new emperor's political and military backing would dissolve. For Niger's legions in Asia, the key to Europe was Thrace—and the key to Thrace was Byzantion. Severus knew this, too.

It must have been unsettling for the Byzantines to have large oppos-ing armies marching toward their city to decide the fate of the entire empire. It was simple enough to maintain a cautious neutrality when Rome's struggles played out over the horizon, but quite another matter to remain aloof when they were in your own lands. Making a virtue of necessity, the Byzantines hailed Niger as emperor when he arrived at their gates. Undoubtedly, Niger promised them rich rewards should he win his struggle against Severus. And should he lose—well, there were always the impregnable walls.

Severus's advance forces settled in at the Greek city of Perinthos (modern-day Marmara Ereğlisi) just seventy miles west of Byzantion, on the north shore of the Sea of Marmara. Niger moved at once, attacking Perinthos and defeating Severus's army. Flush with victory, Niger and his men returned to Byzantion, which he declared to be his new military headquarters in Europe. Yet Severus had not begun to fight. Marching from Rome along the Via Egnatia, he first secured Perinthos and then sent many of his legions across the Hellespont to invade Asia Minor. Niger countered by sending his own armies to defend the southern shore of the Sea of Marmara. The battle lines were drawn, and Byzantion was in the thick of it. Realizing that his forces were outnumbered, Niger sent envoys from Byzantion to Severus, offering a peace proposal. In return for Severus's withdrawal, Niger would consent to dividing the empire, allowing Severus to keep the western half. Severus declined, but made a counteroffer. He would spare Niger's life if he surrendered immediately. Niger declined. The situation in Byzantion was dire.

In the fall of 193 the core of the warring legions met at Cyzicus, on the southern shore of the Sea of Marmara. At the end of the day, Severus's forces emerged victorious. Quickly they marched northeast, in the hope of trapping Niger at Byzantion. Before the noose could be tightened, though, Niger fled to Nicaea, where he regrouped his forces. Severus's legions at Perinthos, failing to find Niger at Byzantion, demanded that the city surrender. The Byzantines refused. Severus's armies then laid siege to the city, surrounding it on both land and sea.

The Byzantines' stubborn support for Niger has long puzzled historians. After the defeat at Cyzicus, many of the cities that had previously rallied to Niger switched allegiance to Severus. Even more of them defected after December 193, when Severus's forces again defeated Niger near Nicaea. As Niger and his remaining legions retreated behind the Taurus Mountains to Antioch, it must have seemed unlikely that he would ever be in a position to make good on his promises to Byzantion. Why then resist the inevitable? But resist Byzantion did. Month after month the Byzantines refused to submit while the rest of the empire was falling in behind Severus. Nicomedia (modern-day İzmit) had already defected, and was quickly followed by dozens of other cities, including Tyre in Syria. In early 194, Egypt switched to Severus. Finally, in May 194, at Issus in Syria, came the final battle of the war. Once again Severus was victorious, forcing Niger to flee to Antioch, where he packed his bags and headed east for the Parthian Empire. Captured on the way out of town, Niger was decapitated and his head sent to Byzantion. Still the Byzantines refused to surrender.

Niger's rotting head perched on a pike outside Byzantion's main gate is good evidence that the Byzantines were not resisting Severus because they expected the fruits of Niger's gratitude. There must have been something more to their decision than is readily apparent today. Dio Cassius, who had a friend in Byzantion at the time, implied that the Byzantines simply considered their city to be impregnable, due not only to its geography, but also to its massive and much-beloved walls. Severus's besieging forces were never able to launch an effective attack on Byzantion itself. Cut off from the Golden Horn by the great chain, the Roman fleets could only assault the seawalls along the Bosporus and the Sea of Marmara, where the current was too swift for them to do any real damage. As Dio Cassius wrote, "In a word, the Bosporus is of the greatest advantage to its inhabitants, for it is absolutely inevitable that once anyone gets into its current he will be cast up on the land in spite of himself. This is a condition most satisfactory to friends, but most embarrassing to enemies."

It was equally impossible for Severus's legions to approach Byzantion's land walls. Apart from their size and many towers, the walls were crowned with a host of machines that flung all manner of missiles. Dio describes these fearsome constructions (which his friend designed) as belonging to two groups. The first hurled great stones and stout wooden beams short distances, obliterating anyone daring to approach. The second consisted of a variety of devices that fired spears and rocks with such force that they could hit enemies far away from the fortifications. Together, these weapons kept the attackers well at bay. The Romans' strategy, then, was simply to cut off all travel into or out of Byzantion, and wait for its inhabitants to become hungry enough to surrender.

It was a long wait. Byzantion was a wealthy city, willing to pay premium prices to merchants not averse to smuggling. When the Romans clamped down on late-night deliveries, the Byzantines hit upon another scheme to keep themselves fed. Across the Golden Horn and to the south were makeshift harbors to supply the legions and their commanders. Under cover of darkness, Byzantine divers went in teams to the merchant vessels docked there. Slipping silently under the waves, they would identify a well-laden ship, cut its anchor line, and then pound large nails into its hull. Around these they secured strong ropes attached to winches along the walls. When the signal was given, the winches would wind and the merchant vessel would quietly glide away, landing at the city, where it was instantly emptied. According to Dio, this practice became so common that some merchants placed their vessels at optimum locations for hijacking so that they could sell their goods without incurring the wrath of the Romans. Eventually, though, this, too, was discovered and the practice quashed.

The civil war was over. Septimius Severus was the new emperor, busy with events on the eastern frontier of the empire. And yet the Byzantines continued to resist. Surely they did not believe they alone could withstand the might of Rome. We can only assume, then, that no terms of surrender were offered. They were the last and most troublesome of Niger's partisans. Severus meant to make them pay. Indeed, he had for some time pursued a policy of harsh reprisals against those who had sided with Niger. The cities that switched over to him had their privileges, and in most cases their freedom, stripped. Any private citizen who had supplied funds to Niger, even the lawful and required payment of taxes to Niger's government, was forced to pay four times that amount to Severus. Most of the senators in Rome were stripped of their property, and a great many Romans were convicted of treason who had never willingly supported Niger at all. And of course Severus executed Niger's family and confiscated all their property. What could Byzantion, which had been Niger's European headquarters and which had backed him until the bitter end, expect from Severus?

The inescapable conclusion is that, for whatever reason, the Byzantines had lost their opportunity to switch sides. Now they would be an example. So the siege of Byzantion stretched on. The defenders' only hope lay in a new rebellion elsewhere in the empire. It was not an unreasonable hope; rebellions were common enough in those turbulent times. The governor of Britain, Clodius Albinus, was at that very moment planning to make a bid to unseat Severus in Rome. But after a two-and-a-half-year siege, Byzantion was running out of time—and supplies. To keep their vessels in good repair, the people tore apart their homes for wood. Women shaved their heads, weaving their hair into much-needed rope. When ammunition for machines ran low, citizens dismantled their theaters for stones and even loaded the catapults with heavy bronze statuary from temples. More worrisome were the depleted food stores. Conditions became so bad that some resorted to eating boiled leather. It was winter 195/196, and the end was in view.

Escape was the only answer, yet it would not be easy with Roman forces arrayed in all directions. So it was that one night, when a vicious storm blew up, the majority of the inhabitants made their desperate decision. With anguish and tears, they piled onto their vessels and sailed out into the deadly and dark waters of the Sea of Marmara. The storm was so fierce that the Romans would have been crazy to follow them. Their escape was an act of pure desperation. Few survived the trip, but those that remained behind fared no better. Disease and starvation took their toll, and those who lived fed on the corpses of those who did not. Byzantion, the wealthy town of delights, had become a gruesome place of horror.

A few weeks later, during another fierce storm, thousands more Byzantines decided to take their chances on the sea. Yet only a fraction of the city's vessels remained in the harbor. They were filled to bursting with desperate people and their meager possessions. Overloaded, the ships sailed awkwardly out and were quickly capsized by the storm or rammed by the Roman galleys. Those who remained in the city could hear the screams of their countrymen all through the night. According to Dio, "The next day the terror was increased still more for the citizens, for when the waves had subsided the whole sea around Byzantion was covered with corpses, wrecked vessels, and blood. Many of the gruesome remains washed up on the city's shore, so that the disaster seemed even worse to the people than it was in fact." After nearly three years of defiance, the last inhabitants of the proud city opened their gates and walked out under a banner of surrender.

The surviving soldiers and government officials were lined up and summarily executed. The rest of the citizens lost all their property, and many were sold into slavery. They watched with bitter sorrow as the legions pulled down their magnificent walls. "[Severus] caused no greater grief to the inhabitants than in the demolishing of their walls, for they lost the glory and the fame that they received when anyone saw them." In the unkindest cut of all, the rancid shell of Byzantion was handed over to its enemy, the city of Perinthos, which treated it as a pathetic, tributary village. Thousands of miles away in Mesopotamia, Emperor Severus received the report of Byzantion's fall. He laughed heartily, tell, ing one of his generals that it would be a very good day.

As far as Severus was concerned, Byzantion had met the fate befit, ting all his enemies. Still, its location remained so important that it could not be abandoned. The following year, in the summer of 197, the em, peror visited the ruins and declared that he would found a new Roman city there. Severus put as much energy and resources into the recon, struction of Byzantion as he had into its destruction. Within a year, the old ports were filled with transport vessels bringing cut stones, food, stuffs, and of course plenty of wine. Byzantion was once again teeming with activity as crews not only rebuilt the old, but greatly expanded the city toward the west. This was not Byzantion. It was a new place, Anto, niniana, named for Severus's young son. It was to be a new stronghold for the heir of the emperor. Indeed, according to some sources, it was Seve, rus's son, later known as Caracalla, who convinced the emperor to restore the city's former privileges, removing it from the clutches of Perinthos.

The construction of Antoniniana was a large undertaking, one that remained unfinished at Severus's death in 211. The land walls that had been laboriously torn down were now painstakingly rebuilt, although farther west. They cut directly across the peninsula from the Golden Horn to the Sea of Marmara. The main city gate, which still opened to the Via Egnatia, was now very near the modern-day Çemberlitas tram stop. Inside the gate, the main street (the Mese) was colonnaded on both sides and richly decorated with statues before opening up to the refurbished Tetrastoon Square. The latter was given porticoes on all four sides, for markets and meetings out of the hot sun. Shrines and artwork and perhaps fountains adorned the open area. In the center was a glittering statue of Helios, the Greek personification of the sun. One can still get a feel for this forum, for it occupied the modern-day Sultan, ahmet Park as well as the open square on the southwest side of Hagia Sophia. The colonnaded Mese still lies beneath the modern-day street of Divan Yolu.

Severus's new city was to be a showplace, a worthy headquarters for a Roman emperor. The dilapidated Baths of Zeuxippus were restored and expanded. For ancient Romans, the baths were not simply a place to clean. They were an experience, an extension of the forum, an amenity of civilized life. The Baths of Zeuxippus were decorated with bright frescoes, columned hallways, and every sort of rich artwork. Severus also saw to the public spectacles, so necessary to Roman life. The theaters and open amphitheater on the eastern side of the acropolis were rebuilt on grander scales. A new gymnasium appeared on the western slope of the acropolis, toward the growing main city. On the acropolis itself Severus expanded the governmental complex, including constructing a palace for imperial use. The many temples there were restored, and we may assume more were added.

Roman cities of this size also required a circus, where the citizens could watch the charioteers race dangerously around the long course. Severus laid out Antoniniana's racecourse just southwest of the Tetrastoon. Large wide tracks were run southwest and northeast around a central *spina*, or "spine." On the *spina* were more statues, monuments, and probably fountains as well as the pyramid-like structures that visibly marked out the laps of the racers. On either side of the tracks, ornate stone seating rose up with room for thousands of spectators. The starting gates were on the northeast end of the track, while on the far southwest side a curved boundary of some sort was erected. Severus's engineers were unable to build stands around the curved end of the track because there the ground quickly sloped down to a lower plateau near the sea. This racetrack, known as the Hippodrome, became a centerpiece of civic life and a source of pride to the inhabitants. Its basic plan can still be seen today in the Atmeydani area to the northwest of the Blue Mosque. Little is known about the races in Severus's day, but the mere presence of a circus placed the city among the largest and most prestigious in the Roman world.

Severus's refounding of Byzantion as Antoniniana was the first large-scale fusion of cultures in a city that would be defined by its cosmopolitan diversity. Built by the Romans for their own purposes, Antoniniana was a hybrid of East and West set firmly on the boundaries of both. Thousands of Byzantines and other Greeks from the greater Byzantion area came to live and work in the city. It was no longer a Greek polis, but rather, a Roman *urbs*. Greek was no longer the only language spoken on the streets, in forums, and in official buildings. Latin had arrived in force, filling the city that its speakers had remade.

Byzantion's resurrection was no act of charity, but rather a clear-headed recognition that the city's location made it a potential citadel from which an emperor could maintain control of a large empire. Still, the city narrowly escaped becoming a partisan in the next great struggle for power. Septimius Severus had two sons very like him. Caracalla and his younger brother, Geta, fought continually. Their mother, Julia Domna, was the peacemaker, but that became increasingly difficult as the boys entered their twenties. When Severus died in 211, the two were proclaimed joint emperors in Rome, a solution neither was willing to accept. As each intrigued against the other, Julia Domna suggested that they divide the empire, with Geta taking the East and Caracalla the West. Both seemed agreeable to this at first. Rome would remain the Western capital, but Caracalla proclaimed that Antoniniana/Byzantion would be his military headquarters. Geta replied that he would establish his base, then, at Chalcedon, just across the Bosporus. The titanic struggle of emperors seemed about to erupt again at the city of the Byzantines.

They were saved only by Caracalla's treachery. On December 19, 211, he suggested a meeting with Geta in their mother's apartment in Rome to finalize the plans for division. The conversation had hardly started, however, when members of the Praetorian Guard loyal to Caracalla stepped in, drew their swords, and moved toward Geta. Julia blocked their way, demanding that the armed men leave immediately. Seconds later, Geta's blood-soaked body lay motionless in the arms of his sobbing mother. Caracalla departed, now sole emperor of Rome.

It was to be a short reign. On his deathbed, Septimius Severus had told his sons to make certain that the soldiers were happy and to ignore everything else. Caracalla followed this advice, raising the pay and benefits of the legions. To afford all this, he hit upon a method of increasing his tax base. In 212 he decreed that all free men anywhere in the Roman Empire were henceforth Roman citizens. This edict swept away the last remnants of the old Roman alliance structure, fusing the empire into one entity—all of it taxable. Antoniniana/Byzantion, like everywhere else, was henceforth a Roman city filled with Roman tax-paying citizens. It would remain so for the next twelve centuries.

The remainder of Caracalla's reign did not dramatically affect the city named for him. Harshly violent and increasingly mad, Caracalla became convinced that he was the reincarnation of Alexander the Great. To prove the point, he dressed his legions as Greek hoplites (in-fantrymen). After massacring thousands of Alexandria's citizens in retaliation for a popular satire about his madness, he headed east to Persia, where he executed his own wedding party. Finally, in 217, while urinating by the side of a road in northern Syria, he was assassinated by a disgruntled military officer. Few mourned his passing. In Antoniniana they celebrated, officially changing the name of their city back to Byz-antion.

As the Roman government crumbled under the weight of its civil wars, the Germanic barbarians began to press in from the north. The frontiers were buckling; indeed, in some places they had already bro-ken. In the 250s one of the barbarian tribes, the Goths, overwhelmed Roman Dacia and poured into the western Black Sea and Thrace. Sud-denly trade vessels stopped coming from the troubled north, and few were the merchants brave enough to sail there to do business. Without healthy trade, Byzantion was becoming merely an entrepôt of conquest, a crossroads for invaders.

In 255, Gothic pirates started raiding Bithynia and the cities of the Sea of Marmara. Across the Bosporus the people of Byzantion could watch these fearsome vessels preying on locales unaccustomed to exter-nal threats. In 257 the Goths sacked Chalcedon, although they were too few to threaten Byzantion itself.

Ten years later they returned with a much larger force: around five hundred vessels. Caught by surprise, the Byzantines were unable to keep the Goths from capturing the harbors and sacking the city. But the invad-ers had not come to stay. Eager to move on to fresh targets, the Goths sailed away, only to be destroyed by a Roman fleet patrolling the Aegean.

It escaped no one's attention that Rome was no longer able to defend its borders. As the Byzantines cleaned up their city and repaired the walls, a still-larger invasion of barbarians was forming in the Black Sea.

In 268 it came—unlike any that had come before. To the north, the Bosporus was covered in ships, each bearing Germanic warriors eager for plunder. Were it not so deadly, it would have been an inspiring sight. Altogether, the barbarian fleet probably numbered more than two thousand major vessels, although some sources put it as high as six thousand. The invaders attacked both Byzantion and Chrysopolis, but whether they captured or sacked the cities is unknown. Either from poor weather or an effective counterattack, the barbarians lost a good part of their fleet at Byzantion. The survivors headed south, fanning out across the Aegean and bringing fire and sword to the heart of the old Greek world. The islands of Crete, Rhodes, and Cyprus were devastated. The magnificent city of Ephesus was sacked, and the Temple of Artemis, one of the Seven Wonders of the Ancient World, was burned to the ground. Eventually the Romans rallied under the emperor Claudius II, who defeated the invaders. In commemoration of his victory, Claudius erected a column on the eastern point of Byzantion, looking out to the sea that he had liberated. That column remains there today.

As the third century came to a close, the eternal Roman Empire was in utter disarray. For the Byzantines this was serious, for they profited when Rome was stable and suffered when it was not. It would not take a prophet to predict that the city would decline as rapidly as the empire that put it at the crossroads of the world.

In truth, though, the city had only begun to flourish.

PART II

BYZANTINE CONSTANTINOPLE

330–1453

Nor do I think myself that in the forty richest cities of the world there had been as much wealth as was found in Constantinople. For the Greeks say that two-thirds of the wealth of this world is in Constantinople and the other third scattered throughout the world.

Robert of Clari, *The Conquest of Constantinople*

Behold the Spring, the goodly Spring, once more appears!
Prosperity and Joy and Health it brings!

Fragment of a song sung in the Hippodrome
on the anniversary of the city's founding

Chapter 5

Founding a New Rome

In September 324, two Roman emperors came to Byzantion to settle the fate of the Western world. As was customary in those troubled times, the discussion would be one of swords, armor, and blood. These were commodities with which the people of Byzantion had become exceedingly familiar. For as the Roman Empire groaned and cracked under the strain of its buckling frontiers and internal divisions, the fault lines seemed always to converge on the city on the Bosporus.

In 324 the warring parties were Emperor Constantine I and Emperor Licinius. Having two emperors was a relatively new practice in the Roman Empire. In the early 290s, Emperor Diocletian divided the Roman Empire into two halves, each governed by an emperor (known as an augustus) and assisted by a vice emperor (known as a caesar). The hope was that this rule by four (known as the tetrarchy) would reduce the temptation of generals far from the imperial court to set themselves up as rival emperors. As the heirs of the augusti, the caesars would have the opportunity to forge ties with the legions, thus forestalling rebellions among lesser officers. A sound idea, yet it never worked. Almost from the beginning, the tetrarchy was plagued with infighting and outright rebellion. Still, the Romans maintained the system because there was simply no better alternative.

Constantine, the emperor of the West, and Licinius, the emperor of the East, had each won his title through warfare. Constantine's situation was different in one truly world-shaking way. He was a Christian. The religion of Jesus Christ had long prospered under the peace that the Roman Empire afforded. It was along Roman roads, aboard Roman vessels, and in Roman forums and theaters across the known world that missionaries had spread the Gospel. The Romans generally preferred as much religious diversity as possible, a philosophy not shared by most Christians, of course, who believed that pagan gods were either nonexistent or demons. Yet, for the most part, Christianity settled well into the larger religious landscape of the Roman world during the first two centuries. By the third, however, tensions between the growing religion and the waning empire became severe, leading to occasional persecutions.

The final break came in 303, when Emperor Diocletian outlawed Christianity, ordering all Scriptures to be destroyed, all churches burned, and all Christians banned from assembling or practicing their faith. The Roman Empire appeared to have lost the favor of the gods, and the Christians' willful refusal to accept those gods' existence was likely the cause. Across the empire, soldiers rounded up Christians for execution, driving the religion underground. In most places, the decrees were strictly enforced, but in Britain and Gaul, where Constantine had ruled as caesar, the authorities often looked the other way. Back then, Constantine was not yet a Christian, but he clearly had sympathy for their plight. Across the empire, one could watch martyrs face their deaths with a sublime certainty that they were going somewhere much better. It was difficult not to be struck by that.

Civil war between Constantine and the Western emperor Maxentius broke out in 312. At first there was nothing particularly noteworthy about so common an event. Then, as Constantine led his troops across the Alps and into Italy, he had a profound religious experience. In a vision he saw Jesus Christ, who gave him the mark of the Greek letters *chi* and *rho* superimposed one over the other (☧). With this symbol, which represented the first two letters of the Greek word for Christ, Constantine believed that the Christian god would grant him victory over his enemy. He ordered it placed on all battle standards and shields of his legions. It was a strange sight indeed, for Roman legions usually adorned their standards with statues of eagles, snakes, or gods. Maxentius was puzzled by the change, but determined to defend his reign at any cost.

On October 28, 312, one of the world's most momentous battles took place at the Milvian Bridge, just north of Rome. There Constantine soundly defeated Maxentius and rode into Rome as the new emperor of the West. He credited Jesus Christ with the victory and immediately announced his own conversion to Christianity. His family joined him in the faith. The following year, Constantine and the Eastern emperor Licinius officially ended the persecutions. Almost overnight, Christianity's situation had been dramatically reversed. Formerly a scorned religion popular among the uneducated poor, it had become the faith of the imperial sovereign. Powerful men and women who would previously never have considered Christianity now gave it a second look. Many converted and were baptized. From the beginning of his reign, Constantine took a keen interest in the well-being of the Church, donating buildings in Rome, including the original Church of St. John Lateran and the first shrine of St. Peter.

For a time, there was peace between Constantine and Licinius, both of whom chose their sons as caesars. But neither was a man who shared power well. After a few skirmishes and treaties, a major civil war broke out in 324. Constantine mustered his legions, now all marching under the Christian labarum, and prepared to conquer the other half of the empire.

Licinius was determined to defeat Constantine before he could cross over into Asia Minor. Like many emperors before him, Licinius made Byzantion his military headquarters, mustering his troops and stationing his naval forces in the city. In the summer of 324 he sent his fleet south to the Hellespont, to keep Constantine's navy, under the command of his son, Crispus, out of the Sea of Marmara. Licinius then led his legions, consisting of some 160,000 men, to Adrianople, in Thrace. There he waited for Constantine.

Once again Byzantion was the stage on which an imperial struggle played out. Yet this time, more than the Roman Empire was at stake. The shape of Christianity's future also hung in the balance.

Licinius had the advantage: his army and navy were significantly larger than those of Constantine. Yet Constantine was still driven by the zeal of the convert, certain that Christ would continue to lead him to victory. At Adrianople he destroyed Licinius's legions, forcing the Eastern emperor to return to the safety of Byzantion. Farther south, Crispus led his fleet to a resounding victory, scattering Licinius's navy and sailing triumphantly into the Bosporus. Unable to maintain the offensive, Licinius crossed over to Chalcedon, where he called for more troops from Asia. As fall approached, Constantine and Crispus loaded their forces onto hundreds of vessels and ferried them across the Bosporus just north of Chrysopolis. Licinius was ready for them. His reinforced legions marched forward, engaging Constantine's men on September 18, 324. Once again Constantine bore the symbol of Christ to victory. Thoroughly defeated, Licinius surrendered, agreeing to live out his days as a private citizen. Constantine thus became the sole ruler of the Roman Empire (Illustration 2).

After so grand a victory, most expected Constantine to return to Rome for a glorious triumph. Instead, he and his court went directly to Byzantion, where they would remain, at least for the foreseeable future. Constantine knew this region well, having spent his childhood at Nicomedia, only forty miles to the east. After many years in England, Gaul, and Italy, and now in his fifties, he may have welcomed the opportunity to return to the beauty of the Sea of Marmara. Most important, though, was Byzantion's location. As the emperor of both East and West, Constantine needed a headquarters that would allow him to react quickly to both. In such uncertain times, Byzantion was the perfect choice.

Roman emperors were already in the practice of basing their administrations somewhere other than Rome. Byzantion had been handsomely rebuilt by Septimius Severus as the imperial residence for his son Caracalla. Constantine meant to expand that practice. On November 8, 324, crowds gathered outside the Severan land walls of Byzantion. Constantine, his family, and dozens of leading officials were dressed for the time-honored Roman ceremony of the founding of a city. Byzantion, they solemnly declared, was to be founded anew, this time by the ruler of the Western world. The pagan priests performed their customary rituals, and Christian clergy were enlisted to give their blessings. The imperial party then processed to the ceremonial plow pulled by a team of powerful oxen. As tradition dictated, Constantine drove the plow to mark out the *pomerium*, the boundaries of his new city. Septimius Severus had rebuilt Byzantion's new land walls about four hundred yards farther west than they had been, adding somewhat to the size of the old Greek city. Constantine proceeded westward across the open grasses *one and a half miles* from the Severan walls and then dug a north–south furrow from the Golden Horn to the Sea of Marmara. This was no mere refurbishment. Constantine meant to quadruple the size of Byzantion. It was scarcely believable. With the ceremony complete, the new city was officially renamed: Constantinople, the city of Constantine.

The scale of the refounding of Byzantion as Constantinople was unprecedented in the ancient world. Fleets of vessels brought armies of engineers, carpenters, stonemasons, and workers—and the raw materials necessary to build a magnificent city. The hilly plains outside the Severan walls had overnight become the world's largest construction site. It would take decades to complete, but all the plans were laid out by Constantine. He intended to build a well-defended, well-supplied showplace that could serve as the administrative center of the Roman Empire. Rome, of course, would remain the capital. No one, not even Constantine, could dethrone the Eternal City; yet Constantinople would serve as a permanent center for government, a home for Constantine and his sons after him.

As the city echoed with the sounds of hammers, saws, and workmen, Constantine headed in 325 to the beautiful town of Nicaea (modern-day İznik), about fifty miles to the southeast. He had invited the Christian bishops of the empire to gather there for the first ecumenical council since the time of the Apostles. There was much to discuss. Christianity had been not only afflicted by persecutions, but also splintered by internal divisions over matters of the faith. As the successors of the Apostles, the bishops convened under Constantine's protection to discuss the theological disputes, pray for guidance from the Holy Spirit, and make a final ruling on them. Constantine attended the ceremonies, though he took no direct part in the discussions or decisions. Here at Nicaea was laid the foundation of the West's unique concept of the separation of church and state: as an emperor, Constantine found that his power was temporal. He was not a priest or bishop, and therefore was unable to perform the sacraments or to rule on matters of faith. Only the bishops of the council could declare Arianism (a belief that Christ was less than God) heretical, which they did. As the secular authority, Constantine could exile the Arians, which he did.

The year after the council met, Constantine and his family traveled to Rome to celebrate the twentieth anniversary of his reign. During the festivities, Constantine uncovered a plot, or perhaps simply a love affair, between his young wife, Fausta, and his adult son (by a concubine) Crispus. Whatever happened, it caused Constantine to issue a *damnatio memoriae*, which legally erased all physical memory of the two. Fausta and

Crispus were tried and executed in Rome in 326. Constantine had had enough of Rome. Like any emperor, he had beautified the capital with monuments and even built his mausoleum there. Now he eagerly left it behind. He would never return.

Since his boyhood, Constantine had always had as his closest adviser his mother, Helena, now in her seventies. He had recently bestowed on her the title "Augusta," which corresponded to "empress." With Crispus and Fausta gone, Constantine relied even more heavily upon Helena, and the two decided that Constantine would return to Constantinople to oversee its construction. Helena went to Jerusalem, where she visited the sites made holy by the life of Christ. While there, she spent liberally on repairing churches and founded several new ones. At the Grotto of the Nativity, the Emperor Hadrian had long ago built a temple to Adonis. Helena ordered it destroyed, and replaced it with a new basilica that would take six years to complete. On the Mount of Olives, she commis-sioned an open-air shrine on the site of the Ascension. Most famously, she sought Golgotha and the Holy Sepulcher, the place of the crucifixion and resurrection of Jesus. Local Christians and Jews knew the site well, as did previous Roman emperors. Hadrian had built a magnificent tem-ple to Venus on it. Upsetting many pious Romans, Helena ordered the temple demolished. Below it, the workmen found not only the rocky crag of Golgotha and the nearby tomb of the Savior, but also the True Cross on which he had hung. Small pieces of the Cross were sent to churches across the empire. Helena ordered the construction there of two churches, which would later be joined into one magnificent structure, the Church of the Holy Sepulcher. She then returned to Constantinople, having forged an enduring bond between the two cities.

During the next four years, Constantine remained busy in his new city. He personally oversaw the building of the new land walls, which stretched mightily across more than a mile and a half of the peninsula. There is no longer any trace of those giants, but they survived for many centuries. Like their Severan and Byzantine predecessors, they were studded with towers and pierced by imposing gates. To the north they began at the Golden Horn, in the Petrion area, just northwest of the present-day Atatürk Bridge. From there the walls snaked southward, jutting between the current mosques of Sultan Selim and Fatih and then roughly following the modern-day streets of Oguzhan, Kizilelma, and Etyemez. Near the southern end of the walls was a large ceremonial portal, known as the Golden Gate. Here the Via Egnatia entered the city, becoming the wide boulevard that emperors would henceforth use for their extravagant triumphal processions. Fragments of this Golden Gate survived until the sixteenth century, but they, too, have disappeared. The gate stood near the modern-day intersection of Zizelema Caddesi and Koca Mustafapasa Caddesi. Undoubtedly there were several other gates along the wall. We hear only of the northern gate of Polyandri, where another wide main road entered the city and proceeded southeast until meeting the Via Egnatia at a square later known as Philadelphion. The intersection of these two roads was the most important in Constantinople, and perhaps also the busiest. Towering over it were two columns, part of a temple complex known as the Capitolium. Embedded in the columns were porphyry statues of the tetrarchy. In each, two rulers embraced, leading to the complex's popular name, "place of brotherly love." Amazingly these statues survive, today embedded on the exterior of the Basilica San Marco in Venice. For centuries the stony monarchs watched over the two main roads of ancient Constantinople.

The main streets of Constantinople were designed to be centers of civic life. All were flanked with long rows of monumental columns, stretching two or more stories into the air and topped by ornate wooden roofs to keep out the sun and rain. These covered streets echoed with conversations and the calls of merchants, who set up their wares between the columns. Constantine and his successors lavishly decorated these routes with statues, fountains, and bright tapestries. These were not avenues; they were malls. More than that, they were forums that stretched on for miles. One could, of course, get from one place to another on these porticoed streets, or *emboloi*, as the local Greeks called them. But carts and beasts of burden were forbidden, banished to the hundreds of side streets in the open air. The Via Egnatia, called the Mese (Central), was the most beautifully adorned road. At several spots along its way the colonnade opened up to embrace a wide-open square, only to close in again on the avenue on the opposite side. These were the great forums of Constantinople, set like pearls along the string of the Mese. The largest was the Forum Tauri (Forum of the Bull), a massive forum roughly corresponding to the modern-day Beyazit Square.

As the Mese approached and then passed through the Severan walls of old Byzantion, it was even more heavily adorned with artwork. One can imagine that along with the armies of masons and builders whom Constantine recruited, there were also thousands of sculptors and painters to decorate his new home. Yet there were not enough artists in the empire to produce all the masterpieces set into Constantinople's public spaces and private palaces. The troubles of the fourth century had not been kind to artists' workshops, leading to a steady decline in numbers and technique. Instead, Constantine requisitioned thousands of antiquity's greatest artworks, to be taken from cities across the Mediterranean and brought to Constantinople. Year after year, vessels unloaded monumental bronzes and lifelike marbles onto the city's docks. These were the works of legendary artists, such as Phidias and Lysippos. Their new home was truly grand, although their old homes were noticeably less so. As St. Jerome noted at the time, Constantine's new city had left all other cities in the Roman Empire naked.

In the wide-open hills and valleys between the Severan fortifications and the new Constantinian walls, Constantine had a free hand to design the city that bore his name. That was much less true in the easternmost area of old Byzantion. There he was constrained by a landscape already well built up. The choicest area was, of course, the acropolis (the site of the current Topkapi Palace), the towering site of the original Greek settlement still reigning over two continents and the waterway that separated them. As the Ottoman sultans later appreciated, this was the perfect location for an imperial palace. Yet in Constantine's day it was heavily populated by pagan temples, holy sites for the majority of Constantinople's new citizens. Constantine had already received bitter criticism for his mother's demolition of temples in Jerusalem. Those, however, had rested on Christian holy sites. There was no such imperative in Constantinople. Constantine was a pious Christian, but he never forgot that Christianity remained a minority religion. He built churches, but he also took care to support the state cults and had no qualms about decorating his city with the gods and goddesses of the Greco-Roman world. It is sometimes said that Constantine built his new city to be a Christian imitation of pagan Rome. Nothing could be more false. Constantinople was just as pagan, and just as Christian, as the faraway city on the Tiber.

This was evident enough in Constantine's embellishments of Byzantion's ancient forum, the Tetrastoon. There Constantine extended and beautified the square's porticoes and built two new pagan shrines, one to Rhea and another to Tyche. After his mother's death around 331, the grief-stricken emperor ordered the construction in the Tetrastoon of a tall column topped by a colossal statue of Augusta Helena. The square was henceforth known as the "place of the Augusta," or the Augusteion. It would forever remain the open forum at the center of the old city. Today, as Hagia Sophia Square, it still buzzes with activity, although much of that now catering to the tourist trade. Dating back to the early Greek village, it is the oldest public space in Istanbul.

Just to the west of the Augusteion/Tetrastoon were the ancient Baths of Zeuxippus. Constantine expanded these significantly, adding lavish new halls and an outdoor enclosed gymnasium adorned with every kind of artwork. Already embellished by Septimius Severus, the Baths of Zeuxippus became under Constantine one of the most opulent public spaces in the empire. Christodorus of Coptos, the author of a later description of Constantinople known as the *Patria*, described eighty individual statues in the baths, depicting gods, heroes, and famous men and women.

Just southwest of the baths was Byzantion's Hippodrome. Here, too, Constantine greatly expanded on what Severus had begun. The stands on both sides of the racecourse were built higher and reinforced with passages behind and below the seats. The *carceres*, or "starting gates," were richly decorated with a tall marble superstructure that served as the new face of the Hippodrome to all who passed by. The *carceres* themselves were topped by a magnificent life-size bronze statue of a charioteer in his gleaming chariot, pulled by a quadriga of four prancing steeds. Of particular difficulty was the completion of the sphendone, the rounded portion of the stands at the far end of the racecourse. Because the ground dropped quickly toward the sea there, Severus had simply left the area open. Constantine ordered the construction of a complex substructure stretching down the steep hill, holding up the monumental sphendone at the Hippodrome level. When completed, the entire Hippodrome flowed seamlessly together, hiding the dramatic difference in elevation below it. Altogether, the Hippodrome could seat more than one hundred thousand people—five times more than had lived in the old city of Byzantion.

Although the stands are long gone, one can still see the sphendone by walking down the hill on Nakilbent Sokak. It survives because it continues to provide a substructure for numerous modern buildings, including Marmara University. The Hippodrome can also be seen in the long open area of the Atmeydani to the northwest of the Blue Mosque. During the games, four charioteers raced around a central *spina*, thrilling the spectators with their daring turns and frightful colli, sions. In a typical race, the chariots circled the *spina* seven times, for a total distance of approximately one and a half miles. The winner would then be crowned with a laurel wreath by the emperor or his representa, tive from the imperial loge, a magnificent box from which the emperor and his court watched the games. For most citizens, the Hippodrome was the only place one could actually see the emperor. In subsequent centuries, crowds would take the opportunity to shout their grievances, and if these were not met, they might forget all about the games and engage instead in destructive civil unrest (as we shall see).

Constantine was determined that the Hippodrome rival the Circus Maximus in Rome. Because the *spina* ran the length of the racecourse, its beautification was essential to the overall magnificence of the space. Excavations in 1927 revealed that Septimius Severus had already provided the *spina* with a number of fountains. A common feature in circuses, fountains not only enhanced the scenery, but also cooled the air for the spectators. Constantine likely kept those fountains, and per, haps added more. The wide low wall of the *spina* was also broken in two places to make room for Egyptian obelisks, in imitation of the circus in Rome. Constantine already had transported one porphyry obelisk, yet that was placed at the Philadelphion with a large cross affixed to its top. It appears that he ordered that an additional pair of ancient obelisks be brought from Egypt, but they did not arrive before his death.

Directly between the two planned obelisks and opposite the imperial box, the *spina* was broken again to make room for the bronze Serpent

Column of Delphi. This extraordinary artifact was forged by the free Greek cities in 479 BC, after the Persian Wars, as a votive offering to Apollo. Cast in one piece, the column depicts three serpents twining their bodies together thirty feet into the air before the heads jut out in opposing directions, thus forming a base for a holy tripod. According to Herodotus, the allied cities inscribed their names on the lowest coils. Constantine ordered this famous relic removed from Delphi and placed at the ceremonial center of the Hippodrome. Although a Christian, Constantine had formerly worshipped a sun god, so it is not surprising that he sought out this famous item dedicated to Apollo. Mangled and broken, the base of the Serpent Column still stands where Constantine planted it seventeen centuries ago. And on its lowest coils, it still bears witness to an ancient war for the survival of the West.

The Serpent Column was by no means the only bronze statue along the Hippodrome's *spina*. Indeed, there were so many that later observers had difficulty identifying them. Usually they simply described crowds of brazen men, gods, and animals. All the statues were likely brought from other cities. Among them was a massive statue of Hercules produced by Lysippos. Adorned in a lion's skin, Hercules was shown despondent after learning of his labors. We are told that a man's belt could just barely be fastened around the statue's thumb and that Hercules's shin was as tall as a man. Sharing the *spina* with Hercules was a bronze ass and driver that had been placed in Actium by Rome's first emperor, Augustus, to commemorate his victory over Marc Antony. There were also several she-wolves evoking the memory of Romulus and Remus, the legendary founders of Rome. A hippopotamus, elephant, lion, and several sphinxes could also be seen. One group depicted an eagle taking flight with a venomous snake in its talons attempting to strike; while another, a hippopotamus and crocodile locked in a struggle fatal to both.

The imperial loge on the southeastern side of the Hippodrome was directly connected to the palace complex on the site of what is today the Blue Mosque. Much of this land had not been part of ancient Byzantion because the terrain there sloped downward toward the sea. Yet no other land was available so near the city center. Placing the Great Palace, as the palace complex came to be called, directly against the southeast side of the Hippodrome had the effect of integrating the emperor's quarters into the civic and religious heart of the city. The Hippodrome became a part of the palace, a grand receiving room where an emperor could address and listen to his people.

The Great Palace was, as one might expect, a magnificent structure designed to strike awe in those who visited. In Constantine's day it consisted largely of a single major building that filled the current Blue Mosque grounds. A ceremonial entrance, the Chalke, stood at the northern corner of the Augusteion. The palace complex branched farther northeast to take up the far side of the Augusteion, where one could find the Magnaura Palace, originally used for court ceremonies and the reception of ambassadors. Within the main palace was a massive throne set with a gold cross encrusted with jewels. There were also large guards' quarters, several council chambers, an imperial chapel harboring relics of the True Cross, and an enormous banqueting hall. In later years the Great Palace would be expanded farther down into two lower terraces, ultimately bringing it to the shores of the sea below.

After four years of intense construction, the cityscape of Byzantion had been transformed into something altogether different. It was Constantinople. But Constantine was not finished. It would have been apparent to anyone who looked carefully that the city the emperor was building was far grander than simply an imperial residence. Emperor Diocletian's old headquarters at Nicomedia, where Constantine often went to escape the din of hammers and the bustle of workmen, was tiny in comparison. Constantine's real plan began to reveal itself only in the spring of 330, when he announced forty days of celebrations and rituals to inaugurate the city upon its completion. Of course it was nowhere near complete, but the site of the ceremonies was finished, and that was enough.

The day so long anticipated came on May 11, 330. All the city's residents were summoned to the Hippodrome to take part in pagan and Christian blessings in which the heavens were asked for eternal favor on the new city. Then, to the roll of drums, the clamor of cymbals, and peals of horns, the emperor and his court processed out of the Hippodrome and down the richly adorned and colonnaded Mese boulevard (modern-day Divan Yolu). The people followed. It was a rich procession, punctuated at various stops by prayers and speeches. The journey was not long. One can walk it today in under ten minutes. At the end of the route, the people poured out of the covered boulevard and into a wide, circular forum surrounded on all sides by double-level porticoes. This was the new Forum of Constantine, built at the summit of a hill just beyond the old Severan walls, on the site of Byzantion's ancient grave-yard. The graves were forgotten, covered over by spotless stone pave-ment, all part of a showplace of Roman architecture. All around the forum, on the ground-level archways of the porticoes, were lifelike equestrian statues of bronze. Numerous other statues decorated the open area, including a bronze colossal depiction of Hera so large that it took four yokes of oxen to move just the head.

The crowds pressed into the forum, filling up the open space, rush-ing to the upper levels of the porticoes, and scrambling onto the nearby roofs. It was a sight not to be missed—one that citizens of Constanti-nople would remember for more than a millennium. Constantine, his officials, and his court then approached the most important monument in the forum. At its exact center stood a giant column base, much larger than a man. On it rose a massive column made entirely of porphyry drums set perfectly one on the other and fastened together by powerful metal bands in the shape of laurel crowns. It rose more than one hun-dred twenty feet over the forum (Illustration 3). At its top was an ornately decorated capital that bore a thrice-life-size bronze statue of Constan-tine, the founder of the city. In the statue's right hand, Constantine held a spear; while in his left, an orb signifying his dominion over the whole world. On his head he wore a crown of seven rays, linking him with not only the sun god Helios, but also the Son of God, Jesus, who was occa-sionally depicted as Apollo pulling the sun across the sky in his chariot. It was an inspired choice, for it evoked pagan and Christian religions while placing Constantine at the center of both. There the assembled performed the final dedication. Yet, it was in many ways a rededication, almost a refounding. For the new city was not named Constantinople, as it had been just a few years earlier, when ground was broken. It was given another name: Nova Roma, "New Rome."

What was in a name? In this case, everything. Although it was set in the sparsely populated and comparatively backward West, Rome was nonetheless the capital of its sprawling empire. Since the days of Julius Caesar, Romans had feared that one of their leaders, seduced by the wealth and allure of the East, might move the capital. The fall of Caesar and then Marc Antony, both of whom had toyed with the idea, had made it so unpalatable that it was never revisited again. Even Diocletian, who had changed everything else about the Roman government, did not tinker with Rome's ancient prerogatives. Constantine did. In the dedication of his new city on May 11, 330, he declared henceforth that there were two Romes, two capitals. It was a stunning declaration that would forever change the city and the empire.

Presumably people called the city New Rome for some time after that—particularly when they were around the emperor. But the name never caught on. Soon after Constantine's death, even the Roman government reverted to the name Constantinople. Nonetheless, it remained the Eastern capital of the Roman Empire. Like a phoenix, the city on the Bosporus had risen from the ashes of its annihilation to be reborn as something more glorious. It was an imperial capital, the ruler of an empire.

In one sense, the founding of a second capital of the Roman Empire was a natural next step after the division of imperial authority. After all, if two emperors were to govern, did that not also suggest two seats of power? Yet the intricately diverse Roman Empire remained so firmly attached to the city of its birth that it seemed impossible to share that glory with any other place. Only an emperor as powerful and secure as Constantine could have made it happen. Only an empire as wealthy as Rome could have paid for it. And only a city as perfectly suited as Istanbul could have made it permanent.

Perhaps the most iconic symbol of Constantinople's new status was the monument placed at the end of Via Egnatia, just to the west of the Augusteion Square (formerly the Tetrastoon). Once, the Via Egnatia had nourished ancient Byzantion, forging a land connection to the Western Roman Empire and elevating the Bosporus Strait to a more strategic and profitable position than the Hellespont to the south. Like all Roman roads, the milestones along Via Egnatia marked the distance to the great "mile marker zero" in Rome, known as the Milliarum Aureum, or Golden Milestone. As the saying goes, "all roads lead to Rome," something that was clearly driven home to travelers as they marked off the miles en-graved on the roadside markers. That changed after 330. Rather than the end of Via Egnatia, Constantinople had become its beginning. Indeed, it was henceforth the beginning of *every* road in the Eastern half of the Ro-man Empire, and marked by a large, beautifully decorated milestone known as the Milion. Like the Golden Milestone in Rome, the Milion in Constantinople was engraved with the distances to all the major cities in the empire. Over it was built an elaborate tetrapylon consisting of four massive arches supporting a golden dome. And over the dome stood a bronze sculpture group depicting Constantine and Helena together hold-ing up the True Cross of Christ. The area around the Milion was likewise richly decorated with various equestrian statues of emperors, such as Tra-jan and Hadrian. No one who saw this impressive monument in the very heart of downtown Constantinople could miss its bold statement. The city was now at the center of the empire, the center of the world.

Chapter 6

Baptized Capital

Constantinople's transformation was staggering. Within the space of thirty years, Constantine and his son Constantius II converted a midsize Greek town of some twenty thousand people into a sprawling megalopolis of more than half a million souls.

Constantine had a great many plans for his capital, yet as he approached his sixtieth birthday he knew that it would be difficult to see them all to completion. Some, however, were more important than others, particularly as he began to contemplate the end of life. The first emperor in centuries who could not expect to become a god, Constantine nonetheless hoped to be welcomed into Heaven by the same Christ who had helped him to win the imperial throne. Although he had a mausoleum in Rome, Constantine was determined to be buried in the city that bore his name. Given that he was frequently away on campaigns against the Goths during his later years, it appears that he gave orders and a strict deadline to architects in Constantinople to produce for him a mausoleum. However, they appear to have had little oversight: the quality of the finished construction was not good, and within twenty years the mausoleum was considered unsafe to enter.

These long-term structural problems were probably invisible in the 330s, when the tomb was finished. It was built on a prominent hill within the expanded city area very near the gate in the new walls through which the northern avenue passed out. (Today this is the site of the Fatih Mosque.) The design of Constantine's mausoleum was especially striking, breaking dramatically from those of earlier imperial burials. Constantine's monumental porphyry tomb was set in the center of a large rotunda, surrounded by twelve other tombs, like the numbers on a clock. The orbiting sarcophagi were meant to hold the bodies of the twelve Apostles, although Constantine must have expected that many, if not all, of them would remain symbolic reliquaries for the fore-seeable future. The body of St. Peter, for example, was housed in a shrine in Rome that Constantine himself had constructed; he made no attempt to have it sent to Constantinople. Near the imperial tomb was an altar for the celebration of Mass. Adjoining the mausoleum was a richly decorated basilica-style church dedicated to the Apostles. Some have suggested that Constantine was asserting architecturally his own equality with the Apostles. Yet the bishop and historian Eusebius, who knew Constantine, reported that the emperor simply wanted his body to be close to the many prayers that would be offered in so marvelous a sanctuary.

Holy Apostles was not the only church that Constantine founded in the new capital. Two of the most important were in the old portion of the city, where space remained at a premium. Although there was little room left on the acropolis, the emperor managed to squeeze a Christian church into its southern end. This was the church of Hagia Eirene, or "Holy Peace." It was to serve as the city's cathedral until the second, much larger church was finished. This was founded just to the south of Hagia Eirene and north of the Augusteion. An imposing basilica-style structure, it was given the name Hagia Sophia, or "Holy Wisdom." Nei-ther of these early churches survives, although they were built on the sites of the current versions. When completed in 360, Hagia Sophia became Constantinople's new cathedral.

Despite the structural provisions for his death, Constantine had not yet completed his spiritual preparations. He had converted to Christi-anity two decades earlier, yet remained unbaptized. This was not as unusual in the fourth century as it may seem in the twenty-first. Chris-tians believed that baptism washed away from the sinner all sin, both original and subsequent. They also believed that baptized Christians could have their sins forgiven through confession and penance. Dis-agreement remained concerning the Church's authority to forgive the most serious sins against God, such as blasphemy or murder. There was also some debate over what constituted grave sins. Was a soldier fighting in war guilty of murder? Or a judge who condemned a criminal to death? In time these questions would be settled, but in Constantine's day the uncertainty led to a natural anxiety about the state of one's soul. It was for this reason that powerful men often put off their baptism until they were aged or near death. At the age of sixty-five, Constantine was, it seemed, at last prepared to be baptized. Yet, as with all things in an emperor's life, he wished it to be a truly remarkable event. In 336 he began preparations for a major military campaign against Persia. Along the way, he planned to stop at Jerusalem to be baptized, like Christ, in the Jordan River.

Matters did not go as planned. Just after Easter 337, the emperor fell ill. At first he did not consider it serious, but traveled to nearby Aquae to take in the hot mineral baths, just to be safe. His condition contin-ued to deteriorate, though. Since the waters were ineffective, he went to Helenopolis (modern-day Altinova) to pray for deliverance at the Church of St. Lucian. That, too, did not help. Realizing that his time was short, and wanting to die in his beloved city, he ordered his men to return him to Constantinople at once. As his ornate carriage, surrounded by war-riors and priests, rolled along the road to the city of Nicomedia, a call came from the doctors to halt. The emperor could go no farther. He was laid in a bed in a small rural house and made as comfortable as pos-sible. Several bishops who had accompanied him came to his bedside urging him to be baptized. He told them how he had hoped to receive the sacrament in the Jordan, but that if God willed it, he would receive it now. Still optimistic, he promised that should he recover, he would lead a good life without endangering his soul. With the waters of eternal life poured peacefully upon his head, the founder of Constantinople passed away.

The body of Constantine I was welcomed back to Constantinople with bitter tears and lavish ceremonies. His son Constantius II presided over the funeral, laying his father to rest in the round mausoleum, now topped with a golden dome and decorated with images of the Apostles. It was a glorious event. Yet when the ceremonies had concluded and the tears were dried, it fell to Constantius to complete his father's building program—a formidable task, one that would remain with him the rest of his life. Year after year the city grew, alive with the racket of rapid construction. What had recently been grassy or wooded hills were quickly covered over with streets, homes, and public spaces. By Constantius's death in 361, the city had largely filled the walled area that seemed so vast when his father traced it out just fifty years earlier.

The dramatic expansion of Constantinople required the creation of an extensive infrastructure, about which we know little or nothing. Food was, of course, a major concern. Cities of this size cannot live on local produce, but require constant grain and other food shipments. For Constantinople these came largely from the fertile Nile Basin in Egypt, which also supplied the hungry mouths of Rome. By the end of the fourth century, Constantinople had twenty public bakeries distributing some eighty thousand free loaves daily. Food shipments alone would have required around three thousand cargo vessels annually, all docked at the city's increasingly crowded ports. Constantius built new warehouses and granaries at the city's ancient wharfs at Neorion and Prosphorion. Yet food was but one commodity that a city of nearly half a million people required. Best estimates suggest that around five hundred major cargo vessels loading and unloading their goods would have been docked in Constantinople at any given time—something that would have required between two and three miles of wharf facilities. Byzantion's ports were much too small to handle this traffic. Constantius, therefore, ordered the construction of an entirely new, walled port built on the southern side of the city, directly on the Sea of Marmara. Although it no longer exists, the lines of Sophia Harbor, as it was called, are still marked out by the modern-day street Kadirga Limani. This new port was instantly busy.

Still it was not enough. We can imagine the hundreds of vessels turned away from Constantinople's ports, forced to anchor offshore or to sail to other nearby ports to await a free landing. Near the end of the fourth century the emperor Theodosius I (379–95) ordered the construction of a new harbor west of Sophia, at the natural bay formed by the mouth of the Lycus River. The river itself was covered over, placed deep under the city, where it still remains. This new Harbor of Theodosius (or Eleutherios, as it was sometimes called) was a massive affair, with hundreds of landings and at least a mile of wharfage. Like all Constantinople's ports, this one no longer exists. It was situated in the modern-day Yenikapı district. Some idea of its extraordinary size and traffic, however, came to light in 2004, when a plan to lay a subway line and station through Yenikapı was abruptly halted by the discovery of numerous shipwrecks buried in the earth. Since then, the Yenikapı excavation has become one of the largest in Europe. Dozens of vessels of all types have been uncovered, some with intact cargoes. Other discoveries include hundreds of anchors and dozens of massive cut stones, some belonging to the walls built by Constantine. Perhaps most interesting, though, are the thousands of daily-use items such as combs, shoes, and simple tools packed aboard ill-fated journeys into or out of Constantinople's largest harbor.

The Harbor of Theodosius solved the problem of food imports, but did nothing for the increasing need for freshwater. Half a million people require a great deal of water, both for their own personal consumption and for a sewer system. In antiquity, civilized urban life required lavish public baths and elaborate public fountains (known as *nymphaea*), which dotted ancient urban landscapes. Some of the latter were small, yet many were massive, ornate monsters spewing water in all directions. Think of the Trevi Fountain in Rome, which, while modern, is supplied by ancient aqueducts. As a general rule of thumb, ancient Romans in elite cities required approximately 265 gallons per person per day. (By comparison, modern Americans use approximately 100 gallons per day.) Multiply that by 500,000 people, and the amount of water required by Constantinople was truly staggering. As in Rome, it was necessary to seek out freshwater sources farther and farther from the city, building extensive aqueduct lines to carry it underground and over valleys. A major water project was completed in 373, named for the current emperor Valens. Although it is commonly thought that the Aqueduct of Valens is simply the impressive structure that today stretches across Atatürk Boulevard, it was in fact a complex of water lines that stretched more than sixty miles to the Istranca and Balkan Mountains.

So extensive a network of aqueducts could pose a strategic risk should an enemy discover their locations and cut off the supply. The Romans responded to this risk in innovative ways. Large underground cisterns were dug in Constantinople to hold water for easy retrieval from wells and for use in times of drought or danger. The most famous of these is the Basilica Cistern, very near the Milion and the Augusteion in ancient Constantinople. To visit that hushed space today is to step back into another age, far removed from the noisy Turkish city above. Its arched brick ceiling is supported by 336 columns that collectively prop up the buildings above. This one cistern could hold more than 100,000 tons of water, yet it was just one of many midsize underground cisterns scattered across the vast city. The columns themselves, so serene today, illumined by colored lights and accompanied by the sound of dripping water from above, are justifiably famous for their diverse shapes and designs. Yet virtually all of them were recycled from older buildings. Indeed, as beautiful as the Basilica Cistern is today, it was never meant to be visited on foot, with but a few inches of water along the floor. All the columns that inspire such wonder among modern tourists were for centuries underwater. The purpose of the cistern, after all, was to be full.

It is still not known how many underground cisterns were built in Constantinople. Fewer than a hundred are known, but there were undoubtedly several thousand. Over the centuries some collapsed, others were repurposed, and still others remain to be discovered. But in the fourth and fifth centuries their function was simple: to store large amounts of water for the ready use of the citizens and for cases of emergency. These underground cisterns were only part of Constantinople's water storage strategy. There were at least three massive open-air cisterns as well. These deep rectangular pools not only held large amounts of surplus water, but also provided a rudimentary filtration system for water bound for the smaller underground cisterns. The open-air reservoirs were so large that one of them, the Cistern of Aetius, is used today as a soccer stadium (modern-day Vefa Stadyumu).

When Emperor Constantius died in 361, the city was in many ways as his father, Constantine, envisioned it. Byzantion had become Constantinople. As the city changed, so, too, did the empire it ruled. Nowhere was this more evident than in the startling rise of Christianity. What had been a hated, persecuted faith of the underclass became in a few short decades the beloved creed of the majority of Romans. Churches sprang up by the thousands across the empire, nowhere more rapidly than in Constantinople.

The conversion of the Roman Empire meant that Christian heresy was serious business. The discredited doctrines of Arianism, con-demned at the Council of Nicaea in 325, were resurrected under Em-perors Constantius and Valens, both of whom appointed Arian Christian bishops in Constantinople. Arianism held that Christ was less than God, a demigod of sorts, the firstborn of creation. Arian missionaries were sent to the barbarian homelands, where they converted the Ger-manic Goths to their brand of Christianity. That is why Emperor Va-lens responded to the pleas of his Gothic coreligionists by allowing many thousands of them to enter the Roman Empire to settle in the Balkans. Yet once they had arrived, they began to quarrel with the Ro-man authorities responsible for their refugee camps. In the end, they turned their anger toward their benefactor, attacking nearby Roman cities and finally meeting Valens himself in battle near the Thracian city of Adrianople in 378. It was the worst Roman defeat in centuries. The Goths wiped out the Roman legions, murdered the emperor, and began rampaging across Greece. The citizens of Constantinople feared the worst for their new city, but Greece was full of soft targets, so there was no need for the Goths to attack the heavily fortified capital city.

Emperor Valens was succeeded in the East by Theodosius. A West-erner, Theodosius was forced to fight his way across Goth-plagued Greece to take up his position in Constantinople in 380. The Roman army in the West was so depleted after the disaster at Adrianople that Theodosius had to hire other barbarians to win his victories and ulti-mately to settle the Goths in Greece under treaties of alliance. Theodo-sius then claimed victory and entered Constantinople in triumph. He was determined to put things right in the East.

One of his greatest problems remained the Arian heresy. For de-cades this dispute had turned Romans against Romans, caused Chris-tian rulers to reject the decrees of the Council of Nicaea, and most recently led an Arian emperor to invite barbarians into the Roman Empire, with cataclysmic results. It had to stop. Theodosius, who was an orthodox believer in the Nicene Creed, had previously issued a joint decree with the emperor in the West, Gratian, that the inspired decisions of the Council of Nicene must be accepted by all Christians, thereby outlaw-ing Arianism. Within days of his entry into Constantinople, Theodo-sius removed the Arian bishop of the city and replaced him with a

Catholic. He then summoned a new ecumenical council, which met the following year in Constantinople's church of Hagia Eirene, very near the palace. This was the first of many ecumenical councils that would convene in Constantinople and its suburbs. Although the city had come late to Christianity, it quickly became the center of the faith in the Roman East simply by virtue of its population and political clout.

As with the Council of Nicaea, the hundreds of prelates who arrived to take part in the Council of Constantinople were meant to represent the successors of Christ's Apostles. In practice, though, the attendees were almost exclusively from the Eastern half of the empire. No representatives from Pope Damasus I in Rome took part. The core issue of the council was Arianism, which it firmly condemned. Backed up by an unfailing imperial will, this time the decree stuck. Arian clergy across the East were ejected from their churches and replaced with Catholics. Although other heresies would stir in the Eastern Roman Empire, the problem of Arianism had at least been solved.

The pope, who was (and is) the bishop of Rome, did not have as much at stake in this council as his colleagues in the East. Or so it seemed. Arianism had never taken root in the less populous and less Christian West. But the fathers of the Council of Constantinople also turned their attention to a matter that would long affect the relationship between Rome and the Eastern capital. Since the earliest days of Christianity it had been recognized that certain bishops had greater authority than others. These "metropolitan sees," as the name suggests, were found in big cities, and could often trace their foundation to a specific Apostle or one of his disciples. At the top of this hierarchy were the three "patriarchal sees," defined at Nicaea as Rome, Antioch, and Alexandria. In 325 these were the three largest cities in the Roman Empire, each with political authority over extended regions. More important for the fathers of the council, though, was that all three of these sees were believed to have been founded directly or indirectly by St. Peter, the prince of the Apostles. It had been to Peter that Christ gave the special authority of "binding and loosing" as well as "the keys of the kingdom of God" (Matthew 16:13–19). This authority was further attested by Peter's actions in the Acts of the Apostles and confirmed by the Letters of St. Paul. According to tradition, Peter had been the first bishop of Antioch before leaving for Rome, where he was also the first bishop (i.e., pope). In Rome he was martyred. Peter's disciple Mark was believed to have been the first bishop of Alexandria.

The foundation of Constantinople, however, introduced a troubling wrinkle into this system. When Constantine and the Christian leaders had met at Nicaea in 325, only a fraction of the empire was Christian, and the new capital had not yet been founded. By 381, when a council convened in Constantinople, the large majority of Romans were Christians. Indeed, it was difficult to find a member of the old pagan cults outside of ancient patrician families, academy scholars, and rural peasants. Likewise, Constantinople had become not only one of the largest cities in the empire, but also the new governmental center of the East. It was, therefore, considered not right that the bishop of Constantinople should have the same rank as any other local bishop. He was the pastor of the emperor himself. The Council of Constantinople dealt with this problem in its third canon, which read, "The bishop of Constantinople shall have the primacy of honor after the bishop of Rome, because Constantinople is New Rome."

This simple canon constituted the very earliest salvo in a struggle that would ensue between Rome and Constantinople for centuries, even unto today. With a marvelous economy of words, it elevated Constantinople above two ancient sees and degraded Rome's authority while seeming to defend it. The three Nicene patriarchates were based on apostolic, specifically Petrine, succession. Constantinople had no apostolic succession. Byzantion was never mentioned in Scripture; nor were there any early traditions of visits by Christ's Apostles. Indeed, the city never had a particularly noteworthy Christian population. The council's third canon, therefore, cleverly posited that the authority of the patriarchates was based on Roman political authority rather than Petrine succession. It also asserted that Rome's position over Constantinople was simply one of "honor," rather than of any real authority over matters of the Church—something Rome had always claimed. When news of the council reached Pope Damasus he ratified all the canons except the third. He insisted that the bishop of Constantinople had no right to elevate himself above Alexandria and Antioch simply because he resided in the new capital. His complaints fell on deaf ears. Although the Christians in the West continued to object across the centuries, the bishop of Constantinople soon donned the title "ecumenical patriarch." Constantinople was already the political leader of the East. It was becoming its spiritual head as well.

By 381, Theodosius could celebrate his successes on the battlefield as well as the victory of Catholic Christianity. It is sometimes said that he made Christianity the official religion of the Roman Empire. He did not, largely because that was unnecessary. The Roman Empire was already thoroughly Christian before he came to the throne. Instead, Theodosius and his colleague in the West separated Rome from any official religion. Since the earliest days of the Republic, the pagan cults had been funded by the Roman government. By the late fourth century this had become grossly anachronistic. Great temples were maintained for the sake of a few devotees or a group of priests with government jobs. Theodosius, therefore, cut off government funding of the pagan cults. Since many of the temples were public property, that meant that they were either closed, sold, or given over to Christian worship. The eternal fire in Rome's Temple of Vesta was allowed to die, and the aged college of Vestal Virgins disbanded. The once-mighty pagan cults had become an antiquarian shell, a tradition rather than a practice. Theodosius simply defunded them, while at the same time strongly supporting the new religion of the Roman people, Christianity. Never again would paganism be more than a curiosity.

Victories of these sorts demanded monuments, and Theodosius undertook several projects in Constantinople to commemorate them. One still stands. The Hippodrome had been in business for decades, with regular chariot races most weeks and a variety of other public amusements. But in 380 the structure still had some noticeably missing elements. Constantine had left two gaps in the racecourse's *spina* to accommodate two Egyptian obelisks. Fifty years later they remained empty. Romans had a passion for obelisks, because of not only their beauty, but also the bold statements they made about the extent and power of the empire. Carved out of a single stone, Egyptian obelisks were massive yet fragile creations. To remove one from an Egyptian temple, transport it across the desert, load it aboard a specially constructed network of barges, sail it across the Mediterranean Sea, and then reerect it elsewhere, all without breaking it, was an exceptionally difficult and expensive task. For his new city, Constantine had ordered two obelisks transported from the ruins of Karnak to the bustling port of Alexandria. They probably did not arrive there until after his death in 337. Although they were both destined for Constantinople's Hippodrome, Constantius II ordered one of them sent instead to Rome, where it was erected in the Circus Maximus in 357. It is today the Lateran Obelisk, relocated and adorned with a cross by Pope Sixtus V in 1588. The second obelisk remained for decades on the Egyptian beach, too heavy to steal and too expensive to move. It even began attracting its own cult of devotees, who slept at its apex in the hope of acquiring mystical power.

Although emperors made plans to send the remaining obelisk to Constantinople, the strife and turmoil of the late Roman Empire always intervened. Theodosius, too, had his share of difficulties, but it appears that he made the transport of the obelisk a priority. It arrived in Constantinople's Hippodrome in 390, a decade after Theodosius came to power. There appear to have been a number of difficulties along the way. Originally almost one hundred feet tall, the obelisk arrived at the Hippodrome with its bottom third missing, making it a little over sixty-four feet. Then it took more than a month for the city prefect, Proclus, to find a way to lift the massive stone and set it on a pedestal prepared for it. The process was so laborious that the pedestal's two inscriptions, one in Latin and the other in Greek, both refer to it. For those who could not read, the process of lifting the obelisk was graphically depicted on the lower portion of the pedestal's north face.

This magnificent monument remains the only Egyptian obelisk in the Roman world that has not fallen or been moved since it was first placed. It is all the more remarkable given that it sits atop four bronze coated cubes, held there for centuries only by the enormity of the obelisk's weight. Although the stone pedestal on which it rests wears heavily its sixteen centuries of weather, fire, and earthquakes, the obelisk above, which was already seventeen hundred years old when it arrived in Constantinople, still looks new, its hieroglyphs still perfectly etched, still proclaiming the victories of Pharaoh Thutmose III. As for the obelisk's base, although it is badly damaged, it remains a marvel, for it

opens a window into the world of the Hippodrome, now passed completely away (Illustration 4). All four sides depict the imperial loge, the
grand box from which the emperor and his family watched the games.
Yet each side depicts different activities. On the south face, the imperial family is flanked by honor guards and the senatorial class. The
north provides a scene from the games, showing the crowds below waving their colors to cheer on their team of charioteers. On the west face,
a delegation of barbarians grovels before the emperor; while on the east
side, the emperor stands, preparing to crown the game's victor accompanied by a band of musicians playing strings, horns, and an organ. The
base even includes a depiction of the games themselves on the lower
south side. It is a truly remarkable artistic piece, made more so by its
continued existence after so many centuries on public display.

The erection of only one obelisk in the Hippodrome raised the question of the arrival of the second. After all, there was a space for it, and
the pageantry of the arena would certainly have been off-center with
just the one. Yet the days of harvesting Egyptian obelisks were over. It
was simply too difficult and costly for an empire faced with so many
other challenges. It was probably at this time, then, that a second obelisk
was constructed out of stone blocks. Carefully built to balance the Egyptian obelisk, the manufactured obelisk was covered in bronze plates,
which shone brightly in the sun. On its peak a globe was set, probably so
that it could be used as a sundial of sorts during the games. Like its colleague, the built obelisk still towers over the open area near the Sul-
tanamhet (Blue) Mosque, although stripped of its proud, glistening
raiment. Subsequent emperors continued to beautify the Hippodrome
through the centuries, adding additional statues and fountains. Yet with
the erection of the two obelisks, the arena was essentially complete.

Theodosius also made his mark on the growing city with the construction of a lavish public forum, which opened in 393. Along the main
street (the Mese) between the Forum of Constantine and the Philadel-
phion/Capitolium was a wide-open area, probably used as a livestock
market, known as the Forum Tauri, or Forum of the Bull. It is today
partially filled by Beyazit Square and parts of Istanbul University. Theodosius's new forum was modeled on the Forum of Trajan in Rome, well
known as the largest and most awe-inspiring in the world. Theodosius

was determined to rival it. The entire square north of the Mese was paved in marble and decorated with dozens of statues and a variety of fountains, including the Nymphaeum Maius, the largest in the city. Around the entire forum were placed beautiful porticoes, and to one side a richly decorated basilica. At the entrance to the forum was a massive triumphal arch consisting of three adjoining arches supported by monumental columns carved in the shape of tree trunks. It was the largest arch in the Roman world. Even today pieces of it can be seen beside the modern roadway. Near the center of the forum was a monumental column rising nearly one hundred feet, modeled on the column of Trajan in Rome. At its summit was a colossal statue of Theodosius. Like its twin, the column of Theodosius was covered in spiraling reliefs depicting the emperor's victorious campaigns. It was also hollow, with a door at street level that opened to a spiral staircase allowing one to climb to an observation deck at the top. The column, like everything else in the forum, no longer exists. It was pulled down by the Ottoman sultan Bayezid II around 1504. However, fragments of it were used in the construction of the Baths of Bayezid. During the twentieth century, the modern road (Ordu Caddesi) was widened and resurfaced, which had the effect of exposing some of the foundation stones of the baths. There the Roman soldiers who served under Theodosius, who for centuries had surveyed his majestic forum, stare out once more. One can see them easily along the sidewalk and on the nearby stairs.

Theodosius was the last emperor to rule a unified Roman Empire. He died in Milan in 395. His body was returned to Constantinople, where it was laid to rest in the Church of the Holy Apostles. The transfer of the imperial remains was an omen of the rapid decline of the empire in the West and its continued survival in the new capital of the East. Rome would indeed fall, but it would live on for a thousand years in the city of Constantinople.

Chapter 7

East of the Fall of Rome

Emperor Theodosius the Great, who had made his mark so indelibly on Constantinople, was powerless to halt the decline of the empire that it governed. Gothic tribes still roamed the Balkans, made up key segments of the Roman military, and invaded the western portions of the empire. When he died in 395, Theodosius left the troubled Roman Empire to his two young sons, Honorius to rule in Italy and Arcadius to rule in Constantinople. Arcadius had the better deal. The city of Rome was so beset by crime and civil unrest that Honorius, like his father, preferred to rule from Milan. When the Goths invaded Italy in 402 he moved the Western capital to Ravenna, a middle-size coastal town that was the home port of the Western fleet. Germanic tribes of Alans, Suevi, and Vandals invaded Gaul (today's France) and Spain, while Britain was in revolt. In 408 the Gothic leader Alaric led his war bands into Italy and surrounded Rome. Two years later he captured the Eternal City and brutally sacked it. It was the first time the city of Rome had been conquered in eight hundred years.

The world was ending—or at least it seemed that way to Romans in the western half of the empire. Even in the East, the sack of Rome went down hard. Some wondered if the old gods, who had overseen the glories of Roman expansion, were wreaking their vengeance on a traitorous empire. But there was never any serious consideration of abandoning Christianity. Indeed, Rome's new faith offered a completely different perspective on the calamities of the age. In his influential work *City of God*, St. Augustine advised his countrymen not to look at the fall of terrestrial cities, but to focus on the heavenly city of Jerusalem promised by Christ. Rich rewards awaited those who endured and were faithful to the end. These were words of comfort for a difficult era, one in which the fabric of civilization seemed to be slipping quietly away.

News of Rome's plight was on every tongue, but in Constantinople it was merely a topic of conversation, not an experienced reality. Situated at the political, cultural, and economic centers of the Eastern empire, Constantinople continued to grow at an amazingly rapid rate. It was difficult for those in its busy markets and forums to imagine that times were hard for their empire, and the same was true of Emperor Arcadius. He made no attempt to help his brother in the West. Leaving the government to his ministers and wife, Aelia Eudoxia, Arcadius spent much of his time enjoying the pastimes of the palace in Constantinople and planning out the construction of a new forum of his own. Naturally he placed it along the Mese, setting it on the southern arm of the covered main road headed to the Golden Gate, in what is today the Cerrahpaşa district. Little is known about the Forum of Arcadius, which was also sometimes called the Forum Bovi, or Forum of the Ox. Although it was much smaller than the Forum of Theodosius, Arcadius was determined to grace it with a similar column. The problem was that the spiraling reliefs on these sorts of columns always depicted the victorious campaigns of those who commissioned them. Arcadius, who preferred to remain amid the luxuries of his city, had no such exploits. No matter. His ministers had previously ejected a number of Goths stationed in Constantinople under the command of one Gainas. The Goths were subsequently hunted down and massacred, thus providing a makeshift victory. It was stretched out to fit the column. Today only the base survives, wedged between modern buildings like a broken tree stump.

So, while Honorius cowered in the swamps of Ravenna, Arcadius busied himself with appointing his forum, attending games, and entertaining at court. While Goths carried fire and sword down the streets of Rome, Constantinople's rich avenues were filled with multitudes seeking bargains or rushing off to the theater, baths, and races.

By 400, Constantinople had three or perhaps four theaters and at least one open-air amphitheater. All were government funded and therefore richly decorated. Particularly favored among the middle and lower classes were the mimes, the ancient equivalent of sitcoms. These bawdy low-brow comedies were filled with plenty of physical gags, raucous humor based on current events, and sexual jokes. In antiquity Roman mimes sometimes performed sex acts onstage, although whether that was still allowed in Christian Constantinople is an open question. Disdaining such vulgarity, the upper classes attended other theaters, which performed pantomimes, big-budget extravaganzas with full orchestras and masked actors embellishing their plays with singing and dancing, but no sex. As for the amphitheater, traditionally Romans used these for gladiatorial battles and wild animal fights. These spectacles were never very popular in the eastern half of the empire, and even in Rome gladiator games had fallen out of favor with a disapproving Christian audience. It is unclear, then, what attractions Constantinople's amphitheater offered.

No theater in Constantinople, however, could compete with the massive Hippodrome. Set like a jewel into the downtown palace area, this extraordinary stadium could seat one hundred thousand people, and often did. It was not just a place for chariot races, although the citizens were mad for those. It was also a meeting place for the city, a drawing room for the masses to come together as one and occasionally even to address their emperor, who would appear in the imperial loge. Chariot racing had long been popular in the Greek East. Charioteers, highly trained professionals, were grouped into teams and used equipment that was exorbitantly expensive. Victorious charioteers, like sports heroes today, could reach a mythic status of popularity. A number of statues of the great charioteer Porphyrus, for example, have been found in Istanbul. A local favorite, he also competed with his team in other cities.

Across the ancient Roman Empire there were only four chariot teams, each designated by a color. By the fifth century, those had been reduced to two, the Blues and the Greens. At least once a week the gates of the Hippodrome would open, allowing thousands of Constantinople's citizens to file in. To the left were the seats reserved for aristocrats and governmental officials. The closer that one could sit to the imperial loge, of course, the better. To the right were the sections for the regular citizens. Here, too, there were sharp divisions, first by team supporters and then by social status. And the divisions went deeper than that. The Blues and the Greens were not simply teams, but highly competitive clubs of sports fans, whose activities extended well beyond the games. They were, as historians refer to them, circus factions, and they had a clear organization. The faction leaders sat directly opposite the emperor; they were present for the award ceremonies and, in later centuries, took part in virtually all civic ceremonies inside and outside the Hippodrome. Emperors usually expressed a preference for one faction or the other (usually the Blues), and in later years the favored faction could occasionally provide an emperor with armed support against urban insurrections. It is not true, as one sometimes reads, that the factions were political parties. Instead, they were extremely enthusiastic fan clubs whose members, when unhappy, could become very, very dangerous.

The games would begin with prayers and ceremonies and then a blare of trumpets and an announcement of the first race. Then, as the line of twelve gates crashed opened and the chariots thundered out onto the wide track, the crowds would roar their encouragement, waving the brightly colored flags of their team. On most days, there would be between thirty and forty races. Each took only a few minutes, so there was plenty of time for other entertainments such as drinking, socializing, and watching side shows: acrobats, jugglers, trained animals, and mimes.

Not everyone was happy with the raucous events of the Hippodrome. The most famous critic was the patriarch of Constantinople John Chrysostom. A highly acclaimed preacher, Chrysostom ("the Golden Mouthed") was much loved by the common people of Constantinople, for his sermons often appealed to the simplicity of Christ's message of love. Even better, he was a frequent critic of the habits of the wealthy and the excesses of the games. During Mass in Hagia Sophia, he often lamented that attendance in the church was nothing compared to the thousands crowded into the nearby Hippodrome. He complained about the fans who left the race track "so frenzied that they fill the whole city with their shouting and disorderly racket." He particularly condemned those wealthier citizens in the prime upper seats, where Constantinople's many prostitutes and gold diggers could be found "bareheaded and with a complete lack of shame, dressed in golden garments, flirting coquettishly and singing harlots' songs with seductive tunes." These women, the patriarch warned, not only brought the sins of lust and adultery to the games, but they broke up good Christian marriages. The patriarch refused to allow those who attended the games to receive Communion without repentance and absolution.

Hippodrome-goers were not the only targets of John Chrysostom's sermons. He frequently berated clergy more interested in wealth, finery, and banquets than in the care of Christ's flock. What made him most popular among the common people, though, was his barbed, even mocking condemnation of the lavish ostentation of Constantinople's wealthy elite. He ridiculed the rich vestments and heavy jewelry of the aristocracy, which they proudly wore even in the church. After one such sermon, the empress Eudoxia concluded (probably correctly) that his barbs were directed at her. She was, after all, the best-dressed woman in the city. With silent rage she conspired with John's enemies in the church to convene a synod to discern whether he held heretical views. Realizing that he would be condemned regardless of the facts, John refused to attend, instead condemning the whole affair in his weekly sermons. As expected, the synod in 404 found the patriarch guilty, deposed him of his office, and banished him from the empire. Outraged at the ouster of their beloved patriarch, the city mobs took to the streets outside the Hippodrome. In the confusion, someone thought it a good idea to burn down Hagia Sophia. The horrible destruction, and a subsequent powerful earthquake, convinced Eudoxia that she had made a mistake. John was allowed to retain his position in Constantinople— that is, until the next year, when he condemned Eudoxia as a self-serving manipulator of the emperor after she convinced him to erect a statue of her in the Augusteion. The banishment order was instantly renewed. No earthquakes followed.

These were the controversies that pestered the minds of Constantinopolitans while the Roman Empire in the West was carved up by barbarian invaders. It is remarkable that in old Rome, Goths plundered, burned, and killed, while in New Rome the pressing problem was a lack of space for new constructions. The population of Rome was dwindling, while that of Constantinople skyrocketed. The wealth of the city on the Bosporus now rivaled Rome in its best days. To give but one illustrative example, in the early fifth century, Antiochus, an official at court in Constantinople, decided to build a new home. Just north of the Hippodrome, the structure was no mere mansion—it was a palace. At its center was an open-air semicircular portico one hundred fifty feet in diameter with numerous halls radiating out from it. The entire structure was so large that in later centuries it was converted into a magnificent church. Next door was the palace of another government official, Lausus. His home boasted a domed rotunda sixty-five feet in diameter that led to a magnificent dining hall one hundred fifty feet long, with seven great apses and a collection of classical sculpture renowned throughout the city.

These were the domiciles of simple imperial officials. The palace of the emperor, which was already opulent in Constantine's time, was repeatedly expanded under Arcadius and his son Theodosius II (408–50). Since the terrain sloped steeply downward to the sea east and south of the Great Palace, this area was cut into six different terraces, provided with marble stairs, and planted with grass, trees, fountains, and lush gardens. It afforded a beautiful view of the Bosporus for the imperial family and other high-ranking members of the government. At the lowest level, a small private port allowed for easy transportation of the emperor and other important people without the necessity of using the public harbors. Later called Bucoleon because it was decorated by enormous statues of a bull and a lion, the harbor also afforded a handy means of escape should an uprising threaten the life of the emperor. Theodosius II had no need of it, but many of his successors did. They would also do their part to fill up the green spaces of the terraces, each adding to the beauty of a sprawling complex that became renowned throughout the world.

The emperor had something in his palace that was an increasingly scarce commodity in fifth-century Constantinople: space. Amazingly, the city had completely filled up the empty territory between the old city of Byzantion and Constantine's new expansive land walls. Invariably, this led to structures being built outside the walls, but that was not a permanent solution, particularly in an age as dangerous as this. The burgeoning city needed two things above all: additional room to grow and better security. It may have been news of the sack of Rome that finally led the government to provide both. Since Theodosius II was only nine years old, his Praetorian prefect, Anthemius, gave the order to construct an entirely new wall system, one that would dwarf any before it in the Roman world. After decades of construction, these would be the famous Theodosian Walls, giants of stone and marvels of engineering that would forever be a symbol of the megalopolis, and remain so today (Illustration 5).

Entire books have been written about the Theodosian Walls of Constantinople, and whole careers have been devoted to unlocking their secrets. The project was not simply to build new land walls farther west, thus greatly expanding the physical size of the city. It was also to completely enclose Constantinople in a system of impregnable fortifications to ensure its safety no matter the situation in the empire. When finally completed around 450, these walls would run almost twelve miles over hills, down valleys, and all along the shores of the city. There was to be no border of Constantinople unwalled.

Because the land portion of the walls still survives (some of it in a state of restoration), it is easier to describe. It consisted of a network of three walls stretching three and a half miles from the Sea of Marmara to the Golden Horn. The largest of the three was about seventeen feet thick and rose to an average height of about forty feet. It was studded with ninety-six towers that jutted out from the wall, commanding the area before it. Most of these towers were approximately sixty feet tall and thirty-six feet wide. About sixty feet in front of this main wall was another, lower wall. This second structure had reinforced archways to give it greater strength and a wide walkway along the battlements. It was about seven feet thick and forty feet high and had more than ninety towers, each designed to complement the larger towers of the main wall behind it. Sixty feet in front of the second wall was a third, small, crenelated wall about six feet high. And directly in front of the third wall was a moat that stretched more than sixty feet across and was about twenty feet deep.

A fortification system like this was simply unassailable in the ancient world. An attacker would first have had to fill in the moat, while thousands of soldiers on three walls and numerous towers rained down missiles of every sort. Then the first, small fortification would have had to be captured. The assailants would then have found themselves in a wide, flat area with no cover and a forty-foot wall to scale. Assuming that this was possible (which it was not), a victorious attacker would have found himself in possession of only a middle wall, with another wide-open area and an even larger and more formidable wall to capture next. The extraordinary strength of these walls and the inherent redundancy in their defenses were so great that no army ever breached even the walls' first line of defenses before the age of gunpowder. They would steadfastly guard Constantinople for a thousand years.

The Theodosian Walls had about a dozen gates (two or more no longer exist). Some of these were smaller military gates, while others accom-
modated grand boulevards filled with traffic. The largest gate was found
at the far, southern end of the walls, where the ancient Via Egnatia snaked
into and out of the city. This was the new Golden Gate, the magnificent
entryway through which triumphant emperors processed into their city.
So different is the Golden Gate from the others along the land walls that
some believe it was originally a freestanding triumphal arch constructed
by Theodosius I and only later incorporated into the fortifications of Theodosius II. It consisted of three separate openings flanked by two massive
square towers. The central portal was much larger than the other two,
making it resemble other victory arches, such as the Arch of Trajan in
Algeria and the Arch of Constantine in Rome. Although the entire
stretch of the Theodosian land walls was decorated with distinctive banks
of alternating brick and limestone, the Golden Gate was completely covered in white marble. The gate complex was further embellished by
winged victories and many large reliefs of mythological scenes and was
topped by a bronze statue group depicting an emperor in a chariot drawn
by four elephants. The main portal had massive golden doors that were
opened only during a triumphal procession. Over the inside main portal
was the inscription THEODOSIUS DECORATES THIS PLACE AFTER THE DEATH OF
THE TYRANT. The identity of the tyrant depends a great deal on the identity of the Theodosius. It could refer to Theodosius I's defeat of Magnus
Maximus in 388 or Theodosius II's defeat of John in 425. Over the outside portal was an inscription (now lost): HE WHO BUILDS A GATE WITH GOLD
RULES A GOLDEN AGE. During most of the Golden Gate's history its side
portals remained open for traffic. Today the structure, bereft of all decoration, is part of Yedikule (Fortress of the Seven Towers). Some of the
portals are bricked shut (Illustration 6).

To the north of the Golden Gate, the Theodosian Walls climb up the
seventh hill, reaching their peak at the Gate of St. Romanus (modern-
day Top Kapısı), so named for a church nearby. From there the fortifications descend sharply downward into the valley of the Lycus River. This
is the Mesoteichion, or "middle wall," the weakest portion of the defenses. Here the walls are actually lower than the plains outside, making
them more vulnerable to missile fire. Defenders, therefore, traditionally

manned the Mesoteichion heavily, so as to repulse any attacks. From the valley, the walls climb quickly back up toward the summit of the sixth hill, the highest point in the city. Here one found the Gate of Charisius, also known as the Gate of Adrianople (modern-day Edirnekapı). This was the busiest of all the gates, for it was here that the northern branch of the Mese exited the city. As the name suggests, this is also where travelers embarked on the journey toward the Thracian city of Adrianople. As the Western empire collapsed, this road overtook the old Via Egnatia in importance and traffic.

From the Gate of Adrianople, the Theodosian Walls make their way down the hill toward the shoreline of the Golden Horn. Only half of that stretch survives today. At some point in later centuries a large single wall was extended northward to include the affluent suburb of Blachernae, home to an imperial palace and the Church of St. Mary of Blachernae, believed to hold the mantle and robe of the Virgin. The original Theodosian Walls there were later dismantled, much like the Constantinian walls made obsolete by the expansion of the city.

As amazing as these architectural wonders remain, the land walls were but one portion of the Theodosian project. The remainder were the seawalls running the entire nine miles of Constantinople's shore. Interestingly, the city appears to have had no seawalls before. On the eastern and southern borders of the peninsula the waters run so swiftly southward that it was impossible to launch a seaborne attack against a city that jutted so dramatically up and out of the waters. The Golden Horn, where the current was slow, was protected, as we have seen, by a massive chain fastened to towers in the city and across the water at Galata. Why seawalls were necessary at this point is not completely clear. It is possible that news of the barbarian Vandals having taken to the sea to attack North Africa may have convinced the people of Constantinople that they needed additional defenses against the new threat. The government had recently paid off the Huns, but they, too, remained a threat just beyond the Danube. The new seawalls were built very close to or even in the water. For the most part they were tall, strong single walls with dozens of towers along their long course. In a few regions, such as Petrion, there were double walls, and additional fortifications stretched into the sea to defend the city's main harbors. The seawalls had many gates, especially along the Golden Horn. Except for tiny isolated fragments, the great seawalls have completely disappeared today.

Thanks to Theodosius II and his advisers and engineers, Constantinople was the best-defended city in the known world. It needed to be. Just to the west, the old order was crumbling away under the relentless attacks of Germanic barbarians and the Huns from Asia. The latter posed an awesome threat to the survival of not just Constantinople, but its empire as well. Under Attila and his brother Bleda, the Huns invaded the Balkans in 441, forcing Theodosius to recall troops from the West and raise more forces among his Gothic "allies." The campaign to eject the Huns was a disaster. Only with thousands of pounds of gold did Theodosius finally convince Attila to withdraw. But the warlord returned again, ready for fresh conquests, in 447. After more failed Roman attempts to defeat the invaders, the Huns broke through the Roman resistance, riding into Greece and finally heading straight toward Constantinople. The great walls would have their first test.

It was to be more frightening than any supposed. As Attila and his hordes ravaged the cities and countryside on their approach to the great prize, a violent earthquake shook Constantinople, bringing down many buildings and a whole section of the new land walls. The situation was desperate. Day and night, workers and citizens banded together to rebuild the shattered fortifications. An inscription on the walls still commemorates the effort, proclaiming, BY THE COMMAND OF THEODOSIUS, IN LESS THAN TWO MONTHS CONSTANTINE (THE CITY PREFECT) TRIUMPHANTLY ERECTED THESE STRONG WALLS. When the Huns arrived, they found the work completed, and Constantinople impregnable. After skirmishing with Roman forces brought up from Isauria, in Asia Minor, the Huns finally agreed to accept the usual tribute payments and withdrew from the vicinity. No other city would fare so well against Attila.

As thousands of horses bearing frustrated Huns turned away from the walls of Constantinople, Theodosius II could take some solace, but there were still many dangers to navigate. Although the city continued to grow and prosper, there were internal problems that needed attention. Christianity in the East had divided itself again as churchmen, nobles, and commoners continued to fight over the specifics of Jesus Christ. At issue was the relationship between Christ's human and divine natures. Pope Leo I in Rome had already ruled that Christ was both fully man and fully God. Yet many in the East rejected this formulation. They held that Christ's human and divine natures were bound together in one—a belief generally referred to as Monophysitism. As with all doctrinal disputes in the Christian Roman Empire, this was a matter not simply of religion, but of power and identity. It drove faction against faction, and only added to the divisions of the troubled state. Theodosius, who understood the quarrel but a little, was powerless to stop it.

The emperor died in 450. He was succeeded by Marcian, a middle-aged, battle-hardened general who had married Theodosius's sister Pulcheria. Marcian was a man of action. He boldly sent word to Attila, who was presently on his way to wreak havoc in Gaul, that Constantinople would no longer be sending tribute payments. Let him come and try his strength against the walls of the capital to collect his due. A devout Catholic, Marcian was also determined to deal with the problem of Monophysitism. Together with Pope Leo, he summoned the bishops of the Christian world to attend an ecumenical council in Constantinople. Because of the danger of the Huns, the fathers of the council decided to convene across the Bosporus, in the ancient suburb of Chalcedon. The Council of Chalcedon in 451 would be one of the most important in Christian history. The unanimous decision of the prelates in attendance was that Leo's ruling on Christ's human and divine natures was correct, and that Monophysitism was a heresy. More than that, Chalcedon defined the Incarnation and the Trinity, neither of which is made explicit in Scripture, in a way that would fundamentally shape Christian doctrine. Virtually all Christians in the West, including most Protestants, still accept the decisions of this council on the Bosporus.

Since it was held in Constantinople, the council, it is perhaps not surprising, once again took up the question of the authority of the patriarch of Constantinople. Waiting for the pope's delegates to take their leave for their long trip back to Rome, the remaining fathers decreed that Constantinople was no longer second to Rome in honor, but equal. Canon 28 based this, as the Council of Constantinople had done before, on the fact that the power of the empire had moved from Rome to New Rome. Like his predecessors, Pope Leo refused to ratify this canon, although he did ratify all the other decisions of the council. Within the Church two models of authority were being forged, one in Constantinople and one in Rome. They would, of course, eventually collide.

The pope had been unable to attend the council in person because he was needed in Rome to muster a defense against Attila the Hun. After leaving a pillaged Gaul, the Huns had crossed into Italy in 452. They captured and burned to the ground the beautiful Roman port city of Aquileia, at the head of the Adriatic. The survivors of this and other nearby cities fled the carnage to seek safety in the scattered sandbars of the nearby lagoons. There they built rude shelters on the thousands of islands that dotted this brackish, watery landscape. Out of those refugees and their pitiful huts would come the magnificence of Venice, a city that would centuries later have a vitally important relationship with Constantinople.

Leaving the Veneto region in smoldering ruins, Attila and his armies headed south toward Rome. Roman forces, which were made up largely of German contingents, were powerless to stop the advance. In a desperate but courageous move, Pope Leo I traveled north to meet Attila near Mantua. The two men spoke in private for some time, but to this day it is unknown what was said. All that is certain is that immediately after the meeting, Attila gave his men the order to withdraw completely from Italy. Rome was saved—but at the peril of New Rome. Enraged at Emperor Marcian's refusal to pay tribute, Attila headed east to train the full force of his power against Constantinople. He never made it there. Within a few months he was dead, and the Hunnish threat died with him.

In Constantinople a column was erected in honor of Marcian. At one time the imperial city had forests of columns dedicated to various emperors and other great men and women. The Column of Marcian is remarkable only because it survives. Known as Kız Taşı (the Maiden Stone), it is just south of Fatih Camii, in an area seldom frequented by tourists. Consisting of a square base supporting a column, Corinthian capital, and square marble statue pedestal, the largely intact monument rises about thirty feet in the air. On its heavily worn base can be seen two winged victories holding the monogram of Christ, with the monogram also appearing on the other three sides. At the top of the column the marble statue base is decorated with eagles looking down from its four corners. Marcian's statue once rested on this base, staring north at the nearby Church of the Holy Apostles. An inscription on the base reads, BEHOLD THE STATUE AND COLUMN OF EMPEROR MARCIAN, A WORK DEDICATED BY THE PREFECT TATIANUS. In later centuries, when the statue was lost and Latin was forgotten, the column was believed to be a magical detector of a woman's virginity (thus the modern-day Turkish name). When a nonvirgin woman approached the column, it was said, the wind would blow her garments up, even over her head.

Under Marcian's careful administration Constantinople not only was saved from the fate of a hundred Roman cities in the West, but was preserved, too, against any future barbarian attacks. Under his successor, Emperor Leo I the Thracian (457–74), the German generals and their forces were finally ejected completely from Constantinople. Breaking their reliance on unreliable barbarian allies was a feat that New Rome managed, but Old Rome never could. There was little left of the western Roman Empire. North Africa and Spain had been lost to the seafaring Vandals. Britain had earlier been abandoned to the tender mercies of the Anglo-Saxon tribes. Gaul, the Balkans, and much of Italy were overrun by Goths. In 475 the German commander of Roman forces in Ravenna proclaimed his ten-year-old son, who had a Roman mother, the new emperor in the West. The reign of young Romulus Augustulus (475–76) marked the end of the Roman Empire in western Europe.

In Constantinople the aged Leo died in 474 and was succeeded by his son-in-law, Zeno. Two years later a remarkable gift and letter arrived in the lavish throne room of Constantinople's Great Palace. It was accompanied by several Gothic emissaries, who hailed the emperor and told their tale. Their master, the chieftain Odoacer, had led his Gothic bands in Italy against the Roman government in Ravenna (Rome having been long abandoned by the emperors). At first Odoacer was content to make peace if he was given control over one-third of Italy. But the government's refusal forced his hand. He captured Ravenna and the child emperor, but rather than murder him, as was the custom in these times, Odoacer came upon a better solution. Since he had no suitable candidates to take the imperial throne in the West, he was sending to Emperor Zeno in Constantinople the purple robes, golden crown, and jeweled scepter of Romulus Augustulus. Henceforth, Odoacer's letter proclaimed, let there be but one emperor of the Roman Empire, glorious Zeno, and one capital, magnificent Constantinople! For his part, Odoacer was content to be Zeno's humble servant, the administrator of Italy.

The truth, of course, was rather different. Odoacer was simply another warlord who would rule Italy as he saw fit. But the fiction of Roman continuity was an important one—important for Odoacer, whose Goths equated political power with Rome; important for the Roman population the Goths ruled; and important for Zeno and the people of Constantinople, who did not have to face the insulting fact that Italy, the homeland of their empire, was lost. Rome, any history book will report, fell in 476. Yet that, too, is a fiction. The Roman Empire was very much alive in the eastern half of the Mediterranean, where the troubles of the West seemed a world away. For the millions of Romans in Egypt, Syria, and Asia Minor, very little had changed. Their capital was strong, wealthy, and growing. It was just that now the opulent city of the Bosporus was the sole capital of the Roman Empire.

Chapter 8

City of Justinian

On a bleak morning in early January 532 a few hundred men gathered in an open area in Sycae, a suburb on the north shore of the Golden Horn (modern-day Galata). The layers of woolen tunics and mantles they wrapped about themselves to keep out the damp cold were decorated with the blue and green sashes of the circus factions. But today their gathering had nothing to do with cheering on the chariot teams. They had come to watch the execution of their friends.

The execution was a sign of the times. As Constantinople grew into a massive, cosmopolitan city, it attracted poor, unskilled workers from the countryside searching for a better life. Some found it, but most were trapped in a spiral of poorly paid and intermittent day labor supplemented with free government bread and regular chariot races and other amusements in the Hippodrome. These castoffs became intensely loyal to their fan clubs. In the previous century, John Chrysostom had complained of the loud, drunken, disorderly, and immoral behavior of the crowds that poured out of the games. In the sixth century these postgame festivities often erupted into open brawls between members of the competing factions. Gangs of fans roamed the streets, singing team songs and engaging in property damage, thievery, and even outright murder.

A few weeks before this morning's execution a particularly nasty brawl had erupted in the heart of the city. By the time it was over, many lay dead. The seven perpetrators were arrested, tried, and found guilty by the city prefect, Eudaemon. It was he who read the charges and the convictions at this somber assembly as three of the men had nooses fitted around their necks. (The other four had already been beheaded by the government.) In earlier decades an emperor might have avoided this sort of show, for fear of upsetting the faction leaders. The current emperor took a different approach, for he understood these low-born ruffians all too well. He was one of them.

Emperor Justinian I (527–65) was born a peasant in the Latin-speaking northern Balkans. His uncle Justin had worked his way to prominence in the Excubitors, an elite military force charged with the protection of the emperor in Constantinople. Childless, Justin adopted young Justinian, bringing him to the capital, where he was well educated and prepared for government service. When Emperor Anastasius died without an heir in 518, the well-connected Justinian convinced the military to support his uncle as the new ruler. Justin and Justinian worked together so closely over the next nine years that it is difficult to attribute their actions to one or the other. Given his origins, Justinian knew how to build support among the common citizens of the city. When he became consul in 521 he personally paid four thousand pounds of gold to sponsor a day of games and spectacles in the Hippodrome that included twenty lions and thirty leopards. When the aged Justin died in 527 there was no question that Justinian would succeed him.

A short, attractive man with curly hair, Justinian had the friendly but firm demeanor of one who had come from humble beginnings. He had an appreciation for those who worked hard and overcame obstacles, and little patience for the preening elites of the senatorial aristocracy. His wife, Empress Theodora, was much the same. She was a child of the theaters, the daughter of a bear trainer. At about the age of thirteen she became an actress, which in the ancient world meant that she was also a prostitute. Working her way through the seedy underbelly of Constantinople, she attracted the eye of a minor governmental official when she was sixteen years old. He took her with him when he was sent to North Africa, but after three years he tired of her and cast her out into the streets. There she remained, plying the sex trade for the next few years in cities such as Alexandria and Antioch, before she returned to the capital. It may have been the birth of her illegitimate daughter that convinced Theodora that she needed to find honest work. Or it may be that at the age of twenty-two, she was unable to garner employment in Constantinople's highly competitive theaters and brothels. In any case, she took a job spinning wool in a downtown shop, where one day she happened to meet the forty-year-old city consul, Justinian. He was instantly taken by her good looks and resilient character. No doubt he was also attracted to her sad story, and the determination she exhibited to make something better of herself. The two fell deeply in love.

It was all well and good for an emperor or his heir to have mistresses; they could have them by the dozens. Yet no one believed that Theodora was the sort of woman Justinian should marry. He, however, disagreed. The dismissive insults with which the senatorial aristocracy ridiculed Theodora enraged Justinian, for he knew well that they said the same of him when he was not in the room. Despite their objections, in 525 the two were married. Two years later, in a magnificent ceremony in Hagia Sophia, the patriarch of Constantinople placed the imperial crowns on the heads of a peasant and a prostitute.

Justinian and Theodora were intensely disliked among the aristocracy, not least because of the tax hikes they soon imposed on the wealthy. This, of course, made them rather popular among the common people, who could see themselves behind the purple raiment and richly jeweled crowns of the imperial couple. Indeed, the thousands who frequented the Hippodrome already knew Theodora well. She had long been a regular performer in the circus. Her parents had even dedicated her to the Blue faction. Justinian and Theodora's familiarity with the lower classes, however, did not translate into leniency with the factions' hooliganism and riots. Justin and Justinian had already begun deploying military forces to break up faction violence. One of Emperor Justinian's first actions was to stiffen penalties for postgame disturbances and to reiterate that they would be applied equally to both factions, no matter the royal family's preference in the Hippodrome.

That is what led to the executions in early January 532. Once the nooses were fitted, the ropes were likely threaded through a pulley and then tied to a team of horses or oxen. When the sentence was read and the final prayers uttered, the order was given to hoist the condemned up, where they would eventually suffocate. But all did not go as planned. Two of the ropes broke or became untied, depositing their cargo on the ground with a thump. A surprised cry went up from the onlookers, who quickly ran to their friends. The guards moved in, pushing the spectators out of the way and replacing the nooses. Once again the two men were hung, and once again they fell to the ground still alive. Monks of the nearby monastery of St. Conan rushed into the open area, picked up the two men, placed them in a nearby boat, and rowed across the Golden Horn to the Blachernae suburb, at the far northern end of Constantinople's land walls. There the twice-hung criminals were placed in the sanctuary of the Church of St. Laurentius. One of them was a Blue and the other a Green.

City officials had plenty of experience with criminals using churches to avoid capture. They would not defile the sanctuary, but neither would they let the fugitives go free. Instead they simply closed off the church, waiting for those inside to starve or surrender. That is how matters stood for the next several days. Faction members visited the church, but they were not allowed to enter. There was no further violence. There appears to have been a feeling among the two factions that the emperor would pardon the men during the next games, which were scheduled to be held on the Ides (thirteenth) of January.

The Hippodrome on that day was packed as usual. The two men trapped in St. Laurentius were a major topic of conversation among the thousands of spectators. As usual, Justinian and Theodora appeared, along with their court, in the imperial box, known as the Kathisma, which was connected via a secure passageway directly to the palace. They were hailed joyously by the people, who then settled in for a day of races and shows. After the opening ceremonies and before the first race, there was an unexpected interruption. The leaders of the two factions and many of those in the stands began crying out to be heard by the emperor. Since emperors were generally seen by the populace only in the Hippodrome, it was an occasional platform for appeals or complaints. The faction leaders ran out onto the track and pleaded with Justinian to have mercy on their friends trapped in the church, men whom God had clearly delivered from the hangman's noose. The emperor ignored the request, and the guard whisked away the petitioners. Yet that was not the end of it. After each subsequent race the cry went up again from the stands, making it increasingly difficult to keep to the day's program. Each time, the emperor ignored the growing commotion. Finally, after the twenty-second race, thousands of fans poured out of their seats and onto the track, begging the emperor to hear them. He did not, or at least he did not appear to. Finally someone cried, "Viva the merciful Blues and Greens!" Almost at once this cry was repeated across the stadium, shouted ever louder as the crowds were pushed back into the stands. Something unprecedented had happened. The bitter rivalry between the two factions had melted away in the heat of this shared insult. During the remainder of the races, there appear to have been meetings between the faction leaders and plans hatched. When the games finally concluded and the fans started to leave, the Blues and the Greens began chanting one simple yet dangerous word, *Nika!* Conquer.

Exiting the Hippodrome, hundreds of chanting faction members marched down the Mese to the city Praetorium, near the Forum of Constantine. There they demanded to see the prefect, who eventually emerged, only to order them to disband and return to their homes. The faction leaders shouted him down, demanding to know whether their friends were to be pardoned and released. Eudaemon had no answer, so he gave none. He simply turned his back on the seething crowd and reentered the Praetorium. Once again the chant rose up, stoking the angry mob into a burning frenzy. "Nika! Nika! Nika!" Like a violent storm, they surrounded the nearby prison, broke down its gates, killed many of the guards and officials inside, and released all the prisoners. Flush with success, they then roared down the Mese, overturning stat- ues, stealing from local shops, and spreading mayhem. So began the Nika Revolt, the most destructive riot in Constantinople's history.

Coming to the end of the Mese, the rioters assembled in the beauti- fully decorated Augusteion, which was flanked by the Great Palace on the east and south and the great church Hagia Sophia on the north. Wielding torches and swords, they shouted their slogan loud enough to be heard even in the imperial apartments. Unable to break into the palace, which was heavily fortified against such disturbances, they set fire to the Chalke, the ornate ceremonial entrance on the east side of the square. The blaze was whipped up by a cold north wind and spread its fiery destruction to the nearby Senate house and finally to Hagia Sophia. The inferno raged all night and could be seen by passing ships and those across the Bosporus and the Golden Horn. By morning the heart of Constantinople had been transformed into a blackened land- scape smoldering in the cold January light.

To keep the rioters occupied, Justinian announced that there would be a special second day of games in the Hippodrome on January 14. As expected, the angry mobs arrived, but they had lost interest in the races. They chanted their slogans, vandalized the stadium, and even set fire to the northern portion of the structure. The flames spread to the nearby Baths of Zeuxippus, the great boast of Constantinople. It is likely that Justinian did not attend the games that day, but the leaders nonetheless demanded that the emperor dismiss three of his closest officials. Eudaemon was, of course, at the top of their list, since it was he who had convicted the men and overseen some of their executions. They also demanded the firing of John of Cappadocia and Tribonian the Quaestor. The addition of these two names is good evidence that members of the senatorial aristocracy were pulling strings among the circus faction leaders. There was no reason for sports fans to have heard of Tribonian, who was busy working on a codification of Roman law. John of Cappadocia was well known to the factions, for he was an ardent supporter of the Blues, and as the architect of new taxes on the wealthy, one would have expected the commoners to favor him. But John and Tribonian were hated by the city elites. Justinian, in any case, was no longer in a position to argue. All three men were instantly dismissed.

Since most of the rioters had never cared about these dismissals, they saw no reason to stop the looting, raping, killing, and burning. Looters broke into and destroyed numerous mansions, churches, and forums in the central city. All was chaos. Justinian had enough soldiers in the palace guard to crush the mobs, but the guards were unwilling to attack fellow citizens and, more to point, were fearful of reprisal should Justinian lose his throne. So they simply did their job, defending the palace while the city descended further into anarchy. Justinian's most trusted general, Belisarius, had recently returned from Persia and had at his command some fifteen hundred Gothic mercenaries, who had no qualms about killing Romans. Belisarius led them several times against the mobs, once in the Augusteion and another time in the burned ruins of the Mese. Yet both skirmishes were indecisive.

Matters could not remain as they were. A group of aristocrats suggested to the faction leaders that the mobs collect one of the nephews of Emperor Anastasius and crown him emperor. Many of the senators hated Justinian, not simply because of his low birth and high taxes, but also because he had been edging them further out of power and into useless ceremonial roles. Some of the aristocracy were undoubtedly also frustrated with the emperor's inability to stop an insurrection that was destroying their homes and businesses. Energized by this new strategy, the crowds rushed to the home of Anastasius's nephew Probus, to inform him of his impending elevation to the throne of the caesars. But he had heard of their intentions and wisely fled the city. Frustrated by his absence, the rioters burned his house down. Anastasius's two other nephews, Pompeius and Hypatius, were already tucked away in the Great Palace with Justinian. They, too, wanted nothing to do with the rioters or the royal power they offered.

Or so it seemed. By January 17 Justinian became convinced that Hypatius was working with the palace guard and other members of the court to murder him and seize the throne for himself. That evening, he ordered both nephews and all the aristocracy out of the palace. Hypatius begged the emperor to reconsider, which only further convinced Justinian that the young man was preparing a coup. The next morning, the Greens and the Blues were surprised to receive an invitation to come to the Hippodrome and speak directly to the emperor. Tens of thousands of them poured into the circus, drunk with victory and plenty of wine. Dressed in his imperial finery, Justinian solemnly entered the Kathisma bearing in his hands a jewel-covered Gospel. He addressed the crowds, whom only a few days before he had ignored, swearing on the Gospel that he would faithfully grant all their demands and give complete amnesty for all crimes committed during the riots. The mobs loudly ridiculed him, calling him a liar and worse before declaring that they would no longer have him as emperor. It was during this humiliating spectacle that word arrived at the Hippodrome that Hypatius had been ejected from the palace and was now in his home. Leaving a trail of destruction, the rioters rushed from the stadium to the mansion. There they seized and carried the reluctant emperor to the Forum of Constantine, where he was crowned in a makeshift ceremony. Then it was back to the Hippodrome, where Hypatius and his senatorial supporters were installed in the Kathisma. The mobs loudly proclaimed him the new Roman emperor.

Their joyous acclamations could be heard clearly in the Great Palace, only a short distance away. Justinian and Theodora met with Belisarius and a few other members of their trusted inner circle to decide on their next move. The situation seemed hopeless. Already the factions were arming themselves in preparation for a full attack on the palace. The guard would do nothing to stop them. In a matter of hours, it seemed, Hypatius would reside in these walls. The only recourse was flight. A small fleet stood ready at the palace (Bucoleon) harbor. Beaten, Justinian gave orders to collect as much money as possible in preparation for departure to the provinces. All his councilors agreed that it was the best course of action. The reign of Justinian had clearly come to an end.

Yet Theodora emphatically disagreed. She stepped forward into the group of men and boldly spoke out against the plan. It was so startling for a Roman empress to contradict her husband and his court that Belisarius well remembered her words and, later, it appears, recounted them to the historian Procopius. Theodora was disgusted by the cowardice on display. Everyone dies, she said, but for an emperor to become a fugitive was worse than death. She continued:

> Let me never be without this imperial purple garment, and let me never live to see the day when all those who greet me do not do so with the words, "Your majesty." So now, if you still want to save yourself, O Emperor, there is no problem. We have plenty of money. There is the sea and here are your ships. But consider whether, once you have managed to save yourself, you might not later prefer death to safety. As for me, I hold to the old saying, "Empire is a glorious death shroud."

We can only imagine the stunned silence that followed as Theodora's dark eyes, which still stare out from the mosaics of San Vitale in Ravenna, flashed across the startled room. Nothing had changed. The mobs were still in possession of the city and were still poised to capture the palace. But Theodora's boundless determination, which had brought her from Constantinople's seediest fleshpots to its most glorious pinnacle, was a force to be reckoned with. Justinian turned to Belisarius and announced that they would stay, they would fight. What were his options?

Although he still had strong doubts, the loyal general presented his master with a battle plan.

The mobs were jammed into the racecourse of the Hippodrome, celebrating their victory, hailing their new emperor, and otherwise engaging in drunken revelry. The time to strike was now, while they were packed closely together and suspecting no danger. Ideally, Belisarius would lead a small force through the passageway to the Kathisma and simply pluck the imperial pretender off his throne. However, the palace guard controlled access, and they would not allow an attack on what appeared to be the new emperor. Belisarius, therefore, suggested a three-pronged attack. First, much of the money that had been gathered for the escape would be given to the palace eunuch Narses, who would use it to bribe the leaders of the Blue faction. He would remind them that Hypatius, like his uncle before him, was a strong supporter of the Green team. What could they expect from him after he no longer needed the support of the Blues? Second, Belisarius was to lead his Goths out the Chalke, the main palace entrance, which was now a burned ruin. Third, another military leader, Mundus, was to lead a small force of Germanic Heruli out the same way. These two forces were to split up and seek any entry they could find into the Hippodrome. Once in, they were to seize Hypatius.

It was, of course, a desperate plan—one likely to give Theodora the shroud she sought. Yet the expertise of Belisarius and the discipline of his Goths turned the tide. They exited the crumbled Chalke and then, with great difficulty, made their way over the blackened ruins of the Augusteion. Belisarius then led his men through a western gate of the Hippodrome and toward a passageway that led directly up to the Kathisma. So crowded was the Hippodrome that their entry went completely unnoticed. The passage to the emperor's box, though, was barred shut, and guards stood on the other side. Breaking it down would take time and make a loud clatter, alerting the mob to their presence. So Belisarius made a desperate move. He ordered his men to draw up their ranks, turn toward the people, and begin killing. It was completely unexpected. Hundreds fell under the Gothic swords before most people learned of the danger. By the time they discovered their peril, the rioters were too disorganized or too drunk to respond effectively. Those who fled for the eastern gates were met by Mundus, whose men began hacking their way through them. It was a systematic, well-ordered slaughter. Hypatius watched with horror as his raucous subjects fell to the power of Justinian's men. When he was finally arrested and led back to the palace, nearly thirty thousand people lay dead on the raceway of the Hippodrome. The Nika Revolt was at an end.

In an astonishing reversal, Justinian now sat in judgment over Hypatius, Pompeius, and eighteen senatorial ringleaders of the revolt. Hypatius pled innocent, saying that he would have much preferred to remain in the palace, yet Justinian himself had thrown him to the revolutionaries. He professed to have sent word from the Hippodrome that Justinian should move against the mob, but that his messenger had returned with a report that the emperor had already fled the city. Given the circumstances, he had had no choice but to accept the royal title. Hypatius's plight, swept up into a power play that he never wanted, was tragic. Justinian could not allow him or his brother to live. Whether they wished it or not, they would always be a tinder for revolution. They were beheaded and their bodies cast into the sea. As for the senators, their properties were confiscated and they were banished. Word was then sent to the cities of the empire that Justinian had crushed the rebellion and punished the traitors. His reign, once hanging by a thread, was completely secure.

His city, however, lay in ruins. It took nearly six weeks for workers to clear away the rubble and charred debris that the riots had left behind in the Augusteion. Justinian rebuilt the stoa (portico) around the great square, decorating it with new, beautiful statuary. On the southeastern side, the ceremonial entrance to the palace, the Chalke, was completely rebuilt. Outside its massive bronze doors were placed statues of emperors and one of Belisarius. A cross surmounted the gate along with images of Christ. Through the entrance was an imposingly large room that served as an antechamber to the palace. Its walls rose heavenward to a golden dome. The room was lavishly decorated with marbles of every color and bright mosaics. The latter portrayed Justinian's later military victories in North Africa and Italy. At the center of the room was a depiction of Justinian and Theodora celebrating the victories, surrounded by jubilant senators and other members of court.

Many of the palace rooms and barracks near the Chalke had suc‚
cumbed to the flames or other violence. Justinian rebuilt them all. We
are told that he expanded and renovated the palace complex, although
precise details are sparse. It is possible that he built a room or courtyard
with a peristyle floor decorated with lush pictures of animals and scenes
of daily life. These floor mosaics were discovered in the 1930s and to‚
day can be seen in situ in the Great Palace Mosaics Museum. Their
rich colors and sensuous depictions recall a dwelling of extraordinary
opulence difficult to imagine today. Outside the Chalke, Justinian built
a new and much larger Senate building to replace the one incinerated
by the rioters. He did the same for the Baths of Zeuxippus, building
them even greater than they had been before their destruction.

The Augusteion was significantly beautified with art and probably
fountains. In the next decade, Justinian built there his own monumental
column, which rose some 230 feet in the air. It was very thick, made
completely of bricks but covered in bronze that glistened in the sun. It
rested on a monumental marble base, which was itself on a pedestal of
seven steps. At the top of the column was a thrice‚life‚size equestrian
statue of Justinian wearing the clothing of Achilles; on its head, a feath‚
ered *toupha* signified victory. In the statue's left hand was an orb sur‚
mounted by a cross. Its right hand was outstretched in a warding gesture
to the East, commemorating Justinian's pacification of the Persians. The
column and statue were so large that they could be seen for miles out at
sea. They became one of the most recognizable features of the city.

Yet all these constructions pale in comparison to Justinian's project
on the north side of the Augusteion. For the second time, the church of
Hagia Sophia had been destroyed by civil unrest. Justinian meant to
rebuild the city's cathedral on a scale unheard of, not just for a Chris‚
tian church, but for any building ever made. Ten thousand workers
were hired to clear away the ruins of the old church and tear down
blocks of residences and buildings near it. The greatest architect of the
age, Anthemius of Tralles, was placed in charge of the project, assisted
by Isidore of Miletus, also renowned for his engineering skill. The new
Hagia Sophia was begun in 527. It was completed five years later, an
impossibly short time for so monumental an undertaking (Illustration 7).

Words fail when describing the glory of Justinian's Hagia Sophia.

Measurements and architectural features cannot convey the awe-inspiring enormity of a building that for one thousand years was the largest in the Western world and still today towers over the modern city of Istanbul. Pictures, too, are powerless to depict its grandeur. It simply must be experienced firsthand—although even then with the knowledge that the building is today without the extraordinarily rich decorations that embellished it during its centuries as a Christian church.

But words must suffice. At its core, Hagia Sophia is a Greek cross roughly 250 by 225 feet. In the center of the cross is a square 100 by 100 feet, surrounded by arched colonnades that 180 feet up support the largest domed cupola that had ever been built (100 feet in diameter). This created a vast area of unsupported space, more than any other structure in history. Indeed, it was not surpassed until the completion of St. Peter's Basilica in Rome more than ten centuries later. All this was further supported by semidomes on the east and west sides and massive buttresses to the north and south. Materials from across the empire were employed in the construction. Marbles of every color and from numerous locales were used to decorate the floor and walls. Beautiful mosaics were installed, although most of the ones that survive today were executed well after Justinian. The extraordinary monolithic columns were also imported. Some of these were taken from the ruins of the Temple of Diana/Artemis in Ephesus. Hundreds of windows brought into the stone interior bright sunlight, which danced and reflected on the gold-covered dome and the multihued marbles. The dome was ringed by windows, giving one the impression that, as Procopius remarked, it was suspended from heaven by a golden chain. On December 27, 537, it was dedicated with great ceremonies and festivities by Justinian and Patriarch Menas. Upon entering the church, Justinian is reputed to have exclaimed, "Solomon, I have outdone you." (Illustration 8.)

And he had. Procopius, who was also present at the dedication, lent his considerable expertise with the pen to an attempt to describe Hagia Sophia in the sixth century.

> Who could tell of the beauty of the columns and marbles with which the Church is adorned? One would think that one had come upon a meadow of flowers in bloom. Who would not admire the

purple tints of some and the green of others, the glowing red and glittering white, and those, too, which nature, like a painter, has marked with the strongest contrasts of color? Whoever enters there to worship perceives at once that it is not by any human strength or skill, but by the favor of God that this work has been perfected. His mind rises sublime to commune with God, feeling that He cannot be far off, but must especially love to dwell in this place which He has chosen.

According to one report, Justinian spent 320,000 pounds of gold on the construction of Hagia Sophia. That is the equivalent of $6.5 billion in 2016. It was, in any case, well worth it. Hagia Sophia became the most important building in the Eastern Roman Empire, the focal point for Orthodox Christianity. It was not just the cathedral of Constantinople; it was also the common church of all Greek-speaking faithful no matter where they lived. So, just as Constantinople became known throughout the empire as simply "the City," so did Hagia Sophia come to be known as "the Great Church." No further description was necessary.

Hagia Sophia is remarkable because of not only its splendor, but its continued survival over fifteen centuries in an area frequently struck by violent earthquakes. Like any building, it has needed repairs. After several tremors, a powerful earthquake cracked the central dome on May 7, 558, causing it to crash down upon the ambo, altar, and ciborium below. Isidore the Younger, the nephew of Isidore of Miletus, oversaw the creation of a new, sturdier ribbed dome that rose thirty feet higher than the original. This new dome allowed for larger and more numerous windows along its base, which not only let in more sunlight during the day but at night allowed the thousand lamps within the dome to shine so brightly that the church was used as a navigational aid along the Bosporus. Other changes were made over the centuries, although from the outside, the church still looks very much as it did in the sixth century. Four minarets now stand guard around it, and of course a crescent replaces the golden cross that for a millennium graced its powerful dome.

Hagia Sophia was only the most famous of the thirty-four churches Justinian either built or significantly restored. The nearby Church of Hagia Eirene had also perished in the flames of rebellion. Justinian rebuilt it as a domed basilica, making it the second-largest church in Constantinople. Like its nearby sister, Hagia Eirene survives today, and is occasionally open to the public. Unlike Hagia Sophia, though, Hagia Eirene was never converted into a mosque. Constantine's Church of the Holy Apostles, the burial place of emperors, was not damaged in the riots. Yet it suffered from poor construction and punishing jolts. Justinian had the entire structure pulled down, building a massive cross-shaped temple topped with five domes in its place. It survived for the next nine centuries, still in good condition, before it was destroyed by Sultan Mehmed II. One can still, however, visit a copy of Holy Apostles today. It was built by Greek architects in Venice to house the holy relics of St. Mark: the famous Basilica San Marco.

Most of Justinian's buildings have disappeared, along with the ancient city he knew. Still, they were astonishingly numerous. The Hippodrome was not only repaired but beautified. The colonnaded Mese, which suffered badly during the Nika Revolt, was completely restored. The covered road was rebuilt, as were the buildings and shops on both sides of the avenue. By the time of his death in 565, Justinian had not only repaired the injured city, but refashioned it. It was already the largest, most beautiful city in the known world. Now it was legendary.

So great a capital implied a great empire, and Justinian meant to restore that, too. Although the Roman Empire had fallen in the West, Justinian and his successors never considered that a permanent situation. In 533, just one year after the Nika Revolt, while Constantinople was filled with the sounds of hammers and saws, Belisarius led a massive fleet to the West. Within a year he had liberated all of North Africa from the Vandals and recaptured Corsica, Sardinia, and the Balearics. Upon his return, he received a triumphal procession and celebration in the Hippodrome—the last to be allowed to one who was not the emperor. Belisarius then returned for the invasion of Italy. The Goths, now beset by their own divisions, were unable to stem the Roman tide. Naples was quickly restored. With the help of Pope Silverius, the city of Rome also returned to Roman rule. Seriously depopulated and in poor shape, it could not be restored as the capital. That honor had been firmly transferred to the city on the Bosporus.

Business was booming in Constantinople. Efficient tax collection filled the imperial coffers, while stable borders to the east allowed trade routes to extend all the way to China. The Romans had a passion for fine Chinese silks, which were produced from silkworms closely guarded by the Chinese government. Yet in 555, Roman agents managed to smuggle silkworms from the Far East into Constantinople. Thus began the city's long and lucrative silk industry.

Trade routes of that length can bring not only prosperity, but also danger. In 541, in the port of Pelusium in Egypt, a new disease was first noticed. The afflicted exhibited dark swellings in their groins, behind their ears, or on their necks. These "buboes," as they were later called, were the hallmarks of bubonic plague. The flea-borne disease moved rapidly aboard ships, all of which had a full complement of host rats. It quickly spread to Alexandria, then Syria, and within the year, cases were showing up in Constantinople. Few places in the East were spared, and the deadly disease was also delivered to the reconquered West aboard Roman vessels. The devastation was unprecedented in the Mediterranean. Within a few years an estimated twenty-five million people died from the plague.

Constantinople was hit worst of all. Procopius tells us that when the first cases were seen, there were emotional funerals to mourn those struck down in the prime of life. Within a month, the deaths were so common that the streets were littered with corpses. The government was forced to clear them, delivering thousands of bodies to open pits in Sycae. When the pits were full, the roofs of wall towers across the Golden Horn were torn off and the bodies dumped inside. So many towers were filled with rotting corpses that the stench permeated the capital. On average, five thousand people per day died in Constantinople during 542. By the time the plague was over, roughly half of the population was wiped out. Even Justinian contracted the disease. He was one of the lucky ones, for he survived and thus became immune.

Theodora had cared for Justinian, the empire, and herself during the emperor's convalescence. But in 548 she died of cancer. Part of Justinian died with her. Although he did not govern as wisely or well in his later years, he completed most of his ambitious projects. Constantinople was rebuilt on a scale unimaginable during the dark days of the riots. By 555, his forces had wrested all of Italy from Gothic control and had even captured southern Spain. For the first time in more than a century, the Mediterranean was once again "Mare Nostrum," our sea.

When he died in 565, Justinian left a Roman Empire, now based in Constantinople, that was resurgent on all fronts. The plague had devas‹ tated the city and the empire, but since it had done the same to many of Rome's enemies, there was reason to hope. As for the city, it had reached a level of wealth and beauty that it would not see again for many centuries. The world was changing. Antiquity was passing away, replaced by a new medieval age. Justinian was the last emperor to speak Latin as his native tongue. The Romans who had formed Constantinople into an unrivaled imperial city were becoming Greek. The language of old Byzantion became that of medieval Constantinople.

Chapter 9

Surviving the Middle Ages

The decline in Constantinople of the Latin language was not a sign that the city had become less Roman. It was, after all, the solitary capital of the Roman Empire, whose borders stretched from Spain to the Red Sea. Yet, after centuries of barbarian invasions, the Western empire was so broken and so poor that it no longer ruled, but begged the Easterners for aid.

They were increasingly unable to offer it. The loss of nearly half the population of Constantinople to plague would have serious repercussions. The severe space shortages in the city that had led Theodosius II to build his new land walls disappeared almost overnight. By 600, the newly acquired territories that made up the western half of the city still remained undeveloped, and property values in the western outskirts were so low that much of the area was donated to monastic communities. There black-robed monks built their convents and churches, tilling the land and harvesting their crops within the monumental walls of the capital. Most of the city's population lived within the eastern confines of the old fortifications of Constantine. This new era of Roman history is (for no really good reason) referred to by modern historians as "Byzantine," a term we will use henceforth. It is important to remember, though, that it is an adjective that no one, least of all the "Byzantines," used in the Middle Ages. They remained ever the Romans.

Decimated by plague, Byzantine forces in Italy were unable to restrain the new barbarian invasion of the Germanic Lombards, who had captured much of the peninsula. Constantinople held on to Rome and parts of southern Italy, Sicily, and the Veneto. In the early seventh century the Goths invaded Spain, ejecting the Byzantines once and for all. Closer to the capital a new Central European tribe, the Avars (from the present-day Caucasus region), rode into Thrace and the Balkans, bringing destruction to these ravaged areas. Like the Huns, they wanted further tribute payments to halt their raids. Unlike the Huns, they continued to raid whether paid or not. Justinian's hard-fought victories quickly unraveled.

The greater danger to the capital arose from the East. After a long and uneasy peace, the Persians at last invaded the Byzantine Empire, quickly conquering Syria, Palestine, and Egypt. Jerusalem was sacked, the holy places desecrated, and the True Cross carried off to Persia. All that was left in the East was Anatolia. The effects of the conquest were felt immediately in the streets of Constantinople. Without grain ship-ments from the Nile, the government could no longer provide free bread to its citizens. Instead, mild subsidies were offered on loaves from Anato-lian grain, forcing people to pay for what they had come to believe was their due. This was a significant break with the Roman past, and it did not go over well among Constantinople's poor and unemployed. There were riots, though none of the intensity of the Nika Revolt.

Under threat of so much calamity, the people of Constantinople looked to their emperor. They were fortunate to have an able one. He-raclius (610–41) was the son of the exarch (governor) of Carthage. He had previously led a coup against his incompetent predecessor, Phocas, and seized the throne. During the first decade of his reign, Heraclius did little but manage disasters. The Persian victories were crushing, but they were in no small part due to divisions among the Byzantine people. Once again a theological dispute had split the empire. Monophysite Christians, who dominated in Egypt, Palestine, and parts of Syria, be-lieved that Christ had only one nature, a fusing of human and divine. The Council of Chalcedon had already defined Christ's dual nature, both fully human and fully divine. All attempts at compromise had failed. As with earlier such disputes, these were bound up as much in politics as in religion. Smarting under higher taxes and other levies, Egyptians and Syrians were increasingly opposed to the Orthodox em-perors of Constantinople. Many of these Monophysites, therefore, strongly supported the non-Christian Persians, whom they viewed as liberators. The Persians returned the favor by giving them positions of authority in the new government.

With only a fragment of his empire remaining, Heraclius was faced with waging a two-front war against powerful adversaries. To the west he sent emissaries to pay off the Avars and put his trust in the mighty walls of Constantinople. To the east, he set off on a bold offensive strategy, ignoring the captured territories and bringing the war to the Persian homeland. To raise the troops and mercenaries necessary to make that gamble, the emperor needed will and money. He found both in an alliance with the patriarch Sergius of Constantinople. This was no ordinary war, after all. With the help of heretics, the Persians had captured and desecrated the Holy Land, the land of the Savior. With the aid of the church, Heraclius promised to rescue the precious relic of the True Cross and punish the enemies of Christ. In return, Sergius blessed the war, giving miracle-working icons of Christ and the Virgin to aid the emperor on the march, and handing over vast sums of wealth, including holy vessels and rich vestments stored in Constantinople's churches.

In 626, Heraclius led his considerable forces across Asia Minor, into Armenia, and then finally toward Persia. The unexpected move required the Persians to recall some troops, but the Persian ruler, Khusrau, seized the opportunity to capture the remainder of the Byzantine Empire. While Heraclius raided the Persian countryside, Persian forces invaded Anatolia and marched west toward Constantinople. Near the end of the year, thousands of Persian troops arrived within sight of the capital, capturing the evacuated city of Chalcedon, and prepared to cross the Bosporus. They were not alone. A vast army of Avars stretched across the plains to the west, just outside the Theodosian Walls. The two attackers made common cause. The Avars sent their fleet to Chalcedon to ferry the Persians over for the final attack.

Shorn of its empire and with most of its forces a thousand miles away, Constantinople was forced to defend itself almost entirely alone. It was, in a very real sense, founded for just that purpose. The impregnable fortifications and strategic position on the swift Bosporus made any attack on the city highly problematic. Yet that did not make the situation any less frightful. Stretching over seven hills, the great city had always afforded its residents spectacular views of the surrounding sea and territories. Now those vistas included nearly one hundred thousand soldiers determined to wipe out the last stronghold of the Roman Empire. The people rushed to the churches as often as they manned the fortifications. They prayed earnestly to the Virgin Mary, begging her to intercede with her Son to destroy the pagan assailants of the "God-guarded" city of Constantinople. Holy icons were paraded through the streets and along the walls as priests sang out their desperate prayers.

As it happened, neither of the attacking armies was able to find suf-ficient supplies, since almost everything in the region had been packed into the walls of Constantinople before their arrival. A Byzantine naval victory in the Sea of Marmara kept the Avar fleet from rendezvousing with the Persians, thus ensuring the two sides could never effectively combine forces. Then came word of additional Byzantine victories in Mesopotamia and Persia. Clearly, Constantinople was no ordinary city. It would require far more time and money to conquer than the Persians or the Avars had to spend. The Persians retreated, preparing to catch up to Heraclius and put the war back on track.

Khusrau's gambit on the Bosporus had doomed both his war and his reign. As Heraclius approached the Persian capital of Ctesiphon, a coup overthrew Khusrau's government. When the dust settled, the new re-gime offered Heraclius highly favorable terms of peace. All the Persian conquests (Egypt, Palestine, and Syria) were to be handed back to Con-stantinople. The borders were to return to prewar status. Rivers of gold poured forth from the Persian treasury in reparation for the war—and of course the True Cross was immediately returned. In March 630, Heraclius entered the recovered Jerusalem and solemnly placed the cross back within the Church of the Holy Sepulcher. He then sailed to Constantinople, where he celebrated a glorious triumph, while giving praise to God and His Virgin mother. Henceforth, the Virgin Mary was universally recognized as the special protectress of Constantinople.

Byzantium's great holy war had come to a seemingly miraculous end. On the brink of utter destruction, the city had seen the desperate strug-gle completely reverse itself. The Eastern empire was restored, Persia was no longer a threat, and Persian treasure had paid in full the debt to the patriarch of Constantinople. As for the Avars, internal divisions weak-ened them, allowing the Slavs to step into the vacuum in the Balkans. They would remain there permanently. With the restoration of Byzan-tine control over the eastern Mediterranean, Orthodox Christianity was again imposed in Egypt and Syria by imperial law. Monophysites were arrested and their churches closed. Given the Monophysites' willingness to collaborate with the enemies of God, Heraclius was no longer in a mood to compromise.

After so many challenges and now in his fifties, Heraclius had good reason to expect some measure of peace and security for the remainder of his years. But it was not to be. Another, far larger threat was preparing to unleash its fury on a battered world. This was not simply the rise of a new ethnic group or a difficult coalition of raiders. Those the emperors of Constantinople understood well enough. On the horizon was a new idea, a new belief—one that would dramatically change the history of Constantinople.

In Mecca, the largest town in the Arabian Peninsula, a man named Muhammad began claiming to receive prophecies and instructions from the Jewish and Christian God. This was not a popular position among the polytheist Arabs, who worshiped various nature spirits and revered a black rock they believed had fallen from Heaven. (Since it may have been a meteorite, they were perhaps correct.) The rock was housed in Mecca, and the people there profited from pilgrimages to it. When the situation become too dangerous, Muhammad fled (Hegira) to Medina, where he became the religious and political leader of the town. There, Islam became both a faith and a state—a state that sanctified its wars. Jihad was both an internal struggle to live a good life and an external war against pagans and those who persecuted Islam. Muhammad and his men waged vigorous jihad against Mecca for several years, finally capturing it in 630. All the conquered residents were forced to convert to Islam. Henceforth, Mecca was the holiest city of Islam. The pilgrims returned, and it became a duty for Muslims to visit Mecca.

By the end of his life in 632, Muhammad had done the seemingly impossible. He had unified the Arabian Peninsula and built a powerful army energized by boundless religious zeal. Historically, the peninsula had been a rough place, periodically sending its nomadic warriors out for plunder and conquest. Yet in recent centuries the considerable power of the Roman and Persian empires had hemmed in the desert people, reducing their attacks to mere border nuisances. Those days were over. Muhammad directed his followers to continue their conquests and spread Islam across the entire world. They followed that commandment with great success. It was a perfect time to do so. Exhausted by their recent war, Rome and Persia were incapable of defending against this new, vibrant threat. Within five years of Muhammad's death, Muslim armies had completely conquered the Persian Empire. They were almost as successful against the Romans/Byzantines. At the Battle of Yarmouk in 636, the Arabs decisively defeated the Byzantines. Within a year, they went on to conquer Syria, including the cities of Antioch and Damascus. Heraclius may have underestimated the danger. He did, however, send additional troops to defend Egypt and ordered the True Cross and other holy relics transported from Jerusalem to Constantinople. No place was safer. Constantinople was well on its way to becoming a massive storehouse of Christian relics, and a pilgrimage destination for centuries to come.

In 638 the Arabs conquered Palestine and captured Jerusalem. Although they feared the worst, the Christians were allowed to keep the Church of the Holy Sepulcher. Arab custom was for the greatest church in a conquered city to be consecrated as a mosque. Caliph Umar, who ruled the Muslim empire between 634 and 644, made a point of not entering the church, instead building a mosque nearby. Muslim law, as set out in the Koran and elaborated in various later hadith, allowed conquered monotheists, such as Christians and Jews, to retain their religions provided they accepted a second-class status and paid an additional head tax. It was this policy, in fact, that had made the conquest of the Byzantine Empire that much easier. Monophysites were still in the majority in Christian Egypt and made up significant minorities in Syria and Palestine. With persecutions against them stepped up in Constantinople, they had every reason to favor Muslim conquest. The Arabs made no distinction between the two Christian camps, so they were happy to tolerate the Monophysites.

From the Great Palace in Constantinople, Heraclius received news of one calamity after another in the East. All that he had fought to preserve was crumbling away. In 641 he died heartbroken. Egypt fell a few months later. The great city of Alexandria now answered to a caliph. And since he allowed the Monophysites (later known as the Coptic Christians) to worship in peace, they were glad to serve him. Over the centuries some Christians would convert to Islam, although a significant Christian population remained in the region well into the modern age.

The Arabs were by no means content with Syria and Egypt. Their forces pressed farther west during the seventh and early eighth centuries, capturing all of North Africa and crossing over the Strait of Gibraltar to conquer most of Spain. Within a century of Muhammad's death his followers had conquered two-thirds of the Christian world and all of the Persian Empire. The vast Muslim state stretched from India to the Atlantic Ocean. Islam had become the superpower of the Mediterranean, and would remain so for nearly a thousand years.

Because world conquest was the ultimate aim of the Muslim campaigns, Constantinople was a natural target. Without it, Muslim armies were forced to enter Europe the long way around, across Africa and through Spain. This meant they were so far from the center of the Muslim empire that they could not project significant power against the Europeans. Constantinople also represented the greatest and most powerful city in the Christian Empire of Rome. Muhammad had repeatedly prophesied its conquest in the hadith narrations. The caliph who could capture mighty Constantinople, it was believed, would be greatly blessed and forever revered.

Caliph Mu'awiya wanted to be that man. Emerging victorious from a difficult civil war, Mu'awiya had established a new Muslim dynasty, the Umayyads, based in the new capital city of Damascus. In 669 he sent his son Yazid with a large army to invade Asia Minor. Yazid was extremely successful, raiding the countryside and making it as far as Chalcedon, Constantinople's suburb across the Bosporus. The appearance of the Arabs so close to the capital sent waves of fear among the citizens. The Muslims seemed to be everywhere. Even while threatening Constantinople, Muslim forces were waging war on Byzantine Carthage and Sicily.

Heartened by his son's success, Mu'awiya invested an enormous amount of wealth and resources in the conquest of Constantinople. He correctly calculated that any attack on the heavily defended city would need to be carefully planned and to use both land- and sea-based forces. In 672 he dispatched three sizeable fleets, which spent the next year securing sea-lanes and establishing supply points between Syria and the Aegean. They arrived in the Sea of Marmara, catching their first glimpse of Constantinople in 674. Meanwhile, another Muslim fleet captured Rhodes, using it as a base from which additional raids could be launched against Asia Minor. The plan was to destroy crops and disrupt food production in Asia Minor, which had become the bread-basket of Constantinople after the fall of Egypt. Simultaneously, the fleets in the Sea of Marmara would halt all shipping into or out of Constantinople while delivering armies to the European side, where they could begin their assault of the city.

Fortunately for the people of Constantinople, the Arabs arrived at one of the few times when the city had a strong and stable government. Since the death of Heraclius, Constantinople had been awash in intrigue, murder, and unrest. Yet few things unify like a common enemy. As the Sea of Marmara filled with the sails of Arab galleys, the citizens of the city rallied around their emperor, Constantine IV. A young man in his early twenties, Constantine took swift action. The Byzantine navy had been diminished by Arab victories, but the emperor still had fleets available in Constantinople's harbors and north along the Bosporus. Recalling troops from Thrace and the Balkans, he was also able to resist the Muslim armies that landed, ensuring that the warfare was limited to the northern shore of the Sea of Marmara, not far from the Golden Gate. These battles, we are told, were waged almost daily. Both sides seemed evenly matched, so the bloodshed was considerable. Still, the Byzantines' resolve to defend their capital meant that the Muslim forces were never able to move north along the Theodosian Walls. They were therefore unable to cut off supplies coming into the city from the Thracian roads.

Since the Muslim forces, though great, were unable to surround or cut off Constantinople, this was not a siege, as it is often called. It was worrisome, though, and could easily have resulted in Muslim victory. Every fall for the next four years, the Muslim fleets and armies retreated to Cyzicus, a peninsula on the southern shore of the Sea of Marmara. Every spring they returned, attacking shipping by sea and attempting to capture the lands to the west of the city. The caliph's money and patience seemed limitless. The patience of the Byzantine people was not. Muslim forces in Asia Minor had caused substantial damage there, bringing food prices in the threatened capital to new highs. Something had to be done.

In 678, Constantine launched a two-pronged attack. Several Byzantine armies in Asia Minor came together to attack Muslim forces there, successfully forcing the marauders to retreat to Syria. Meanwhile, the navy stationed at Constantinople sailed out into the Sea of Marmara to attack the Arab fleet. Given the detailed accounts, the people of the city must have watched the battle unfold from their high hills and sea walls. The Byzantine vessels were outnumbered, but they had a new secret weapon. "Greek fire," as it was known in Europe, consisted of a mixture of flammable liquids manufactured in Constantinople under the greatest secrecy. Divulging the recipe for Greek fire was punishable by death—and indeed, it is still unknown. The liquid was loaded aboard special vessels with large holding tanks below and teams of men who worked bellows to pressurize the tanks. Up top, specialists operated complex tubes, which were opened to project the liquid great distances while it was simultaneously set ablaze. The effect was dramatic. From their prows, hundreds of Byzantine vessels emitted fearful torrents of fire that not only consumed enemy vessels foolish enough to come close, but also set the very sea on fire. For captains unfamiliar with the weapon, it was as devastating psychologically as militarily. To enhance the mental distress, the prows of Byzantine vessels were sometimes adorned with bronze heads of terrible monsters, each with an open mouth vomiting forth the hellish fire.

With a combination of naval skill and Greek fire, the Byzantine fleets defeated the Arabs, forcing them to return to their base at Cyzicus. Since their forces in Asia Minor were similarly defeated, there seemed no hope in the foreseeable future for a conquest of Constantinople. The attackers withdrew. On their way back to Syria a violent storm destroyed a good portion of the Arab fleet. Accepting defeat, the caliph made a truce with Constantine that included the return of Rhodes and all the other islands captured as well as a token tribute payment. It was a stunning victory for the Byzantines and an uncharacteristic loss for the Muslims. In the decades that followed, the Byzantines were able to restore and reinforce Asia Minor. They had lost most of their empire, yet they had survived.

The Arab attacks had proven the wisdom of Constantinople's founders and fortifiers, but without a large empire, how could a classical megalopolis survive? The elements of ancient civic life were fading away in medieval Constantinople, not only because the empire was smaller and poorer, but also because the world itself was changing. Without free bread or the seemingly limitless construction work they had once enjoyed, thousands left Constantinople to find a new life in the hills and countryside of Greece, Thrace, or Anatolia. How far the city's population declined in the seventh and eighth centuries is still a matter of debate. Because the water supply had been damaged by war and time, some have suggested that it may have declined to as little as 50,000. That seems excessively low, but a population of 100,000 to 150,000 would not be surprising. Since Constantinople had never been conquered, it had never experienced the sort of destruction that Rome or other once-great ancient cities endured. Yet the decline in population and wealth meant that some areas and buildings in the city were abandoned and allowed to fall into ruin. Others were repurposed.

Baths, for example, were not much use in a city trying to conserve water. In any case, the culture of baths, so integral to ancient civic life, completely disappeared in Constantinople by the ninth century. The Baths of Constantine were shuttered, and a hermit was recorded to be living in the ruins of the Baths of Dagistheus. In the tenth century an anonymous resident wrote a treatise, the *Patria*, on the marvels of Constantinople. He had never in his life seen a public bathhouse, although he had heard stories of their magical waters. Even the monumental Baths of Zeuxippus were abandoned in the late eighth century. They were later converted into a barracks and prison.

The lavish forums remained open areas for citizens to gather, though they, too, found new purposes. The double-storied porticoes surrounding the Forum of Constantine became retail space. The area around the Column of Constantine remained a place revered for its sanctity and served as the starting point for the annual celebrations held every May 11 to commemorate the founding of the city. At the base of the column was a small Chapel of St. Constantine, where the emperor and patriarch met each year during the rituals. The much larger yet equally adorned Forum of Theodosius was used as the city's pig market. A hay market was set up not far from there. Sheep were sold at the ancient Strategion, while slaves could be purchased at the Milion. The Augusteion remained a beautifully decorated forum, yet because it led directly to the Chalke and the Senate House, it was closed off to the general public.

Constantinople's theaters also declined in the seventh century. Since the government owned the theaters, it is not surprising that they were the first of many institutions to be cut when times became hard. By mid-century all of Constantinople's theaters had closed. Actors took to the streets, providing short farces for the coins they could catch. Yet even they were banned by a church council in 692. Later, Byzantine authors could not say just what a pantomime was. Mimes, though, still worked the streets. A twelfth-century writer, Zonaras, described them as people who dressed up as Arabs or Armenians and hit one another over the head.

Perhaps the most visible changes in civic life, however, were found in the games of the Hippodrome. Like modern professional sports, ancient chariot racing existed across numerous city stadiums, all in some measure connected to one another. However, by the eighth century only Constantinople still had a working racecourse. In cities such as Ephesus, Miletus, and Thessalonica the stadiums had long ago ceased operations, and most were destroyed or severely dilapidated. Even the Circus Maximus in Rome had become a swampy ruin. Constantinople's Hippodrome, on the other hand, remained well maintained and lavishly decorated. Dozens of bronze statues still decorated its *spina*; ornate fountains still sprayed water into the air. What it lacked was chariots and people. Without an empire of avid fans, it was difficult to make a living as a charioteer. Without leisure time, it was nearly impossible for fans to show up. As a result, the number of races declined steadily. By the end of the seventh century the games were no longer entertainment, but civic ritual. Rather than weekly, they were held only a few times a year—on the festival before Lent, just after Easter, and on May 11. Mobs of unruly drunks were replaced by citizens in their best clothing filing into the arena for choreographed ceremonies. Jubilant cheers from the crowd were transformed into precise acclamations voiced by the people and led by the deacons of Hagia Sophia. The emperor and his court attended of course, but no one would have thought to address him or in any way go off script. On these occasions only eight races took place, four in the morning and four in the afternoon. No statues or monuments to charioteers were dedicated. The wild and raucous games that engendered such condemnation from St. John Chrysostom had become a day-long liturgy. Little wonder, then, that the clergy not only began attending, but also had their own section in the stands. The Hip-podrome was no longer the arena of the people, but a highly regimented chamber of the palace complex. As such, it was closed and kept locked when not in use.

The virtual absorption of the Hippodrome into the Great Palace made sense, for the palace was the only place where ancient civic life had not declined. There, baths still functioned; beautiful outdoor fo-rums and manicured gardens still provided refreshment for the emper-ors and aristocracy. In the famous Hall of the Nineteen Couches the emperors still reclined at table, in the ancient manner, and hosted feasts, featuring every kind of delicacy, all served on solid gold tableware. If anything, the Great Palace had become more opulent as each emperor added his own contribution to the growing complex. The extravagant luxury of the palace, combined with the occupants' rich clothing and elaborate rituals, was explicitly designed to impress upon foreign envoys the majesty and power of this most ancient empire. Nowhere was this clearer than in the great throne room known as the Magnaura. Just be-yond the imposing Chalke gate, the Magnaura was a long and sumptu-ously decorated hall at the end of which rested an enormous throne, reputed to have been that of Solomon. Descriptions of it date from the tenth century, but it was probably in use as early as the seventh. When foreign dignitaries approached the imperial throne, water organs played and mechanical birds sang from intricately crafted golden trees while automated lions roared and beat their mighty tails. The throne itself could be raised into the ceiling, providing for dramatic entrances and exits of the sacred emperor. As the real power of the Byzantine Empire declined, this sort of diplomatic spectacle became more important than ever.

Chapter 10

Byzantine Plots

Constantinople continued to haunt the Muslim imagination in the eighth century. Damascus, the capital of the Umayyad Empire, was outfitted with palaces and gardens in imitation of those found in the Byzantine imperial city. As the caliphate expanded in all directions, crushing every foe, it was unnerving to the faithful that Constantinople continued to resist. To some, this seemed a sign that God was reserving this glorious victory for a truly blessed and worthy caliph. Until that man appeared, Muslim border raids against Byzantine territories in eastern Asia Minor continued regularly.

In 717, determined at last to cut off the head of the troublesome Christian empire, Caliph Suleiman launched a massive campaign against Constantinople. He spared no expense and made clear that he was willing to spend all that he had, indeed all that his empire had, to win this victory. Around 120,000 men and 1,800 vessels headed west from Syrian ports, a force larger than the combined army and navy of the Byzantine Empire. Under the command of the caliph's brother Maslama, the Arab armada arrived at the Hellespont in the summer of 718. After securing the area, the great fleet ferried the armies over into Thrace. Opposed only by Bulgarian raiders, the Arabs then marched in good order to within sight of the Theodosian land walls. They had no intention of attacking them. Even 100,000 men could not successfully storm those tripled giants. Instead, they built their own walls across the peninsula, cutting off all land traffic into Constantinople. They would starve out the defiant city.

It was a good plan, but it required complete control over the sea sur-rounding the city, a feat that no assailant had ever been able to achieve. Thousands of sails billowed in the winds, propelling their Arab masters past Constantinople to the Bosporus ports and those of other nearby suburban landings. As they sailed north past the city, the winds sud‚ denly ceased, becalming a number of the vessels in the rearguard. Un‚ able to fight the strong Bosporus current with their oars, the Arab ships floated helplessly back toward the small Byzantine navy in the Golden Horn. At once the chains were lowered, and the Byzantine galleys sped out, spraying Greek fire liberally over their enemies. Many of the Arab vessels were lost that day. Unwilling to risk any similar disasters, the Arab fleets remained some distance from Constantinople. As a result, they were unable to keep the city from receiving steady supplies by sea.

Nonetheless, the Arabs still had a mighty army in Thrace, and an‚ other one was making its way through Asia Minor, devastating the countryside as it went. Byzantine emperor Leo III had little to work with, but he did understand the Arabs. Like so many emperors of his day, he had come to the throne through a mixture of intrigue, bribery, and military favors. The specifics are not clear, but it appears that Maslama believed that Leo would deliver Constantinople to him in ex‚ change for a governorship in the new Arab government. Negotiations and communications between the two leaders dragged on, and eventu‚ ally the Arab army ran perilously short of food, forcing its soldiers to consume horses, camels, and even their own dead. It did not help mat‚ ters that the winter of 717/18 was one of the coldest in memory.

A new caliph, Umar II, sent additional fleets laden with supplies to support the siege. They arrived in the spring, docking near Chalcedon, far from the threat of Constantinople's Greek fire. However, the bulk of the crews in those vessels were Christians who, upon their arrival, de‚ fected to the Byzantine side. They brought with them vital intelligence regarding the locations of Arab vessels and the land‚based army march‚ ing across Anatolia. Leo seized upon this information, sending out his navy against the supply ships, now unable to defend themselves with only skeleton crews. The Byzantines captured the provisions and then defeated the bulk of the Arab fleet in the region. The sea was once again opened to them. A Byzantine force of regulars and mercenaries marched eastward to defeat the Arab relief army. As for the Arabs in Thrace, their numbers had already been decimated by a mixture of disease, starvation, and Bulgarians. Without those supplies, they could not continue. After thirteen months, the caliph recalled them. The attack had failed. It was not lost on the joyous citizens of Constantinople that their delivery occurred on August 15, the feast day of the Dormition (Assumption) of the Blessed Virgin. Henceforth, on every anniversary of that day, the patriarch of Constantinople would recount to the citizens the victory won for them by Theotokos (Mother of God).

No simple telling of the events of 717–18 can adequately describe their powerful significance for Constantinople, or the modern world. For a second time, the greatest power on earth had launched a well-planned and heavily funded effort to conquer a city. The failure to do so preserved not only the Byzantine Empire, but all of western Europe. Had Constantinople fallen, the Arab conquests would likely have continued across the shattered West, meeting those in Spain, where Muslims already ruled. Eighth-century Europe was poor, fractured, and pitifully weak. It had no defense against powerful armies launched from a Muslim megalopolis on the Bosporus. Constantinople, the impregnable fortress of the Roman world, could not have saved its far-flung empire. But it did save itself and Europe from Muslim conquest. Without the foresight and resolve of the citizens and rulers of Constantinople, the world would be very different today.

The second Arab siege of Constantinople was the last Muslim attempt for more than six centuries to conquer the Queen of Cities (as it was now often called). The seeming immediacy of Muhammad's prophecies concerning the conquest of the capital were reinterpreted as a future event that would signal the end of the world. With that settled, Arab/Byzantine relations transformed into predictable border wars that satisfied the needs of perpetual jihad without disrupting the status quo overly much. Still, for Constantinople, times remained difficult. Given the continued successes of Muslim armies elsewhere, Emperor Leo came to the logical conclusion that God was displeased with the Byzantine Empire. To rectify that, the emperor reworked Byzantine laws to put them more in line with biblical commandments. This led him to consider the biblical prohibitions against graven images. The Muslims had taken those seriously, banning all images from their mosques and holy places. By contrast, Byzantine churches were densely populated with mosaics, paintings, and wooden icons of Christ, Mary, and the saints. The icons especially were intensely venerated by all the faithful, who saw in them a powerful connection to the spiritual world. Was this the reason for God's wrath?

Leo believed so. In the years after the Arab attack, he began empty, ing Constantinople's churches of all images. In 730, without a church council or even the support of most clergy, he decreed a complete ban on all religious icons. Byzantine troops stormed into the beautifully deco, rated monasteries and churches across the city and empire, destroying every image they could find. The damage was total. No Christian reli, gious art dating back earlier than the eighth century remains in Istanbul.

The destruction of holy images was intensely unpopular among most Byzantine people, clergy, and monks. Aside from the emperor and his son the co-emperor Constantine V, the only supporters of icono, clasm were the military and the civil bureaucracy of Constantinople. They, of course, were paid to support it, and they had the means to impose it on the city. In Italy, where Byzantine power had dramatically waned, it was impossible to enforce the imperial decrees. Pope Gregory III flatly rejected the emperor's ban, even after Leo confiscated papal prop, erties in southern Italy. This controversy, coupled with relentless Lombard attacks in Italy, led the popes to question their continued association with Constantinople. Papal elections were no longer confirmed by the emperor, and the pope no longer expected Constantinople to help de, fend Rome. Finally, in 751, the Lombards conquered the Byzantine capital of Italy in Ravenna. Faced with a full-scale invasion, the pope turned to the Catholic barbarian tribe known as the Franks. They had settled in Gaul, forming a new kingdom eventually named for them, France. Their leader, Pepin the Short, obligingly conquered the Lom, bards in Italy and then, in 754, gave to the pope in perpetuity the city of Rome and its surrounding lands. The pope thus became a monarch, the ruler of his own independent state. Henceforth, Old Rome and New Rome went their separate ways. The city of the popes was no longer the city of the caesars.

Back in Constantinople, Leo and Constantine remained unpopular, but their success in securing the borders against the Arabs, and even recapturing some territories in northern Syria, inoculated them from overthrow. Perhaps there was something to their diagnosis of God's wrath. It certainly seemed that way in 746, when the bubonic plague again crawled out of the ports and onto the streets of Constantinople. The devastation was horrific. For almost a year, dead bodies littered Constantinople's walkways and forums. The afflicted, both physically and mentally, roamed the avenues and back ways, forgetting their family members and attacking their friends. Crosses began to appear on the tunics of the sick, which always signified an impending death. This enigmatic sign only confirmed the widely held belief that God was smiting his sinful people. Tens of thousands of bodies were piled up in empty cisterns across the hollow city. When those were full, the dead were carted out to pastures and abandoned fields in the open western section of the walled space. Already depopulated, Constantinople was left a virtual ghost town by this latest plague.

It could not, of course, remain that way. After the disease dissipated, thousands from rural areas in Greece and Asia Minor moved to the great city, seeking advancement close to the imperial government. Iconoclasm was finally repealed in 787, under the Empress Irene, the first woman to rule the Roman Empire in her own right, though the practice would continue to flare up here and there before finally succumbing in 843. Not long after the repeal, a beautiful fresco of the Virgin and Child was placed above the high altar of Hagia Sophia. Uncovered and restored, it remains there still.

The lifting of iconoclasm did little to mend relations between Constantinople and Rome. Bound together by a common faith and history, the two cities were separated by everything else. No longer able to rely on Constantinople, the popes had turned to the Franks, who dutifully protected and supported the leaders of the Catholic faith. In gratitude, Pope Leo III gave an imperial crown to the Frankish king Charlemagne. On Christmas Day 800, Leo solemnly proclaimed the illiterate warlord "Emperor of the Romans." It was a title that German rulers would don for centuries. Empress Irene, of course, rejected it—just as she rejected the proposal of marriage "Emperor" Charlemagne later offered to her. But the continued use of the imperial title in the West was yet another irritant between the Latin and Greek halves of Christendom.

The rapid decline of Constantinople in the eighth century had left the city with vistas of territory completely depopulated. Many homes, shops, warehouses, and other structures stood empty, decaying and overgrown through neglect. In spite of this, the city had no shortage of power strug-gles. Indeed, this period ushered in a golden age of treachery and intrigue amid the lavish halls of the Great Palace. A stereotype of Constantinople was forming, as a place where a complex, corrupt, and deadly game of power consumed all but the most ruthless and cunning. Politics had be-come, in other words, positively byzantine.

Irene had come to power as regent for her son, Constantine VI. When at the age of twenty-four the young man began asserting his right to rule, Irene ordered her men to seize him and gouge out his eyes. The Byzantine custom of blinding to disqualify someone from the imperial throne was already a century old. But in this case, the assailants were too aggressive. Horribly disfigured, Constantine died of his wounds a few days later. Grief-stricken by her role in her son's death, Irene be-came a shadow of herself. She continued to rule, but scarcely noticed or cared when a palace coup was hatched to unseat her in 802. Accepting her fate willingly, she lived out her remaining year of life in a monastery that she had founded on the island of Lesbos.

Her successors did not fare much better. While they fought over the scraps of a fading city, the empire slipped away. Resurgent Arab armies captured Cyprus and Sicily, shrinking further the Byzantine world. Em-peror Michael III (842–67) perhaps best typifies this period. Popularly known as "the Drunk," the twenty-something ruler neglected every as-pect of statecraft, focusing instead on the amusements of the Great Pal-ace. As his nickname suggests, he was particularly fond of late-night revelries with friends and favorites, during which many jugs of fine wine were consumed. He was also, anachronistically enough, a devotee of chariot racing. He frequently financed race days in the Hippodrome and even occasionally took the reins of a chariot himself. The holy and aus-tere patriarch Ignatius of Constantinople rebuked the hedonistic em-peror from the pulpit of Hagia Sophia, but to no avail. When Michael ordered his own mother forcibly sent to a convent, Ignatius refused to allow it. Since many of Michael's bad ideas came from his uncle Bardas, Ignatius excommunicated him. Fed up with the pious moralizing of Con-stantinople's leading churchman, Michael sent word to Hagia Sophia that Patriarch Ignatius was to resign immediately. The emperor then appointed a layman, Photius, as the new patriarch of Constantinople.

Probably by accident, Michael had appointed a diligent, intelligent, and highly educated man to the patriarchal throne. Nonetheless, Pope Nicholas I in Rome refused to ratify the change, arguing correctly that the forced resignation and the appointment were irregular and invalid. He insisted that Ignatius be restored. Photius responded by calling a synod in Constantinople to examine the state of the Catholic Church in the West. It concluded that among other problems, the western Europe-ans had added a word to the Nicene-Constantinopolitan Creed: *filioque.* At issue was the procession of the Holy Spirit. In the creed, the Holy Spirit proceeded from the Father. The addition of the new word meant that in Rome, the Holy Spirit was said to proceed from the Father *and the Son.* Theologically it was a minor point. Indeed, Greek Fathers of the Church had frequently argued for the double procession of the Holy Spirit. But the pope's willingness to accept the addition touched a nerve, for it suggested that Rome's authority was greater than Constantinople's and even than that of an ecumenical council. Ignatius's synod declared the pope a heretic, and called on him to resign his office. Nicholas, of course, had no intention of complying. As the successor of St. Peter, he alone had the binding and loosing authority given by Christ. He did not recognize the ravings of an excommunicate appointed by a drunkard. Rome and Constantinople were no longer simply estranged but positively hostile.

Emperor Michael paid little attention to the ecclesiastical dustup. The delights of the palace were much more pressing. Among his favor-ites there was a particularly affable man, a well-apportioned former athlete and horse tamer, now in his fifties. Basil was of Armenian stock, although he was born and raised in Macedonia. His charms and hearty wit helped him to advance through the palace hierarchy, and he quickly became one of the emperor's closest friends and confidants—perhaps too close. Michael III made it abundantly clear to Basil that he did not like his empress, Eudocia Decapolitissa. He much preferred his mis-tress, Eudocia Ingerina, who had a deeper appreciation for the emper-or's amusements. Not surprisingly, the imperial mistress became pregnant. Michael could not bear the thought of his love child denied the imperial throne simply because of illegitimacy. He therefore de-vised a rather bizarre plot. He ordered his trusted friend Basil to marry his mistress, Eudocia Ingerina. Then he crowned Basil co-emperor. In this way his child would be thought to be Basil's, and therefore a legitimate heir to the purple.

Michael's scheme, however well conceived, was not well executed. When the child, a boy whom he named Leo, was born, Michael was so overjoyed that he opened the Hippodrome for a day of lavish games— a gesture that would have seemed excessive, if the boy were indeed Basil's son. In the subsequent weeks, Michael noticed that now-emperor Basil, who was thirty years his elder, was rather efficiently taking over the reins of government. Indeed, it seemed that the co-emperor no longer had time for his young drinking buddy. In a rage, Michael warned Basil not to take his position too seriously. He was, after all, merely a placeholder for the legitimacy of Michael's son. Basil was immediately dropped from the guest list of the emperor's all-night parties, and there materialized a new group of favorites, who played on the emperor's gullibility to promote their own interests. Fearing that he would soon be the victim of one of the palace's not-infrequent assassinations, Basil decided to act first. After one of Michael's binges, the co-emperor and a few armed men entered the imperial chamber and murdered the emperor. According to one account, the assassins first cut off Michael's hands before running him through with a sword.

Basil I's reign marked the beginning of a new imperial dynasty, the Macedonians. They would rule in Constantinople until 1025. Under Basil and his successors, Byzantium's sharp decline was halted and indeed fully reversed. Almost immediately Basil ended the strife with Rome by removing Patriarch Photius and restoring Ignatius. Basil allowed young Leo to grow up in the palace, but he crowned his own son by a previous marriage, Constantine, as junior emperor. Basil personally led the Byzantine armies against their foes, stabilizing the frontiers in the East and West. He remained married to Eudocia Ingerina, and had a number of additional children with her—although it is sometimes difficult to sort out which he fathered and which belonged to Michael III. Basil's succession plans were crushed, however, in 879, when Constantine died at the age of fourteen. The seventy-year-old emperor was devastated, for Constantine and he were much alike. The patriarch obligingly declared the deceased a saint, and a local bishop claimed to be able to summon his ghost so that Basil could speak with him. Next in line for the throne was Leo, a precocious but highly intelligent young teen who could not hide his happiness over his "brother's" death. Basil hated the scholarly and sneaky Leo, who returned the sentiment by devising plots against him. These schemes were always discovered, earning the heir a house arrest, yet no blinding.

Basil died in a hunting accident in 886. As he lay dying, he insisted that it was no accident and that it had been stage-managed by Leo. That may be true. Or it may be that Basil was attempting one last time to disinherit the young Leo. If so, it failed. Leo VI was immediately crowned amid glorious splendor in Hagia Sophia. His younger half-brother Alexander, the son of Basil and Eudocia Ingerina, was crowned junior emperor, but in practice he had no real power. Leo detested him and was determined to have a son quickly, to forestall any chance that Alexander would succeed him. That project did not go well. His first wife, Theophano, gave birth to one daughter before her death in 897. Soon after, Leo married his longtime mistress, Zoe Zaoutzaina. She, too, had a daughter and then died. The custom in the Orthodox Church was to allow only two marriages, so the emperor was in some difficulty. He petitioned the patriarch, who in this case made an exception, allowing him next to marry Eudocia Baeana. Much to the emperor's relief, Eudocia became pregnant. The Great Palace and the whole city prepared for the joyous event in 901, only to learn that the empress had died tragically in childbirth. The child, a son, died a few days later.

Seemingly out of options, Leo could not bear the thought of his hated half-brother coming to the throne. Leo was the son of a true emperor, Michael III, while Alexander was the son of that peasant upstart Basil I. Of course, under the law, Leo was also the son of Basil, yet he made no pretense of hiding the truth of his parentage. He even ordered Michael III's mutilated body brought from its resting place in the city suburbs and placed with all pomp in Constantinople's Church of the Holy Apostles. Leo needed a son, and for that he needed another wife. Patriarch Nicholas refused to allow it, and actively supported conspiracies in favor of Alexander. Leo took another mistress, the formidable Zoe Carbonopsina (of the Coal Eyes). Soon enough she became pregnant and gave birth to a daughter. Finally, in 905, Leo was at last rewarded when Zoe gave birth to a healthy baby boy. To underscore the child's right to rule, they named him Constantine.

The birth of Constantine only intensified the plotting and intrigue in the palaces, mansions, and churches of Constantinople. Alexander and his partisans worked feverishly with the patriarch to bar the baby from the throne. Nicholas only reluctantly agreed to allow Constantine to be baptized, but he would never consent to recognize a marriage between his parents. Exasperated, Emperor Leo sent envoys to Rome to seek the pope's permission to marry Zoe. Pope Sergius III promptly granted it, since the Western Catholic Church had no limit on the number of marriages one might have after a spouse died. When Patriarch Nicholas still refused to recognize the marriage, Leo used the pope's ruling to force the patriarch to resign. The new patriarch naturally blessed the emperor's fourth marriage, to Zoe, thus legitimizing Constantine as the heir. This caused such scandal in Constantinople that the patriarch had to demand the emperor issue an edict henceforth forbidding fourth marriages. Leo was also required to undertake a number of penances. One we can still see today in Hagia Sophia: Over the great imperial door leading from the narthex into the nave, Leo commissioned a rich lunette mosaic. In gold, silver, and deep reds and greens, the mosaic depicts the emperor groveling on the ground, pleading for mercy from Christ, who is seated on an imperial throne, flanked by the Virgin Mary and an archangel (Illustration 9). With this act of humility and many others, Leo got his heir. On May 15, 908, he crowned the two-year-old Constantine co-emperor.

Still, Basil I's son Alexander refused to give up. He, after all, had been crowned co-emperor decades earlier. Matters worked themselves out in his favor in 912, when the forty-five-year-old Leo became deathly ill. He had no choice but to leave Constantine under the care of Alexander, the new senior emperor. No sooner was Leo laid to rest than Alexander lashed out at his enemies. Leo's entire inner circle of advisers and officers were fired or imprisoned. Zoe was sent to a convent. The new emperor planned to make his own way. Like Leo, Alexander was immortalized in Hagia Sophia. Yet, rather than begging for mercy, he appears in a corner of the north gallery wearing the rich imperial vestments of Easter. He stands alone, without his junior emperor, Constantine. Alexander also omitted Constantine's image from his coins. There is no doubt that he planned to remove the troublesome child from the scene, probably after he had produced his own heir. Then, scarcely a year after Leo's death, Alexander was playing polo on the grounds of the Great Palace when he suffered a heart attack.

Coal-eyed Zoe was out of her monastery within the year, ruling the Byzantine Empire in the name of her young son, Constantine VII. She planned and oversaw several military campaigns against the Arabs in the East and the Bulgarians in the West, but none went well. In 919 a palace coup led by the admiral Romanus Lecapenus toppled her, returning her to the convent. Romanus married off his daughter Helena to Constantine. Then, as the imperial father-in-law, he was crowned co-emperor. For the next two decades Romanus governed wisely and well, leaving the scholarly Constantine to partake in the pleasures of the Great Palace. Unlike Zoe, Romanus's campaigns were crowned with success. Indeed, he extended the borders farther east, capturing Edessa from the Arabs. In 944 he triumphantly returned to Constantinople with Edessa's most precious relic, the Mandylion, purported to be the burial shroud of Christ. It is possible that this is the same relic today known as the Shroud of Turin.

Constantine VII ruled in his own right after Romanus's death in 948, although none of his military campaigns came to much. He is best remembered for his patronage of scholars and his own literary works. His *Book of Ceremonies* remains a fascinating text, for it describes in detail the many rituals and processions that had become an integral part of life in medieval Constantinople. These included processions on the feast of the city's foundation on May 11 and other religious and secular holidays. Similarly, his *Book on the Administration of the Empire* provides an overview of the peoples and regions that remained to the rulers of Constantinople. Both books were meant for the use of Constantine's son, Romanus II. Constantine was also likely the author of a biography of Basil I, which appears in the larger history of *Theophanes Continuatus*. It extols the emperor's many achievements. And for those who could not read, Constantine had many of them depicted in bronze and placed on the brick obelisk in the Hippodrome.

The time of the Macedonian emperors was one of renewal for Constantinople and its empire. Under Constantine's son Romanus II (959–63), the empire recaptured the island of Crete and even sacked the Arab city of Aleppo. Nicephorus II Phocas (963–69) pushed the Arabs out of Antioch, reclaiming the ancient city for the Byzantine Empire. John I Tzimiskes (969–76) invaded Syria and briefly restored the Holy Land, although he was unable to capture Jerusalem before his untimely death in 976. Basil II "the Bulgar-Slayer" (976–1025) was the longest-reigning emperor in Roman history. After crushing several armed rebellions, he went on (as his name suggests) to subjugate the Bulgarians, extending the empire across the Balkans and incorporating protectorates in Dalmatia, along the Adriatic Sea. By the end of Basil's reign, the Byzantine Empire had strong borders and fabulous wealth. It was an amazing change from just a century before.

Under the Macedonian emperors, Constantinople the ghost town was transformed back into Constantinople the megalopolis. The city grew to become even larger than it had been during the heady days of Theodosius II. By the year 1000 the population within the walls was probably around four hundred thousand, with well over a million in the greater metropolitan area. This required enormous expenditures for the repair of the neglected city. Aqueducts and cisterns had to be cleared, forums restored, warehouses rebuilt. The colonnades along the Mese once again stretched the miles between the Milion and the Golden Gate. The emperors poured treasure troves into the expansion of the imperial palace and the repair of Constantinople's many mansions of the elites. Just as in the days of Constantine the Great, the city was a hive of construction. Yet the character of this growth was very different from what came before. There was no thought of restoring Constantinople's ruined or missing baths, which would have been the first priority of an ancient leader. No new forums were laid out, no theaters or amphitheaters constructed. There were no new columns reaching to the skies bearing the statues of triumphant emperors. Those were the structures of antiquity. The new monuments to emperors and the new gathering places for citizens were churches and monasteries.

During his reign, Basil I built or restored more than thirty churches in Constantinople as well as many other buildings. Seventeen chapters of his biography are devoted just to these building projects. They included a lavish restoration and expansion of the monastery of St. Diomedes, near the Golden Gate. The monks of this house had kindly taken in Basil when he first arrived nearly penniless in Constantinople. He repaired earthquake damage on a number of churches, including Holy Apostles and Hagia Sophia. In the Great Palace, he built the monumental New Church, dedicated to Christ, the Virgin Mary, Elijah, St. Nicholas, and Gabriel the Archangel. He also began the practice of constructing a new monastery within the city to house his family members in life and their tombs in death. The fashion of massive imperial sepulchers in the Church of the Holy Apostles was replaced by emperors laid to rest in humble monastic graves, in the hope of easier entry into Heaven. Leo VI built yet another church in the palace, dedicated to Lazarus, and a Church of All Saints, near Holy Apostles. Romanus Lecapenus built the Myrelaion (Place of Myrrh) Monastery. Its church still exists, now a mosque called Bodrum Camii. John I Tzimiskes dedicated a Church of Christ the Savior next to the Chalke gate of the palace. And these are only a few of the nearly one hundred churches and monasteries founded or restored during the reign of the Macedonians.

The sudden rejuvenation of Constantinople in the tenth century was in large part due to the expansion of an empire that no longer had any other major cities. Conquered and sacked repeatedly, the cities of the Byzantine Empire were little more than large towns. Impregnable Constantinople, therefore, became the empire's lone urban landscape, its indispensable nerve center. It was the empire's focal point of attention and activity, the safe storehouse for religious relics and worldly wealth. It had long been known as the Queen of Cities. Now it was increasingly referred to simply as the City. The Roman Empire could continue without Rome, but it could no longer continue without Constantinople.

Chapter 11

Dining with Barbarians

On Saturday afternoon, July 16, 1054, in the great church of Hagia Sophia, the black-robed clergy of Constantinople's cathedral bustled through the cavernous interior, preparing it for the next day's liturgy of the Mass. Candelabras were lowered and filled with oil, incense prepared, precious vessels of gold and jewels purified and laid out. Michael Cerularius, the patriarch of Constantinople, was also there, sometimes overseeing preparations, other times seated on his throne examining the Sunday liturgy, Scripture readings, and his own homily. It was a Saturday like any other in this most remarkable of all churches.

Then came the determined, quick footsteps of several people marching across the church headed straight for the high altar on which the Body and Blood of Christ would soon be offered to God. They wore brown robes cinched with leather belts. One donned a red mantle, and all were tonsured, which identified them as Catholic clergy. Several of the nearby Greek clergy approached them curiously, but the Catholics pushed past them, determined to get to the altar and the patriarch seated near it. Patriarch Michael knew the one in red well enough. He was Cardinal Humbert of Silva Candida, a legate sent to Constantinople by Pope Leo IX—or at least that is what he said he was. Over the past several months Michael had had his fill of this proud barbarian. He refused to take his proper place during ceremonies, insisting that since he represented the pope, his position was superior even to that of the patriarch. He had written a Greek tract that he circulated around the city on the errors of the Greeks. No wonder, then, that most of the people of Constantinople were eager to see him go. It was only the soothing words of Emperor Constantine IX, who hoped for a military alliance with the pope, that kept this troublemaker in town. Now he looked dressed for travel. That was promising.

There was no mistaking the anger on the face of the cardinal. His face seemed to become darker with every step. Finally, he and his fellow clergy came to the iconostasis before the altar. They flung it open, entered the sanctuary, and mounted the marble steps to the jewel-encrusted altar. There Cardinal Humbert reached into his satchel and produced a rolled parchment threaded through with a papal seal. With great ceremony, he turned to the patriarch and slammed the parchment down on the altar. Then, with a final look of disgust, he marched out the way he'd come. The parchment unceremoniously rolled off the altar and onto the floor. A cathedral canon quickly retrieved and read it. Letting out a cry, he ran to catch the cardinal and block his way. The patriarch could hear the pleas for the cardinal to take back the parchment. Indeed, the canon thrust it into the prelate's hands several times. But each time, it simply fell back to the pavement. Finally, the angry Catholics made it to the door of the church. There they shook the dust from their sandals in a ritual condemnation of the place and its people. And with that, they were gone. Michael ordered one of his men to bring the parchment to him. It was as he expected. In the name of Pope Leo IX, the good cardinal had excommunicated the patriarch of Constantinople and all his cathedral clergy. Michael smiled, rolled the parchment back up, and let it fall once more to the stone floor of Hagia Sophia.

The dramatic scene that took place that day has cast a long shadow over the history of Christianity. Today it is common to date the break between the Catholic and Orthodox Churches to the mutual excommunications of 1054. In truth, though, it was not much noticed outside Constantinople at the time. Ironically, Cardinal Humbert had been sent to the East on a mission of friendship and reconciliation. The tensions between the Churches of Rome and Constantinople had continued to grow, particularly in the eleventh century, as a new and more confident reform papacy came to power in the West. The *filioque* clause was one bone of contention, but there were others. Greek priests were allowed to marry before ordination, while marriage was completely forbidden to European priests. In the West, the clergy were tonsured and clean shaven, while Eastern priests refused to cut off their beards, considering it a sinful vanity. The bread of the Eucharist in Constantinople was leavened, while in Rome it was unleavened. Added to these were a host of minor issues, such as whether to warm the water added to the wine during Mass, as well as imaginary ones, such as the belief in Constantinople that Europeans baptized their children with wolf saliva. The deep animosity that grew between Humbert and Michael during the former's visit to Constantinople only made things worse. Michael had refused to meet with the cardinal, claiming that he was an imposter. Surely, he reasoned, the pope would never have sent such a caustic and stupid man to the Queen of Cities. Later, news arrived that Leo had died and a new pope had yet to be elected. As a result, Humbert was a legate to no one. That did not, however, stop him from excommunicating Michael in Leo's name before riding out of town.

It would be more accurate to say that a schism existed between Michael and Humbert. Future popes continued to work with future emperors and patriarchs in Constantinople. There were problems, of course, but these centered more on authority than doctrine. The popes refused to recognize the patriarchs as "ecumenical," or universal, as they called themselves, insisting that the patriarchs were merely the archbishops of Constantinople. For their part, the patriarchs rejected the papacy's insistence that all clergy be obedient to the "head and mother" Church of Rome, insisting that the pope was a co-equal "brother," not a master. What the events of 1054 demonstrated, though, was that the West was emerging in a way that it had not since the barbarian invasions plunged it into chaos. For six centuries Constantinople had looked on western Europe with a mixture of pity and derision. Those days were over. A new, vibrant culture forged in Roman, Christian, and Germanic traditions was flourishing in the West. Western monarchies and the Catholic Church were rapidly growing in strength. Towns had sprouted up along European trade routes, while bustling cities in northern Italy conducted business across the Mediterranean. Western Europeans had for centuries been focused on their own miserable conditions. Now they were reaching out to the wider world. They would be major players in the history of Constantinople for the next four hundred years.

The world was closing in on Constantinople during the eleventh century, even as the city grew to new levels of population and wealth. Threats seemed to come from every quarter. The Pechenegs, a Turkic people from Central Asia, began regular raids into Thrace and Greece. The Normans, Christian descendants of the Vikings, conquered Sicily and southern Italy, displacing both the Arabs and the Byzantines. For the first time in five hundred years the Roman Empire no longer had a presence in Italy.

From the East came both a threat and, ultimately, a new era in the life of the City. Another Turkic people, the Seljuk Turks, invaded the Abbasid Empire, capturing Baghdad in 1055. Having converted to Islam only a few generations earlier, they were fired with the zeal of converts. With amazing energy, they conquered Syria and Palestine, making Jerusalem and the Holy Land a dangerous place. Their empire soon stretched from the Eastern frontiers of Anatolia across Mesopotamia and all the way to Persia. In 1071 their leader, Arp Arslan, led his forces west into Asia Minor, where he met the mostly mercenary army of the Byzantine emperor Romanus IV Diogenes. The subsequent Turkish victory at the Battle of Manzikert opened Anatolia wide for further conquests. But that was not the only reason Constantinople would lose its heartland. Indeed, Arp Arslan had no immediate desire to press westward. Although he defeated the Byzantine army and even captured the emperor, he released Romanus IV on the promise that the latter would send back a modest ransom and an annual tribute. It was the ruthless state of Byzantine politics that led Constantinople to unseat Romanus, force a destructive civil war, and then refuse to pay the Turks anything. Over the course of the next decade, Byzantine plotters and pretenders would turn often to the Turks, using them for their own immediate purposes while inviting them to extend their conquests ever farther into Asia Minor. By 1081, Turkish forces had captured virtually the entire region, including the city of Nicaea, which they established as the capital of a new Sultanate of Rum (i.e., Rome).

The loss of Asia Minor was disastrous for Constantinople, for the city relied on its rich soil for produce and its people to man its armies. The wealthy residents of Anatolia fled to Constantinople, thus enriching the capital further. All the rest made peace with their new Muslim masters. Constantinople had already become dependent on Western mercenaries to fight its wars. This trend only accelerated with this latest rise in wealth and loss of manpower. Indeed, the citizens of Constantinople quickly gained a reputation for elite snobbery, refusing to dirty their hands with manual labor or difficult warfare, preferring to outsource both. The Jewish traveler Benjamin of Tudela noted when he visited Constantinople around 1170:

> Wealth like that of Constantinople is not to be found in the whole world. Here also are men learned in all the books of the Greeks, and they eat and drink, every man under his vine and his fig-tree. They hire from amongst all nations warriors called Loazin [barbarians] to fight with the Sultan Masud, King of the Togarmim [Seljuks], who are called Turks; for the natives [Byzantines] are not warlike, but are as women who have no strength to fight.

Constantinople had become a historical oddity, a rich and populous capital of a small and relatively weak empire. It managed that contradiction because it remained geographically situated to command the increasingly lucrative trade conducted in the eastern Mediterranean, Aegean, and Black Sea. Those traders included new faces from western ports—most notably the Italian merchants of cities such as Genoa, Pisa, and Venice.

Protected by the city's mighty walls and enriched with foreign capital, citizens of Constantinople might easily forget that the enemies of the empire continued to close in on them. Fortunately, their new emperor did not forget. After a decade of palace intrigue and internal struggles, Alexius I Comnenus fought his way to the throne in 1081. As so frequently happened in the history of Byzantine Constantinople, the city acquired a competent ruler just when it needed one most. A dark-skinned man with a beard worthy of a Greek priest, Alexius was a talented general and a gifted politician. He came to power the usual way—through tricks, lies, bribes, and a ruthless mercenary army. Once possessed of power, he used those same mechanisms to hold on to it. He was determined to do whatever it took to defend his city and his empire.

His challenges were profound. In the summer of 1081 the Norman leader Robert Guiscard and his son Bohemond crossed the Adriatic Sea to lay siege to the Byzantine city of Durazzo (modern-day Durrës), the beginning of the ancient Via Egnatia, which still ran across Greece directly to Constantinople. The great city was, of course, the Normans' ultimate goal. Alexius moved quickly, assembling a large mercenary army to relieve Durazzo by land. Naval support was more problematic. During the previous decade the once-great Byzantine navy had been scandalously neglected by admirals who diverted appropriated funds into their own pockets. The Normans' attack fleet, on the other hand, was massive. Alexius could not hope to break the siege of coastal Durazzo without control of the sea. He turned, therefore, to Venice.

From the perspective of the people of Constantinople, western Europe was a land temporarily lost to the Roman Empire, presently in the hands of Germanic barbarians. Before the twelfth century, Byzantine authors used ancient place names when writing about the West, and referred to Europeans as Germanic tribesmen. Venice had always stood apart. The city of the lagoons was founded in the fifth century by Romans who had fled from Attila the Hun and later from the Lombard invasions. Because it was literally built out in the water, Venice was spared the barbarian incursions that smothered the West. Venetians were proud of the fact that they were Rome unfallen, loyal subjects of the emperor in Constantinople. They were fishermen and salt farmers, but most of all merchants. They could be found making deals in marketplaces across the eastern Mediterranean, but nowhere more than Constantinople. As the centuries passed, however, Constantinople was unable to control Italy or its seas. Venetian trade relied on a safe Adriatic. Faced with an economic disaster, the Venetians built their own navy and began policing the waves themselves, thus becoming increasingly independent. Many of the cities along the Dalmatian coast soon came under Venetian control. By Alexius's day, the people of Venice were generally viewed in Constantinople as poor cousins of the empire—not barbarian, but not altogether Roman, either.

Alexius dispatched envoys to Venice promising rich rewards if the Venetians joined him in his war against the Normans. The leader of Venice, Doge Domenico Silvio, accepted the offer at once. Beyond a sense of duty, the Venetians were eager to eject the warlike Normans from the

Adriatic Sea. Venice outfitted a large war fleet, and Doge Silvio personally commanded it. It reached Durazzo in the late summer or autumn
of 1081. Although outnumbered, the Venetian fleet defeated the Norman armada and seized control of Durazzo's port. On October 15,
Alexius arrived with his mercenaries. He immediately attacked the
Normans besieging the land walls. It was a miserable failure. Robert's
men not only scattered the Byzantine forces, but even managed to
wound the emperor. Alexius retreated to Constantinople. The Venetians remained, supporting Durazzo until February 1082, when the
Normans finally captured it. The war would continue for several more
years. In 1084, Alexius returned to the area with a makeshift navy,
which he joined to the Venetian fleet. Although they twice defeated the
Normans, Robert was able to capture the strategic island of Corfu, killing thousands of Venetians there. Meanwhile, his son Bohemond led
Norman forces eastward along the Via Egnatia, capturing cities and
territories on his way toward Constantinople.

Then the war ended. In January 1085, Robert Guiscard unexpectedly died. Many of the Norman troops returned to southern Italy to
support Robert's son Roger, the heir to his Italian holdings. Bohemond,
who was to inherit all Norman territories east of the Adriatic, could not
defend his new conquests with a tiny army. Within a year, Alexius
pushed the last of the Normans out of Greece and restored control over
Durazzo and Corfu. Bohemond ended up with nothing.

Yet the lasting impact of the Norman war had nothing to do with
territories won or lost. Rather, it fundamentally altered the role Italians
would play in the history of Constantinople. Venice had paid dearly for
its alliance with the Byzantine Empire—thousands of Venetians had
lost their lives, thousands more were cruelly mutilated, and even the
doge himself was overthrown. Alexius had promised rich rewards, and
he was true to his word. For Doge Vitale Falier and his successors, Alexius granted an annual stipend and bestowed on them the much-vaunted
(but utterly meaningless) title of *protosebastos*. He also supplied a stipend
for the head of Venice's church, the patriarch of Grado, and annual
tithes for various Venetian churches. In Constantinople he granted the
Republic of Venice a group of buildings and properties clustered in the

Perama district, near the Golden Horn seawalls (in the area of modern-day Rüstem Paşa Camii). In response to increased trade in Constantinople, the ancient Neorion and Prosphorion harbors were extended farther west along the Golden Horn. Just outside the walls, wharfs and loading docks sprang up in quick succession. Over the next several decades this urban area would become the nucleus of a substantial Venetian Quarter (literally a city within a city), in which thousands of Venetians lived and did business. A quarter provided Venetian merchants with a place to dock their vessels close to their own warehouses and residences and ensured that many more Venetians would come to settle permanently in Constantinople. They were not alone. In subsequent years Byzantine emperors offered neighboring quarters to the Amalfitans, Pisans, and Genoese. The Italians had come in numbers, and they had come to stay.

Yet even a quarter in Constantinople was not Alexius's greatest gift to the Venetians. He also gave them a privilege. Henceforth, he decreed, Venetian merchants could do business in all ports of the Byzantine Empire tax free. This was an enormous concession: the Venetians were handed a commercial advantage over not only their Italian competitors, but even the Byzantines themselves. Surviving business contracts demonstrate that Venetians began shifting most of their trade to Constantinople and other Greek cities. By the mid-twelfth century it was common to see wealthy Venetian residents all across Constantinople. The Greeks naturally resented the haughty nouveau riche ways of these Westerners, many of whom acted as if they were the true masters of the City. Venetian bad manners paled, though, in comparison to those of the Genoese, who positively swaggered through the streets and forums. Alexius and his successors tolerated it for one simple reason: they needed Italian naval power.

Indeed, they needed a great deal more than that. Despite Alexius's attempts to manage the Turkish threat in Asia Minor, it continued to grow. Saved from the Norman menace to the West, Constantinople was in grave danger from the Turks, who had established themselves on the eastern shores of the Aegean. Alexius needed a powerful army to push back the recent Turkish conquests. He still hoped to recover Asia

Minor completely. But where to find the troops for so large an operation? In 1095 he took another unprecedented step in Constantinople's evolving relationship with western Europe. He sent imperial envoys to Piacenza to meet with Pope Urban II. The envoys informed the pope of the grave danger posed by the Turks and begged him to have mercy on the Christian people of Asia Minor now oppressed or enslaved by their Turkish conquerors. Moved by their plight, the pope promised to do all he could.

Several months later Urban convened the Council of Clermont. After conducting the planned ecclesiastical business, the pope invited the knights and barons of southern France to attend an open-air sermon, which he would deliver. Hundreds came to hear what would be one of the most famous orations in medieval history. The precise words are not preserved, but later recollections make clear that Urban gave a stirring account of the persecutions endured by the Eastern Christians. He told the assembled warriors about the relentless Turkish attacks that had captured the heartland of the Byzantine Empire, including the cities of Nicaea, Ephesus, and Antioch. He recounted the recent Turkish conquest of Jerusalem, which had for centuries been under Arab rule. Ending the Arabs' toleration of Christians, the Turks had attacked churches and monasteries, killing priests, nuns, and a great many pilgrims. These massacres had themselves come on the heels of the Muslim destruction of Christianity's holiest site, the Church of the Holy Sepulcher, built by Constantine and his mother, St. Helena. Eastern Christianity was in trouble. Urban called on the knights of western Europe to leave aside their petty wars and prepare themselves for a mighty armed pilgrimage that would restore all that the Turks had captured and rescue those they had conquered. This pilgrimage, Urban told the warriors, would serve as penance for their many sins. The grassy plain outside Clermont erupted in a roar of approval. The excited knights chanted, "Deus vult!" God wills it! Thus began the First Crusade, the beginning of a movement that would forever change Constantinople.

According to Alexius's daughter Anna Comnena, who later wrote a biography of her father, the emperor had hoped for an army, not a movement. He certainly never envisioned the creation of a new form of

Christian holy war. But his request as voiced by Urban II struck a chord with western European nobles, who lived by the sword and thereby feared for the health of their immortal souls. The Crusade, as an act of charity and love for the Christians of the East, provided a means for these men to use the one thing they knew well, warfare, for their own spiritual benefit. Urban's call echoed in the sermons of a thousand preach⁄ers all across the West, but most especially in France. Tens of thousands took the vow of the Cross, in which they promised to make a pilgrimage to Jerusalem and wore a cloth cross to signify that commitment. They would all be heading to Constantinople.

Pope Urban II set August 15, 1096, as the departure date for the armies of the Crusade. Hurried and costly preparations were under way, not only on the estates of western knights but also in the cities of the Byzantine Empire, where Alexius ordered his people to gather pro⁄visions and set up markets for the thousands of soldiers who would march across their lands. The First Crusade was shaping up to be the largest and most ambitious military operation launched from western Europe since the days of the Roman Empire. The costs in resources and manpower were truly enormous. Not all who took the cross were trained warriors. A mesmerizing preacher, Peter the Hermit, rode from town to town on his donkey recruiting any who would heed his call. Miracles followed Peter wherever he went. Demons were exorcised, sicknesses healed, and confirmed sinners turned to God. It was widely believed that Peter carried with him a letter sent from Heaven in which God exhorted all Christians to move quickly against the Turks so that He could take vengeance upon them. Peter's preaching drew thousands into a makeshift army that followed him. Some of them were nobles, but most were poor people armed with improvised weapons. The absurdity of their campaign did not dissuade them, for they believed their success was assured.

This so⁄called People's Crusade marched across Europe, a storm of religious enthusiasm impelled by simple faith and Peter's spellbinding personality. In 1095, long before the official departure date, they crossed Hungary, Bulgaria, and Greece, leaving chaos in their wake. The mob finally arrived at Constantinople on August 1 and made camp in the western suburbs. Food, of course, was plentiful there, so these ragtag Crusaders broke into markets and caused general mayhem until the emperor at last sent provisions. Alexius invited Peter the Hermit into the Great Palace, showing him every deference. Unlike his predecessors, Alexius had a keen interest in the youthful culture of medieval Europe. He was impressed by Peter's sanctity, but not his timing. He advised the preacher to wait until the main body of the Crusade arrived the following year. Although Peter was convinced, his unruly followers continued to pillage the suburbs, demanding to be transported across the Bosporus so that they could cover themselves with glory in a war against the Turks. Within the week, Alexius gave them their wish. More than ten thousand of them were deposited on the Asian shore, where they rushed deep into Turkish territory. They were quickly wiped out. The only survivor of the People's Crusade was its leader. Peter the Hermit spent the next year in Constantinople as the houseguest of Alexius.

The main body of the Crusade began to arrive in the fall of 1096. Hugh of Vermandois, the brother of Philip I of France, was the first major noble to appear outside the walls of Constantinople. His army was small, as most of it had been lost during a crossing of the Adriatic Sea. Alexius invited Hugh into the Great Palace, where he engaged in the time-honored Byzantine practice of overawing foreigners with the fabulous wealth of the ancient empire. Hugh was impressed but not distracted. Like the other Crusade leaders, he was curious about the role the emperor planned to play in the expedition. Alexius professed his desire to add imperial forces to the Crusade's numbers and to personally lead those armies against the infidel. Before he transported the Crusaders across the Bosporus, though, Alexius felt only justified in asking them to show their good faith. He politely requested that Hugh swear an oath that any lands the Crusade captured that had previously belonged to the empire should immediately be returned to the emperor. He also asked for an oath of loyalty to him while the Crusade remained in his domains. Since the Crusaders did not plan to go beyond the far-flung borders of the old Roman Empire, this oath would effectively give all conquests to Alexius. Hugh stalled, not certain what other magnates had planned and not wanting to go out on a limb himself. In the meantime, the emperor kept him in sumptuous luxury in the city, but refused to allow him to return to his troops. Hugh at last relented and took the emperor's oath.

A few days before Christmas 1096, Godfrey of Bouillon, the power, ful Duke of Lower Lorraine, arrived with a sizeable force. Once again, Alexius sent a messenger, this time inviting Godfrey to the Great Pal, ace, where he planned to extract the same promises. From Hugh, God, frey knew the emperor's intentions, and he did not much care for the particulars of the oath. He declined the invitation, but the emperor was not so easily put off. Alexius sent word that he would not transport Godfrey's army across the Bosporus until Godfrey had sworn loyalty and given his word that reconquered territories would not be stolen from the Roman Empire. When Godfrey remained aloof, the emperor cut off provisions to his army. In retaliation, the Crusaders pillaged the suburbs, forcing Alexius to reopen the markets. For the next three months, Godfrey stubbornly waited, all the while demanding to be taken to Asia. Exasperated, Godfrey finally ordered his troops to attack Constantinople itself. In January 1097, the Crusaders assaulted the northernmost portion of the mammoth land walls. Godfrey's troops, however, were far too meager to seriously threaten the largest and best, defended city in the Western world. In retaliation, the emperor ordered a sortie of imperial soldiers. After his forces were roughly pushed back from the walls, Godfrey at last decided to come to terms. On January 20 he took an oath to Alexius, and he and his men were promptly trans, ported across the Bosporus.

The next to arrive was the Norman Bohemond of Taranto, the same Bohemond who a decade earlier led his men against Alexius in an attempt to conquer the Byzantine Empire. Now he arrived at Constan, tinople as a Crusader and ally. Alexius naturally distrusted Bohemond, but establishing control over the Crusade was his paramount interest. From the emperor's perspective, the timing of the crusading leaders' arrival at Constantinople could not have been better. One by one, he was able to negotiate with each in isolation. As one leader agreed to take the oath, it made it more difficult for the next to refuse. Bohemond was not op, posed to taking the oath in any event. It seems likely that the Norman prince suggested that Alexius appoint him commander in chief of the imperial forces in Asia, something that would have given Bohemond effective control over the entire enterprise. Yet Alexius was not willing to go that far in this friendly reconciliation. Instead, he replied cordially and in a noncommittal fashion, and Bohemond took the oath. His troops were then taken across the Bosporus to join the other Crusaders assembling in Asia Minor.

The last major leader to make the rendezvous at Constantinople was also the most powerful. Raymond, the fifty-five-year-old Count of Toulouse, had spent most of his life extending his power over thirteen counties in southern France—almost the entire region. His wealth, lands, and armies were greater than those of most kings, including the king of France. Moved by the preaching of the Crusade, Raymond decided to finish his life in the service of God. By now, Raymond had heard of the progress of the other Crusading lords and was aware of the oath that they had sworn to the emperor. He probably also heard of Bohemond's attempt to take control of the Crusade. More mature and powerful, the Count of Toulouse would not be so easily manipulated by Alexius. When asked to take the oath, Raymond responded that he had come to serve God; he would not take another as his lord. The other crusading magnates across the Bosporus urged Raymond to relent, so they could get under way. He refused. Raymond clearly saw himself as the natural leader of the Crusade. He did not want to be forced to accept Bohemond as commander in chief if Alexius decided to appoint him as such. Instead, Raymond proposed that if the emperor himself took the cross and commanded the Crusade, then he would gladly take his oath. Alexius replied that nothing would make him happier, but that he could not leave Constantinople at present. A compromise was reached: Raymond swore to respect the property and person of the emperor, a lukewarm oath not uncommon in southern France. With that, Raymond and his forces were transported across the Bosporus. The First Crusade was at last assembled.

There is no doubt that the Crusade made an impression on the people of Constantinople. Westerners were a common sight in the city, but never before had so large and powerful a force arrived from the barbarian world. Alexius's daughter Anna Comnena remarked on the rude manners and rustic ways of the Europeans. These were people, after all, who for the most part could not read, or even eat with a fork. But she was also impressed by their bravery and sturdy moral character. The Crusades would bring western Europeans and Byzantines together much more frequently and in much greater numbers. Although they shared a common religion and a common enemy, the cultural divisions between East and West would prove a constant irritant. In the streets of Constantinople in the twelfth century, this would manifest itself by an increasing level of "anti-Latinism," a visceral hatred of all western Europeans.

In Constantinople's ever-treacherous political climate, Alexius could not afford to be absent for a long campaign. Instead, he sent his most trusted lieutenant, Taticius, to lead the Byzantine armies accompanying the First Crusade. Their first target was Nicaea, the capital of the Turkish Sultanate of Rum. The sultan himself, Kilij Arslan, was away when the Crusaders came within sight of the well-fortified town on the lake shore. They invested the land walls while Taticius brought Byzantine vessels overland to cut off Nicaea's port. On May 21, 1097, Kilij Arslan arrived with a powerful relief force. Yet these Crusaders were made up of Europe's finest warriors, not the motley collection of Crusaders whom the Turks had recently dispatched. Kilij Arslan was ultimately forced to retreat to gather more forces. With no hope for rescue, the Turkish garrison handed over the city to Taticius in return for their lives and a promise not to let the unruly Europeans inside.

The recovery of Nicaea was a major boon to the Byzantine Empire, for it formed the basis on which Constantinople would regain control over western Asia Minor. For their part, the Crusaders were intent on pressing on, all the way to Jerusalem. Most of the Byzantine forces remained at Nicaea or returned to Constantinople, although Taticius commanded a small contingent to represent the emperor on the Crusade. Alexius promised to raise a large army and to meet the Crusaders in the East. So from Nicaea, the Crusaders set out across the plains of Central Anatolia, baking in the summer sun and stripped of every sustenance by the retreating Turks. Many died of starvation and many others were forced to eat horses, dogs, and even the enemy dead. They arrived at the great city of Antioch in December 1097. For the next six months the

Crusade remained outside the walls, the target of frequent Turkish raids, while suffering further depredations. Food remained scarce, and the Crusaders stripped the countryside bare for miles around with their foraging. Disease also took many lives. In the spring, the Crusaders learned that the Turkish ruler of Mosul, Kerbogha, was marching to relieve Antioch with a massive force. The news caused a panic among the weakened forces. Desertions reached an epidemic level. Even Peter the Hermit, who still bore his letter from Heaven, slipped out of camp and ran for home. He was captured and returned. With profuse tears, he begged the Crusaders to forgive him for his loss of faith, and they did.

Taticius did not desert—at least not openly. He and his men boarded vessels bound for Cyprus, claiming that they would bring back supplies and support from the Byzantine island. They never returned. Taticius's relationship with the Crusade commanders had been deteriorating for some time, as they demanded to know where his master was with his promised support. As a skilled general, Taticius knew the hopelessness of the Crusaders' predicament. Like many others, he made his escape.

The situation was dire, but it was also fluid. On June 3, 1098, Bohemond managed to bribe a Christian garrison commander to allow him and his men to scale the walls under cover of darkness. Once inside, they opened the main gates, and the rest of the Crusaders stormed in, capturing the dozing city. Unfortunately for them, there were scarcely more supplies in the city than outside. When Kerbogha and his armies arrived, they completely surrounded Antioch. Fear, hunger, and despair racked the city. Some fled and managed to escape; others were captured by the Turks and cruelly tortured and mutilated in view of their comrades manning the city walls.

One of the Crusade leaders, Stephen of Blois, and some four thousand Crusaders under his command were in nearby Alexandretta when Antioch was taken. They returned to discover that although their comrades had captured the city, the Muslim forces camped outside were so vast that they were certain to destroy the Crusade. Like Taticius, Stephen concluded that the situation was hopeless. With great sorrow, he abandoned the enterprise and began his journey home. On the way, he learned that Alexius was marching to Antioch with a sizeable army.

Fearing that the Byzantines would be ambushed by the victorious Turks, Stephen made a special trip to rendezvous with the emperor at Philomelion. There he related the heartbreaking news of the arrival of Kerbogha and the sure destruction of the Crusade at Antioch. He urged Alexius not to continue on to what was certain doom. Alexius thanked Stephen for the warning and ordered his men to return to Constantinople. Stephen went back to France.

Stephen was wrong. Although seriously outnumbered, the hungry and weakened Crusaders were determined to die fighting rather than surrender to the hated Turks. When they learned of Alexius's retreat, they cursed both him and Taticius. Most of the commanders now repudiated their oaths to the emperor, claiming that they would not keep faith with a traitor. This single event had an enormous impact on the relationship between Constantinople and the West. It nourished an image among Europeans of Byzantines as treacherous, craven, duplicitous, and weak. The Crusades, which Pope Urban had envisioned as a means to bring the Christians of the East and West together in a common cause, was driving a wedge between them. Even as he retreated, Alexius believed that Antioch should belong only to him. The Crusaders huddled behind its walls were determined to keep it for themselves.

On June 28, with equal parts courage and folly, the First Crusade marched outside the walls of Antioch, drew up its ranks, and charged against the numerically superior adversaries. Kerbogha's emirs, who had not expected a bloody fight, began withdrawing their forces, leaving the *atabeg* to fight the Crusaders alone. He could not hold the line. With his retreat, Antioch fell completely into the hands of the Crusaders. They bestowed it on Bohemond of Taranto, who at last built a kingdom on former Byzantine property. The Principality of Antioch would remain under European control for the next century and a half. The Crusaders also captured Edessa, in Armenia, and several months later, in July 1099, went on to conquer Jerusalem. They did all this on their own. Alexius and Taticius had made rational judgments based on the available information. The Crusaders, on the other hand, had made irrational decisions based on the sure knowledge that God would grant them victory. Without Alexius's help, the First Crusade laid the foundation for a new Christian Kingdom of Jerusalem that would span the entire eastern Mediterranean shoreline and survive for nearly two centuries. The Holy Land was restored to Christianity, but not to Constantinople.

Alexius may have fumed about the Crusaders' unwillingness to hand over their conquests, but he still reaped benefits from their efforts. Turkish power in western Asia Minor was broken, allowing him to restore the Aegean and Mediterranean coasts, including important cities such as Ephesus and Smyrna (modern-day İzmir). The farms of Asia Minor once again fed the mouths of Constantinople. The Turkish threat to the City was neutralized—for the moment.

Chapter 12

————◆————

Treasure and Treachery

No one who lived in twelfth-century Constantinople could miss the steady immigration of western Europeans into the city. The influx reflected the rise of the medieval West, a land where powerful kingdoms flourished, Gothic cathedrals reached to the heavens, and universities echoed with the debates of learned scholars. The reach of the West even extended to Constantinople's imperial family, anointed by God to rule over the empire of the Romans. Emperor Alexius I Comnenus's son and heir, John II, took as his empress Piroska, a red-haired Hungarian princess who assumed the Greek name Irene. (A glimmering mosaic of the couple still greets visitors to Hagia Sophia's south gallery.) Their son Manuel I married a German princess, Bertha of Sulzbach. After her death in 1159, Emperor Manuel married a tall, blonde-haired Norman princess, Maria of Antioch. Little wonder, then, that Constantinople's twelfth-century emperors focused ever more intently on the Catholic world, both in western Europe and in the Crusader states to the east.

This is not to suggest that western Europe had anything to rival Constantinople. In the twelfth century, the largest cities in the West were Rome and Venice, each with a population of around fifty thousand. Constantinople, by comparison, had some four hundred thousand living within its walls, with another six hundred thousand or more in the greater metropolitan area. It was by a wide margin the greatest Christian city in the world, one in which the glories of antiquity were still on display (Illustration 10). Fountains danced in spacious forums, people marveled at colossal bronze statues and gaped at giant columns adorned with imperial images. Although used only for civic ceremonies, the Hippodrome remained a showplace, with its stunning obelisks and nearly a hundred bronze statues crowded onto the central *spina*.

Yet the people of Constantinople had changed with the times. The magnificent statues, no longer admired for the stories they told of ancient glories and gods, were instead cultivated as talismans, believed to have been devised by ancient magicians for their own mysterious purposes. When the Norwegian king Sigurd visited Constantinople around 1111, residents informed him that the Hippodrome's statues had once been alive, and indeed used to take part in the games. The Byzantines frequently rubbed, touched, or buried items near or within the city's hundreds of statues, hoping to reap arcane benefits. One statue depicting a woman with her hands outstretched was said to be a mystical arbiter of fair prices—at least before one of the arms was lost. A palace oracle advised an emperor afflicted by impotence to clothe all the naked statues in the Hippodrome. Numerous statues of mice, rats, and snakes were thought to protect the city from the ravages of their living counterparts. Even the beautifully adorned Golden Gate, opened only for triumphant emperors, was transformed into a talisman. Since imperial victories had become a rarity, it was commonly thought that anyone who walked through the main archway was destined to become the emperor. The great door was, therefore, always locked and under guard. Emperor Isaac II became so obsessed by it that he ordered the door removed and the entire Golden Gate sealed up with stone. On display was a thoroughly medieval approach to pagan antiquities: they were viewed with deep suspicion, yet also sought for their protective powers.

In the eleventh century, Constantinople's emperors shifted their construction attention to monasteries, often where they hoped to be buried. Romanus III built the extensive monastic complex of St. Mary Peribleptos, in the southwest part of the city. Michael IV founded the monastery of Saints Cosmas and Damian, just outside the Theodosian land walls near the Golden Horn. Constantine IX placed the beautiful St. George of the Mangana on the eastern slopes of the First Hill, looking out toward the Bosporus. The Comnenian emperors accelerated this trend, building monasteries throughout the city, such as St. Mocius, Christ Philanthropos, and Christ Pantepoptes (probably modern-day Eski Imaret Camii). A hospital and orphanage dedicated to St. Paul on the old acropolis was so large that Anna Comnena described it as a city within a city. All these religious complexes have disappeared. The

greatest of the Comnenian monasteries was the magnificent Christ Pan,
tocrator, set high between the Third and Fourth Hills, just north of the
Aqueduct of Valens. Although that monastery no longer exists, its ex,
traordinary triple church does. The three joined sanctuaries consist of
a large main building, an adjoining chapel to St. Michael, and another
church dedicated to the Virgin.

Emperor John II Comnenus was an energetic leader who believed
that by co,opting the youthful yet often erratic energy of western Eu,
rope he could harness it for the benefit of his city and his empire. He
concluded that his father, Alexius, had given the Venetians too much
for their help against the Normans. By 1118, when John took the throne,
the Venetians in Constantinople were richer and more numerous than
ever before. They were contemptuous of Byzantine officials, many of
whom, because of Alexius's privileges, had no power over them anyway.
John refused to renew their privileges. The Venetians, of course, did not
take that decision well. As it happened, Venice had prepared a powerful
Crusade fleet in 1122, which was to transport some fifteen thousand
Venetians to the Holy Land to help the Kingdom of Jerusalem. They
decided to make war on John along the way. During the winter of 1122/23
the Venetian fleet besieged Corfu, although trouble in Syria forced it to
leave later that spring. On the way back from their Crusade in 1124 and
1125, the Venetian fleet raided the Aegean islands and the island of
Rhodes. Plundering, burning, and stealing relics, the Venetians had be,
come a major threat to Constantinople. John could do little to stop them
without a viable navy, and he was utterly reliant on Italian naval power.
Finally, in 1126 he relented, renewing all Venice's trading privileges.
Peace was restored to Byzantium's waters and to the Venetian Quarter
of Constantinople. But John had planted the seed of a response to Ven,
ice's arrogance. He granted to Venice's commercial rival Pisa its own
quarter in Constantinople. In later years, other quarters would similarly
be given to Genoa and Amalfi. Lined up along the southern shore of
the Golden Horn, Constantinople's Italian quarters attracted more
Western businessmen to the bustling city. More important from John's
perspective, it broke Venice's monopoly. Henceforth, emperors would
play the Italian city,states against one another.

Manuel I Comnenus succeeded his father, John, in 1143. The son of a

Hungarian princess and the husband of a German princess, Manuel was as much a product of the West as he was of Constantinople, and he could not hide his fascination with Western ways. Chivalric poetry was intro' duced in the palace, and knightly tournaments staged in the Hippo' drome. Like John, Manuel believed that harnessing the West was key to rebuilding the Roman Empire. His first order of business was to restore southern Italy to Byzantine control—no small feat now that it formed the basis of a Norman kingdom. Manuel allied with the German king Conrad III to begin an invasion, but other matters intervened. In 1144 the Muslim leader Nur'ed'Din captured Crusader Edessa and threat' ened Antioch. Two powerful Crusade armies were raised in Europe, one led by Conrad and the other by King Louis VII of France. Rather than reclaiming Italy, Manuel was thrust back into the role of supporting a Crusade. He pivoted gracefully, ensuring that markets were well stocked for the armies as they marched across Greece. Nonetheless, the unruly German troops caused a fair amount of damage, especially in Constanti' nople's suburbs, where they attacked people, businesses, and homes. Since Conrad was eager to be on his way, Manuel obligingly transported the German army across the Bosporus. In central Anatolia, they met a powerful Turkish force and were completely wiped out. Only Conrad and a few others survived. Louis and Queen Eleanor of Aquitaine ar' rived at Constantinople with their French Crusaders on October 4, 1147. Manuel invited the royal couple into the city, where they were housed in a lavish palace and treated to every luxury and entertainment the wealthy and cosmopolitan city could offer.

It is possible that Manuel entertained the king and queen of France in the sprawling Great Palace complex. It was, after all, unrivaled in splendor anywhere in the Christian world. Yet Manuel himself no lon' ger spent much time there. Byzantine emperors had long had multiple palaces, many outside the capital, where they could go for relaxation, away from the crowds, noise, and smell of Constantinople. For reasons that are still unclear, Manuel Comnenus moved the main imperial resi' dence to the Blachernae suburb, which a century or so before had been enclosed in the expanded land walls at the far northern tip of the city. The Blachernae Palace was ornate, but also more compact than the Great Palace. Built on a hill against the mammoth walls, the palace looked out over the harbors on the one side and the plains outside the city on the other. Tekfur Saray, a three-story annex of the Blachernae complex, is all that remains of the many palaces that once dotted the landscape of medieval Constantinople. From its second floor one can peer out windows aligned directly along the Theodosian land walls, getting a magnificent view of the exterior of the walls while remaining safely within them.

The royalty of France departed Constantinople cordially and set out with their countrymen on their great expedition. Unfortunately, Louis's Crusade was almost as disastrous as Conrad's. Harried by Turks, it clung to life along the Aegean and Mediterranean coasts of Asia Minor. When food ran low, the Crusaders attacked the Byzantines, taking what they wished. Louis became convinced that Manuel was actively seeking to destroy the Crusade, something that was completely untrue. When the Second Crusade later failed to capture Damascus, and the survivors returned to Europe in shame, Louis placed the blame for the debacle on Manuel's shoulders. He even argued for a new Crusade, against Constantinople. The pope and the rest of Christendom rejected the idea.

With the Second Crusade at an end, Manuel could again focus his attention on matters in the West. During the 1160s he attempted to coax the Germans, Italians, and papacy into a partnership that would restore control of southern Italy to Constantinople. Meanwhile, he continued to campaign in the East and West. In 1167 he conquered Bosnia and Dalmatia, reestablishing the Byzantine frontier on the Adriatic Sea. For the first time in living memory, a direct attack on the Norman kingdom seemed feasible. Of course, for that he would need a powerful navy. He sent three ambassadors to Venice to ask for the "customary aid" in a war against the Normans. Yet times had changed. Italy was convulsed in a war that pitted the pope, Lombard cities, and the Normans against the Germans under their emperor Frederick I Barbarossa. To attack the Normans was tantamount to attacking the pope, which the Venetians would not do. They politely declined Manuel's request.

When the three ambassadors returned to Constantinople and informed Manuel of the Venetian response, he was beside himself with rage. Venice had enriched itself in the markets of Constantinople, enjoying unheard-of privileges as the gift of the Byzantine emperor, and now it had the temerity to refuse so trifling a request? Manuel had had his fill of Italian merchants. They brought their crass manners, money-grubbing ways, and deep and petty animosities to the streets and forums of the Queen of Cities. Indeed, street fighting between the Genoese and Pisans had become so fierce that in 1162 Manuel expelled them all from Constantinople, confiscating their quarters and warehouses. The Venetians had prospered by their absence, yet now they would not lift a finger to help the people of Constantinople. Why should Manuel honor the promises of his grandfather Alexius if the Venetians would not renew their support of the Byzantine Empire? In Venice, Doge Vitale Michiel knew Manuel's mind on this. He issued a warning for his countrymen that they should avoid doing business in Byzantine ports, lest they fall victim to the emperor's wrath. The sway of profits was simply too great to significantly reduce the number of Venetians conducting trade there, though, and when Manuel later assured Venetian envoys that he had no intention of striking out against them, the doge lifted his warning.

In 1170, Manuel struck up a new alliance with Venice's enemy, the German emperor Frederick I Barbarossa. He followed this up by restoring to Genoa and Pisa their quarters in Constantinople, while warning their people that he would tolerate no more violence in his capital. Venice, as it happened, was no longer necessary. Several weeks later, a mob of Venetians in Constantinople descended on the newly restored Genoese quarter with torches and swords. That was the last straw. From his palace, Manuel sent hundreds of secret messages to Byzantine officials across the empire ordering them to arrest, imprison, and confiscate the property of every Venetian in their jurisdiction on March 12, 1171. When Venetian envoys arrived in the imperial court to excuse the violence in the quarters, Manuel smiled sweetly and assured them all was well. Then, right on time, the arrests began. In Constantinople and every other Byzantine port, Venetian men, women, and children were thrown into prison, and when the prisons were full, they were piled into monasteries. Their houses, shops, merchandise, and vessels were confiscated. Well over ten thousand Venetians would remain in custody for years.

Venice's response was swift. It outfitted a powerful armada designed to raid and pillage the Byzantine Empire while the Venetian doge sent envoys to Constantinople to negotiate the release of the captives. But the mighty fleet was beset by a pestilence that it could not shake, even after hopping from one Aegean island to another. Those lucky enough to survive brought the dread disease home with them. Disgusted by the failure, the people of Venice murdered their doge. A state of war would exist between Venice and Constantinople for the next decade.

It was largely a cold war, one that Emperor Manuel could safely ignore. All his attentions were focused on preparations for a large-scale military campaign to conquer Muslim Asia Minor and Egypt. It was an uncharacteristically bold move for a Byzantine emperor, particularly for Manuel, whose efforts had always been so focused on the West. Yet this new offensive, although it headed east, was meant to increase his authority in Europe. With Europe torn by wars and papal schisms, its inhabitants bitterly regretted their continued failures in the Eastern Crusades. Manuel meant to deal a blow to the Muslim kingdoms that would not only reestablish his power in the East, but also forge his reputation in the West as the true defender of the Christian faith. His agents had already discussed with Pope Alexander III the possibility of papal support for Manuel as universal emperor of East and West. A stunning victory against the Muslim enemy would seal that deal.

It was not to be. A Turkish army crushed the Byzantine advance at the Battle of Myriokephalon in 1176. This crippling defeat left Manuel with large debts, a shattered reputation, and almost no military assets. It permanently erased Constantinople's influence on the affairs of western Europe and the Crusader states. All that Manuel had striven to build up now crumbled around him. In Europe, both sides in the continuing struggle between pope and emperor could safely ignore Constantinople. Manuel was isolated, with few friends, eager enemies, and no allies. For the moment, the Normans of southern Italy were involved in Italian matters, but when they again turned their attention to the conquest of Greece, Manuel could rely only on the unreliable Genoese for help. Faced with this calculus, Manuel made a halfhearted attempt to negotiate a peace with Venice. He released a few Venetian prisoners, who returned home after eight years in captivity. But soon after, on September 24, 1180, the emperor fell ill and died. He left an eleven-year-old son, Alexius II, and his Norman wife, Maria, as regent.

The mood in Constantinople in 1180 was hardly conciliatory toward western Europeans. Although Manuel had managed to maintain order in the city, his attempts to court favor with Westerners and even to bring their customs into the Queen of Cities was highly unpopular. Anti-Western sentiment had been growing steadily among the native Greeks of Constantinople. The Europeans had swarmed into the city with their uncouth ways and barbarian tongues, flinging their money about and arrogantly demanding respect and service. Much of Constantinople's population blamed their empire's decline on Latin influence. It was a hatred born of impotence, which is among the most virulent. The accession of Alexius II, the son of a Norman empress and a half-European emperor, was bad enough. But the barbarian regent, Maria, immediately began favoring the Genoese and other Italians in the city. She also began having an affair with Manuel's cousin, despite the fact that she had taken a vow of celibacy as a nun after her husband's death. It was intolerable. A rival faction arose around another Maria, Manuel's elder daughter by his first marriage, to Bertha. The two Marias were roughly the same age, so it is not surprising that step-daughter and stepmother did not get along. Supported by the patriarch of Constantinople and her Italian husband, Renier of Montferrat, Maria Comnena attempted to overthrow her stepmother. The plot was foiled and the conspirators forced to hide out in Hagia Sophia for months until they were granted a pardon.

The failure of the coup further enraged the Greek mobs, who refused to be ruled any longer by Western barbarians. Riots broke out across the city. Regent Maria's attempts to put them down failed, as her Greek soldiers were increasingly unwilling to move against citizens with whom they generally agreed. She did, however, have the Varangian Guard, an elite mercenary corps responsible for the protection of the imperial family and the palace. The Varangians were all western Europeans, usually from Scandinavia or England. Trained from an early age, they were adept at a number of fighting techniques, but were best known for the single-edged axes they carried on their shoulders. To the people of Constantinople, they were simply "the axe bearers." They took a solemn vow, which they passed down from father to son, to protect and defend the emperor. Given the number of plots and attempted coups, that was a full-time job. Although they numbered around five thousand, they were much too few to deal with the growing urban unrest in Constantinople.

Generally, on these occasions, a Byzantine official or member of the aristocracy would raise an army and march on Constantinople in an attempt to seize the throne. That is how Alexius I Comnenus had come to power in 1081, and although his family had retained the throne ever since, they were required to fend off numerous armed revolts of this kind. In 1182, Andronicus Comnenus, a cousin of Manuel I Comnenus, decided to make his bid. Andronicus was a remarkable man. Although in his mid-sixties, he remained extremely strong and vigorous. According to the Byzantine senator Nicetas Choniates, who knew Andronicus, he was bald on top and had a long gray beard, which he parted down the middle. He was well known not only for his military skill, but also for his extraordinary charisma, which brought him the admiration of men and a long line of distinguished mistresses. In his late twenties and early thirties, he had been a regular in the court of Emperor Manuel, who appointed him to various tasks in Constantinople and abroad. It was then that he had an infamous affair with his cousin Eudoxia. In 1153 he was caught participating in a conspiracy against the emperor and imprisoned. Year after year he staged ever-more-daring escapes, until finally, in 1165, he managed to get away. He then traveled between various courts, ultimately ending up in the Principality of Antioch, one of the Crusader states. There he met and seduced Philippa, the beautiful daughter of Prince Raymond, who was the sister of Maria, the second wife of Manuel and the mother of young Alexius II. Outraged by the insult, Manuel ordered him arrested and returned to Constantinople. So Andronicus fled to Crusader Jerusalem, where King Amalric I liked him so much that he made him lord of Beirut. While still in the royal palace, Andronicus met the beautiful twenty-one-year-old widow of the previous king, Baldwin III. Theodora, who was a niece of Manuel I's and therefore a cousin to Andronicus, was enchanted by the fifty-something swashbuckler. When their affair was discovered, the two fled Jerusalem, first to Damascus, then Georgia, then Trebizond on the Black Sea.

After so exciting a career, a bid for the imperial throne may have seemed mundane to Andronicus. Yet the unrest in Constantinople was too great an opportunity to pass up. He raised troops in Trebizond and their numbers increased as he marched toward Constantinople. Only a few halfhearted skirmishes were fought, as the real struggle was on the streets of the megalopolis. There the people hailed Andronicus as their savior. To avoid unnecessary bloodshed, he proposed that Empress Maria return to her convent, allowing him to take on the burden of the regency government of her son, Alexius II. She had no choice but to obey. Across the Bosporus, in Chalcedon, Andronicus waited for preparations to be concluded for his arrival. He waited for something else, too. The mobs had given him the capital—now they wanted their reward.

They got it. In April 1182, Andronicus sent agents into the city to spread the news that the people were free to cleanse Constantinople of its western European filth. The carnage began early in the morning. Tens of thousands of Greeks poured into the streets and swarmed into the Italian Quarter along the Golden Horn. No Catholic was safe. The mob broke into their homes, churches, and hospitals, killing, raping, and torturing those they found. Thousands were killed in their beds before they even knew what was happening. The easiest targets were women, children, and the aged, who were cut down mercilessly. Catholic priests and monks were brutally massacred. Even the papal legate, who was in the city on an official embassy, was dragged into the streets and decapitated. His head was tied to the tail of a stray dog, who was then chased for miles by the blood-drenched Greeks. The massacre was not finished until every Westerner in Constantinople was dead or had escaped. A Venetian merchant vessel bound for the city met a returning ship crammed with refugees. They warned them, "If you do not flee you are dead!" One contemporary estimate put the number of dead at sixty thousand, which may be too low. Thousands more were captured and sold as slaves to the Turks.

Genoa immediately declared war against Constantinople. Across Europe, the horrific massacre was recorded angrily in the chronicles of monasteries and royal courts. The hatred that the people of Constantinople felt for Europeans could not have been more apparent. Unsurprisingly, Westerners began to see Byzantines as much an enemy as the Muslims. Andronicus, for his part, did not hate Westerners—many of his mistresses were Europeans, and he had been welcomed in the Western courts of Antioch and Jerusalem. But he knew where the power in Constantinople lay. The mobs had raised him up and, unless appeased, could as easily bring him down.

Firmly installed in the palace, Andronicus at once turned against every possible rival. Manuel's elder daughter, Maria, and her husband, Renier of Montferrat, had supported Andronicus's coup, but he had them poisoned anyway. Although Empress Maria was cloistered in her monastery, Andronicus nonetheless ordered her arrest. He then drew up her death warrant and forced her eleven-year-old son to sign it. The beautiful Maria was either strangled or sewn up in a sack and thrown into the sea. And these were only the highest-profile of his victims. With vengeance, he moved against the aristocracy of the city. The slightest hint of disapproval or betrayal was enough to warrant an arrest. Hundreds of Constantinople's elite were blinded, mutilated, tortured, impaled, or otherwise dispatched. As the reign of terror spread, Andronicus became increasingly paranoid, which led him to order more arrests and executions.

To secure his position, Andronicus decided that it was time to take the throne for himself. In a grand and thoroughly staged ceremony in the Augusteion, under the gaze of the magnificent mosaic of Christ the Victor, young Alexius II and a host of slavish courtiers begged the aged Andronicus to become co-emperor so that he could better protect the God-guarded city. He refused, of course. After many more requests, he agreed to enter Hagia Sophia and receive the crown. Shortly thereafter two of Andronicus's henchmen stole into young Alexius's room and strangled the boy with a metal wire. The grieving Andronicus decided to do the honorable thing. He married Alexius's betrothed, the twelve-year-old Agnes, daughter of the king of France.

Andronicus ruled Constantinople as boldly as he had lived. Yet the City was no young princess, to be won over easily by his charms. Andronicus's enemies were legion, far more than before his purge. And they were not only in Constantinople, for most of Europe also decried him as a villain. Some took action on that belief. Genoese corsairs plundered Byzantine ports and cities at will. The Hungarians attacked and conquered Constantinople's Dalmatian territories, hard won by John II. Even worse, the Normans, under King William II of Sicily, launched an ar⸗ mada against Durazzo, planning this time to achieve their dream of conquering Greece and then Constantinople. They would do a good job of it, bringing chaos and destruction across the region. In 1185 they even captured and sacked Thessalonica, the second city of the empire. Andronicus had no allies and an increasing number of enemies. Desper⸗ ate, in 1184 he turned to Venice. Although thousands of Venetians re⸗ mained in Byzantine prisons, they had not suffered much from the massacres of 1182. In return for naval support, Andronicus released all the prisoners, restored Venice's old quarter in Constantinople, re⸗ instated all Venice's privileges in the empire, and promised to make repa⸗ ration payments to all Venetians harmed by Manuel's actions against them. With their position restored, Venice's merchants and families returned to the lucrative markets of Constantinople. Within a few years the population of the Venetian Quarter rivaled that of Venice itself.

Still, Venetian support could not save Andronicus from his own peo⸗ ple. By 1185 the mobs had soured on the autocrat, particularly after thousands of Venetians began moving back to Constantinople. News of the approaching Normans also filled the city with dread, yet the em⸗ peror did little but assure the citizens that the approaching army was falling into his well⸗prepared trap. Rather than defend the city, however, he left it frequently for pleasure trips with a whole troupe of beautiful women, who, the Byzantine senator Nicetas Choniates tells us, followed him everywhere "like a cock by barnyard hens." As the people of the capital were beset by a potent mixture of anger and fear, Andronicus energetically "sought to attain the sexual prowess of the cuttlefish." An elderly man, he had some difficulty keeping up with his many women, "so he also sought help in revitalizing his genitals for the purpose of sexual intercourse by resorting to ointments and extravagant prepara⸗ tions." The latter included a steady diet of lizards imported from Egypt.

The end wasn't far off for Andronicus and his dynasty. While out of town, he ordered some of his enforcers to arrest and execute a young, red⸗haired twenty⸗something aristocrat named Isaac Angelus. His crime: one of the palace's fortune⸗tellers had assured Andronicus that a man named Isaac would overthrow him if left unchecked. Yet the arrest went poorly: Isaac mounted a horse, grabbed his sword, and charged upon his attackers, killing one and injuring several others. Then, with extraordinary bravery and skill, he galloped down the crowded Mese brandishing his bloody sword and declaring to all that he was being set upon by the emperor's assassins. This naturally caused a stir, leading thousands to follow him, if only to see how it would all turn out. After reaching Hagia Sophia, Isaac fled into the sanctuary and mounted a pulpit, where he loudly proclaimed his innocence and begged his fellow citizens to protect him from the bloodthirsty emperor. Word spread across Constantinople of Isaac's daring ride, leading thousands more to jam into the great church and spill out into the Augusteion. By the next morning, when Andronicus sailed into the Great Palace's harbor on an imperial trireme, a full-scale riot was raging in the city. Aside from the usual looting and violence, the mobs had broken open the imperial prisons and stormed the gates of the Great Palace. The palace guard refused to fight, and the Varangians were too few. The soothsayer, it would appear, had been correct about Isaac.

Taking as much gold as he could carry, his wife, and a sizeable cadre of concubines, Andronicus disguised himself as an Italian and boarded his imperial vessel, fleeing north toward the Black Sea. Meanwhile, the mobs broke into the palace, looting many of the rich rooms and chapels and even a mint. In Hagia Sophia they cut down the crown of Constantine, which hung on a golden chain over the main altar, and forced the patriarch to place it on Isaac's head. Thus began the troubled career of Isaac II Angelus, one that would ultimately bring Constantinople to its knees.

On that September day of 1185, however, the mood was jubilant. In a storm of fury, the people had deposed their once-beloved emperor, replacing him with an unknown whose main qualification seems to have been that he was reasonably young. Their fury had yet to be spent. When Andronicus was captured and returned to Constantinople a few days later, he was subjected to (as the historian Donald Nicol put it) "a frenzied and horrible bestiality unparalleled even by Byzantine standards." He was shackled head and foot with heavy chains normally used for lions and other beasts and paraded through the streets, slapped, kicked, and punched by any who desired. He was then led before Isaac, where his right hand was cut off with an axe. Several days later one of his eyes was gouged out. He was then dressed in rags and placed on a mangy camel, which was led through the city. Once again the mobs poured out to accost him. According to Nicetas, "Some struck him on the head with clubs, others befouled his nostrils with cow-dung, and still others, using sponges, poured excretions from the bellies of oxen and men over his eyes." Onlookers threw stones, and one prostitute flung a pot of boiling water into his face. He was then led into the Hippodrome in a mock triumphal ceremony. He was helped off the camel, at which point the crowd tied his feet together and suspended him upside down between two columns. Again Nicetas: "[R]emoving his short tunic, they assaulted his genitals. A certain ungodly man dipped his long sword into his entrails by way of the pharynx; certain Europeans raised their swords with both hands above his buttocks, and, standing around him, they brought them down, attempting to see whose cut was deeper." Thus ended the Comnenian dynasty, which had brought Constantino-ple to new levels of prosperity and treachery.

The new emperor moved quickly to neutralize the greatest threat to the city. He sent his general Alexius Branas to engage the Normans, forcing them back to Durazzo. He also made a treaty of friendship with the new leader of Egypt and Syria, Saladin. Indeed, he even built a small mosque on the shore of the Golden Horn, near the old Genoese Quarter. None of this, of course, endeared him to the western Europe-ans, who naturally viewed Saladin as a threat to the safety of the Holy Land. And they were right.

In 1187, at the Battle of Hattin, Saladin's forces crushed the armies of the Kingdom of Jerusalem. Thousands of European Christians were killed in the battle or the mass executions thereafter. Saladin later ad-mitted to killing forty thousand. He also captured the precious relic of the True Cross, which was sent to Damascus and there destroyed. De-fenseless, most of the Crusader kingdom quickly fell, including Jerusa-lem. A new Crusade was preached across western Europe, and it attracted Christendom's mightiest rulers. King Richard I Lionheart of England and King Philip II Augustus of France joined together to produce one of the largest war fleets of the Middle Ages. That, at least, was not a direct threat to Constantinople, although Richard did conquer the is-land of Cyprus, henceforth lost to the Byzantine Empire. Emperor Frederick I Barbarossa of Germany, however, was a threat. He raised a powerful Crusade army and began marching along the time-honored Crusader path, directly toward Constantinople. Isaac did not trust Frederick, and Isaac's friendship with Saladin obligated him to hinder the Crusade's progress toward the Muslim leader. This he did, all the while claiming to support the Crusade. When Frederick learned of Isaac's treachery, he diverted his Crusade to the city of Adrianople, in Thrace, which he captured. In return for restoring the city, Frederick wrung promises from Isaac to supply the Crusade army and peacefully ferry it across the Hellespont.

The Third Crusade was not as disastrous as the Second. Frederick died on the campaign, but Richard was able to restore most of the lost territories, although Jerusalem remained in Saladin's hands. The end of the Crusade brought a truce between the Muslims and Christians, which suited Isaac well enough. He made peace with the Pisans and Genoese, welcoming them back to their own quarters and playing them off the Venetians. For these businessmen, the capriciousness of Constantinople's emperors and people was becoming a serious liability. Still, there was nowhere in the world where one could make the sort of money that could be found in the wharfs and bazaars of the Queen of Cities. Once again, the city prospered while the empire crumbled. Indeed, what was left of the Byzantine Empire in Greece and Asia Minor was almost always in one state of rebellion or another from Constantinople. Isaac spent much of his time defending against or putting down these rebellions.

It was during one of those campaigns that he lost his throne—at least the first time. His brother, Alexius Angelus, accompanied him on the journey. An unscrupulous and power-hungry man, Alexius hatched a plot to overthrow his brother. In 1195 he and a number of supporters captured Isaac and blinded him. They then returned to Constantinople and announced the succession of Alexius III Angelus. Given the depths to which politics in the city had descended, the viciousness of the coup was ignored by the people. Isaac was given a reasonably pleasant confinement under house arrest, still allowed to converse with family and friends.

In terms of population, size, and wealth, the twelfth century brought

Constantinople to its zenith prior to the modern era. It was a place of every piety and virtue and every vice and cruelty. Its streets were filled with riches and poverty, lined with palaces and beggars. With its pockets full of commercial gains, Constantinople purchased its warriors and wares from others while its empire cracked under the strain of providing for a world capital that governed only a small region. Something had to give.

Chapter 13

Blind Men

Since the earliest days of Byzantion, the gentle waters of the Golden Horn have provided a secure harbor set apart from the swift current of the Bosporus Strait. Always crowded with vessels arriving and departing, loading and unloading, the harbor was especially busy on July 17, 1203, with one disturbing difference. One onlooker, Nicholas Mesarites, described masts of a fearful armada arranged in a line on the opposite shore, as a great forest of trees, each bearing poisonous fruit. Flying from the tops of those deadly masts were crimson banners depicting the winged lion of St. Mark, the symbol of the Republic of Venice. And in their holds they bore an army of Crusaders. Their target was Constantinople.

The seeds of the dramatic events that would bring these hostile forces into Constantinople's inner harbor were sown in the treacherous rebellion of Alexius III against his brother, Isaac II, back in 1195. Although Alexius had usurped the crown of the caesars, it was his wife, Euphrosyne, who masterminded the coup. As the new empress, she took charge over much of the government—so much so that, during state ceremonies, she and the emperor presided from identical thrones. Husband and wife reveled in the luxury of the imperial palaces, spending seas of money on idle pastimes, extravagant amusements, and sumptuous banquets. Euphrosyne took it upon herself to deal with the armed rebellions and palace intrigue that were part of daily life in twelfth-century Constantinople. To safeguard her husband's position, she often took part in arcane rituals designed to reveal threats and provide mystical tools to thwart them. Sometimes these involved the mutilation of ancient statues. In the Hippodrome, for example, she sentenced a bronze boar to have his snout cut off and a statue of Hercules to be flogged. Other statues lost arms or were decapitated by hammer blows. By these enchantments, Euphrosyne meant to stay in power.

For his part, Alexius III put as little effort into government as possible. He obligingly rewarded those who helped him seize the throne, then sold imperial titles to the highest bidder, delegating important matters to his wife or those she suggested. He did not have the heart to murder his deposed brother, so he gave him a comfortable confinement in the suburbs across the Bosporus. Isaac's son, who had been named after Alexius in happier times, seemed to get along well with his uncle. It did not escape the teenage Alexius's attention, however, that the ruthless deposition of his father had barred the young man from succeeding to the throne. Not surprisingly, Alexius and his blind father spent frequent evenings hatching schemes of revenge. One plan materialized around some letters sent to Isaac's daughter (and young Alexius's sister) Irene, who was the wife of Philip of Swabia, one of two rival kings of Germany. In them, Isaac and Alexius bemoaned their condition in Constantinople and asked Irene to stir up her husband to help them.

Feeling particularly avuncular, in the summer of 1201 Alexius III suggested that his namesake accompany him on a short campaign in Thrace. Shortly after their departure from Constantinople, the young Alexius sneaked onto a Pisan merchant vessel, cut off his beard and cropped his hair to appear Italian, and sailed to the West. The Pisan sailors obligingly dropped the refugee off at Ancona, where he sent word of his flight to his sister at the German court. Irene dispatched a contingent of soldiers and plenty of money to bring the young man to her. Back in Constantinople, Alexius III was apparently unconcerned by the sudden disappearance of his nephew. He may have even welcomed it. The emperor had just recently named his son-in-law Theodore Lascaris as heir to the Byzantine throne, and the disappearance of his nephew meant one less reason for a coup to develop.

Meanwhile, young Alexius Angelus arrived at the rustic but comfortable hunting lodge of Philip of Swabia at Haguenau in October 1201. There he was reunited with his loving sister Irene, and warmly acquainted with her royal husband. He also met another of Philip's distinguished guests, Boniface, the Marquis of Montferrat, a mature man in his early fifties and one of the most powerful nobles in northern Italy. Spending the winter together, the two learned that they had much in common. Boniface's brother Conrad of Montferrat had served as caesar in Constantinople for the young Alexius's blinded father, Isaac II. Boniface's brother Renier of Montferrat had also been a caesar and, with his wife, had attempted to overthrow Alexius II. Renier was later poisoned on the orders of Emperor Andronicus II. Although Boniface had probably never visited Constantinople, he was intimately aware of the treachery of its politics and the allure of the imperial throne.

There was more to talk about on the long, cold Alsatian nights than the injustices of Constantinople's rulers. Boniface had recently secured a new job. He was the commander in chief of a forming Crusade, called by Pope Innocent III to win back Jerusalem. Europeans had come to believe that the state of the Holy Land was a reflection of God's pleasure with them. Because of their sins, God had taken the Holy City from them, handing it over to the Muslims. Innocent was determined to "avenge the injuries of the Crucified" by launching a massive new Crusade to recover it. Calling the Crusade had been Innocent's first act as pope back in 1198, but the project faltered for some years, largely because of a war between England and France. By 1201, though, recruitment and preparations were well under way. The Fourth Crusade (1201–4) was to travel by sea, thus avoiding Constantinople altogether. Delegates from the French Crusade leaders had already contracted with the Republic of Venice to provide an enormous war fleet and tons of provisions so that the entire army could sail directly to the East without the Byzantine entanglements that had delayed previous Crusades. The costs were, of course, enormous, but since each Crusader would pay his own passage, they were manageable. The Venetians also joined the Crusade, contributing fifty war galleys. They were led by their aged and blind doge, Enrico Dandolo.

Boniface told his winter companions of the preparations for the great Crusade, which was to sail out of Venice that very summer. When the snows had melted, he planned to return home to settle some matters and then head off to Rome to consult with the pope on the Crusade's destination. The Crusade leaders had decided to target Egypt, the base of Muslim power in the Middle East. With Cairo under their control, they believed that Jerusalem would fall to them easily. Alexius eagerly told the marquis that he was himself the rightful emperor of Constantinople, for his uncle was a vile usurper and his father blind. He assured Boniface that the people of Constantinople hated Alexius III and longed to welcome him as their new ruler. If Boniface and his Crusade made a minor diversion to transport young Alexius to the great city, the people would overthrow Alexius III. Once crowned, the young man would show Boniface the gratitude that only a Byzantine emperor could afford. Beyond the customary money and titles, Alexius would join the Crusade with his own forces and restore Jerusalem to Christendom. All this for a simple detour.

Boniface was intrigued. As commander in chief, he could not steer the Crusade where he willed; as with all Crusades, decisions were made in a council of the leading barons and a papal legate. The person to convince was Pope Innocent III. Alexius made plans to do so. After spending Christmas at Haguenau, the Byzantine prince took an armed retinue of Germans and several pouches of Irene and Philip's money and traveled to Rome. The royal couple bid good-bye to the young man, wishing him every success.

Alexius Angelus arrived in Rome in early March 1202 and was quickly granted a papal audience. In his mid-thirties, Innocent III was one of the youngest popes to take the throne of St. Peter. Well educated, well spoken, and deeply pious, Innocent was also a good judge of character. He politely listened to Alexius's tragic tale of betrayal and his fervent promises that the citizens of Constantinople longed to overthrow his uncle the tyrant. If only the pope allowed the new Crusade to right this terrible wrong, Alexius would use all the resources of the Byzantine Empire to support the expedition's holy work. Even better, he would end the division between East and West, forcing the patriarch of Constantinople to acknowledge the pope as his ecclesiastical superior. Innocent was unimpressed. The lad had passion but little else. The pope doubted that Constantinople's people were longing to crown this teenage refugee. Alexius's claim was weak from the start. After all, he was born before his father became emperor—therefore not "born to the purple." Also, an assault on the city would likely be necessary to topple the current emperor, and that was utterly foolhardy. Constantinople was impregnable; everyone knew that. The rumor in Rome was that Constantinople had enough fishing boats alone to defeat a Crusade fleet. The Crusaders had taken the cross to serve God, not to become a tool of Constantinople's poisonous power struggles. Innocent told Alexius to go home to his sister. When Boniface of Montferrat arrived in Rome a few weeks later, the pope ordered him to have nothing further to do with the young man's scheme.

The wayward pretender to the throne of Constantinople did not take the pope's advice. Rather than returning to Germany, he took up lodging in Verona, a day's ride from Venice. There he watched as hundreds of Crusaders marched past daily on their way to the lagoon city. It was heartbreaking to think of this great armada sailing off to Egypt when the young prince could have made so much better use of it in Constantinople. The pope's support would have been helpful, of course, but young Alexius was convinced that it was by no means necessary. Boniface of Montferrat likely visited Alexius in Verona, assuring him that he would promote the Constantinople plan in Venice when the time was right.

Would the time ever be right? Although Crusaders began arriving in Venice in May, they were not as numerous as expected. By June 29, the planned departure date, only about 10,000 were camped on Venice's Lido. The French leaders, however, had ordered a fleet that could carry 33,500 men and more than 10,000 horses. The Venetians had undergone enormous expense to produce that fleet, and they could not renounce payment. With a fleet now three times too big, the Crusaders could not afford what they had ordered. So they waited month after month for additional Crusaders to arrive. Some did; thousands more decided to avoid the whole mess, finding their own transportation from other ports. Thus, the Fourth Crusade stalled until the end of August, when the sailing season was quickly coming to a close. By then, the Crusaders were no closer to the Holy Land, out of money, and quickly consuming all their provisions. Finally, Doge Enrico Dandolo came up with a solution to save the Crusade. The Venetians agreed to defer payment for the vessels and food provided the Crusaders helped them to conquer Zara, a town on the Dalmatian coast that had rebelled against Venice and was currently under Hungarian control. The Crusade could then spend the winter of 1202/3 in Zara and head to Egypt in the spring. With much grumbling, the Crusaders agreed.

During the next few weeks, the Crusade fleet was prepared for departure. It was then that the young Alexius Angelus sent a few German envoys to meet with the leading Crusade barons in Venice. They recounted for the lords the heart-wrenching story of poor Alexius Angelus, the rightful ruler of Constantinople, who now sought aid for his people, oppressed by the tyrant Alexius III. The Crusade leaders expressed amazement at the tale. Boniface was among those leaders, pretending that it was all new to him and not a scheme twice forbidden by the pope. The envoys suggested that the Crusade leaders send their own representatives with Alexius back to the court of Philip of Swabia to receive assurances of his support and consider the outlines of a possible agreement. This they did. Shortly thereafter, in the first week of October 1203, the Fourth Crusade set sail.

In Constantinople, Alexius III received word of his nephew's activities. It did occur to him that a powerful Crusade bearing an imperial pretender might pose an inconvenience to his social schedule. To avoid that eventuality, he sent an embassy to Pope Innocent to discuss the matter. Innocent had previously exchanged correspondences with Emperor Alexius and Patriarch John Camatarus of Constantinople. They were cordial, though not productive. Innocent had urged the emperor to support the Crusade so that, thus united, they could defeat the Muslims and redeem Jerusalem. He also warned him that the Greeks must cease their stubbornness and show proper obedience to the Holy See in Rome. Alexius had excused himself from the Crusade and declined to place Orthodoxy under Catholic control. In his own letter, the patriarch of Constantinople lectured the pope on Church history and the organizational structure of Christianity. As always, there was a certain haughtiness to the Byzantine response, the norm when addressing Westerners. Now, however, the mighty Crusade was a clear threat to Alexius III's throne. Many of Constantinople's statues would need to undergo amputations to avoid so terrible a tragedy. The Byzantine envoys informed the pope about the young troublemaker's activities and urged him not to fall for his promises. A Crusade, after all, should not attack fellow

Christians. Innocent responded that he had already forbidden the Crusaders to take up the young man's cause, so the emperor had nothing to
worry about on that score. He did point out, though, that the pretender
promised aid for the Holy Land and reunification of the Churches under Roman obedience. That was much more than Alexius III had done.
He urged the emperor to see to those matters. Relieved by the pope's
response, Alexius III and Euphrosyne returned their attentions to the
pleasures of the imperial palaces.

Where the pope and emperor erred was in believing that either had
any control over the Fourth Crusade. When Innocent learned that the
expedition was planning to attack Zara, he sent a letter to the Crusade
leaders strictly forbidding it under pain of excommunication. Zara, a
Catholic city, was under the protection of the king of Hungary, whose
lands were under papal protection. Since wintering at Zara was the only
means of preserving the Crusade, the Crusaders ignored the pope, conquering the city on November 24. They were immediately excommunicated.

During the winter of 1202/3 envoys from Philip of Swabia arrived at
Zara and addressed a large assembly of leading Crusaders, including
Boniface of Montferrat, Baldwin of Flanders, and Doge Enrico Dandolo.
They stressed the duty of Crusaders to aid the downtrodden and, with
much emotion, related the oft-told tale of Alexius Angelus and his poor
blinded father. If, in their charity, the Crusaders made a simple detour
to Constantinople, the people of the city would throw off Alexius III
and joyously welcome their new emperor. In return for this righteous
deed, the young man would pay them two hundred thousand silver
marks (fifty-one tons of silver) and fully supply the Crusade at his own
expense. He would also join the Crusade with an army of ten thousand
men, and for the rest of his life maintain a force of five hundred knights
in the Holy Land. And, of course, he would restore the Orthodox
Church to Roman obedience.

On its face, it was an extremely attractive offer. The Crusade was
running low on provisions and even lower on money. However, it would
also mean delaying further this already delayed enterprise. The large
majority of Crusaders wanted nothing to do with Constantinople. Their

duty, as they saw it, lay in the Holy Land. There they could complete their vows and return home. Most of the Crusade leaders saw things rather differently, though. The Crusade's dwindling provisions meant that if they sailed for Egypt as planned, they would land with nothing to eat for man or horse. They would also have no means of return, since the lease on the Venetian fleet expired in June. Supporting Alexius Angelus, on the other hand, would solve all their problems. It seemed to be the only viable option. So, without the approval of the rank and file, a handful of the leading barons signed and sealed agreements with the runaway pretender to the throne of Constantinople.

In April 1203, Alexius Angelus joined the Crusaders and the fleet made its way down the Adriatic, stopping occasionally at Byzantine cities such as Durazzo and Corfu to proclaim the right of the young man to rule, receive some halfhearted acclamations, and put aboard supplies requisitioned by the true emperor. They did much the same in the Aegean throughout the month of May before finally casting anchor near the Abbey of St. Stephen, about seven miles southwest of Constantinople. The people of the capital rushed to the seawalls to see this extraordinary armada, which had more than two hundred major vessels and many smaller ones. The largest fleet to enter the Sea of Marmara in centuries, it was a magnificent, although worrisome spectacle for everyone in the city. The pennons and banners of the lords, with their lively and variegated colors, were unfurled. The shields, each furbished with the arms of its owner, were ranged around the bulwarks like a wall of steel. The richly decorated sails were puffed with air, mightily pulling the vessels against the Bosporus's relentless current. It was a sight to behold.

If the citizens of Constantinople were intrigued by the Crusaders, that was nothing beside the stunned amazement of the Crusaders themselves. They were dumbfounded by the grandeur of the scene before their eyes, for they had never imagined there could be so beautiful a city in all the world. They had never beheld so many and such magnificent palaces, and the many domes of the Orthodox churches were also a strange and marvelous sight. Constantinople was simply outside the ken of the Westerners. This teeming megalopolis was greater than the ten largest cities in western Europe combined. One of the Crusade leaders, Geoffrey de Ville-hardouin, wrote in his memoir that no man was so brave and daring that he did not shudder at the sight of the sprawling city. A poor knight, Robert de Clari, who later dictated his experiences, tried to describe for his Western audience the enormous size of Constantinople and its vast numbers of palaces and marvels. At last he simply gave up, proclaiming, "[I]f anyone should recount to you the hundredth part of the richness and the beauty and the nobility that was found . . . in the city, it would seem like a lie and you would not believe it."

The next day, the Crusade fleet lifted anchor and sailed directly under the seawalls of Constantinople, on their way to make camp at Chalcedon, on the other side of the Bosporus. Their path was completely unimpeded. Alexius III had ordered the imperial navy to engage the enemy, but had overlooked the fact that the navy lacked war vessels. There were of course myriad exalted naval functionaries drawing large stipends for doing nothing. They vaunted their proud titles and posed as admirals and captains, but there was no fleet. The brother-in-law of Empress Euphrosyne, Lord Admiral Michael Stryphnos, had the chief responsibility for seeing to the maintenance of the imperial navy. According to Nicetas Choniates, the admiral had an amazing ability to turn anchors into gold and ropes into silver—in other words, he sold off whatever was apportioned for the fleet. As a result, in the spring of 1203, Constantinople's navy consisted of twenty decaying and worm-eaten ships incapable of putting out into open water.

The Fourth Crusade remained camped near Chalcedon for the next week, waiting for the popular uprising that would depose the tyrant. It never came. Eventually, Alexius III sent an envoy to the Crusade leaders to express amazement that they had come to Constantinople, for he was a Christian just as they were. He knew their holy mission was to deliver Jerusalem, and would of course support them with provisions and supplies. But if they had come to do mischief in his lands, he proclaimed that he had the power to destroy them, even if they were twenty times more numerous. That was a bit of an exaggeration. It is true that Alexius III had troops in Constantinople that outnumbered the Crusaders by more than three to one, but their quality was uneven.

He did, however, have the legendary walls that had shrugged off invaders twenty times more numerous than this army. The Crusaders responded by demanding that he relinquish the throne he had treacherously usurped. The emperor naturally declined.

A few days later the Crusaders took their case directly to the people of the City. All the Venetian war galleys rowed out, impressively taking their places on the waters of the Bosporus just outside the acropolis. As expected, thousands of Constantinople's citizens thronged the walls and nearby rooftops to see the spectacle. On the richly adorned galley of the Doge of Venice stood the ancient Enrico Dandolo and the leader of the Crusade, Boniface of Montferrat. Between them was the young prince. "Behold your rightful lord!" they loudly proclaimed to the people. They cried out the crimes of Alexius III and stressed that they had not come to do harm to Constantinople, but to defend and assist it against the tyrant. They urged the Byzantines to take action against the usurper. If they refused, the Crusaders promised to do as much damage to the city as they were able. Yet the Crusaders had seriously misjudged the mood of Constantinople's citizenry, still seething with anti-Western hatred. The Byzantines threw a fierce volley of stones at their unwanted saviors. Their projectiles were outnumbered only by their insults, catcalls, and obscene gestures.

On the morning of July 5, 1203, the Venetian war galleys began crossing the Bosporus, each towing behind a barge packed with archers and crossbowmen. Their plan was to attack Galata, on the north shore of the Golden Horn. Alexius III arrayed a large force along the shoreline to contest the landing, but his troops fled when fired upon. With the way clear, the Crusaders' horse transport vessels sailed to the shore and opened their doors. Out charged the mounted knights, who quickly captured most of Galata. After setting up stone-throwing machines, they pounded the Tower of Galata for several hours until it fell. The harbor chain was then lowered, and the entire Crusade fleet poured into the Golden Horn. It was the first enemy fleet ever to enter Byzantium's secure harbor.

On July 17 the Crusaders launched a two-pronged attack on Constantinople. The knights attacked the far northern portion of the land walls protecting the Blachernae district. The Venetians outfitted their transport vessels with flying bridges on which they could climb to the top of the masts and cross over to the top of the seawalls. About a hundred of these vessels advanced across the Golden Horn and toward the city. Artillery mounted on the city walls fired stones at the transports while crossbowmen and archers from both sides filled the air with missiles. The ferocity of the Byzantines' missile fire kept the Venetian transport vessels from pressing too closely to the shore. A few vessels grazed the walls with their bridges, but they quickly retreated to avoid the deadly shower of stones.

At this point, the blind doge of Venice, Enrico Dandolo, did a remarkable thing. Standing on the prow of his galley, fully armored and with the banner of St. Mark waving in the wind before him, the old doge had been listening intently to the sounds of battle and the description of events from his men. When the transport vessels halted, he ordered his own galley to advance to the shoreline and run aground beneath the walls. Not surprisingly, his men questioned the wisdom of this tactic. Dandolo erupted in fury, promising to personally do harm to anyone who did not obey his order. So the rowers put their back into it, and the ducal galley moved swiftly forward. All along the line, Venetian sailors watched in surprise as the doge's vessel came out from behind the transports and sped toward shore. Amid the torrents of missiles, they could see the winged lion of St. Mark and behind it the figure of their doge, still standing bravely on the prow. As soon as the galley made landing, several men grabbed the standard and planted it onshore. This incredible display of courage gave heart to the Venetians. At once the great transports moved forward, and the marines again rushed to the flying bridges. This time some managed to gain a foothold on the walls, while others came ashore and scrambled up ladders. The Byzantine defenders fled, allowing the Venetians to move quickly across the fortifications and capture twenty-five towers of the seawall.

As the Venetians began flooding into the Blachernae and Petrion districts, collecting horses and booty, Alexius III dispatched reinforcements, which probably included the elite Varangian Guard. The Venetians retreated to their boats, setting fires along the way. A strong wind fanned the flames into a massive and uncontrollable inferno, which quickly reduced a wide area of the northern city to smoldering rubble.

It was the first of many wounds the Crusaders would inflict on the Queen of Cities.

The people of Constantinople were well accustomed to palace coups and armed rebellions. They were not accustomed to having their city harmed in the process. Alexius III's inability to defend Constantinople against these barbarians was magnified by the devastating damage the latter had inflicted on it. The emperor saw the danger. He also recognized that his regular Greek troops were poorly trained and unwilling to suffer losses. He needed more mercenaries. Late that night he packed a thousand pounds of gold and as many precious stones and pearls as his wagons could carry and slipped quietly out of the city. The plan was to hire more swords in the provinces and then return to destroy the Crusaders. He left his heir, Theodore Lascaris, and his wife behind to manage the defense of Constantinople in his absence. But a coup was already under way. As soon as Alexius III's absence was detected, Euphrosyne was arrested and blind Isaac II released and restored to a throne he could no longer see. The next morning, imperial messengers arrived in the Crusader camp. They brought expressions of gratitude from Isaac II and a request that they bring his son to him. He would be pleased to offer them every hospitality. The gates of Constantinople opened wide for the Crusaders, transforming the conquerors into tourists.

No visitor to Constantinople before 1203 offered so rich a description of the city as the knight Robert de Clari, who had a Greek guide to show him around. Robert was astounded by the richness and vastness of Constantinople. With wide eyes and gaping mouth, he fully believed everything he was told, even about those things he did not see. The Great Palace, he records, had "fully five hundred halls, all connected with one another and all made with gold mosaic." He tells of the palace's "Holy Chapel, which was so rich and noble that there was not a hinge nor a band nor any other part such as is usually made of iron that was not all of silver." Crammed with relics, he assures his reader, the chapel had pieces of the True Cross, the Holy Lance, nails of the Crucifixion, the blood of Christ, His seamless garment, the Crown of Thorns, the Virgin's Robe, John the Baptist's head, Veronica's Veil, and an icon of St. Demetrius which "gave off so much oil that it could not be removed as fast as it flowed from the picture."

Robert was astounded by his visit to Hagia Sophia. Every column in the church, he claims, cured a sickness of some sort, simply by one's rubbing against it. The main altar, he reports, was fourteen feet long and "made of gold and precious stones broken up and crushed all together." He describes the altar's silver canopy, which resembled a church spire, the gorgeous ambo, and more than a hundred chandeliers, including one that was so large that it required a chain the width of a man's arm to suspend it. A pipe "such as shepherds play" hung on the main door of Hagia Sophia. According to Robert, if a sick man put this pipe in his mouth, it instantly began "sucking out all the sickness and it made the poison run out of his mouth and it held him so fast that it made his eyes roll and turn in his head, and he could not get away until the tube had sucked all of the sickness out of him."

Outside Hagia Sophia, Robert toured the Augusteion. He was particularly impressed by the Column of Justinian, with its giant equestrian statue at the top and its hand outstretched to the East. According to Robert, it was of the emperor Heraclius, and his gesture was a warning to the Muslims of the East. By the thirteenth century, people in Constantinople commonly believed the statue provided magical protection for the city against Muslim conquest. Robert did not visit the Church of the Holy Apostles, which he believed was called "Seven Apostles," but he knew that Constantine the Great was buried there. He was most impressed by the city's various talismans. On one gate he saw a bronze statue with a golden mantle and an orb in an outstretched hand. According to Robert's guide, the orb protected Constantinople from all lightning strikes. The statue had an inscription that read, ANYONE WHO LIVES IN CONSTANTINOPLE A YEAR CAN HAVE A GOLDEN MANTLE JUST AS I HAVE.

Robert was amazed by the Hippodrome, although he had no idea what "games" were once played there. Upon the *spina*, he explained, "were figures of men and women, and of horses and oxen and camels and bears and lions and many other kinds of animals, all made of copper, and all so well made and formed so naturally that there is no master workman in heathendom or in Christendom so skillful as to be able to make figures as good as these. And they used to play [in the games] by enchantment, but they no longer play." Farther down the Mese,

Robert saw the spiraled columns of Theodosius and Arcadius. The military campaigns portrayed on those columns had long ago been forgotten, transformed by the common people into images of mystical prophecies. "But no one could understand the event [depicted on the column] until it had happened, and when it had happened the people would go there and ponder over it."

Having thousands of rude Westerners walking their streets, peering into their churches, and pawing their merchandise was not much appreciated by most citizens of Constantinople. Anti-Western sentiment remained a potent force, becoming even more so with the arrival of the Crusaders. To reduce the possibility for violence, a few days later Isaac asked the Crusaders to make their lodging across the Golden Horn, in Galata, which they did. Overall, the mood was good among the Westerners. Isaac had already ordered the patriarch of Constantinople to send a letter of submission to the pope in Rome. Now all that was needed was payment of the promised reward, and they could be on their way.

Then they hit a bit of a snag. Shortly after the young refugee was crowned Alexius IV on August 1, 1203, he began making payments to the Crusaders. Half the promised sum, one hundred thousand silver marks, arrived almost immediately. Yet after that, it became increasingly difficult to raise funds. Alexius IV had already confiscated the wealth of his enemies; he could not do the same to his friends. Instead, he turned to the Church, sending armed men into Constantinople's sanctuaries to collect sacred vessels and altar adornments, and had them melted down for coin. Yet that, too, was not enough.

Isaac and Alexius quickly found themselves in a difficult bind. The mobs in Constantinople seethed at the Western presence, and the Byzantine nobility were shocked by the extraordinary payments. The emperors realized that they were almost certain to be overthrown when the Crusaders departed. Indeed, Alexius III was in Greece raising troops for precisely that purpose. They needed more time to collect funds and firm up their hold on power. They therefore convinced the Crusaders to remain at Constantinople until the next sailing season, in March 1204. In return, they promised to provision the army and extend the lease on the Venetian vessels for an additional year, at their own expense. After much debate, the Crusaders agreed.

The agreement did nothing to quell the growing frustration of Constantinople's people, who began assembling in ever-greater crowds, demanding that something be done to send these barbarians packing. Finally, in mid-August, the anger on the streets boiled over. Thousands of rioting Byzantines decided to repeat the anti-Western massacre of 1182. They poured into the Italian Quarters, making no distinction between friend and foe. The Amalfitans and Pisans had recently helped them defend Constantinople against the Crusaders. No matter. The mobs torched all their quarters, hoping to cleanse their city of the Westerners. Their churches, homes, hospitals, warehouses, and shops all along the Golden Horn were quickly reduced to ashes. The Italians themselves fled toward the harbor, where the Venetian fleet gave them safety. Nearly thirty thousand of them were relocated to Galata. The people of Constantinople had rid their city of the Westerners, and in so doing had formed them into a unified and angry group.

Out of that anger would erupt the greatest fire ever to rage across the landscape of Constantinople—or any medieval city. On August 19 a large group of Flemings, Venetians, and Pisans boarded fishing boats and rowed across the Golden Horn. Their initial target was the mosque built by Isaac II to commemorate his friendship with Saladin. It was outside the walls on the harbor shore. While the Flemings burned down the mosque, the Venetians and Pisans entered the city and began torching the homes of their former Byzantine neighbors. As they retreated to their boats, a powerful wind blew up from the north, whipping the blaze into a mighty inferno. The flames, Nicetas Choniates reported, "rose unbelievably high above the ground . . . While in the past many conflagrations had taken place in the City . . . the fires ignited at this time proved all the others to be but sparks." Shifting erratically, the strong winds blew the enormous fire in a zigzag path. Buildings that seemed to have been spared were again turned upon and destroyed. Columns, statues, great structures "went up in smoke like so much brushwood." "Nothing," Nicetas lamented, "could stand before those flames." Across the Golden Horn the Crusaders looked on with horror. Villehardouin recorded that the barons "were extremely grieved and filled with pity, seeing the great churches and the rich palaces melting and collapsing, the great streets filled with merchandise burning in the flames, but they could do nothing."

The fire raged southward during much of the first day, destroying a vast number of buildings, including the palace of Nicetas Choniates, just northeast of the Forum of Constantine. The flames then darted down the covered Mese all the way to the Milion. They destroyed the atrium of Hagia Sophia, but the church itself was spared. The Forum of Constantine was not so fortunate. Its covered walkways were leveled. The Mese became a river of fire. A little farther west, the ancient and splendid Church of St. Anastasia was destroyed. To the east, the Hip^{podrome} narrowly escaped destruction. The next day, the wind shifted again, blowing the fire westward. The blaze ran along the southern por^{tion} of the city, destroying homes, churches, and warehouses along the Sea of Marmara. Finally, it halted at the Port of Theodosius.

By the third day the fire had largely subsided. The citizens, using the many cisterns in the city, got to work extinguishing the last of the flames. Localized fires continued to erupt here and there for another week. Approximately four hundred fifty acres of Constantinople's most opulent and congested areas had been reduced to ashes and rubble. The material cost was enormous; so, too, were the human costs. Some one hundred thousand people saw their dwellings destroyed. Some, such as Nicetas Choniates, had alternate accommodation. Others simply left the City. Most returned to the devastation, building squatters' camps and tent villages in the pathetic ruins of their former neighborhoods.

As the embers cooled, the people of Constantinople erupted in a fiery rage. For the sake of his throne, Alexius IV had brought these bar^{barians} to New Rome, urged them to attack it, and paid them seas of coin when they had finished. No wonder they felt completely at liberty to burn the City down. The residents of Constantinople would stand it no longer. Alexius had to make the Crusaders pay for their crimes. Per^{sonally} fond of the Crusade leaders, the young emperor did not want to break with them. Yet in his court at Blachernae, the nobles and officials were nearly unanimous in their desire to see an end to the Westerners.

Frozen by indecision, Alexius did nothing. Although provisions continued to arrive at the Crusader camp, the young emperor stopped visiting the leaders and making additional payments. As for his father, Isaac, he was slowly losing his mind. He spent his days listening to mystics who promised him a miraculous restoration of his sight and his impending elevation to the throne of ruler of the world.

Unwilling to be ignored, in November the Crusaders sent to Alexius a six-man delegation. They were received in the sumptuous throne room of Blachernae Palace, which was filled with dozens of richly dressed nobles and lined by the axe-wielding Varangian Guard. The envoys recounted all that the Crusaders had done for the emperor and all that he had promised them. Would Alexius honor those promises? If so, then a word from him was enough. But if he would not, they warned him that they would attack his lands in an attempt to "pay ourselves." At this, the whole room exploded in shouts of anger. Never had the ears of a Roman emperor been wounded by threats in the sanctum of his own throne room. This is what came of befriending barbarians! The decorous meeting quickly devolved into a brawl, forcing the envoys to flee for their lives. When they returned to Galata they informed the Crusade leaders that the deal was off. "And so began the war," Villehardouin declared.

It was a war that would drag on throughout the winter months. The rich villas and splendid churches that surrounded the capital in every direction were stripped of all wealth and burned to the ground. Occasionally the Byzantines would attempt to defend their property, but they usually failed. Although Alexius boasted to his people about impending strikes that he would lead against the Westerners, he never left the palace. By December 1203 the area around Constantinople was picked clean for miles. Requiring provisions for more than thirty thousand people, the Crusaders began sending out foraging expeditions on Venetian vessels that ravaged the coastlines of the Bosporus and Sea of Marmara. Since the emperor would do nothing to stop the chaos, groups of citizens began assembling to hatch schemes to wage war without troops. In the last week of December, under cover of night, they loaded a few old vessels with dry wood, old barrels, pitch, fat, and whatever else would burn. They then hoisted sail, moved out into the dark waters of the Golden Horn, and set the vessels ablaze before diving overboard. These fire ships moved swiftly north and nearly crashed into the Crusader fleet. The Venetians, who were consummate sailors, leaped aboard the burning vessels and steered them out into the current of the Bosporus. On January 1, 1204, the Byzantines launched another blazing flotilla, although this one consisted of seventeen vessels chained together in a line of fiery destruction. It took the Venetians most of the night to separate and tow these fire ships out of the Golden Horn. As they did so, the Byzantines shot arrows from the shore, wounding many. In the end, one Pisan merchant ship was sunk; otherwise, the Crusade fleet was unharmed. Resorting to these dramatic but ineffective attacks on the Crusaders demonstrates clearly that, in Constantinople, the secret of Greek fire had been lost.

Constantinople no longer ruled its empire, now in open revolt, and the emperor no longer ruled Constantinople. The people of the city had taken matters into their own hands while Alexius IV cowered in his palace. Seething with frustration, the mobs even sought to wage magical warfare against their enemies. Near the Forum of Constantine, a colossal bronze statue of Athena, believed to be the work of the ancient master Phidias, was sacrificed to that effort. In one hand Athena had previously grasped the shaft of a long spear, but the weapon had long ago been lost. The empty hand, therefore, appeared to the mob to be beckoning someone, and they assumed that it was the Crusaders. The fact that the statue was facing south, with its back toward the Westerners, was of no consequence. The mob shattered the priceless antiquity without remorse. The reliefcovered columns of Theodosius and Arcadius were also vandalized. Since their images were believed to be prophecies, people grabbed ladders and smashed with hammers any that appeared to foretell a Crusader conquest of Constantinople.

Every day brought more raids outside the City and more uprisings inside. Finally, on January 25, a massive crowd descended on Hagia Sophia, forced its way into the sanctuary, and demanded that the clergy and aristocracy choose a new emperor. Nicetas Choniates was one of the aristocrats present. He sympathized with the sentiment, but he and his colleagues knew that it was unrealistic. The minute they put forth a name, the crowds would crown him. That unfortunate would then be an emperor with neither an empire nor an army—a perilous position. Alexius would undoubtedly turn to the Crusaders if things became too dangerous. Frustrated by their silence, the mob's leaders berated the clergy and aristocrats, demanding that they name someone, anyone, to rule them. With tears streaming down their cheeks, they refused. The rebels declared that no one would leave the great church until a new emperor was anointed. So they remained there for the next three days.

Exasperated, the crowds finally began proposing nobles who were absent, thus forestalling their refusal. At first they settled on an aristo‹ crat named Radinos. When news reached the unlucky man, he immedi‹ ately dressed himself as a monk and fled the city. Not finding him at home, the delegates of the revolution seized his wife and brought her to Hagia Sophia for questioning. She refused to reveal her husband's whereabouts. The rebels then turned to another young nobleman, Nicholas Canabus. Here they had a bit more luck. On January 27 he was seized and brought to Hagia Sophia for his coronation. Patriarch John Camaterus refused to crown the unwilling man, so the people grabbed a nearby crown and did it themselves. Poor emperor! His do‹ minion never extended beyond the confines of Hagia Sophia.

At Blachernae Palace, Alexius weighed his limited options. The mobs had already taken over much of Constantinople, and now they had their own emperor. He did not trust his regular troops to defend him or to disperse the crowds. Instead, he decided to make a deal with the Crusaders. In return for their help suppressing the rebellion, he promised to give them the Great Palace as security against his outstand‹ ing debt. On the morning of January 29 they were to assemble outside the city gates, which would then be opened to them. That never hap‹ pened, though, for the evening of January 28 was Alexius's last as em‹ peror. That night, one of his court officials, Alexius Ducas, called Mourtzouphlus (Unibrow), launched his own coup in Blachernae. By morning, the young Alexius was safely locked up in the dungeons. Since Isaac II had conveniently died a few days earlier, Mourtzouphlus de‹ clared himself the new emperor. For the next several days, Constanti‹ nople split itself between him and Nicholas Canabus. But by February 2, Mourtzouphlus had managed to bribe and bully enough leaders to support him. Nicholas, who had never wanted the crown, was arrested and decapitated. Three days later the new emperor was formally crowned as Alexius V.

The new emperor celebrated his elevation by leading a major force outside of Constantinople against the Crusaders. He even brought along the celebrated icon of the Virgin Mary, believed to have been painted by St. Luke himself. The Western knights soundly defeated the Byzantines, forcing Mourtzouphlus to flee back to Constantinople and even to lose the miracle-working icon to the hated Catholics. (This icon is quite possibly the one known today as *Madonna Nicopeia*, venerated in the left transept of Basilica San Marco in Venice.) Since a direct attack had failed, Mourtzouphlus met with Doge Enrico Dandolo to discuss terms of the Crusaders' withdrawal. The Westerners demanded that Mourtzouphlus restore Alexius IV and pay the remaining ninety thousand silver marks still owed them. Mourtzouphlus refused. A few nights later he ordered the young emperor strangled, proclaiming to the Crusaders that he had died of natural causes. They were not fooled.

Now it was the turn of the Westerners to be outraged. After so much effort, danger, and heartache, they had put Alexius IV on the throne of Constantinople only to have him treacherously double-cross them. In this city of treason, it was hardly surprising that the traitor was himself betrayed by his own court official. Now the Crusaders had nothing to show for all their trials. The Crusade clergy, which included several abbots and bishops, ruled that since Mourtzouphlus was a murderer and his people abettors of murder, and since the city of Constantinople had once again broken with the pope in Rome, a war against it was right and just. This judgment was in direct opposition to several letters that Pope Innocent had sent to the Crusaders forbidding them to attack Constantinople under any circumstances. Yet those parchments no longer mattered. Without their promised payment, the Crusaders lacked the means to sail to Egypt. Their goal was no longer on the Nile, but on the Bosporus.

Throughout the early spring the Crusaders prepared their fleet for a massive attack all along the seawalls of the Golden Horn. The great transport vessels were again outfitted with flying bridges as well as rock-pitching machines. Heavy vines were draped over stout timbers to deflect and absorb flying missiles. Mourtzouphlus likewise prepared Constantinople's defenses, increasing the height of the seawalls and building out additional wooden stories that overhung the stone wall and allowed the defenders to pour down pitch and hot sand on anyone who landed. He also brought in thousands more troops from the other areas of the empire he still controlled.

Before launching their attack, the leaders of the Crusade drew up an agreement, known to historians as the Pact of March, which laid out in detail the ground rules for the conquest of Constantinople. It committed all Crusaders to a vigorous attack on the city and specified the division of any booty that could be gathered. Should the entire city fall to them, the pact described an election of a new emperor by a committee of six Venetians and six non-Venetians. The Crusaders would then remain in the emperor's service for one year, after which they could return home.

The long-anticipated attack came on Friday, April 9, 1204. In a line, the Venetian vessels made their way amid fierce missile fire toward the walls of Constantinople. The fighting raged most of the day, but in the end the Crusaders were unable to breach the city's defenses. An unusual south wind hampered operations, driving the transport ships back from the walls. To many on both sides, it seemed to be the hand of God protecting the City. After suffering heavy casualties, the Crusaders retreated. Suddenly the Pact of March looked hopelessly idealistic.

On Monday, April 12, the Crusade fleet tried again, although this time they bound the transport vessels two by two, so greater force could be brought to bear on individual towers. Once again the fighting was fierce all along the walls, both at their foundations and at the highest reaches of the towers. At about noon a north wind arose, blowing the transport ships toward shore. Two of the largest vessels, the *Paradise* and the *Pilgrim*, bound fast together, were able to position a flying bridge directly on a reinforced tower. After much bloodshed, a group of Crusaders scrambled onto the walls and captured a few towers. Mourtzouphlus, who was commanding the defense from the hill of Christ Pantepoptes monastery, swiftly sent additional troops to keep the Crusaders from entering the city.

The defenses of impregnable Constantinople then broke down in a bizarre, almost comical way. Robert de Clari was one of about ten knights and sixty sergeants led by the courageous warrior Peter of Amiens, who landed on a narrow strip of ground at the base of the walls. There they discovered a postern gate that had been walled up. They fell on it with picks, crowbars, and even swords. It was hard going and dangerous, for above them, the Byzantines rained down large stones and boiling pitch. While some picked away at the gate, others covered them with their shields. Soon they succeeded in making a hole. Peering through it, they saw a huge crowd of Byzantine soldiers inside. According to Robert it seemed that half the world stood on the other side of that wall. They dared not enter. Robert's brother Aleaumes, an armor-wearing, sword-wielding monster of a man (and also a Catholic priest), pushed forward to claim the honor of first entry. Fearing for his brother's life, Robert begged him not to go in. But Aleaumes got down on his hands and knees and began crawling through the hole. Robert grabbed his foot, trying to pull him back, but with a shake, Aleaumes broke free and entered the city. With a thousand eyes looking on, he stood up, drew his sword, and charged the Byzantine troops standing there—one man against a multitude. They fled like cattle. The story Robert tells seems so improbable that one is tempted to disbelieve it, but the prideful words of the lowly knight are corroborated by the lamentations of Nicetas Choniates. Poorly trained and martially inept, the largely provincial elements in the imperial army were willing to fight only when the danger to themselves was minuscule. Most of them had little stake in Constantinople and therefore refused to risk their lives for the sake of the capital. Instead, as Nicetas puts it, "they took to their customary flight as the efficacious medicine of salvation."

Quickly Aleaumes's companions slithered through the hole. When the Byzantine troops stationed at other posts along the walls saw that the Crusaders had gained entry, they fled as well. Soon a domino effect spread all along the walls as one tower after another was evacuated. Seeing the impending collapse of his forces caused by such a tiny leak, Mourtzouphlus tried to put his finger in the dike. At first he sounded his trumpets and beat his timbrels to frighten Peter and his men, but it had no effect. Finally, he spurred his own horse and charged toward the group of Crusaders at full gallop. He was all alone. Peter of Amiens ordered his men to stand their ground. They relished the opportunity to prove their mettle against "Mourtzouphlus the traitor." Sensing their resolve, the emperor pulled back on the reins and retreated. Peter's men rushed to the nearest gate, which they tore open. The Crusaders swarmed into the city like killer bees.

The unthinkable had happened. Constantinople had fallen.

Chapter 14

---◆---

Latin Occupation

Unthinkable is precisely the word to describe the fall of Constantinople. Armed rebellions, palace coups, bloody riots—these were regular, even expected events in the lives of Constantinople's people in 1204. Yet none had ever tarnished the luster of the greatest city in the known world. True, the hated Westerners had breached the walls, but they had done the same one year earlier, when they ousted Emperor Alexius III and placed his brother and nephew on the throne of the caesars. To replace an emperor was the reason all armies in the last several centuries had made war on Constantinople. If the attempt was successful, the winner protected his newly won capital. He had every reason to do so.

Since the days of the rebellion of Alexius I Comnenus in 1081, the response in Constantinople to a successful military attack on the city was always to shift the capital's allegiance to the victor. That was infinitely preferable to hosting a destructive war across the vast urban landscape. It was commonly accepted that an emperor who could not defend Constantinople was simply unworthy of it. As the shadows lengthened on the evening of April 12, 1204, the city's hundreds of thousands of residents prepared to welcome their new victorious emperor. Mourtzouphlus's short reign was over.

Mourtzouphlus disagreed, naturally. He knew well that the Crusaders had not yet conquered Constantinople. Some twenty thousand of them had entered the city and made camp in the northern region left barren by the Venetians' fires of the previous spring. One of their leaders, Baldwin of Flanders, had occupied Mourtzouphlus's colorful tent at Pantepoptes monastery—a symbolic gesture. Mourtzouphlus and the Crusade leaders understood that there was much more to conquering Constantinople. The Western knights needed broad, open spaces on which to charge their horses. They were nearly useless in the densely packed streets of Constantinople's core, and Crusade leaders had already forbidden their soldiers from venturing into the city's snarl of backstreets and broad avenues, where they could easily be picked off by lone assassins, tumultuous mobs, or residents throwing down roof tiles. Instead, they would post guards overnight and, on the morrow, draw up their battle ranks in the open, burned region. There they would demand that Mourtzouphlus meet them on the field of honor. If he refused, they would set fire to the city, burning out its defenders.

A few renegade Crusaders decided to employ that strategy early. That night, they set fire to buildings along Constantinople's northern seawall. The fire spread quickly to the east, along the lower elevations, stopping only when it reached the charred desolation left behind by the great fire of the previous August. This was the third fire the Crusaders had inflicted upon Constantinople. Geoffrey de Villehardouin estimated that more houses were destroyed in the three blazes than existed in the three largest cities in France. He was close to the mark. Altogether the Crusaders had turned one-sixth of Constantinople into smoldering ruins and eliminated one-third of its dwellings. Looking out over the charred wastelands, Nicetas Choniates mourned for his beloved city, crying out, "[N]ow your luxurious garments and elegant royal veils are rent and torn; your flashing eye has grown dark, and you are like an aged furnace woman all covered with soot."

Emperor Mourtzouphlus rode to the Great Palace, where he met with his advisers to take stock of the situation. It was grim. Most of the imperial army had already fled or was in the process of doing so. They were largely provincials who believed that the matter was settled and therefore were eager to get back home. There remained about ten thousand Byzantine mounted troops permanently garrisoned in Constantinople. Whether they would obey Mourtzouphlus's commands was another matter. Of course he could count on the elite Varangian Guard, which stood at about six thousand men. While formidable, the Varangians were still insufficient to turn back twenty thousand Crusaders. Mourtzouphlus needed the army and the population, which still numbered some four hundred thousand, to back an effort to expel the invaders. As every Byzantine emperor knew, Constantinople's mobs could be dangerous adversaries when roused. It was his job to rouse them.

That evening, the opulent Chalke gates swung open onto the ornately decorated forum of the Augusteion. The emperor rode out on his best horse. Through the streets of the city he charged, calling out the danger and rallying his people to the defense of their city. There was, of course, more than the usual buzz of activity in Constantinople that night. Some people, particularly those who had lost their homes in the great fire, were gathering their few belongings and leaving the city. Others, perhaps remembering the three days of looting that followed Alexius I Comnenus's coup, were burying their wealth. Still others were preparing for the next day's ritual procession of the new emperor to Hagia Sophia for his coronation. Into all this rode Mourtzouphlus. The battle was not lost, he claimed. If they worked together they could still crush the invaders between the irresistible populace and the immoveable walls. When the people refused to join him, he ridiculed them for their fickleness. Had they forgotten their hatred for the Europeans? Where was their Roman courage? From place to place, Mourtzouphlus rode, but everywhere he received the same reply: silence or scorn. The commoners ignored his exhortations, and the aristocrats fled, so as to avoid any association with the defeated emperor that could be used against them later.

Nothing Mourtzouphlus said could convince the Byzantines to defend their city. As they saw it, it was only his reign that was at stake. Neither he nor they envisioned the conquest of Constantinople or the fall of the Byzantine Empire. They expected instead the imperial coronation of the Crusaders' commander in chief, Boniface of Montferrat. Boniface, after all, had an excellent imperial pedigree. His two brothers had married into the Angelus dynasty, and both had received the title caesar. From the Byzantine point of view, Boniface, a member of the Angelus dynasty by marriage, was attempting to overthrow Mourtzouphlus, the murderer of the Angeli emperors. It seemed that Boniface had at last won the throne that had eluded his brothers. The fact that Boniface was Catholic and backed by a Western army was reason enough to oppose him if it cost little, but insufficient if it meant warfare within the city. The same citizens had, after all, joyously accepted Alexius IV, who had been backed by the same army and had promised the submission of the Orthodox Church to Rome. Constantinople's populace had no moral obligation to support the current emperor when another had militarily bested him. While many undoubtedly felt pity for Mourtzouphlus, the red glow of fire from the north told of the fate of their city should they continue to support him.

Mourtzouphlus returned to the Great Palace in anger and sorrow. The City had already forsaken him, preparing as it was to crown his successor. With the Varangian Guard, he could hold the palace complex for a while, just as Andronicus I had done in 1187, but that would only postpone the inevitable. As Nicetas put it, the emperor would be "put into the jaws of the westerners as their dinner or dessert." It was time to flee the capital. With Euphrosyne, the wife of Alexius III, and her daughter Eudocia, whom he married soon after, he boarded a small fishing boat docked at the palace wharf and faded into the gloom of the Bosporus night.

Amid the glittering splendor of Hagia Sophia, the remnants of the city's government struggled to find some means of survival. Those most closely associated with Mourtzouphlus or with the anti-Western party in the imperial court naturally feared the accession of Boniface of Montferrat. They urged Patriarch John Camaterus to crown a new emperor who could rally the people against the Crusaders. Since the patriarch had publicly repudiated the submission of Hagia Sophia to the pope, he was very willing. After casting lots, they chose Constantine Lascaris, the brother of Theodore Lascaris, the heir of Alexius III. Yet when the patriarch moved to crown the victor, he refused the insignia. The young Lascaris knew what Mourtzouphlus knew: the emperor, whoever he was, would suffer mightily if the Crusaders took the city. Lascaris would accept the crown only if he was assured of the support of the people and the Varangian Guard. So, accompanied by the patriarch, the emperor-elect walked out of Hagia Sophia and into the torch-lit throngs in the Augusteion.

There, near the gilded arch of the Milion, stood the Varangian Guard, the only cohesive fighting force on which Constantinople could still rely. There also were a large number of citizens, some confused and frightened, others preparing for the next day's ceremonies. Like Mourtzouphlus, Lascaris appealed to the people. He enjoined them to fight the Westerners who had already done them such injuries. Not a single person responded to his exhortations. Lascaris then turned to the Varangian Guard, urging them to support him, for a Westerner would have no appreciation for the "far-famed gifts or honor of the imperial guard." The Guard agreed to honor their oath to support any emperor. So Lascaris told them to prepare for battle in the morning.

As it happened, the Guard would never have to fight that hopeless battle. Shortly after entering the Great Palace, Constantine Lascaris came to the same conclusion as Mourtzouphlus only a few hours earlier. He could not hold power without popular support. So he and his brother Theodore boarded a vessel in the palace harbor and rowed out of the city and toward Asia. Their journey would end in Nicaea, where Theodore Lascaris would found a new government-in-exile, known to historians as the Nicaean Empire. It would preserve the flame of the Byzantine candle for almost sixty years before it at last returned to Constantinople.

There was one terrible flaw in the conventional wisdom that ruled Constantinople that turbulent night. The Crusade army had not come to put Boniface of Montferrat on the throne. Their objective was no longer to manhandle Byzantine politics, but to punish the Byzantines for their double-crossing treachery. This was not a coup; it was a conquest. Only a few days earlier the Crusade leaders had sworn to the Pact of March, which committed them to a vigorous attack on the city, the equitable division of its booty, and the later election of an emperor. It is hard to imagine two peoples who understood each other less than the Byzantines and the Crusaders on the morning of April 13, 1204.

Even before the rays of the sun had touched the highest pinnacle of Hagia Sophia's dome, the people of the city were busy preparing for the ritual procession of Boniface of Montferrat. Along the ceremonial route, they turned out in their best clothing, bearing crosses and holy icons to bless and welcome their new leader. A delegation of high clergy and officials arrived at Boniface's camp promptly at sunrise. Bedecked in their splendid vestments and accompanied by the Varangian Guard in dress uniforms, the delegation recited the ritual acclamations, proclaiming Marquis Boniface the new emperor and delivering over to him the city and all its wealth. They then prostrated themselves on the ground in a show of traditional reverence to an emperor.

The marquis drank in the scene, but he could not accept the honor. As much as he hoped to be elected emperor, he had no power to take the throne now. Boniface likely understood the meaning of the ritual, but it was completely lost on the rest of the Westerners. They did not see the ceremony as the first step toward a peaceful coronation, but simply as the surrender of the city to the Crusaders. When the news spread through the camp, the rest of the Crusaders were astonished. They had expected this to be the first day of a very long and dangerous war. They could not believe that the vast city was surrendering itself to them with so much flair and so little fight. At once they fell out of ranks and fell upon the Queen of Cities.

Nicetas Choniates now groaned at the foolishness of his people. The narrow streets, broad avenues, and busy intersections that the Crusaders had so feared were cleared of all traffic to make way for the triumphal procession. Unaware of what was coming, the citizens stood by the side of the roads with their precious vestments and rich icons. The ritual shouts of adulation transformed into screams of terror. Nicetas lamented that the Westerners' "disposition was not at all affected by what they saw, nor did their lips break into the slightest smile, nor did the unexpected spectacle transform their grim and frenzied glance and fury into cheerfulness. Instead, they plundered with impunity and stripped their victims shamelessly, beginning with their carts."

So began the sack of Constantinople. Yet even the violence that the Crusaders would rain down on the city did not immediately shake the Byzantines out of the cultural certainty that Constantinople could not be conquered; it could only change emperors. Days later, the Benedictine abbot Martin of Pairis still noticed that the people of the city would greet a Westerner by making the sign of the cross with their fingers and proclaiming, "Aiios Phasilieos marchio" (Holy Emperor the Marquis). No looting ever experienced by Constantinople or Byzantion before could compare with that of 1204. Indeed, it was one of the richest plunders in premodern history. The reason was simple. The army lacked an imperial claimant to restrain the destruction of his new city. The Pact of March had purposely left the identity of the new emperor up in the air. Even the Crusade's leaders, then, had incentive to pick the city clean, leaving the bones for the dubious winner of the imperial election.

"What then should I recount first and what last of those things dared at that time by these murderous men?" Nicetas Choniates's question still plagues anyone who would describe the Crusader sack of Constan-tinople. For three days the victorious Westerners feasted on the bloated corpse of New Rome. The Crusaders and the Italian refugees were merged into a hideous mob driven by greed, lust, and hate. Oaths sworn on the Gospels to leave women and ecclesiastical buildings unmolested were forgotten in the frenzied anarchy. Many fanned out to the richest houses and palaces, where they found their wealthy owners waiting. They stripped the homes of all wealth, forced the owners to reveal their hidden treasures, and threw them out, taking the dwellings for them-selves. With nowhere to live, these bands of ragged lords streamed out of the city, leaving it to its Western conquerors.

In the holy sanctuaries of Constantinople, the Europeans stripped the altars of all precious furnishings, smashed icons for the sake of their silver or gems, and defiled the consecrated Eucharist and Precious Blood. Patens were used as bread dishes, and chalices as drinking cups. Radiant Hagia Sophia was stripped of everything of value. The price-less main altar was hacked to pieces and divided among the looters. So much wealth was found in the great church that mules were brought in to carry it all away. Unable to keep their footing on the slick marble floor, some of the beasts tumbled to the ground and were split open by the sharp objects they carried, defiling the church with their excrement and blood. According to Nicetas, a French prostitute was even put on the patriarch's throne, where she provided entertainment for the looters with her bawdy songs and high-kicking dances.

Equally sought after in Constantinople's churches and monasteries were hundreds, perhaps thousands of holy relics. It is no exaggeration to say that many, if not most, of the relics preserved in Europe today were stolen from Constantinople in 1204. We know about only the highest-profile ones. Bishop Nivelon of Soissons, for example, took the robe of the Virgin Mary, the head of John the Baptist, and two large pieces of the True Cross from the Church of the Virgin of the Pharos. Bishop Conrad of Halberstadt seized a large number of relics, including hair of the Virgin; pieces of the Apostles Bartholomew, Simon, Thomas, and Paul; and the finger of St. Nicholas. Doge Enrico Dandolo claimed an-other head of John the Baptist and a variety of other relics, which were sent to San Marco in Venice, where they still remain. An unknown

1: Bronze coin of Byzantion from the second or third century AD depicting the city's founder, Byzas.
CREDIT: World Imaging

2: Colossal head of Constantine I at the Capitoline Museum in Rome. In AD 330, Constantine refounded Byzantion as the eastern capital of the Roman Empire.
CREDIT: Jean-Christophe Benoist

3: Column of Constantine, erected at the dedication of Constantinople on May 11, 330. The original Roman base is covered in Turkish masonry and the column itself is supported by modern metal bracings. The marble top is a twelfth-century repair. It is known today as Çemberlitaş, the Burnt Column.

4: A depiction of the imperial box in the Hippodrome found on the base of the Egyptian obelisk. In the center are Emperor Theodosius I and his sons, surrounded on both sides by court officials and imperial bodyguards. Below are spectators. CREDIT: Georges Jansoone

5: Ruins of the land walls of Theodosius II, completed c. 450. They stretch almost twelve miles and are studded by nearly two hundred towers.

6: Ruins of the Golden Gate complex used by Roman emperors for their triumphal entries into the city. The area is now part of the Yedikule fortress.

7: Hagia Sophia, the monumental church built by Emperor Justinian I in 537. It remained the most important building in Constantinople for more than a millennium and still dominates the old city of Istanbul. It is today a museum. CREDIT: Arild Vågen

8: Mosaic in Hagia Sophia depicting the Virgin and Child flanked by two emperors. To the right is Constantine I offering the city of Constantinople. To the left is Justinian I giving the church of Hagia Sophia.

9: Tenth-century mosaic depicting Emperor Leo VI worshipping at the feet of the enthroned Christ, who is flanked by the Virgin Mary and an archangel. The mosaic is directly over Hagia Sophia's main imperial door, through which only the emperor entered the church.

10: Constantinople, c. 1200. In this aerial reconstruction of the Byzantine capital at its peak, the Hippodrome is in the center with Hagia Sophia to the right, the Forum of Constantine above, and the Great Palace complex below. CREDIT: Byzantium1200.com

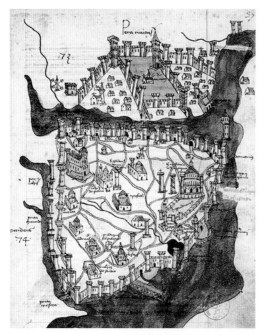

11: One of the earliest surviving maps of Constantinople. Drafted by the Florentine monk Cristoforo Buondelmonti in 1422, it includes landmarks such as the Hippodrome, Hagia Sophia, Holy Apostles, and Blachernae Palace.

12: Sultan Mehmed II, who captured Constantinople, making it the new capital of the Ottoman Empire. The painting was executed in 1480 by the Venetian artist Gentile Bellini.

CREDIT: The National Gallery

13: Pieter Coecke van Aelst's highly detailed depiction of Sultan Suleiman the Magnificent processing through the ruins of the Hippodrome.

CREDIT: The Metropolitan Museum of Art/Art Resource, NY

14: Sinan's masterpiece, the Süleymaniye Mosque, as seen from the Golden Horn.

15: A typical coffeehouse on one of Constantinople's streets, c. 1870.

16: English forces parade down the Grand Rue de Pera (modern İstiklal Caddesi) during the occupation of Constantinople in 1918—the first time the city had been occupied by foreign troops since 1453.

thief stole the famous Burial Shroud of Christ kept at the Church of Saint Mary of Blachernae. This may be the relic known today as the Shroud of Turin.

Among Western writers, only Gunther of Pairis records the rampant theft of relics, and he does so with gusto. Describing the activities of his abbot during the sack, he wrote, "Abbot Martin began to think also about his own booty and, lest he remain empty-handed while everyone else got rich, he resolved to use his own consecrated hands for pillage." Martin, however, piously limited his thievery to sacred relics. Like others, the abbot had heard that many Byzantines had hidden their treasures at the monastery of Christ Pantocrator. By the time he and a chaplain arrived there, though, the conquerors were already busy despoiling the rich buildings of their gold and silver. "Thinking it improper to commit sacrilege except in a holy cause," Martin began hunting for a secluded part of the monastery, where relics might be stashed. He soon discovered an elderly Greek priest, whom he threatened with death unless he revealed the monastery's relics. The frightened cleric took Martin to a large iron chest, which he opened. It was filled with a great storehouse of relics. "On seeing it, the abbot hurriedly and greedily thrust in both hands, and, as he was girded for action, both he and the chaplain filled the folds of their habits with sacred sacrilege." Unwilling to share with his fellow looters, Martin and his chaplain spirited the relics away to his boat, where they venerated their haul for three days.

The rich heritage of classical antiquity was dealt a crushing blow by the sack of 1204. Undoubtedly, many manuscripts were lost, forever consigning some of humanity's greatest authors to oblivion. Most of the Western conquerors were illiterate and so saw little value in Constantinople's libraries of scrolls and codices. Nicetas Choniates records that the Crusaders often ridiculed the Byzantines by taking a quill and "pretending" to write in books. Constantinople also preserved a vast trove of ancient artwork, including pieces from most of the ancient Greek masters. Little of it would survive the conquest. Strapped for cash, the Westerners later melted down nearly all the city's bronze statues. Thousands of them were dumped into the pots for the sake of a few coins. Heartbroken at this cruelest barbarity, Nicetas Choniates wrote a lament

for the statues of Constantinople, describing dozens of the most beautiful. They included the monumental statue of Hera in the Forum of
Constantine and a bronze mechanical device shaped like a pyramid,
replete with warbling birds, piping shepherds, and swimming fish. The
giant statue of Hercules in the Hippodrome was liquidated along with
all the rest of the bronze figures that adorned the *spina* of the racetrack—
all, that is, except one. The bronze Serpent Column of Delphi, forged
by the ancient Greek cities that defeated the Persians in the fourth
century BC, was left unmolested. Sometime before 1204, the Byzantines had hooked the serpents up to a water source, thus transforming it
into a useful fountain. That alone saved it.

Only one other set of bronze statues survived the conquest of Constantinople. Over the starting gates of the Hippodrome was a life-size
group depicting a victorious charioteer before his four prancing char-
gers. The charioteer and chariot were destroyed. But Doge Enrico Dandolo ordered his people to carefully remove the four horses, crate them
up, and ship them to Venice. When they arrived at the city on the lagoon, they were mounted above the main entrance of the church of San
Marco. They became a symbol of the Republic of Venice, remaining
there for centuries until Venice itself was conquered by Napoleon. After a short stay in Paris, the four bronze horses were returned to San
Marco. Today, the astonishingly well-preserved steeds are kept indoors,
to protect them from the elements. Replicas are mounted outside.

These were not the only of Constantinople's treasures that Dandolo
sent back to Venice. Given their long association with the great city, the
Venetians were much more interested in preserving than destroying.
The porphyry statues of the tetrarchs mounted high on columns in
Constantinople's Philadelphion were sent to San Marco, where they are
still attached to an outside corner of the building. The so-called Pillars
of Acre standing outside San Marco were also from Constantinople.
Indeed, a great deal of the marbles and art that adorn the basilica today
are part of the war booty of 1204. Inside San Marco the treasury still
holds hundreds of precious chalices, patens, and reliquaries taken from
Constantinople's churches, preserved there for centuries when all others
were lost.

The proud, yet now humbled, aristocrat Nicetas Choniates gave a detailed account of his own situation during the immediate aftermath of Constantinople's conquest. It provides a rare glimpse into the human side of this tragedy. Unlike many of his friends, Nicetas no longer had a large palace, since it had burned to the ground in the fire of August 1203. Instead, he was living in a modest dwelling not far from Hagia Sophia in 1204. Less ostentatious and better hidden, Nicetas's home was not the first target of the looters. Yet it was not long before he learned of the fate of his city from friends who had been expelled from their own palaces. Realizing that he, too, would soon lose his home, he enlisted the aid of a Venetian resident of Constantinople, a wine merchant with whom he was friendly. The Venetian, who was named Domenico, owed the Byzantine aristocrat a favor. Back in August 1203, when most of the Westerners had fled Constantinople, Domenico and his family had gone to Nicetas Choniates, who had welcomed them into his home. Now in April 1204 the situation had reversed itself. When the Western looters at last came to Nicetas's small house, Domenico dressed himself in armor and pretended to be one of them, insisting that he had already claimed this dwelling for himself. His cleverness and bravado worked well enough with other Venetians and Italians, but the French marauders were much harder to discourage. This was especially true after that area of the city was later allotted to the French. Unable to protect them, Domenico urged Nicetas and his family, as well as other Byzantine families that had come there seeking aid, to leave Constantinople before the French seized the house. They took his advice.

On April 17, 1204, a cold and stormy day, Nicetas Choniates, his family, and his friends prepared to make the long walk along the ruined splendor of the Mese to the Golden Gate. Word on the street was that, in their mad desire to flee the capital, the imperial troops had torn down the bricks that had once stopped up the triumphal gate. The noble refugees needed a ruse, though, to ensure their safety in so much bedlam. So Nicetas, his family, and friends had their hands bound with rope and strung together in a line. Then the good Domenico pulled the party along the Mese as if they were his captives. This worked well through the core of the city. Then, when the danger seemed to have largely passed, Domenico released them and wished them a safe journey.

The ragtag group, which now included such potentates as Patriarch

John X Camaterus, was a pitiful sight. Nicetas's wife was pregnant and very close to term, yet still she had to walk the long road to freedom. As they made their way along the Mese, more friends and relatives came out to join them, expanding their group until it resembled a "throng of ants." Past the Forum Bovis, the Mese had become a gauntlet of armed Westerners randomly stopping refugees to search for precious fabrics or bags of money hidden beneath their tattered clothing. Others were on the prowl for attractive young women. The women in Nicetas's party spread mud on their faces and huddled in the center of the group "as though in a sheepfold." This strategy worked during most of the trek. Yet when they were almost to the Golden Gate, very near the Church of St. Mokios, an armed warrior burst into the group and plucked out the young daughter of a judge. The entire company of Byzantines shouted out in alarm as the soldier dragged the poor girl away. Her aged and sick father pursued the assailant, but he soon stumbled and fell into a mud hole, where he wallowed, helpless to get up. Racked with horror and grief, the old man turned to Nicetas, calling him by name and begging him to stop the defilement of the young maiden. Nicetas went after the criminal and, along the way, convinced some Italian soldiers to help him in the cause. Taking pity on the girl, the Italians followed Nicetas to the house of her abductor. There the criminal had locked the girl inside and stood defiantly in the doorway, prepared to defend his prize. With angry tears and violent sobs, Nicetas denounced the man to the Italians, reminding them of the prohibitions of their leaders against rape and asking them to think of their own children and wives. Moved by Nicetas's pleas, the soldiers demanded that the abductor release the young woman or face the hangman's noose. Seeing their resolve, the assailant handed over the girl, who was returned to her rejoicing father.

After so long and harrowing a trip, Nicetas and his party at last passed through the Golden Gate and out of Constantinople. The tired aristocrat now turned his head to the right and looked across the hills, where the mighty Theodosian Walls stretched on for miles. Their proud strength and iron resolve to defend against any foe stood in stark contrast to the destruction of the city behind them. The absurdity of the events was more than Nicetas could bear. He fell down on the ground weeping and cursing the walls. "If those things for whose protection you were erected no longer exist, being utterly destroyed by fire and war, for what purpose do you still stand?" The silence of the ancient stones mocked Nicetas as he and his company left Constantinople, torn from their beloved city like "darling children from their adoring mother."

After three days some measure of order was restored in the city, although matters would remain dangerous for months. It is clear, though, that even during those three days, the Crusaders did not abide by their own rules. Despite their oaths and the threat of excommunication, they had ruthlessly violated Constantinople's churches and monasteries, murdered many innocents, and raped many women. When Pope Innocent III heard of these crimes he was filled with shame. He angrily wrote to his legate in Constantinople, "For they who are supposed to serve Christ rather than themselves, who should have used their swords against the infidel, have bathed those swords in the blood of Christians. They have not spared religion, nor age, nor sex, and have committed adultery and fornication in public, exposing matrons and even nuns to the filthiness of their troops." Nicetas Choniates contrasted the sack of Constantinople with the fall of Jerusalem to Saladin, judging that his city would have fared better had it been conquered by the Muslims. He lashed out at the Crusaders, who had sworn to deliver Jerusalem, promised to kill no Christians, and even proclaimed that they would refrain from sex until they had completed their vows. "In truth, they were exposed as frauds. Seeking to avenge the Holy Sepulcher, they raged openly against Christ and sinned by overturning the Cross with the cross they bore on their backs, not even shuddering to trample on it for the sake of a little gold and silver."

For Byzantine nobles such as Nicetas Choniates, these terrible events were God's just punishment of Constantinople for centuries of moral decay that had culminated in Alexius IV's shameless plundering of the churches to pay off his Western enforcers. Greek commoners across the countryside saw the fall of Constantinople as the overdue chastisement of the proud aristocracy, which squeezed the provinces for ever more taxes while reveling in its own debauched hedonism. Western Europeans unanimously saw in this victory God's revulsion for the Byzantines' refusal to support the Holy Land and their willingness to ally themselves with the perfidious Muslims. Out of patience, the Lord of All had handed over the Queen of Cities to a people who would use it for the benefit of Christendom. Whatever the explanation, there was no doubt about the final outcome: Greek Constantinople had been transformed into Latin Constantinople.

The Crusaders had previously agreed that if the capital fell to them they would also claim the empire. Historians refer to the Western state created during this period as the Latin Empire of Constantinople. It would last from 1204 until 1261. During those years, the city of Constantinople would suffer mightily. It was not only the wealth of the city that was packed up and shipped off to western Europe. The people, too, abandoned the capital. Various Byzantine successor states sprang up in places such as Epirus, Bulgaria, and Nicaea, each claiming to be the true Roman Empire. The Latin state based in Constantinople struggled from its beginnings. Without a competent bureaucracy or any knowledge of how to run a complex state, the new rulers of Constantinople allowed it to decay into the husk of the vast walls surrounding a landscape of ruin and poverty. Before 1204, Constantinople had a population of some four hundred thousand in the city and around one million in the greater metropolitan area. By 1261, when the Greeks managed to expel the Westerners and take back their beloved city, Constantinople had no more than thirty thousand residents. It would never regain its glory under Christian emperors.

In the first days after the conquest of the city, the Crusade leaders took up residence in some of Constantinople's best palaces. Boniface of Montferrat, who the Byzantines continued to believe was their new emperor, occupied the Great Palace. To solidify his claim, he married Margaret, the young widow of Emperor Isaac II. The other contender for the throne was Baldwin, Count of Flanders. A powerful and wealthy lord, he was beloved by the French soldiers of the Crusade. Baldwin and his men had claimed Blachernae Palace. Enrico Dandolo, the doge of Venice, took up lodgings in the recently vacated Patriarchal Palace at Hagia Sophia.

On May 9, 1204, six Venetian and six non-Venetian electors chose the new emperor of Constantinople: Baldwin of Flanders. Like his brothers, Boniface of Montferrat had been close to the throne, but ultimately it eluded him. He was gracious in defeat—at least at first. Amid cries of joy, Baldwin was carried to the Great Palace, where plans began for his coronation on May 16. The event was meticulously recorded by Robert of Clari, who had never seen anything so splendid, an interesting mixture of Byzantine pomp and Western traditions. The leading barons and Venetian nobles rode in procession to the palace to collect the emperor-elect and then proceeded across the Augusteion to Hagia Sophia. There Baldwin was bedecked in the rich garments of a Byzantine emperor. Precious stones were so copious on his attire that (if Robert is to be believed) it is a wonder he could walk at all. Even his shoes were studded with jewels. His mantle bore the imperial eagles in rubies so brilliant that it seemed to be on fire. Baldwin proceeded through the church to what was left of the high altar, accompanied by French nobles carrying the imperial standard and sword. Baldwin knelt before the altar, where his garments were taken from him one by one until he wore nothing from the waist up. He was then anointed with oils and his robes and mantle replaced. Next, the crown was taken up by the Crusade's bishops and blessed. Then all of them, each holding the crown with one hand, placed it on Baldwin's head. Around the new emperor's neck, they hung a ruby the size of an apple.

According to the Pact of March, if a non-Venetian should be elected emperor, then the Venetians would receive the patriarchate of Constantinople. Enrico Dandolo named around twenty Venetian clergy to be the new canons of Hagia Sophia, which was thus transformed from a Greek Orthodox to a Roman Catholic cathedral. They elected a Venetian monk in Ravenna, Thomas Morosini, who was well liked by Pope Innocent III. Hearing the surprising news of his election to the patriarchate of Constantinople, Morosini traveled to Rome, where Innocent appointed him to his new office. All the other churches in Constantinople were likewise turned over to Catholic clergy. Many of the empty monasteries were soon inhabited by Benedictines from the West and, later, Franciscans and Dominicans.

In western Europe there was much hope that the conquest of Constantinople would lead to a new unified Christendom, one that could organize an effective defense against the Muslim advance from the East—and at first, all seemed to be heading in that direction. After drawing up the Treaty of Partition of the Byzantine Empire, the knights and warriors of

the Fourth Crusade sallied forth to claim their lands. Many of the con-
quests were impressive, establishing Latin control over much of Greece.
Boniface of Montferrat, for example, became the ruler of Thessalonica.
They even managed to capture Emperor Mourtzouphlus. After fleeing
Constantinople, Mourtzouphlus had made his way to Mosynopolis, where
Emperor Alexius III had set up a makeshift court in exile. There he delivered to Alexius his wife and daughter, just rescued from the city before its
fall. Mourtzouphlus had recently married Alexius III's daughter Eudocia,
so the former emperor welcomed his new son-in-law with every hospitality. But as Isaac II had learned years earlier, it was not healthy to be
Alexius III's relation. After their arduous trip, Alexius offered the newly-
weds a comforting bath. No sooner had they settled in, though, than
Alexius's men burst in, thrust Eudocia to the floor, held Mourtzouphlus
down in the tub, and with a sharp knife gouged out his eyes. Alexius reclaimed his screaming daughter and then dumped his blind son-in-law at
the side of the road. It was not long before some Crusaders discovered
their adversary and returned him to Constantinople. There he stood trial
for rebelling against his rightful lord, the young Alexius IV. Mourtzouphlus defiantly proclaimed that he had killed a traitor to the empire
and would do the same to anyone guilty of such crimes. Unimpressed, the
Western court found him guilty and sentenced him to death. He was taken
to the Forum Tauri, walked up the stairs inside the spiraled Column of
Theodosius, and thrown headlong down onto the pavement below. As
many of the Crusaders quipped, "For a high man, high justice!" The
Greeks remaining in Constantinople lamented the death of their former
emperor—and soon enough found an image of a falling man on the prophetic reliefs of the ancient column.

The new leaders of Constantinople proved just as incapable of controlling the chaotic divisions in the Byzantine Empire as their Greek
predecessors. When the Fourth Crusade arrived at the capital in 1203,
virtually the entire empire had been in rebellion, and the city itself was
torn apart by factionalism and unrest. The Crusade's arrival, led there
by that same treacherous factionalism, was a symptom of the political
rot that infected Constantinople. Nothing was improved by its conquest. In February 1205, Kalojan, the king of the Vlachs and Bulgarians, struck up an alliance with independent Greek lords in Thrace to

make a bid for Constantinople. When the cities of Demotica and Adrianople swore allegiance to Kalojan, Emperor Baldwin I recalled all
knights to the capital. In March he led a relief force to Adrianople, but
it failed to recapture the city. On April 10, Kalojan counterattacked,
dealing a devastating blow against the heretofore invincible Crusaders.
The emperor himself was captured and eventually killed. He was succeeded by his brother, Henry of Flanders, but the city of Constantinople
would remain in great danger.

Several weeks later the aged doge of Venice, Enrico Dandolo, died.
He was buried with great pomp and many tears in a tomb in the upper
gallery of Hagia Sophia. He was the first and last person ever to be
buried in Constantinople's greatest church. Today, in the south gallery
of Hagia Sophia, a stone marker embedded in the wall bears his name.
Tour guides routinely inform their clients that it is the grave marker of
the doge, but it is not so. The stone was actually placed there in the
nineteenth century by the Italian Swiss architects the Fossati brothers,
who undertook extensive restorations in the church. Nevertheless, it is
likely that Dandolo's now-lost tomb stood very near there, likely along
the railing.

Constantinople's conquerors managed to hold on to their prize for
more than half a century, but the remainder of the empire broke apart
into warring states. By 1210, Henry of Flanders ruled Constantinople
and much of Thrace, while his vassals controlled a good part of Greece.
A member of the old Comneni dynasty claimed to rule the Byzantine
Empire from a small state surrounding Trebizond, on the southern
coast of the Black Sea. Theodore Lascaris made the same claim from
his new capital at Nicaea. In the West, Michael Ducas set up a state in
western Greece called the Despotate of Epirus. The Genoese seized
Crete, although Doge Dandolo had previously purchased the rights to
the island from Boniface of Montferrat. A war between Venice and Genoa ensued, the first of many between the two Italian maritime powers
over the scraps of Constantinople's shattered empire. By 1211, Venice
had captured Crete, which it would rule for the next four centuries.
Many of the Aegean islands and a few Greek mainland port cities also
became part of Venice's new overseas holdings.

A Latin emperor ruled in Constantinople, but his was not the despotic power wielded by his Byzantine predecessors. Weak and always short on money and men, each new resident of Blachernae Palace approached his position much like other European kings—seeing himself as a first among equals, heavily dependent on his vassals. As laid out in the Pact of March, Constantinople was physically divided among the victors, with the emperor controlling one-quarter, the French three-eighths, and the Venetians the other three-eighths. In practice, this meant that the French/Flemish emperors directly controlled most of the city, while the semiautonomous Venetian Quarter was expanded to include the better part of the northern city along the wharfs of the Golden Horn. The monastery of Christ Pantocrator became the head-quarters for the Venetian governor, called a *podestà*. A similar division was made (at least on paper) for the remainder of the Byzantine Empire. It was for this reason that the doges of Venice added to their titles "lord of three-eighths of the whole Roman Empire."

Aside from the persistence of urban decay, very little is known about Constantinople during its years of Latin rule. The only certain artistic remnant of the period is a cycle of frescoes depicting the Virgin Mary and the life of St. Francis of Assisi in what is today the Kalendarhane mosque. Earthquakes during the 1230s made a bad situation worse, tumbling down many buildings just barely standing. Hagia Sophia suffered especially, which led the French to add new buttresses to prop up its walls. It is possible that the famous *Deesis* mosaic in the south gallery of Hagia Sophia was executed during this period. The evocative depiction of Christ flanked by the Virgin Mary and St. John the Baptist was certainly produced by local Greek artists, but may have been meant as a decoration for a Chapel of the Venetians, which was there, near the body of Doge Dandolo. It is also possible the mosaic was produced just after the Latins were expelled.

Although the Venetians repaired the harbor fortifications, the French neglected the land walls, which were in a ruinous state of disrepair by 1260. Henry of Flanders managed to maintain the two major imperial palaces, but by the 1220s the Latin emperors were so cash-strapped that they could no longer afford to keep up the sprawling Great Palace complex. As its grounds were neglected and its moveable wealth liquidated, it soon fell into ruin. Emperor Baldwin II, who ruled from 1237 until the Byzantine reconquest in 1261, lived only in Blach-ernae Palace—that is, when he was not touring the royal courts of Eu-rope begging for money. He even ordered the lead joints holding together the Great Palace's roofs stripped, melted down, and sold.

Many of the holy relics that were not stolen and shipped off to the West in 1204 found their way there over the following decades. Desper-ate for Western aid, the Latin emperors were forced to use these reli-gious assets to capture the attention and acquire the support of the West. The fate of the Crown of Thorns, preserved in Constantinople for centuries, is instructive. While Baldwin II was in Europe, his nobles in Constantinople borrowed much-needed funds from Venetian mer-chants using this precious relic of Christ's Passion as collateral. In 1238 the loan fell due. Since the emperor had not sent any money back to Constantinople, the nobles were forced to default. Just as the Venetians were preparing to bring the Crown back to Venice, Dominican envoys from the court of King Louis IX of France arrived guaranteeing the repayment of the loan. Baldwin II, who was enjoying the hospitality of the king, had promised to make a gift of the Crown if Louis redeemed it from the Venetians. So he did. In 1239 the Crown arrived in Venice amid much jubilation. But with the debt subsequently paid by French agents, it was transported across the Alps to Paris, where Louis and the entire French court welcomed it as if it were Christ himself. To house the relic, Louis constructed the spectacular Sainte-Chapelle. Amaz-ingly, the Crown of Thorns weathered the later storms of revolution that destroyed so much of France's medieval culture. It remains in Paris still, venerated every Good Friday in the Cathedral of Notre Dame.

As the years passed, the old Byzantine Empire remained a shattered battlefield and Constantinople a decaying wasteland. By the 1240s, how-ever, the rulers of Nicaea had managed to consolidate their position in Asia Minor and defeat their Greek, Latin, and Bulgarian rivals in Thrace and parts of Greece. Latin Constantinople was surrounded on all sides by the Nicaean Empire. Still, the Greek emperors in Nicaea were reluctant to attack the city directly. Although dilapidated, its walls were still formidable. More important, they feared that the reconquest

of Constantinople would prompt the pope in Rome to call a new Cru‚
sade, bringing thousands more Western knights to recover the ruined
city. Instead, all the Nicaean emperors pursued a policy of reuniting
the Roman Catholic and Greek Orthodox Churches. Their hope was
that by their becoming good sons of the Church, the pope would be‚
stow Constantinople on them. It was not to be. Although trains of
university‚educated Franciscans and Dominicans traveled to the court
of Nicaea during the thirteenth century, they were never able to close
the divide between themselves and the Orthodox clergy, who refused to
accept the fullness of papal authority.

In 1258 the Nicaean emperor Theodore II Lascaris died, leaving a
seven‚year‚old son, John IV, as sole heir. In the Byzantine court in exile,
plots and factions naturally crystalized around the unlucky young man.
Although initially under the guardianship of the palace official George
Muzalon, young John's regent was soon toppled by a coup that left him
hacked to pieces by a crowd of mercenaries. The new regent was the
well‚respected general Michael Palaeologus. In good Byzantine fashion,
Michael bribed and bullied his way to the highest office, receiving the
crown of co‚emperor on January 1, 1259. Unlike his predecessors, Michael
dreamed big. He was determined to recapture Constantinople, thereby
forever cementing his hold on power. He personally led an attack on the
capital in 1260, but it failed badly. He quickly realized he needed a
navy to invest the peninsular city. Since Venice controlled much of
Constantinople, its enemy Genoa was willing to support Michael in a
new bid to take it away. Plans were drawn up for a major siege. In an‚
ticipation of the attack, Michael sent one of his generals, Alexius Strat‚
egopoulus, with a small force to reconnoiter the defenses.

The circumstances of Constantinople's fall in 1261 were almost as
bizarre as those in 1204. General Alexius and his men received intelli‚
gence that the Venetian fleet and most of the French forces had left
Constantinople to attack a nearby island. Only a tiny garrison remained
on the land walls. Although he lacked orders, Alexius and his reconnais‚
sance force went to the city under cover of darkness on July 24/25,
1261. Slipping in through the opened Gate of the Pege, they quickly
dispatched the garrison and marched into the city itself. Defenseless,
the Latin residents grabbed whatever they could carry and rushed to

the Golden Horn, where Venetian ships brought them to safety. The last Latin emperor, Baldwin II, fled so quickly that he left behind his crown and scepter in Blachernae Palace. Alexius sent both of them to Michael Palaeologus in Nicaea to announce the surprising victory.

The Latin Empire of Constantinople thus came to a pitiful end. The Byzantine Empire was restored, led by the founder of an imperial dynasty that would last longer than any in Roman history. The Greeks had returned to their beloved capital. Yet no amount of jubilation could hide the fact that the Queen of Cities had become a vacant expanse of rubble and ruin.

Chapter 15

Life Among the Ruins

Every August 15 the Christian world celebrates the death and assumption of the Virgin Mary into Heaven. On that date in 1261, the Virgin Mary rode in an imperial chariot through Constantinople's Golden Gate—or at least her revered icon did. After the Byzantine reconquest of the city, the victors discovered in the monastery of Christ Pantocrator what they believed to be the famous icon of the Virgin Hodegetria, revered for centuries as an image painted by St. Luke. The Virgin had long been the special protector of Constantinople, so Michael VIII believed that it was only right that she receive the glory and honor traditionally due to a victorious emperor. The chariot and its procession entered ceremoniously through the triumphal gate, flanked by the ancient reliefs depicting the labors of Hercules, and rolled joyously over the ground on which Nicetas Choniates had collapsed in grief fifty-seven years earlier. Behind the patroness of Constantinople, Michael VIII walked humbly, adding his voice to those of the assembled spectators praising the Mother of God. After about fifteen hundred feet the procession stopped at the Monastery of St. John Studion (modern-day İlyas Bey Camii), where the icon was lifted from the chariot and deposited in the church with solemn reverence. Then Michael VIII mounted his own horse and led the parade down the Mese, amid the accolades of the inhabitants, at last arriving at Hagia Sophia for his second coronation.

This was the first triumph to be celebrated in Constantinople for many centuries. It was also Michael VIII's first visit to the Byzantine capital. We can only imagine how he greeted the sad spectacle before his eyes. The rich ornamentation of the Golden Gate was only a memory; even its glistening doors had long ago been discarded. The area between the Theodosian land walls and the old walls of Constantine was a landscape of ruins, overgrowth, and grazing livestock. At the Forum of Arcadius, with its spiraled column still reaching to the sky, was the broken rubble of the old porticoes and abandoned buildings for as far as the eye could see. The situation was no better in the Forum of Constantine. The founder's column still dominated the landscape, but everything else was burned-out desolation. Pressing on, the victory march came upon the Hippodrome, the great pride of Constantinople for a millennium. It had been stripped of all ornament and was crumbling from neglect. The imperial loge was no longer stable, the walkways below the stands filled with garbage and vermin. The two obelisks and the Serpent Column still marked out the *spina* around which the chariots of the empire once raced. Yet even these had been battered. The bronze coverings on the "built obelisk" had been melted down by the Latins, leaving the obelisk the blocky stone needle one sees today. Uninterested in civic rituals, the western knights had used the Hippodrome as an area for jousts and other impromptu games. It had become an open public space, something it would remain for the remainder of its history.

Hagia Sophia had been hastily prepared for Michael's arrival. The Catholic Europeans took good care of the great church during their stay, although it needed some rearranging of furnishings to prepare it once again for Greek Orthodox rituals. In that great temple at the heart of the Byzantine Empire, Michael VIII was hailed as emperor, the restorer of Constantinople, and even a new Constantine. After his second coronation, he went outside to the Augusteion to receive the congratulations of the assembled. This, the city's oldest square, had also been badly damaged by decades of Latin rule. Statues had disappeared from their bases, and even the great Milion had lost all its bronze decorations. The colossal bronze equestrian statue of Justinian atop its massive column had remained only because it was too high and too heavy to be safely removed. Michael VIII then entered the nearby Great Palace, where he would live for the next ten years. It was a humble abode. Most of the once-fabulous palace complex was an overgrown, rat-infested wreck tumbling down the terraced hill to the sea below. A few of the churches and clerical quarters in the upper palace had been kept in good repair, and for the time being, these would house the imperial court. Like his Byzantine and Latin predecessors, Michael VIII planned to live in the Palace of Blachernae, along the land walls in the far north ern corner of the city. But the Westerners had so neglected that build ing that it was no longer fit for an emperor. Soot from wax candles and poorly shielded oil lamps covered its walls. Michael ordered Blachernae to be restored, beautified, and expanded. Its new decorations included a fresco cycle depicting the many victories of Michael's career. The only portion of the Blachernae Palace that survives today, known as Tekfur Saray, was probably part of Michael's expansion project.

A landscape of such desolation made it difficult for Michael to proj ect a convincing image of himself as a new Constantine. A ten year old emperor in Nicaea who, unlike Michael, was born to the purple made it doubly difficult. Like many Byzantine regents before him, Michael dreamed of unseating his young charge and founding his own dynasty. But John IV Lascaris was a pious, humble boy much loved by all. His family had presided over the Byzantine government in exile since 1204 and had brilliantly expanded the empire to include much of what had been lost. Surely the Lascaris family deserved the fruits of this precious victory. Michael, however, had three sons, and was determined that one of them succeed him to the throne of Constantinople. On Christmas Day 1261, which was also John IV's eleventh birthday, the young heir was visited in Nicaea by a group of soldiers sent by Michael. They seized the poor boy, gouged out his eyes, and spirited him away to Bithynia, where he was thrown into a fortress prison. In Constantinople, Michael VIII proclaimed the sad news that John IV had been kid napped and was feared dead. It did not take long for the truth to filter back to the capital. When he learned of it, Patriarch Arsenius, who had protected the boy since his father's death, bitterly rebuked Michael VIII for his treachery. He excommunicated the emperor, something common in the West but unheard of in Constantinople.

Although he had reclaimed the capital, Michael VIII now found himself denounced across the city as a treacherous usurper. His re sponse was to demonstrate his worthiness by rebuilding Constantinople with as much zeal as its sainted founder. The problem was that Constan tine the Great had had significantly more assets at his disposal than Michael VIII. Nonetheless, Michael appears to have begun a number of projects to clean up the main areas in the urban core, particularly along the Mese and in the larger forums. He partially rebuilt the wharfs and warehouses along the Port of Theodosius on the Sea of Marmara. Michael restored a few monasteries and churches, and after his death, his empress, Theodora, funded the rebuilding and enlargement of the tenth-century monastery and church of Lips. A new church there, dedicated to St. John the Baptist, was intended as a mausoleum for members of the Palaeologan family. Most of the emperor's meager reconstruction funds, though, were spent on repair of the Theodosian land walls and reinforcement of the seawalls along the Golden Horn.

The emperor was eager to rebuild Constantinople's population to its pre-Crusade levels. Yet the city had previously been a vast megalopolis because it had been the capital of a powerful and wealthy empire. When the empire later dwindled, the city retained its size because of its economic and strategic location, and because its impregnable fortifications offered safety in an uncertain world. Since then, though, the walls had been breached and seriously degraded. Much of the trade that formerly went through Constantinople had since moved to other Greek ports, Syria, or Egypt. For the Greeks of the reconstituted Byzantine Empire, there was little to attract them to the ruined capital. Some estimates suggest that Michael may have increased the population of Constantinople to sixty or even seventy thousand, yet a great many of those people would have been Italians. In return for their acting as his makeshift navy, Michael gave the suburb of Galata, on the north shore of the Golden Horn, to the Genoese. This was not simply a quarter, but an independent city. Michael also expelled the Venetians and handed over to the Genoese their ports along the Bosporus and the Black Sea. The latter were particularly important, for this was the age of the Pax Mongolica, a time when it was possible for traders from the Far East to travel the Silk Road to the ports of the Black Sea. Because the riches that could be made in those ports were substantial, the ports would remain a fiercely contested prize between the Genoese and Venetians for years. Despite favoring the Genoese, Michael could not oust Venice from

Crete or its many other Aegean islands and Greek ports. Genoa's monopoly over Constantinople's naval power also soon become trouble some, as the Italians demanded ever more concessions for their services. Finally, in 1268, Michael restored to Venice its quarter in Constantinople. The returning Venetians, he hoped, would remain a check against the Genoese.

Michael's most dramatic improvement to Constantinople made a decidedly unsubtle statement about him and the legitimacy of his reign. In front of the main door of the Church of the Holy Apostles, the burial spot of Constantine, Justinian, and the other emperors of Constantinople's glorious past, Michael erected a large, very tall column. That in itself was unusual. The days of monumental column building had passed away with antiquity, but it was precisely those days that Michael wished to evoke. This enormous column, of which no trace survives today, became a new feature on the skyline of Constantinople. In the earliest surviving map of the city, drawn by the Florentine priest Cristoforo Buondelmonti in the early fifteenth century, Michael's column juts out of the landscape along with those of Justinian, Constantine, Theodosius, and Arcadius (Illustration 11). With the exception of Justinian's, all the other columns had long ago lost their bronze statues. Michael's new column would have one: a larger-than-life bronze statue of the archangel Michael was mounted at its top. Far below, on a large stone base, a similarly giant bronze statue of Emperor Michael knelt reverently, doing homage to his namesake and protector. It was a striking scene. Scholars have long wondered how Michael VIII could have managed such a project in this city of poverty and decay. The construction of the column was amazing enough, but the technology to produce large bronze statues had been lost long before in Constantinople, and was only just rediscovered in Italy. It is possible that Michael modified an ancient bronze statue of a winged victory, but the production of his own statue remains difficult to explain.

No matter how tall Michael built his column, it failed to convince Patriarch Arsenius to accept him as the rightful emperor of Constantinople. In 1265, after four years of strife, Michael finally deposed the patriarch and sent him into exile, where he died a few years later. Arsenius's many followers were outraged. This was compounded the following year, when Michael appointed his own confessor, Joseph, to the patriarchate of Constantinople. Unsurprisingly, Joseph absolved the emperor of all wrongdoing and proclaimed him the true ruler. The crippled city split down the middle, dividing Orthodoxy between the Arsenites, who rejected both the emperor and the new patriarch, and the Josephites, who accepted both. This gash across Byzantine society would remain unhealed for the next fifty years.

All these problems paled in comparison to the danger from the West. For decades the Nicaean emperors had been negotiating a reunification of the Greek Orthodox and Roman Catholic Churches—one that would allow them to take back Constantinople with the pope's blessing and, most important, no subsequent Crusade. Michael's surprising capture of the city was not well received in the West. The last Latin emperor, Baldwin II, had fled to Europe pleading for a Crusade to retake Constantinople and return him to his throne. Michael saw the danger. Even as Hagia Sophia was restored to Greek Orthodox worship, the emperor sent word to the pope that he was eager to have an ecumenical council to unify the church. Yet his actions in Constantinople and elsewhere suggested otherwise. In 1267, Baldwin II handed over most of his rights in Constantinople to Charles of Anjou, the brother of King Louis IX of France, who had recently become the king of Sicily and southern Italy. With the pope's support, Charles was determined to lead a powerful Crusade against Constantinople to win it back. It was unlikely that Michael's makeshift fortifications could withstand such an attack, and equally unlikely that the Genoese would help him to repulse it. Instead, Michael sent word to King Louis, a man who would one day be canonized as a saint, that he and his brother must focus their efforts on the redemption of the Holy Land, much of which remained in Muslim hands. Louis agreed. Charles was henceforth drafted into service in Louis's new Crusade, which sailed to Tunis in 1270. It was destroyed by a disease that also claimed the life of the king of France.

Without his brother to restrain him, Charles of Anjou again began his plans to capture Constantinople. Only one thing could stop him. In 1272, Pope Gregory X called a new ecumenical council to meet in Lyon in two years. He invited Michael VIII and the patriarch of Constantinople to attend, to settle all matters that separated the churches. Michael accepted immediately. He sent delegates to the council in 1274, where they discussed the items that separated the Greek East and Latin West, and accepted the Roman position on every point. To mark the reunification at Lyon, the Greek clergy celebrated a Mass with the Catholics, signing the creed with the *filioque* clause that they had rejected for centuries. The ecumenical council then solemnly declared an end to the schism. No Crusade could be called against Constantinople, for it was a city under papal authority. Emperor Michael VIII and his people were Catholics—at least on paper. When the canons of the Second Council of Lyon were published in Constantinople, Patriarch Joseph refused to accept them. Michael deposed Joseph. The patriarch's followers, the Josephites, repudiated the emperor, thus further exacerbating Constantinople's divisions. The union was nonetheless enforced in Constantinople and throughout the empire. Although the Greek rite continued to be used in Hagia Sophia and the city's other churches, the creed was altered to fit the Western model and the pope's name was placed into the Eucharistic liturgy. The Josephites and Arsenites naturally disliked each other, but they agreed on the apostasy of Lyon. Supported by the city's monks, they preached in the streets against the faith of the Crusaders, telling the people that they should never attend a church in union with Rome. In truth, it was very difficult for an average person in Constantinople to tell the difference between a Mass in a Greek church in union or not. So the opponents helpfully drew up lists, urging the people that if they valued the purity of their faith, they must not accept the errors of the ecumenical council.

A stronger emperor could have enforced the union, since the opposition was initially small and localized among the monasteries and a minority of the clergy. Yet Michael was so beset by problems from within and without that he was powerless to stop a propaganda war that had as much to do with him as it did the question of union. In the end, he simply stopped trying. Although he remained a Catholic, he did nothing to enforce the council's decrees. This did not go unnoticed in the papal Curia, which sent legates and nuncii to Constantinople to oversee the union. Michael blamed a vocal minority for blocking his efforts and promised to continue to work on the problem. These were precisely the arguments made by generations of Nicaean emperors, with no progress. In Rome many suspected, rightly of course, that Michael was simply stalling to prevent the launching of a Crusade to take back Constantinople.

In 1281 a French cardinal under the control of Charles of Anjou was elected pope: Martin IV. One of his first actions was to demand implementation of the decisions of the Second Council of Lyon in the Byzantine Empire. When this was not done, Martin excommunicated Michael VIII and gave Charles of Anjou permission to launch his long-delayed mission to Constantinople. Charles at once began assembling thousands of vessels for a massive attack. Venice added its considerable power to the cause. Bereft of support at home and abroad, Michael, in a last desperate move, sent agents to Sicily with orders to spend freely to foment rebellion. They did so with great effect. During Easter 1282, a revolt known as the Sicilian Vespers erupted and raged across Charles's Italian kingdom, ejecting the French and ending his Mediterranean ambitions. Almost overnight the threat that had hung over Constantinople for two decades evaporated. Michael, who had restored Byzantine Constantinople, had rescued it once again. He died within the year, still a Catholic and still reviled in the city he had saved.

Michael was succeeded peacefully by his twenty-three-year-old son, Andronicus II Palaeologus. With the immediate danger from the West past and recognizing the widespread unpopularity of union, the new emperor repudiated the Council of Lyon and restored Patriarch Joseph to Hagia Sophia. This healed some wounds, although the Arsenites remained firmly opposed to the Palaeologi until 1310.

The city remained at the center of the Western world. Indeed, this was truer with the coming of the Mongols and the development of the Black Sea ports as the gateway to the Far East. Yet the ancient capital and its derelict empire were so poor and so weak that they could do little but react to events around them.

For centuries the sophisticated citizens of Constantinople had looked upon western Europe with a mixture of disdain and pity. It was the land of their lost ancient empire, now flooded with barbarians; a place of crude, warlike people who scarcely understood the Christianity they professed. These comforting images could no longer be sustained in the

crumbling city of the Palaeologan emperors. The popes had built a bureaucracy that spanned Europe, becoming the true leaders of the West.
Western monarchies, particularly in England and France, continued to
grow in power and reach. The new universities of western Europe produced brilliant minds that expanded the understanding of God and his
universe. The economy in Europe was booming, led by a rapid rise in
population and a vibrant growth of towns and cities. Constantinople
was no longer the largest city in Christendom. Indeed, it was not even in
the top ten. Western merchants had always been a regular sight in Constantinople. By the end of the thirteenth century, they dominated it.

The Genoese continued to patrol the Bosporus, excluding their rivals from the Black Sea and reacting badly to any attempt by the emperor
to build his own navy. Venice naturally found this situation disagreeable. In 1291 the Mamluk Empire out of Egypt destroyed the last remnant of the Crusader states in Syria. Thus cut off from Eastern markets,
Venice was determined to expand its presence in Constantinople and
the Black Sea. Realizing this, the Genoese moved to tighten their hold
on the Bosporus. In 1295 the Genoese crossed the Golden Horn and
waged war on the Venetian Quarter in Constantinople. Hundreds were
massacred, and the remaining Venetians were arrested by Andronicus II
at the behest of the Genoese. Weeks later a Venetian war fleet under
the command of the feared admiral "Malabranca" (Evil Claw) appeared
in the Bosporus. Declaring war on Genoa and Constantinople, the Venetians launched attacks on Galata and preyed on Genoese and Byzantine traffic up and down the straits. They even broke into the Golden
Horn and prepared to attack Blachernae Palace. The emperor had no
choice but to make peace. He released all captives and made reparations to the Venetians.

Although the West was growing, it was itself dwarfed by the continued expansion of Islam in the East. After being dealt a blow by the
Mongols, the Turkish tribes in Asia Minor had reorganized themselves
under one leader. His name was Osman, a name he would give to his
dynasty and his empire: Ottoman. Both would last until the twentieth
century. Osman and his forces pressed westward with increasing ferocity.
In 1302 they defeated Byzantine forces at Nicomedia (İzmit), opening

the way for them to capture everything east of the Aegean. With no navy and few troops, Andronicus was desperate for soldiers to defend Constantinople. He found them—probably more than he wanted. A band of mostly Aragonese mercenaries known as the Catalan Company offered their services to the emperor. Led by the swashbuckling Roger de Flor, the roughly five-thousand-strong warriors were unruly but devastatingly powerful. Andronicus hired them. In the spring of 1303 the Catalan Company attacked the Ottoman forces in Asia Minor and drove them back. But they did as much damage to the Byzantine citizens they liberated as to the Turks they defeated.

Returning to Gallipoli for the winter, Roger demanded that the emperor hire more of his friends, despite the fact that the imperial treasury was nearly empty. Andronicus obeyed, and heaped titles upon the mercenary leader, but the situation grew increasingly extortionate. Finally, in 1305, Andronicus and his son and co-emperor, Michael IX, moved against the Catalans. Michael first coaxed Roger and his retinue to a banquet in Adrianople. Between courses, he ordered the mercenary leader and his attendants stabbed to death. He then led an army of Turkish and Alanian mercenaries against the Catalan Company, although he failed to defeat it. Soldiers from the betrayed company raged across Thrace and Greece, conquering, pillaging, and capturing Greeks for the next several years. In 1310 they even took Athens, which they used as the capital of their new duchy.

What is most remarkable about this dark period in Constantinople's history is that it was also a time of artistic renaissance. For the first time in many centuries, the artists of the city began to experiment with new designs and new media. Little of it survives, but where it does, it is glorious. The church of the Monastery of Theotokos Pammakaristos (modern-day Fethiye Camii) was built during the eleventh century but dramatically restored and expanded sometime after 1310, by Martha Glabas, the widow of one of Andronicus II's generals. The main church is lost, heavily altered when it was converted into a mosque at the end of the sixteenth century. But the Paracclesion, or side chapel, was left relatively unmolested. It has since been restored and is open to the public as a museum. It is a beautiful structure, built along Greek models but with a new emphasis on vaulting and light reminiscent of Gothic ceilings in the West. Its surviving mosaics have a new, more lifelike attitude. A beautiful dome mosaic depicts Christ Pantocrator at the center surrounded by twelve prophets of the Old Testament. Over the altar space is a magnificent mosaic of Christ enthroned, as well as others depicting the Virgin Mary, John the Baptist, saints, and a beautiful scene of the Baptism of Christ.

If Pammakaristos is not much visited today, it is only because it is eclipsed by the extraordinary beauty of the Church of Holy Savior in Chora (Kariye Camii), very near the location of the old Blachernae Palace. Also a monastery church, it was founded in the twelfth century but was remodeled and expanded as a pious offering by Theodore Metochites, the head of the civil administration under Andronicus II. Its walls and ceilings were covered in exquisite mosaics and frescoes—the latter a relatively new medium for Byzantines. They survive because the small, relatively obscure church was quickly converted into a mosque in the sixteenth century, with its walls and ceilings simply covered with plaster. After World War II several American organizations funded its restoration. Aside from Hagia Sophia, it is the only former church turned mosque that is no longer a functioning mosque in Istanbul. The beauty of Holy Savior cannot be described adequately with words. Its rich colors and evocative, action-filled depictions must be experienced. Fresco paintings in the Paracclesion vividly portray the Second Coming, the Harrowing of Hell, the heavenly court of angels, the Virgin and Child, and Moses. The glittering mosaics depict the life of Christ in fifteen scenes and the life of the Virgin in as many. Theodore Metochites, with his wide and flowing headdress, is depicted in another mosaic, kneeling before Christ enthroned while offering a model of the church.

Andronicus II and his son, Michael IX, ruled jointly for five years. To ensure the stability of the dynasty, in 1319 or 1320 they also crowned Michael's son Andronicus as an additional co-emperor. It was hoped that the crown would therefore pass easily from father to son to grandson. However, one evening in 1320 the younger Andronicus was spending a pleasant evening in bed with a married noblewoman when his younger brother, Manuel, came to the house and demanded that the guard posted outside let him in. The drowsy or drunk Andronicus, who did not know who was pestering him at that hour, told his men to kill the man. It was only in the morning that he learned of his mistake. Andronicus II and Michael IX were horrified by the event. Indeed, Michael was so upset that he died. Andronicus II, now in his sixties, was unsurprisingly ill disposed toward his namesake. He seriously considered disinheriting him. Sensing this, Andronicus III fled Constantinople and headed to Adrianople, where he set up his own rival court. From 1321 on, the tiny Byzantine Empire was thus divided between two emperors struggling for the scraps of glory. Only in 1328 did Andronicus II abdicate, allowing his grandson to return to Constantinople.

Andronicus III inherited the throne of a sinking empire. He was powerless to stop the decline, although his general John Cantacuzenus was able to use his own personal contacts with the Turks to acquire their support against the Serbs, Bulgarians, and other enemies. In 1341 the emperor died unexpectedly, leaving a nine-year-old son, John V Palaeologus. Cantacuzenus naturally took the regency, although a subsequent palace coup while he was out of the city forced him to fight a five-year civil war to regain control of Constantinople. In 1347 he was crowned co-emperor in the Church of St. Mary of Blachernae—a first. Hagia Sophia's dome had earlier collapsed, and the government had not scraped together the funds to repair it. During the coronation, John VI Cantacuzenus used costume jewelry. The real crown jewels were in hock to the Venetians. No sooner had he donned the crown than the Black Death arrived in Constantinople, killing about one-third of the already low population. It would continue to claim millions of lives across Europe for the next decade.

In 1351 the twenty-year-old John V Palaeologus demanded that Cantacuzenus abdicate the throne and return all power to him. Cantacuzenus naturally refused, again plunging the Byzantine Empire into civil war. This one, however, was to have long-lasting consequences. As John V was supported by the Serbs and the Bulgarians, John VI turned to his old friends the Ottoman Turks. Ten thousand of them came across the Hellespont and camped near Gallipoli, which Cantacuzenus controlled. He then led them north into Thrace, where he defeated John V's forces. With the victory won, the Turks began pillaging the Thracian countryside, demanding additional payments. Cantacuzenus paid them, and they re-treated to Gallipoli. Then, in 1354, a powerful earthquake brought down Gallipoli's fortifications. Under the command of the Ottoman sultan's son Suleiman, the Turkish army captured the city and reforti-fied it. For seven centuries the city of Constantinople had defended Europe from a Muslim invasion from the East. In 1354 a vibrant Mus-lim power, ferried across the straits by the Byzantines themselves, had at last established a permanent eastern European foothold. The way was thus cleared for the Turkish invasion of Europe.

With Asia Minor lost to the Turks, and Turkish armies pressing northward into Thrace, it was clear that Constantinople's position was dire. Cantacuzenus, the author of this debacle, was deposed and sent to a monastery. John V's strategy was a simple one: beg the West for aid. In a letter to Pope Innocent VI, John V made clear that he was willing to unite the churches and become a Catholic himself in return for military aid. Alarmed at the growing Turkish power, the Europeans had been launch-ing small-scale Crusades and Holy Leagues against the Turks in Asia Minor for decades. With papal support, more were forthcoming. Count Amadeo of Savoy led a Crusade that ousted the Turks from Gallipoli and put that city back under imperial control. But by then the Turks were so well established in Greece that Gallipoli had become irrelevant. In 1369 the Ottomans captured Adrianople (Edirne) and proclaimed it the new capital of the Ottoman Empire in Europe. Constantinople was in desper-ate danger.

Yet John V was not there. Four years earlier he had left for the court of King Louis of Hungary, where he attempted to extract funds and promises of military aid. In 1369 he went to Rome to meet Pope Urban V (becoming the first Roman emperor to visit the Eternal City since Con-stans II, exactly seven hundred years earlier). He made his profession of faith as a Catholic and then, from Rome, traveled through Italy seeking aid until finally coming to Venice. This last destination was a mistake. The Byzantine government owed Venice a great deal of money. For sev-eral years the Venetians had made clear to the emperor that they would erase his entire debt and return the crown jewels if he ceded to them the little island of Tenedos (Bozcaada), near the southern mouth of the Hellespont. Since the Genoese did not want the Venetians to have this strategic island, they refused to allow the emperor to take the deal. Now with the emperor in their city, the Venetians offered again, and placed the debtor under house arrest to underscore the seriousness of the situation. John eventually accepted, although at the last minute his younger son, Manuel, raised the money to pay the Venetians and thereby win his father's freedom. John returned to Constantinople with little to show for his efforts. In his absence, the Ottoman Empire had managed to completely surround Constantinople. The great city had become a little bit of flotsam in a growing Turkish sea. The Turks had already broken Serbian and Bulgarian power in the region, which led both kingdoms to become vassal states to Sultan Murad of the Ottomans. John V had no choice but to do the same. In 1372 he formally did homage to the sultan, declaring himself a vassal of the Turkish ruler.

For the first time in more than two millennia, the Roman Empire was a dependency of another power. Constantinople had sunk to its lowest level yet. The new connection with the Ottoman Empire brought another outside player into the government of desolate Constantinople. In 1373 John's eldest son, Andronicus, teamed up with one of Sultan Murad's sons to topple both their fathers. The fathers won. Murad blinded his son, who subsequently died of his wounds, and demanded that John do the same to Andronicus. Soft-hearted John could not bring himself to be so cruel, so he had Andronicus blinded in just one eye and then imprisoned in Constantinople. Three years later, again strapped for cash, John finally agreed to hand over Tenedos to Venice under the previous terms. The Genoese of Galata, unaccustomed to having Constantinople's emperors disobey their orders, stormed the imperial prison and released Andronicus. With Genoese and Turkish troops, Andronicus seized power and threw his father and younger brother, Manuel, into the same prison from which he had just escaped. When it came time to hand out rewards, Andronicus IV handed Gallipoli back to the Turks and Tenedos to the Genoese. Venice declared war, eventually restoring John V and Manuel, who would later be crowned Manuel II.

The only constant during these intrigues and wars was the relentless expansion of the Ottoman Empire across the Balkans. The Ottomans captured Thessalonica in 1387, and by 1389 they had conquered all Bulgaria. A few years later they did the same to Serbia. Western Europe could not stop them. Constantinople could scarcely defend itself. When John V died in 1391, he left to Manuel II the capital, a few ports in Thrace, part of the Greek Peloponnesus, and a few islands. Constantinople no longer ruled an empire, but a memory.

Chapter 16

———◆———

Empire's End

A side from the imposing dome of Hagia Sophia, the most noticeable feature of Constantinople's medieval skyline was the soaring Column of Justinian, with its massive equestrian statue. Those who approached Constantinople from the sea (as most did) could not fail to be struck by this marvel. Erected in AD 543, the bronze Justinian sat astride a prancing horse with one forefoot in the air. The emperor wore the raiment of Achilles: half boots, bare legs, and a shining breastplate. On his head he donned a magnificent headdress of feathers, the ceremonial toupha worn by Roman emperors during triumphal processions. In his left hand he held a globe surmounted by a cross, while his right hand was boldly stretched out to the East, in a warding gesture. The statue, which commemorated Justinian's victory over the Persians, visually represented the emperor's demand that they never again threaten the borders of the Roman Empire. The globe represented his mastery over the whole world, and the cross, as the contemporary writer Procopius tells us, was "the emblem by which alone he has obtained both his empire and his victory."

Nine centuries later the statue safeguarded Constantinople from Turkish conquest. As with every other ancient statue in the city, the inhabitants of medieval Constantinople attributed to Justinian and his horse a variety of magical properties. Since the Persians were long forgotten, the outstretched hand was thought to threaten the Muslim powers invading from the East. New prophecies were generated claiming that the statue's magic restrained the Turks from crossing the empire's borders. These were disproved time and again, but they endured nonetheless. By the fifteenth century, when the borders of the empire and the walls of the capital were one and the same, the statue and its column were believed to be a mystical talisman preserving Constantinople from Turkish conquest, anti-Muslim magic from a statue older than Islam.

It seemed to work. Sultan Bayezid I "the Thunderbolt" besieged Constantinople for nearly eight years between 1394 and 1402 before fi, nally admitting defeat. Sultan Murad II brought some one hundred thousand Ottoman troops to besiege Constantinople in 1422, but failed to breach its defenses. That a city so large with so few defenders could hold out against such power was truly astonishing.

Justinian and his horse were by no means the only supernatural de, fenders of Constantinople. The greatest of them all was the Virgin Mary, ever the special protectress of the Queen of Cities. The icon of the Virgin Hodegetria was still processed through the streets of the city and along the ramparts of its walls whenever danger approached. Con, stantinople also had an angel. According to the well known tale, centu, ries earlier, during the construction of Hagia Sophia, a group of workmen had decided to break for lunch. The master builder told a boy working with them that he should remain to keep watch over the tools. A little later, a handsome warrior came along and asked the boy why he was not eating with the others. The boy replied that he could not, since he had been ordered to watch the tools. The kindly warrior told him to go eat, promising to guard the tools, the church—indeed, the whole city—until he returned. When the boy joined the other workmen and told them of the warrior, the master builder instantly realized that it was an angel. He ordered the boy never to return to Hagia Sophia. Thus the city acquired an eternal protector from the armies of Heaven.

Not all the mystical augurs in Constantinople were good. In 1316 a strong gale blew the golden orb out of Justinian's hand. It fell with a crack onto the Augusteion's pavement below. The symbol of the empire slipping from the emperor's grasp could not be a good omen. From John Mandeville on, Western travelers invariably remarked on this ominous portent that so neatly summed up Constantinople's weakness. To coun, teract the magic, the Byzantines several times replaced the orb. Indeed, once they strung from the roof of Hagia Sophia a tightrope across which an acrobat walked to replace the fallen talisman. Each time, it would fall again, unwilling to remain in the emperor's hand. The fallen orb also fit nicely with Turkish prophecies of a "golden apple" that would come to the Turks, widely thought to be Constantinople itself.

Magic aside, the situation remained grim for Constantinople in the fifteenth century. The rise of the West meant more travelers visiting the city, thus providing many more descriptions of it, but the old accolades of its beauty and richness were now rare. Indeed, Europeans preferred the Genoese colony in the suburb of Galata to the ruined capital across the Golden Horn. Ruy Gonzáles de Clavijo, a Spanish ambassador who visited the city in 1403, noted that Constantinople "contains many great churches and monasteries, but most of them are in ruins; though it seems clear that, in former times, when the city was in its youth, it was the most renowned city in the world." Gonzáles de Clavijo was the first European to note that "the Greeks do not call it Constantinople as we do, but Escomboli." This word was his hearing of *eis tin Polin*, Greek for "in/to the City." Like New Yorkers who refer to Manhattan as "the city," the Greeks used this familiar shorthand, while foreigners assumed it was a completely new name. The Turks thought the same, later modifying what they heard to "Istanbul." In both cases, it means the same: "the City."

Even the Byzantines had to admit the sad shape of their city when compared to the resurgent West. In a letter to the emperor's son, the Byzantine ambassador Manuel Chrysoloras compared Rome to Constantinople. He did his best to put a good face on it, referring to the few churches and monuments that remained in good repair in Constantinople. But the general desolation remains evident in almost every line. "Many other such statues used to be in the City as shown by their remaining pedestals and the inscriptions on them. These were in different places, but especially in the Hippodrome. . . . How big, precious and beautiful these statues must have been may be surmised from the beauty, height, splendor and magnificence of the bases."

The rise of the Christian West stood in stark contrast to the decline of Constantinople, yet it also offered a ray of hope. Crusades, which the Byzantines had scorned for centuries, seemed to be the means to deliver the city and its faded empire. A steady stream of Crusades had already made their way to the East, primarily under the patronage of the Knights of St. John Hospitaller, who had established a base at Rhodes and others along the southern coast of Asia Minor. Venice and Spain were also active in the Eastern Crusades. The French teamed up with the Hungarians and a few others in 1396 to wage a large Crusade against the Turks, but it was destroyed near Nicopolis. The problem remained that although western

Europe was growing rapidly, it was still dwarfed by the Islamic world. The Europeans were simply no match for the Turks.

Nevertheless, western Europeans were virtually the only other free Christians left in the world, and therefore Constantinople's only possible allies. Emperor John VIII Palaeologus came to the inescapable conclusion that without a firm unification of the Greek and Roman churches and a massive Crusade, Constantinople was lost. As it happened, the fifteenth century was a particularly good time to seek aid from the West. Pope Eugenius IV was a Venetian with no love for the Turks. For seven years the Republic of Venice had poured blood and treasure to defend Christian Thessalonica, only to have it captured and burned to the ground in 1430 by Sultan Murad II. Shortly after becoming pope in 1431, Eugenius used Venetian ambassadors to open negotiations with Constantinople for a new ecumenical council—one so inclusive that no Greek could deny its legitimacy.

As it happened, the pope had a bit of a problem himself. A reform movement growing out of the universities, known as conciliarism, had for years argued that papal power in Europe should be curbed in favor of regular ecumenical councils. The popes naturally opposed this, but after the embarrassment of the Great Schism, which saw Europe split by first two and then three different popes at the same time, they found the concept hard to resist. Eugenius had called the Council of Basel in 1431, but it was poorly attended and quickly dominated by radical conciliarists. With each year it became more of a danger to the authority of the pope. Yet simply dissolving it risked open rebellion and another schism. Constantinople was key to Eugenius's plan to neutralize the conciliarists at Basel. By 1436 he had concluded preparations for Emperor John VIII, Patriarch Joseph II, and six hundred of Greek Orthodoxy's highest clergy to come from Constantinople to attend a truly ecumenical council in Ferrara, one that would permanently repair the division between East and West. The Venetians sent scores of rich galleys under papal banners to pick up these elites of Constantinople and transport them to the West.

For the first time in many centuries, and also for the last time, Constantinople's emperor was directly affecting events in western Europe. Pope Eugenius issued a decree announcing the impending arrival of the

Byzantine representatives and moving the Council of Basel to Ferrara. The conciliarists saw that they had been outmaneuvered. Churchmen from across Europe rushed to Ferrara to be part of the grandeur of the reunification of Christendom, thus further bolstering the pope's author' ity and sidelining the conciliarists' ambitions. They quickly sent their own envoys to Constantinople to beg John VIII to come to Basel in' stead, where they promised to greet him warmly and do all they could for the preservation of his empire. John had no interest in Western church reform; he was counting on a powerful pope in the old medieval mold who could call mighty Crusades against the Turks. He politely declined, expressing the hope that he would see the prelates in Ferrara.

In the summer of 1437 the galleys left Constantinople. They win' tered at Venetian Modon and finally arrived in Venice on February 8, 1438. For the Venetians, who still cherished a history in which their state was the child of Constantinople, it was an unprecedented event: not only had the emperor himself come to the lagoon, but he had brought his court, his clergy, and most of the high officials still left in the once'great empire. The government of Ancient Rome had landed in Venice, and the Venetians were determined to show filial devotion to their aged cul' tural parent. The welcome ceremony itself was demonstrative of the ex' traordinary wealth that Venice now possessed. The entire sea before San Marco was filled with decorated boats ranging from galleys to gondolas. Doge Francesco Foscari came to collect the emperor in his ducal galley, known as the *bucintoro*, a floating palace. Banners bearing the imperial eagle of Byzantium streamed along the sides of the vessel, while on the prow waved the winged lion of St. Mark, the symbol of Venice. John VIII boarded the gilded ship amid drumbeats and horn blares, and was guided to an ornate throne fit for an emperor. Then the doge removed his *corno*, the headwear of his office, and bowed low before the emperor. John bid him sit on a smaller throne to his left. Cheers and music swelled up from the boats and the shore, greater than any triumph in Constanti' nople for many centuries. The Byzantine delegation then paraded down the Grand Canal before arriving at their lodging, a new and very rich palazzo, which is today the Fondaco dei Turchi. The court remained there for nearly three weeks, living the sumptuous life of antiquity's em' perors. Then they were off to Ferrara.

For the next year the Greek Orthodox and Roman Catholic prel‑ ates, theologians, and philosophers worked out their differences at the council. An international collection of well over a thousand leaders of the Christian faith converged upon Ferrara from as far away as Egypt and Ethiopia. For the first time in centuries, all five of the ancient patriarch‑ ates of Christianity were represented at an ecumenical council. Fearing a plague in the area, the council moved to Florence in late 1438. The grandeur of the event was not lost in the cradle of the Italian Renais‑ sance. The artist Benozzo Gozzoli even depicted the richly adorned emperor John VIII as one of the Magi in his famous fresco in the Medici Chapel. Across the Alps, in Basel, the once‑fashionable council withered as its attendees excused themselves one by one to take part in the events in Florence. Finally, on July 5, 1439, amid great celebration, Pope Euge‑ nius and Emperor John formally celebrated the union of the churches. What was left of Christendom was at last one.

Pope Eugenius did not waste time coming to the aid of Constantino‑ ple. He declared a truce across Europe and called on all warriors to take up the Crusader's cross to save their Christian brothers and sisters in the East. Although the Hundred Years' War was preoccupying the French and English, the new Crusade attracted thousands of Poles, Wallachians, Hungarians, and even a few French. In 1444 it met the armies of Sultan Murad II near the city of Varna, in Bulgaria. The Turks utterly crushed the Christians. The king of Hungary was killed in battle, and thousands of captured Crusaders were decapitated. Once again a great Crusade had failed to stop the relentless growth of the Ottoman Empire. Constanti‑ nople continued to plead for substantial Western support, but it seemed that even that was no match for the Sultan.

Emperor John VIII died in 1448. He was succeeded by his younger brother, Constantine XI, a pious, brave, and very humble man. A few years later, in 1451, Murad II also died. If the people of Constantinople believed that the passing of their enemy presaged a time of peace, they were sadly mistaken. Nineteen‑year‑old Mehmed II was known to be scholarly, inquisitive, and deeply interested in Roman history (Illustra‑ tion 12). He was also determined to make Constantinople the capital of his empire. From the moment of his elevation he intensely studied the matter, considering the structure of the city's walls, the extensiveness of its water supplies, and the currents of the waterways that surrounded it. He gave orders to raise tens of thousands of troops, who were to assemble at Constantinople ready for a long siege. In April 1452 the young sultan began construction of a great fortress on a large hill just north of the city. When finished, Rumeli Hisari was an imposing structure, built at the narrowest point on the Bosporus and designed to permanently control the waterway. Atop its highest tower, the Turks mounted a relatively new weapon: gunpowder artillery. Mehmed then announced that no traffic would be allowed on the Bosporus without his approval and the payment of a toll. Doubting the strength of his threat, many merchant vessels sailed through anyway, dodging cannonballs on all sides. Once the guns were properly sighted, though, they missed less often. A Venetian merchant vessel carrying wheat was struck and sank in August 1452. The commander, Antonio Rizzo, and his thirty crewmen were brought before Mehmed in chains. The sultan gleefully ordered the public impalement of Rizzo and the decapitation of his crew.

It was plain to all that Mehmed's preparations were aimed at capturing Constantinople. Constantine XI did all that he could to avoid that, sending embassy after embassy to the sultan to bribe, beg, and warn him to cease his military buildup. Mehmed's response was less than encouraging:

> I am not depriving the City of anything. [Constantine XI] controls and possesses nothing beyond his moat. . . . Why are you trying to stop me? Am I not allowed to do as I please in my own territory? Go tell your king: the present lord does not resemble his predecessors. He will easily accomplish what they failed to achieve. He eagerly wishes to succeed in what they proved unwilling to do. I will skin alive any man who dares to talk to me of this matter in the future.

Mehmed assembled approximately one hundred thousand troops, who were arrayed across the fields outside the Theodosian land walls. Constantinople had withstood larger forces, but not ones armed with cannons. The ancient emperors of the Queen of Cities had attempted to provide defenses that could withstand any adversary, but they naturally did not plan for the transformation of warfare by gunpowder. A Hungarian engineer named Urban, who had previously worked for the emperor in Constantinople, demanded a large increase in pay to remain on the Christian side. Constantine could not afford it, so Urban left to join Mehmed, who paid him handsomely. Urban not only knew how to produce bronze cannons, but he had overseen reconstruction work on the Theodosian Walls, a job that had given him insights into their strengths and weaknesses. Beyond the land forces, Mehmed also had a large navy, which began patrolling the waters of the Bosporus and the Sea of Marmara.

War had not yet been declared, but only a fool could believe that it was not imminent. Constantine XI was no fool. Before the hammer fell he sent one last, brave letter to the Ottoman sultan, boldly stating the obvious:

> Since you have chosen war and I can persuade you neither by flat-tery nor by your sworn treaty, do as you please. I will seek shelter with God. If it is His will to hand this city into your hands, who will be able to oppose Him? If again He inspires peace in your heart, I will gladly welcome it. For the time being, take back your treaty and your sworn statements. From this point on I will close the gates of the City and I will provide protection to the inhabit-ants. Do go on with your oppressive rule until the Righteous Judge will deliver His just verdict to each man—to you and to me.

Mehmed did not reply. By the winter of 1452 the City was completely invested.

The situation was dire. Constantine XI ordered a census of the able-bodied men among his citizens who could fight. The number was 4,973. He had already sent letters to the West begging for additional supplies and forces. The pope sent some men, and the Venetians some arms and armor. But Europe was preoccupied with its own wars. Venice had ex-panded its empire onto the Italian mainland and was laying out many of its resources fighting Milan. Those Venetians who happened to be in Constantinople when the siege began took a vote and decided to remain there to help defend the city. Their leader, Girolamo Minotto, sent word back to Venice that they would hold out as long as they could. The Ve-netian Senate responded by promising to send additional aid. Aside from the local Venetians, Constantine could rely only on a mixed group of other Italians. These did not include the Genoese—at least not those thousands who resided in their colony at Galata; they had refused to assist either side, hoping to keep their lucrative position no matter the outcome of the siege. A contingent of Genoese mercenaries, led by the condottiere Giovanni Giustiniani, did arrive in Constantinople and offered its services for hire. Constantine accepted and even appointed Giustiniani as his military commander. Altogether the Italian defenders numbered some two or three thousand. Roughly eight thousand defenders against more than one hundred thousand well-armed assailants.

Fear stalked the streets of Constantinople, now a tiny island of Christianity in a raging ocean of Islam. The people feared not only for their lives, but for the end of something that had seemed eternal. Sixteen centuries earlier the victorious Roman general Scipio Aemilianus had wept bitterly as he gave the command for his legions to destroy the city of Carthage, the last remnant of a once-great empire. When his Greek friend Polybius saw the tears running down the general's face he earnestly asked him what was wrong. He replied, "A glorious moment, Polybius, but I have a dread foreboding that someday the same doom will be pronounced on my own country." This was a story well known in the Greek capital of the Roman Empire. Manuel II Palaeologus and his son John VIII had prayed to God that he would not allow the empire of Scipio, Caesar, and Justinian to fall during their reigns. Constantine XI made that same prayer, but it seemed increasingly unlikely to be answered. A letter from a citizen of Constantinople, Theodore Agallianos, gives voice to the desperation of the moment:

> The City can expect help neither from inside or outside. Funds
> and men are lacking since the City has been tortured for so long
> by its great poverty, lack of men, attacks of the enemy, and fear of
> the bitter realization of what is to become of us. Our only hopes
> are the merciful and compassionate God, should He return, spare,
> and defend us, and the pure, ever-Virgin Mother of God.

Mehmed II was well aware that Constantine had been sending envoys and letters to the West for more than a year, reporting on the danger and begging for aid. More than one Turkish siege of Constantinople had been scrapped because of a troublesome Crusade. The sultan was determined, therefore, to capture the City quickly. Urban had assured him that he could produce a cannon that could "bring down the walls of Babylon," turning Constantinople's Theodosian fortifications into dust. Laboring for three months in Adrianople, Urban produced a truly massive cannon more than twenty feet long, capable of firing stones weighing more than eight hundred pounds. "The Monster," as many of the eyewitnesses referred to it, was painstakingly transported across Thrace by sixty oxen and set up on a giant mounting to face the ancient walls. It was not alone. Mehmed II had at least a dozen and perhaps many more other cannons of various sizes. Although gunpowder artillery was still a novelty in the Middle East, it had become a regular feature of warfare in western Europe. Indeed, Urban's Monster was old-fashioned by European standards. Westerners no longer produced bronze cannons, but had perfected new iron ones, which were more mobile, accurate, and destructive.

That is not to say that the cannons of Mehmed II were ineffective. The smaller ones especially could be used almost continually, while the Monster had to be cooled for three hours between firings. Even so, it lasted only a matter of weeks before it developed cracks. Iron bands fitted snuggly around its barrel did nothing to halt its disintegration. Constantinople had cannons of its own, but the city's supply of gunpowder was so limited that every shot had to count. There were so few defenders that they could man only the lower outer wall of the Theodosian fortifications. Behind the defenders loomed much higher towers and walls, but given the meagerness of their forces, they were of no use. The outer walls were strong, but they were so pummeled by round-the-clock bombardment that to fire a cannon from their towers would mean costly damage from the recoil. Instead, the defenders carried their defensive artillery to wall portions that had crumbled and were repaired by wooden and stonework makeshift barricades. From these relatively stable mountains of rubble they could fire at will.

It is commonly said that gunpowder killed Byzantine Constantinople. Since the fall of Constantinople is usually considered the last event of the Middle Ages, there is a certain poetry to its proud antiquity falling before the emerging science of modern warfare. Recent studies, though, have demonstrated that Mehmed's cannons, while helpful, were by no means decisive. In the contest between "the Monster" and the walls of Theodosius, it was the belching cannon that crumbled and collapsed. As far as we know, the famous weapon never caused any substantial damage to the walls. Still, it was psychologically devastating. Even from a mile away its thunder shook the City. It was like nothing that anyone had ever heard before. The smoke from its firing was so substantial that it covered the battlefield and poured into Constantinople. For two months the other cannons kept up their barrages, but the defenders were always able to repair the damage, often under cover of night. They also frequently launched sorties, harassing the Ottoman forces should they approach too close to the walls. As the weeks passed, Mehmed became increasingly irritated by the delay. He had expected the Byzantines, who were hardly renowned for their courage, to have fled at the first sound of the Monster or at least after their walls began to crumble. Instead, they continued to fight back with all their strength. He suspected that it was not their doing. "What is at work here," he said, "is the skill of the Franks (Europeans) and not the Greeks, that results in such resistance and fighting. They have no fear of innumerable arrows, or cannon, or of wooden castles, even though there is no end to this siege." In that, however, the sultan was wrong. Greek men fought with determination on the walls, and Greek women helped to repair them at night.

Constantinople was supposed to fall on April 20, 1453. That, at least, is what Mehmed II's sufi adviser had prophesied. In anticipation, the sultan ordered his recently expanded fleet to attack several Italian vessels near the City and to capture the Golden Horn, which was protected by its powerful chain and several Venetian war galleys within. The state-of-the-art Italian vessels managed to destroy a good portion of the Ottoman fleet before it could even approach the chain. The sultan was enraged by this defeat, not least because there were rumors of a Venetian war fleet approaching from the Aegean. He fired his chief admiral and took matters into his own hands.

On the morning of April 22 the defenders of Constantinople awoke to an amazing sight. More than seventy light Ottoman vessels were floating in the Golden Horn, filling everything except the area around the chain, where the Italian galleys were docked. Even worse, Turkish engineers began constructing a bridge across the upper Golden Horn, which would allow easy communication between Mehmed's forces in the northern hills and the main army outside the land walls. How had the sultan managed to bypass the chain and the galleys? To their aston-ishment, the Christians learned that all the Ottoman vessels had been dragged up and over the hills of Pera in a single night. It was an amazing feat. A subsequent attempt by the Venetians to burn the fleet failed miserably, costing many of the Venetians their lives. The presence of the Ottoman fleet forced Constantinople's defenders, who were already stretched thin, to assign men to the harbor walls in order to protect against a seaborne attack.

As the weeks passed, the relentless bombardment of the walls contin-ued day and night. To move things along, Mehmed also sent sappers, who built long tunnels toward the walls in an attempt to undermine them. The Greek and Italian defenders responded by placing wide pots of water along the walls and watching them carefully for any ripples that would betray the blows of subterranean picks. When these appeared, they sent their own countersappers, who broke into the Turkish tunnels and set fire to their wooden supports, entombing those within. Despite many attempts, the Ottoman sappers failed to harm Constantinople's defenses in any way.

Rumors of the expected relief force from Venice continued to swirl around the city and in the camps of the Turks. Emperor Constantine even sent a lone scout vessel to slip past the Turkish blockade to search for signs of the coming fleet. It found only an empty horizon. Captain General Giacomo Loredan had indeed sailed from Venice in April, but experienced infuriating delays attempting to acquire ships in Venetian colonies along the way. In May 1453 he was still in Negroponte, still cobbling together a force.

Mehmed feared that help would arrive soon. Near the end of May, he decided that he could wait no longer. He must risk an all-out attack on Constantinople. For weeks the sultan had been concentrating his fire on the Mesoteichion, or "Middle Wall," an area of the land walls be-tween the Gates of St. Romanus and Pempton. This was well known to be the weakest part of the Theodosian fortifications, for it was where the walls descended into the Lycus River Valley. By this time the outer walls there were piles of rubble and ruin still defended fiercely by the

Christians. On Monday, May 28, the Ottoman land forces began to converge on the area. It was clear that a concentrated attack was coming soon. That evening, the emperor attended Mass at Hagia Sophia. All those who did not have to be on the walls were there. Realizing that it might well be the last Christian worship to echo from the walls of Justinian's great church, the people came together as one, forgetting for the moment their many divisions. Roman Catholic and Greek Orthodox clergy sang the Mass together in Latin and Greek, begging Christ and his Mother to deliver them one more time.

The Turkish assault began early the next morning, Tuesday, May 29. Mehmed came out to the Middle Wall in his golden chariot to shoot the first arrow over the walls. It was followed by thousands more. The Turkish advance was massive and relentless. First came the expendable irregulars: low-quality renegades and riffraff recruited from the Balkans on the promise of booty. The Genoese condottiere Giovanni Giustiniani commanded the defense, quickly dispatching this opening attack. Next came the Ottoman regular troops, who marched in good order and posed a much greater danger. Giant pots of boiling oil and water were rushed to the fortifications and poured liberally on the attackers. By midday, when the Turkish army was finally pushed back, the defenders were jubilant, yet utterly exhausted.

Then came the Janissaries. These fearsome warriors were the elite bodyguard of the sultan. A slave army, they literally belonged to the Ottoman ruler. Janissaries were recruited while still infants. Ottoman officials periodically inspected male offspring born to Christian families under their rule. The strongest boys were taken from their parents and raised in the barracks of the Janissary corps. There they not only learned to be disciplined and deadly soldiers, but became well versed in math, science, Persian poetry, and how to live an exemplary Muslim life. Service to the sultan was their highest goal, one for which they would gladly give their lives. For good reason the Christian West regarded the Janissaries with dread.

While the defenders braced themselves for the fresh onslaught, Constantinople's fate was decided elsewhere. As Giovanni Giustiniani barked orders to his men, a single arrow, or perhaps some other missile, struck him and he began to bleed. The many accounts of this momentous injury are so different that it is difficult to know the precise details. The wound was serious, since he later died of it. What is unclear, though, is why Giustiniani then left the battle, heading straight for his vessel, docked just inside the harbor chain. He was no coward. Indeed, it was his courage and skill that had inspired the Christians to hold out against the Ottoman siege for two long months. Why, then, did he flee at this critical moment? It is impossible to know, but the drastic effects of his decision are all too clear. When his men saw their leader retreat, they quickly did the same. Soon word spread among the defenders that the battle was lost. Panic erupted.

Wielding his sword on the ruins of the City's ancient walls, Emperor Constantine XI watched with sorrow as the Janissaries advanced easily across the broken battlefield and into Constantinople, killing everyone they found there. The vision of Scipio had come to pass. Rome had fallen. Its last emperor cast off his purple mantle, raised his sword in defiance, and plunged into the fray. Like his friends and countrymen, he was dispatched by the ruthless efficiency of the sultan's slaves.

The City's long relationship with Rome had come to an end. Its time as an imperial capital had not.

PART III

OTTOMAN CONSTANTINOPLE

1453–1923

As for the site of the city itself, it seems to have been created by nature to be the capital of the world.

Ogier Ghiselin de Busbecq, *Letters*

Constantinople! Constantinople! . . . It is the empire of the world!

Napoleon Bonaparte

Chapter 17

The Spider's Curtain

Even as the Ottoman forces poured through the battered walls of Constantinople, slaying all who stood in their way, the last citizens of the Roman Empire hoped for a miracle. For the past century, elaborate prophecies had swirled around the City, foretelling the hour when the Turks would finally breach its ancient defenses. The invaders would rush down the Mese, they claimed, in a mad dash to seize the riches of Hagia Sophia. They would never make it. When throngs of marauders entered the Forum of Constantine, passing the great column of the sainted founder, an angel would descend from the skies wielding a fiery sword. With righteous fury, the angel would chase the infidels out of Constantinople, indeed out of the whole Christian empire. In one glorious moment all that had been taken would be mercifully restored. The safest place, then, was the holy sanctuary of Hagia Sophia. Thousands poured into the church and barred its doors.

The prophecies accurately predicted the trajectory of the conquerors, but that is all. No angel made the rendezvous at the forum, no celestial vengeance was exacted that day. Instead, the looters rushed to Hagia Sophia and began battering the great bronze doors of the temple. When they tore them loose from their tired hinges, they were shown the cavernous interior of Justinian's church filled with frightened worshippers still begging God to deliver them. The scene that followed can be well imagined, although it is also described in many accounts. The victors slaughtered the men and the elderly, sparing only attractive women and children for their own sport or to be sold in the slave markets. As the glistening mosaics of Christ, the Virgin, saints, and emperors looked down, the Turks noisily rounded up their pitiful captives, marching and beating them across the marble floor awash in the blood of their loved ones.

Then came the looting. In a city as poor as Constantinople, what riches remained were found largely in the churches—and none had more than Hagia Sophia. Gold and silver vessels, reliquaries, and book covers were smashed or stolen. The story was much the same throughout the fallen city. In accordance with Muslim custom, Sultan Mehmed, who would henceforth be known as Fatih, "the Conqueror," granted his victorious troops three days to sack the city they had captured. For the vanquished, it was three days of horror.

Much was lost. For centuries Constantinople had preserved the writings of Greek antiquity and still had a few libraries holding priceless works. Before the conquest, hundreds of these volumes had been sent to the West. Many ended up in Rome, where they found their way into the Vatican Library. Others went to Venice, where they remain in the Biblioteca Marciana, just off the much-touristed Piazzetta San Marco. Now, in Constantinople, the imperial archives were destroyed, thus erasing the memories of more than a millennium. As a result, modern historians of the Byzantine Empire rely solely on the small amount of contemporary literature that has survived. Beyond a few collections on Mount Athos, not a shred of Byzantium's vast archives outlasted the fall of its state. Artwork not already damaged or carried off by the Crusaders in 1204 also suffered. Islam's prohibition on idols was often interpreted as an imperative to destroy every depiction of the human form. The result in Constantinople was a landscape of mutilation.

The entry of the sultan into his new capital was a moment of enormous importance, so it is not surprising that it formed the basis of many fanciful stories. There is no doubt, however, that Mehmed rode through the streets from the Gate of St. Romanus to Hagia Sophia. It had long been the custom for Muslim victors over Christian cities to visit first the greatest church in order to chant the Muslim prayer "There is no God but Allah. Muhammad is his Prophet." Having thanked God for his victory, Mehmed stood before his people, who acclaimed him the new ruler of the City, the blessed leader that the Prophet himself had foretold would capture the Roman capital. It was a moment of extraordinary triumph, despite the poor condition of the prize. Mehmed believed earnestly that the Ottoman Empire was the natural successor to Rome, and likewise Islam the natural supplanter of Christianity. As New Rome, therefore, Constantinople was the inheritance of the sultans, who walked boldly in the footsteps of the caesars. According to one account, after completing his prayer, Mehmed swore that he would rejoin the younger and elder sisters under his rule. In other words, Rome, too, would soon become a Muslim city.

Various accounts describe Mehmed's survey of his new capital, a city that he had likely not visited previously. Perhaps the most famous describes his reaction to the pitiful ruins of the once-opulent Great Palace. From Hagia Sophia's heights, gazing down on the broken, overgrown landscape that stretched down the hill to the sea, he is said to have chanted the words of the Persian poet Saadi Shirazi:

The spider weaves the curtains in the palace of the Caesars
The owl calls the watches in the towers of Afrasiab

In this desolation and chaos, the Conqueror saw the promise of rebirth. Constantinople, he believed, would rise again to be the envy of the world, led by the Ottoman sultans and enriched by the true faith of Islam. Several stories recount instances of Mehmed disciplining troops who harmed the city's buildings and monuments, ordering them to be content with capturing the moveable goods, but to leave everything else to him. According to one writer, he ordered a tree growing at the base of the Serpent Column in the ruined Hippodrome to be removed lest it harm this ancient monument.

After three days of looting, order was largely restored in Constantinople. There was then the job of cleaning up the bodies. Mehmed was especially eager to identify the corpse of Constantine XI. Rumors among the Greeks claimed that the emperor had survived and would rally his people against the Turks, wresting the City from them. Mountains of the dead had been stacked near the wall breach at the Gate of St. Romanus, so the sultan's men went there to look for Constantine. Although the emperor had cast off his imperial regalia, he was nonetheless identified by the imperial eagles on his purple socks. Yet his head was missing. Zealous soldiers had earlier beheaded the bodies of the infidel defenders, piling the heads up separately nearby. The sultan's men searched through them but were unable to identify Constantine for certain. In the end, they chose a head that seemed close and delivered it along with the body to

Mehmed II. To advertise graphically the end of the old order, Mehmed ordered the head hung from the outstretched arm of Justinian's equestrian statue high above the Augusteion. The message was clear: from this bronze figure that Greeks had believed would save their city from Muslims hung the head of their lord, placed there by their Turkish master. However, the gesture did not have quite the intended response. Several Greeks who had known Constantine insisted that the head hanging from the statue did not belong to him. This, in turn, fanned rumors about the survival of the emperor, and hope for his return.

This hope would sustain the Greek people for centuries; it would even play a part in the formation of the modern Greek state. Based on a group of fortune-telling emblems known as the Oracles of Leo the Wise, many Greeks came to believe that Constantine XI did not die in the conquest, but was, rather, saved by an angel, who transported him to a subterranean cave near the Golden Gate. There the last emperor went into a deep sleep, awaiting the day when the Greeks would have paid fully for their sins. Then the angel would return to Constantinople, awaken Constantine, and bestow on him his sword. What happened next depends greatly on the story and the period in which it was told. In all versions, though, it would be a very bad day for the Turks.

This was only one of hundreds of Greek folk stories concerning the fall of Constantinople and its eventual recovery. Others claimed that the jewel-studded altar of Hagia Sophia had been lifted by angels and deposited in the Bosporus, where it would remain until the church was restored to the Christian faith. One told of a priest singing Mass when the Turks broke into the great church. A shining door miraculously appeared, through which the priest walked, still clutching the consecrated Host. When God returned Constantinople to the Greeks, it was said, the door would reopen and the priest would emerge to finish the Mass. All these tales had at their core an intense belief among the vanquished Greeks that their sins were the ultimate cause of their misfortune, and that God would relent when they had suffered sufficiently under Ottoman subjugation.

Stories and folklore were not simply fireside chatter. They had real effects on the events of the time. This explains why, after graphically proving the mystical impotence of the statue of Justinian, Mehmed II ordered it pulled to the ground. After nine centuries atop its towering column, the magnificent bronze horse and rider shattered onto the stone floor of the Augusteion below. Some of the pieces later made their way to the Ottoman cannon foundries, where they were melted down. The European scholar Pierre Gilles saw a few of them in 1544. He recorded that Justinian's leg was taller than a man, his nose nine inches long, and one of his horse's hoofs nine inches tall. The column itself outlasted Mehmed II, but it, too, was eventually pulled down, around 1520. No trace of it remains today.

Even as the bodies of the slaughtered were carted away and the thousands of captured Christians led to the slave traders, Mehmed turned his attention to repopulating Constantinople. In many ways, Mehmed saw himself as a new Constantine, founding a new capital on the ruins of the old. And it is true that he faced many of the same problems. With enough money, one can build a capital, but how does one fill it with people? Constantine had offered free land and help with housing for the poor, and urged nobles and the wealthy to come to the empire's new center. Mehmed did much the same, although with less success. Although considerable, the sultan's resources could not compare with those of the ancient Roman emperor. Where invitations failed, Mehmed resorted to the use of force. He sent agents across Asia Minor and the Balkans to collect families for relocation—whether they liked it or not. Mehmed was particularly eager to have skilled craftsmen in the city, so his agents made them a priority. Most of those forced to move were Turks but also included thousands of Serbs, Armenians, and Greeks under his rule. Within ten years of the conquest, the Greek population of Constantinople was greater than it had been before it. Jews were also welcome. Many fled to Constantinople after their expulsion from Spain in 1492.

All these groups settled in various ethnic enclaves in Constantinople. As dictated by Muslim law (sharia), non-Muslims were forbidden to have weapons and forced to pay a special head tax. They were also excluded from positions in the government. Other than that, non-Muslims were allowed to live their lives and worship as they chose. Most of the churches in Constantinople were in various states of ruin when Mehmed captured the city. Depending on their location, some were ignored, others converted into local mosques. The mother church of Constantinople, Hagia

Sophia, became the imperial mosque for the Ottoman state. All crosses in the temple were broken, and all images either destroyed or plastered over. The altar and other ecclesiastical architecture were removed, prayer carpets were spread across the rich marble floor, and a mihrab (a niche indicating the direction of Mecca) was placed at the site of the old high altar, slightly shifted so that it would better face the holy city. Mehmed also built a small minaret for the mosque on its southwest corner. Its name, however, remained unchanged: Hagia Sophia. Initially Mehmed relocated the patriarch of Constantinople to the city's second greatest church, Holy Apostles. A few years later, after the Conqueror had moved permanently to his new capital, he thought better of this. Patriarch Gennadius II was evicted from Holy Apostles and given the much more modest Theotokos Pammakaristos (modern-day Fethiye Mosque). Many other churches remained in Christian hands, although all had their bells removed. Only the Muslim call to prayer would henceforth echo across the hills of Constantinople.

Shortly after moving to the city in 1456, Mehmed began several major building projects, something not seen in Constantinople for centuries. Like Constantine, Mehmed gave a great deal of thought to his tomb, which he wanted prominently situated and eternally cherished in the city he was refounding. So much did he wish to imitate Constantine that he chose for his final resting place precisely the same spot. That meant, of course, that Constantine and a host of other Byzantine emperors would have to move. Their bodies were scattered, and their sarcophagi mostly destroyed. Only a few of the most beautiful porphyry tombs were preserved. Today they stand outside the archaeological museum, all that remains of the Church of the Holy Apostles. When the site was at last clear, the new complex, known as a *külliye*, was begun. Like Constantine, Mehmed wanted his resting spot to be the focal point of a bustling area of religious activity. So at the center of the *külliye* he placed his mosque and tomb, known today as Fatih Camii. Over its entrance he inscribed in Arabic the famous hadith of the Prophet CONSTANTINOPLE WILL BE CONQUERED. BLESSED IS THE COMMANDER WHO WILL CONQUER IT, AND BLESSED ARE HIS TROOPS. The mosque was surrounded by a wide square courtyard on all sides, a conscious imitation of the Roman forum, and as such, the first of its kind in Ottoman architecture. On the outskirts of this area were religious schools (*medreses*), a library, hospital, alms kitchen, caravanserai (travelers' inns), a Koran school, and markets. The idea of a mosque as the nucleus of an urban complex was new, but would be imitated often in Constantinople by later Ottoman sultans. As for Mehmed's *külliye*, it was largely destroyed by an earthquake in 1766. All the buildings were subsequently rebuilt on a greatly altered plan.

Mehmed naturally saw to the repair of Constantinople's fortifications, though it was not the priority that one might imagine. The Ottoman Empire's frontier was distant, and those who could reasonably threaten Constantinople few. Naval raids by Western powers were more likely, which is why the maintenance of the seawalls received special attention. The breach in the Theodosian Wall through which Mehmed's forces had entered was never fully repaired. It is all the more surprising, then, that the Conqueror put so many resources into the building of a new fortification complex at the far southern end of the land walls. Yedikule, or Seven Towers, is a self-contained fortress built within the ancient land walls, making use of four of its towers and adding three more to surround them. It is not immediately clear why the sultan would wish to build such a structure so far from the main city. In later years it was used as secure storage, first for treasure and later for people—the Ottoman version of the Tower of London, a prison for nobles and other elites. What is most startling about Yedikule's new towers is that, rather than being built against a solid wall, they perfectly enclose a gate, the Golden Gate. This triumphal entryway had for centuries been attributed mystical properties concerning the conquest of the city. There is no doubt that the Greeks of Mehmed's Constantinople told stories of their resurrected emperor returning through this gate. The Turks often gave much credence to these folk tales. Did Mehmed surround the Golden Gate with towers and garrison them with troops to defend against an emperor reborn? If so, it would not be unlike the walling up of the same gate by Emperor Isaac II in the twelfth century or the sealing of the Golden Gate in Jerusalem by Mehmed's successor, Suleiman the Magnificent. In both cases, rulers sought to forestall prophecies of doom for their reigns.

Mehmed's doleful commentary on the ruined splendor of the Great

Palace was just as appropriate for the Byzantine emperors' other residence, the Palace of Blachernae. It, too, was in a state of advanced decay.
Neither location was fit for an Ottoman sultan. Shortly after the conquest
of the city, the sultan began construction on a new palace, situated at a
high point in the central city found at the northern end of the old Forum of Theodosius, not far from the Aqueduct of Valens and several
ancient fountains. It is possible that Mehmed repurposed a fortress or
palace that stood there at the conquest. There is no doubt, though, that
the new palace was well fortified and included a garden that surrounded
a luxurious residence. It had rooms to accommodate a large number of
slaves as well as the concubines and wives of the ruler. This compound
would remain the sultan's primary dwelling in Constantinople for the
next century or so. After that, it was converted into a home for the
women of the harem. It no longer exists.

Mehmed also began construction on another palace, one that would
serve as the seat of imperial government. For its location he chose one
of the choicest yet strangely overlooked pieces of real estate in the city:
the ancient acropolis. This high area at the tip of the peninsula was the
location of the original Byzantion, and was later sanctified by numerous
pagan temples that for centuries looked out across the busy traffic of
the Bosporus. When Constantine refounded the city, the pagan temples
were still in business. He therefore constructed his Great Palace on the
inconvenient southern slope of old Byzantion, forcing further expan-
sions of the complex to be built in tiers down to the sea. It is not clear
how the acropolis was used during the subsequent centuries of the Middle Ages. The temples were abandoned by the sixth century. Several
monasteries flourished in the area, but much of the acropolis seems to
have remained undeveloped, perhaps for the benefit of the citizens, who
could take in the sights of two continents amid trees and grass.

Mehmed meant his new imperial palace to rival the Byzantine Great
Palace in its heyday. He began by surrounding the grounds with strong
walls that stretched from the seawall along the Golden Horn to the
Bosporus—walls that coincidentally followed those of earliest Byzantion. They cut between Hagia Eirene and Hagia Sophia, where they
were pierced by the large Imperial Gate. Here, too, Mehmed followed
the Byzantine example of the Chalke Gate, placing his own ceremonial

entrance near the city's greatest temple, thus binding secular and religious authority physically together. Within the Imperial Gate was an
expansive outer courtyard. The palace itself was set in the center of the
acropolis. Initially it consisted of one inner court for the Divan, the
sultan's council, and another for audiences with the sultan. Apartments
were also included, as well as the harem. During its first century this
palace was usually referred to as the Sultan's Castle, but it would later
take on the name of the nearby seawall gate, Topkapi Palace. It was but
the seed of a complex that would grow to cover much of the area as the
centuries progressed and the might of the Ottoman Empire grew.

Constantinople took up much of the Conqueror's attention, but it
was only one part of his expansion plans. Although he saw himself as a
successor to the Roman emperors, he was also proud of his reputation as
a *ghazi* warrior, waging jihad to expand Islam. During his reign he added
to his empire the Christian lands of Serbia, the Peloponnese, Trebizond,
Wallachia, Bosnia, Moldavia, and Albania. In a bitter war with Venice,
Mehmed extended the Ottoman Empire to the shores of the Adriatic
Sea and forced the proud maritime republic to accept humiliating losses
and pay heavy tributes. Then, in 1480, Mehmed's forces crossed the
Adriatic and invaded Italy itself. The city of Otranto was quickly captured, creating a beachhead for the coming invasion. It seemed that
Mehmed would make good on his promise to reunite Constantinople
and Rome. The Christians of the West were incapable of defending Italy
against the might of the Ottoman Empire. In Rome the papal curia was
packing up and preparing to flee to France. One can only imagine how
subsequent history would have played out had the Conqueror captured
the last free center of Christianity. But in 1481, just as the invasion was
being prepared, Mehmed died—probably poisoned by his son Bayezid.
The subsequent struggle for the throne sapped all energy for the Italian
campaign. When an army from Naples later arrived at Otranto, the Ottoman garrison abandoned the city and returned home. Rome was saved.

As with Constantine, at the Conqueror's death his grand project at
Constantinople was still incomplete. But the framework of the new Ottoman capital had been developed, and its execution was well under
way. Mehmed's conquests had helped to boost the forced relocations to
the city, expanding its numbers well beyond those in 1453. By 1481

approximately one hundred thousand people lived in Constantinople, restoring it as one of the larger cities in Europe. It still had far to go to rival the megalopolis of Justinian, but a good start had been made.

The return of imperial power to Constantinople brought with it a level of intrigue and treachery not seen since the twelfth century. Mehmed II's grand vizier (prime minister) Karamanli Mehmet Pasha attempted to keep the sultan's death quiet until his younger son, Cem, could travel to Constantinople to secure the throne. The Janissaries, however, favored Mehmed's older son, Bayezid, so they stormed the palace and murdered the vizier. Eventually Bayezid took power in the capital, although Cem seized control of Asia Minor. For the next several weeks a civil war pitted the two halves of the empire against each other. In the end, Bayezid was victorious and Cem was forced to flee to Bodrum, where the Knights Hospitaller, a crusading order, had a castle. They sent him to their base at Rhodes and eventually on to Europe. Cem remained a threat to Bayezid, one that he was willing to pay to have kept out of the way. Pope Innocent VIII took custody of Cem in March 1489 and accepted handsome payments from Bayezid for the upkeep of his half-brother. Those payments included the transfer from Constantinople of the relic of the Holy Lance, believed by Christians for centuries to have been the weapon used to pierce the side of Christ. It remains at the Vatican.

Like his father, Bayezid was determined to leave his mark on the new capital. One of his most disruptive initiatives for the Christians of Constantinople was his widespread annexation of churches. A few were spared, particularly those where Christians could demonstrate previous agreements with the Conqueror. The patriarch, for example, was able to hold on to Pammakaristos in that way. Many of Constantinople's other major churches were seized, however, including Theotokos Chalkoprateia (Acem Ağa Mescidi), the Lips monastery and church (Fenari İsa Camii), St. Savior in Chora (Kariye Camii), the Church of Saints Sergius and Bacchus (Küçük Ayasofya Camii), the Monastery of Stoudios (İmrahor Camii), and Myrelaion (Bodrum Camii). Hagia Eirene, which had been incorporated into the Topkapi Palace grounds, became an armory. As such, it remains the only church in Istanbul never converted into a mosque. Bayezid's drive to evict Christians from their churches would also remain popular with later sultans in the sixteenth century. The patriarchate eventually lost Pammakaristos in 1586 and was moved to the small church of St. George in Phanar (Fener), on the shore of the Golden Horn. By the end of the sixteenth century only three Christian churches remained within the walls of Constantinople.

Bayezid was also a builder. He added a second minaret to Hagia So-phia and continued to expand the Topkapi Palace complex, although he and his family lived in the old palace at the Forum of Theodosius. It was in that great paved expanse of Roman ruins that Bayezid decided to construct his own mosque and tomb. It would be a complex to rival the one just completed by his father. The beautifully elegant mosque and courtyard were augmented with a kitchen for the poor, caravanserai, a public well, *medrese*, and a bath house. Many of the buildings survive, wedged between the busy Ordu Caddesi and the University of Istanbul. It is still called Beyazit Meydani (Square).

Before Bayezid began building in the old forum, one of Constanti-nople's best-known Roman monuments stood there: the relief-covered Column of Theodosius, built on the model of the Column of Marcus Aurelius in Rome. The entire column was pulled down and the pieces used as foundation stones for the new Baths of Bayezid. During the twentieth century, Ordu Caddesi was widened, and the new sidewalk was brought directly adjacent to the closed baths. This revealed many of the broken stones of the ancient column. A careful observer walking along the north side of the street can still notice a variety of Roman soldiers and seaborne warriors staring out amid the stones of the Otto-man building, just as they have done for more than fifteen centuries.

On Monday, September 10, 1509, the rebuilding of Constantinople was dealt a serious blow. One of the most powerful earthquakes ever to rock the city occurred around 10:00 p.m. Modern estimates put it at a 7.4 magnitude quake. The property damage was extreme, although the population of the city was still not dense enough for the quake to claim more than about five thousand lives. A six-meter-high tsunami then slammed into the walls on the Sea of Marmara. Hundreds of houses and mosques were destroyed, and few escaped some damage. One of the minarets of the just-completed mosque of Bayezid collapsed, as did the structure's main dome. Mehmed II's mosque was also badly damaged, losing its roof and several columns. The aftershocks continued for more than a month, bringing down more buildings and rattling more nerves. To the amazement of contemporaries, Hagia Sophia emerged intact. Only its new minarets tumbled down—an event pregnant with meaning for Constantinople's Christians. Justinian's great structure had weathered so many earthquakes over the centuries that its frequent repairs had made it almost immune to their damage. The two minarets were rebuilt several decades later.

By the time of Bayezid's death in 1512, Constantinople's population had grown substantially. It was once again a bustling, cosmopolitan city. Yet with each passing year the capital lost more of its Roman and Christian character, becoming in every way a Turkish imperial center. The ruined Hippodrome still had its two obelisks and the Serpent Column, yet the racecourse had become a grassy area for impromptu games of *jereed*, a favorite among Turkish riders. The great Column of Constantine still towered over the city he founded, but its forum was gone, filled with noisy poultry and slave markets. Even its name was lost, as the Turks called the battered and soot-covered monument Çemberlitas, the "Burnt Column." The Column of Marcian still stood in a small community near the Fatih Mosque, yet its winged victories were identified as maidens and the column itself thought to be a diviner of a woman's virginity. Then as now it was known as Kiztasi, the "Maiden's Stone." In these ways and many others, the Turks were forming Constantinople into something new, something their own. Of course they did this in partnership with the many other ethnic and religious groups who called the city their home, but it was their capital and their empire, so they were the principal architects of this, their inherited city.

Chapter 18

———◆———

City of Suleiman the Magnificent

It is difficult to understand the turbulent environment of Ottoman Constantinople without peering into one of its most iconic institutions, the imperial harem. One thinks immediately of beautiful women, sparkling fountains, perfumed air, and every luxury amid the rich splendor of a sultan's palace. And that image is, in fact, not far from the mark. The ever-changing nature of Constantinople's harems would shape a new age of power and intrigue, one not seen since the middle Byzantine period.

In most historical cases, a fortunate royal dynasty can hope to survive several centuries before a generation fails and it finally dies out. The Ottoman dynasty, on the other hand, ruled for six centuries and never died out. (Indeed, it still exists.) The harem is the reason. Traditionally Ottoman sultans did not marry. Instead, they acquired female slaves, usually from Christian populations, who were chosen for their beauty, health, and strength. These slaves were housed in closed apartments, overseen by a complex organization of women and black eunuchs. This was the harem. By the time of Sultan Selim I (1512–20), the Ottoman rulers had taken up permanent residence in Topkapi Palace. Their harems, however, remained at the Old Palace in the center of the city. When it suited him, a sultan would visit the harem, where he would be presented with a variety of women for his approval, each carefully selected by the chief black eunuch (*kizlar agha*). These would all be virgins with whom the sultan would likely have sex only once, although occasionally a sultan would request someone more often. Should the slave become pregnant, she would instantly rise in the harem hierarchy, receiving more comfortable accommodation and many servants and slaves to see to her needs. When her child was born, he or she would become the sole responsibility of the woman's remaining life. She would never again receive the sexual attentions of the sultan. If the child was a male, the woman became a "favorite," again increasing her status and authority in the harem. She would carefully oversee her son's education, preparing him to rule the empire one day. Years later, when the boy came of age, she would accompany him when he was sent to govern a province in Anatolia, known as a *sanjak*. If all went well, her son would one day become sultan, and she would become the *valide sultan*, or queen mother, the most respected and powerful woman in Constantinople.

It was, of course, difficult to make it that far. Female slave markets were extremely active in Ottoman Constantinople, particularly as the empire expanded into further Christian areas. Catching the eye of the chief black eunuch was no easy task. Many of the harem slaves were not sold in the markets at all, but were sent as gifts by provincial governors eager to win favor with the sultan. Even after making it into the imperial harem, few slave girls were judged worthy of presentation to the sultan. Those who were received a quick education in manners, music, poetry, and, of course, sexual pleasure. The rest became ladies in waiting. These hundreds of rejected virgins were still famed for their beauty, so it was not unusual for a sultan to give them away as gifts or rewards. Even when everything went right for a harem concubine—she was presented to the sultan, he impregnated her, and she bore a son—the danger was still great. Given the nature of the harem, sultans often had many sons ready to take the throne upon their death. The Ottomans had no specific rules of succession. Instead, when the sultan passed away, his surviving adult sons would race from their posts in the provinces to Constantinople to claim the throne. The victor would then, if possible, murder the losers. The mothers of these unfortunates, who naturally supported their sons' cause, were usually executed as well. For the sultan's women, therefore, it was a high-stakes game. From a son's earliest age, his mother would tirelessly work to position him to inherit the throne. Naturally, she would also search for ways to neutralize his competitors.

It was precisely these dynamics that led to the downfall of Sultan Bayezid II. The political maneuvering of his two adult sons, Ahmed and Selim, led to a civil war. In the end it was Selim who emerged victorious. He deposed his father, executed his brother, and seized power in Constantinople. Selim knew firsthand the dangerous treachery that infested the sultan's palace in Constantinople, so he ruthlessly purged anyone suspected of conspiring against him. He routinely executed his grand viziers. Although he was a stern master (winning himself the nickname "the Grim"), he was also an accomplished warrior who led the Ottoman armies with extraordinary skill. His many campaigns culminated in 1517 with the stunning defeat of the Mamluk sultanate of Egypt. In this victory, Selim added to the Ottoman Empire all of Syria, Palestine, Egypt, and much of Arabia, including the holy cities of Mecca and Medina. The Abbasid caliph in Cairo was sent to Constantinople, where he eventually abdicated. Ottoman sultans had for centuries claimed to be the true caliphs of Sunni Islam. Now the last of their rivals had been removed. As a symbol of the new order, the Abbasid caliph gave Selim the sword and mantle of the Prophet. Both remain in Topkapi Palace today.

Selim's victories made Constantinople the ruler of lands that it had lost nearly a thousand years earlier. It was again the capital of a truly enormous empire. Selim busied himself with expanding the army and put enormous effort into building a strong navy. The north shore of the Golden Horn in the area of Kasımpaşa became a vast arsenal for the construction of war vessels. More than a hundred covered docks echoed with the hammers, saws, and shouts of workmen producing the ships the sultan needed to dominate the eastern Mediterranean. But it would not be Selim who would use them. He died unexpectedly in 1520.

Selim's impressive successes were overshadowed by those of his son, Suleiman the Magnificent. Twenty-six years of age, the new sultan came to the throne unopposed, as he had no brothers. He was, according to a Venetian ambassador in Constantinople, "tall, but wiry, and of a delicate complexion. His neck is a little too long, his face thin, and nose aquiline." Suleiman was known to be scholarly, having excelled in all his subjects at the palace school. He was also goodhearted, cheerful, and honorable. Suleiman would continue his great-grandfather's drive westward with unprecedented success. Under Suleiman, the Ottoman Empire would enter its golden age, and Constantinople would be transformed.

Within a year of taking the throne, Suleiman led his forces against Belgrade, capturing it in August 1521. He then turned his attention to the Knights of St. John Hospitaller, who had been a problem for the

Ottomans since the beginning of the dynasty. In recent years, the crusading order had been attacking Ottoman shipping, raiding Turkish army camps, and allying with other Christian powers to wage war on the empire. Unlike all the other Catholic powers, the Knights were based in the East, at their fortified headquarters on the island of Rhodes. Previous Ottoman attempts to oust them had failed. In 1522, Suleiman led an army of one hundred thousand men to the region. They set to work on the construction of a castle and naval base directly opposite the island. After a difficult five-month siege, the Knights finally capitulated. Suleiman was so impressed by their resolve that he allowed the crusading order to march out of its fortress with its banners flying, saluted by his own victorious troops. The Knights boarded their vessels and headed west, where they established a new base on the island of Malta.

Suleiman also headed West, leading armies there many times larger than Mehmed II had done. At the Battle of Mohács in August 1526, the Ottomans defeated King Louis II of Hungary, capturing his entire kingdom. Across Europe, people braced for the final blow from the unstoppable Turks. It seemed to come in 1529, when Suleiman and his armies invaded Austria and laid siege to its capital, Vienna. Torrential rains, though, forced Suleiman to leave behind much of his heavy artillery, which proved to be decisive. In his first defeat, the sultan was forced to withdraw, failing to capture Austria. He tried a second time in 1532, but once again the weather delayed his progress and doomed the siege. It was a critical event in European history. Had Suleiman captured Vienna, as it seemed he would, Germany and Italy would have been at his mercy. Even in his failure, though, Suleiman dramatically changed the history of Europe. Emperor Charles V of the Holy Roman Empire was unable to burn Martin Luther at the stake because he needed the support of Protestant princes to defend against Suleiman's invasion. Without the Ottoman threat, the Protestant Reformation might never have happened. Since Protestants were opposed to Crusades, Suleiman was very much in favor of Protestants—he even offered to protect Luther in Constantinople should he require it.

After consolidating his conquest of southeastern Europe, Suleiman turned toward the Persians in the East. They would remain his enemies throughout his more than four decades of rule. In 1534 he triumphantly entered Baghdad, the traditional seat of the Abbasid caliphate. Over the next few decades Ottoman armies extended the empire to include Mesopotamia (modern Iraq), including important ports on the Persian Gulf. Suleiman's navy was active there, in the Red Sea, and in the Indian Ocean, where they attacked the new Portuguese shipping they found there. Under the brilliant naval commander Khair ad Din (known as Barbarossa for his red beard), Suleiman later pressed into the western Mediterranean and established control over all of North Africa. By the end of Suleiman's reign, Constantinople ruled an empire larger than it had even during the height of Byzantine power under Justinian.

In truth, it is difficult not to compare Suleiman with Justinian. Both were successful empire builders, bringing a new prosperity to their state. Both were lawgivers, overseeing the codification of their respective legal systems. And both transformed the city of Constantinople. As with Justinian, it is impossible to do justice in so short a space to the many building projects undertaken during Suleiman's long reign, but we can explore some of his most profound marks on the evolving cityscape.

Suleiman built Constantinople into a showplace just as Justinian had done, yet his approach was very different. The Romans, like the Greeks before them, conceived of the urban environment as a reflection of their civilization. It was a place for citizens to live, flourish, and interact with the state. It was also a space that celebrated their cultural and political achievements, be it in the Hippodrome, the baths, or the forums. The Turks had no such concept. Traditionally, Muslim city-dwellers differentiated themselves from rural farmers and nomads, but they did not see themselves in a direct relationship with the city or its rulers. Sultans, therefore, did not beautify the streets or adorn open areas of their capital with colonnades and artwork. They did not build streets at all. The notion of city planning was alien to them. Ottoman Constantinople's only straight road was Divan Yolu—the ancient Mese, which was itself the end of the Roman Via Egnatia. Everything else was a snarl of dirt backways and a few cobbled wider streets that snaked through the city. It was up to the locals to work out the roadways, although occasionally the government would knock down homes that were in the way. Building a Hippodrome, theater, or arena for the people would never have entered the head of a sultan. Roman citizens had gone to the games not just for enjoyment, but to participate in a civic ritual in which they expressed solidarity with one another and interacted with their emperor. Ottoman Constantinople had nothing like that. The beautifully detailed engraving, executed in 1533 by Pieter Coecke van Aelst, of Suleiman the Magnificent and his attendants riding through the Hippodrome is instructive (Illustration 13). There is no road, simply an open dirt area at the center of the city. The two obelisks and Serpent Column are visible, but all that is left of the magnificent chariot arena are the overgrown columns of the sphendone and a few other ruins. There are a few onlookers, but many are facing the other direction, busying themselves with their own activities.

This is not to say that sixteenth-century Constantinople was devoid of ceremonies, only that the citizens played no role in them. Grand processions, for example, took place on major religious festivals and smaller ones every Friday, when the sultan would go to the mosque to pray. People often watched these processions to see the finery and with the hope of catching a glimpse of the sultan. They would, of course, shout blessings to the ruler. Similarly, sultans would occasionally parade through part of the city after a victory, and many would turn out to see the spectacle. But this was not a Byzantine procession, where it was the duty of the citizen to attend and call out the ritual acclamations. The city's residents were not participants in the ceremonies, but merely onlookers.

Building projects in Ottoman Constantinople were of two sorts. The first were those structures necessary for the practical functioning of the city and empire. Suleiman greatly expanded the naval arsenal in the Golden Horn to meet the needs of a far-flung Ottoman navy. He ordered the expansion and repair of the Roman aqueduct system that brought the city's water from many miles to the north. Janissary barracks were expanded in the city, as was Topkapi Palace, to meet the needs of the growing imperial government. All these projects were undertaken for practical reasons, although often with impressive artistic results.

The second sort of construction was that undertaken for the benefit of the soul and memory of the benefactor. It was, in other words, about a person, not a community. We have seen this dynamic already in the building of the complexes of Mehmed II and Bayezid II. In both cases an enclosed space was provided with a great mosque, open courtyard, tomb of the benefactor, and various buildings for the public welfare. These *külliyes* were not simply monuments to the sultan (although they were that), but, most important, they were an extravagant donation, a giving of alms—which is one of the five pillars of Islam. The more one has, the more one is required to give. A sultan had a great deal, so his complex was a conscious declaration of his fidelity to Islam and his hope for eternal reward. The structures making it up were not conceived as a means to beautify Constantinople, but instead were understood as comprising a small city unto itself, separate from other *külliyes* and the greater city. With a few exceptions, the various mosques and secondary buildings of the sultans are today largely obscured by the heavily built-up urban environment of Istanbul. Yet, in the sixteenth century, Constantinople still had large open areas marked with small villages. Even in the urban core, the houses were predominantly wooden two-story structures, many with gardens that sheltered fruit trees. In such a city, the new mosques built by sultans and other leading figures dominated.

Suleiman the Magnificent had a good architect, the best that the Ottoman Empire ever produced. Mimar Sinan, the chief architect and head of the Department of Imperial Architects, would serve Suleiman, his son, and his grandson. In that time, he was credited with designing and building nearly five hundred structures in Constantinople and elsewhere. Even given a nearly five-decade-long career, that seems excessive. In truth, he had a large organization at his disposal and was given credit for all its work. Sinan personally designed and oversaw the construction of the great mosques of the sultans as well as many other buildings in the capital. He is universally credited with ushering in the Ottoman classical style of architecture.

Sinan came from humble beginnings. A child of Greek Christians in Cappadocia, he was taken by the imperial government and raised in the Janissary corps. Like all Janissaries, he was well educated, but he showed a particular aptitude for engineering. He served in many of Suleiman's campaigns before he came to the sultan's notice by building a sturdy bridge to convey the armies across a troublesome river. Suleiman sent him back to Constantinople, where he began designing much larger structures. His style was dominated above all by a simple practicality in the service of elegant stability and soaring beauty.

Sinan's first major project was the Şehzade *külliye*. This was probably

begun in 1539, as the *külliye* of Sultan Suleiman. It was placed prominently on the top of Constantinople's Third Hill, just east of the Aqueduct of Valens, on the site of the ancient Nymphaeum. However, in
1543, one of Suleiman's sons, Mehmed, died unexpectedly at the age of
twenty-two. The sultan was grief-stricken, spending forty days at Mehmed's temporary tomb mourning and weeping. It was then that he appears to have decided to give this *külliye*, still under construction, to the
beloved prince (*şehzade*). Considering the procreational habits of the
sultans, it is little wonder that this is the only example of a *külliye* for an
uncrowned sultan's son. It speaks forcefully of the love Suleiman had for
this young man. The Şehzade Mosque was built with a large central
dome surrounded by four half-domes and flanked by two galleries. Outside, there was a *medrese*, hospice, alms kitchen, elementary school, and
tomb within a large open courtyard. Given the size of the mosque, the
complex is somewhat underbuilt, suggesting that it may have been completed quickly to focus resources on the sultan's own *külliye*.

Having ceded to Prince Mehmed the best remaining location in the
city, Suleiman was left with limited options for his own final resting place.
Nevertheless, the sultan wanted his complex to make a powerful mark on
the city's profile. He therefore gave to Sinan the garden of the Old Palace,
perched near the top of the Third Hill. To the north and east of this
plot, the terrain sloped quickly down to the wharfs of the Golden Horn.
It was, therefore, a difficult place on which to build—not unlike what
Byzantine engineers had encountered a thousand years earlier, when constructing the Great Palace. Sinan expanded the area for the mosque and
courtyard with heavy retaining walls, literally cutting a flat surface out of
the fabric of the terrain, and still the other buildings of the complex had
to be situated on terraces at different levels from the mosque.

To honor so great a sultan and exceed the achievement of Şehzade,
Sinan turned to the techniques used by Justinian's architects in Hagia
Sophia. There was a certain justice to this, for both rulers were renowned lawgivers, thus evoking Solomon in the building of their greatest temples. And it is clear in Sinan's writings that the challenge of Hagia
Sophia wore heavily on him. The Ottomans had conquered Constantinople, but the achievement of its greatest church stood undefeated. Europeans, of course, often pointed this out as an example of the superiority

of Christianity. For Sinan, it was Hagia Sophia's dome that drove him. He was determined to construct a mosque that could support a central dome that was larger and higher. This was no small task. Hagia Sophia's dome has a diameter of 102 feet and rests at a height of 182 feet, 5 inches.

Like Hagia Sophia, the Süleymaniye Mosque was built with a central dome flanked by two semidomes and two arches filled with windows. Like Justinian's architects, Sinan ordered massive marble columns and other marble blocks taken from Roman ruins (in this case, ancient Nicomedia) for the new structure. It was a major undertaking, employing thousands of free workers and slaves for eight years. The result was an architectural masterpiece, utilizing new techniques such as the concealment of buttressing into inner and outer walls and the construction of a colonnaded courtyard of exquisite beauty. Unlike the blocky exterior of Hagia Sophia, the Süleymaniye Mosque flows symmetrically in a majestic cascade (Illustration 14). Yet despite Sinan's best efforts, Justinian's central dome remained larger. The Süleymaniye dome is 90 feet in diameter and 174 feet high—about 12 feet smaller and 8 feet shorter than Hagia Sophia's.

The multilayered *külliye* of Süleymaniye was the largest yet seen in Constantinople and would serve as the ideal model henceforth. It consisted of four *medreses*, schools specializing in the study of hadith, a medical school, a hospital, an alms kitchen, a hospice, a public bath, stables, an elementary school, and, of course, the sultan's tomb. This last was itself an innovative reworking of Emperor Diocletian's tomb in Spoleto. Octagonal and surrounded by a columned arcade, it was beautifully decorated with tiles and windows. Taken as a whole, the Süleymaniye *külliye* was a triumph worthy of so accomplished a ruler.

Suleiman and Justinian had something else in common. Both men defied social conventions by marrying women of low social status—women who would acquire unprecedented power in Constantinople. The story of Justinian and Theodora had its echo in sixteenth-century Constantinople with Suleiman and Roxolana. Born in western Ukraine around 1505, Roxolana (a nickname; her real name remains unknown) was the daughter of an Orthodox priest from Poland. At around the age of fifteen she was captured in one of the many slave raids into the region by the Crimean Tatars. She and thousands more such unfortunates were marched to Caffa (modern-day Feodosia), the largest slave market on the Black Sea. There she was purchased by a trader and sent to Constantinople, where she was put on sale at the Avret Pazari, in the central Aksaray district. This large female slave market did a brisk business. Virtually all the slaves were cap, tured virgins. When placed on the block, they were stripped naked and strung together by ropes so that they could be inspected by potential buy, ers. According to tradition, Suleiman's best friend, Ibrahim, caught sight of Roxolana and decided to purchase her as a gift. This was probably in late 1520, shortly after Suleiman had come to the throne.

In the harem, Roxolana was given the name Hurrem, meaning "the laughing/joyful one." She came quickly to the sultan's attention, perhaps recommended by Ibrahim himself. Suleiman was captivated by her. Even after having sex with her several times, he continued to go to the harem and ask only for her. In 1521 she bore him a son, Mehmed. This was, of course, very good news for her. Many of the other harem women were also pleased, since it would mean that the sultan's attentions could be di, rected elsewhere. The custom of one woman, one son was a long and venerable one for the Ottomans. From another concubine, Suleiman al, ready had one son, Mustafa, born in 1515. His mother, Mahidevran Sul, tan, was by virtue of that birth a *kadin*, or "favorite." She therefore enjoyed authority, wealth, and prestige over all others in the harem—with the exception of the valide sultan, or "queen mother," Ayse Hafsa Sultan. She now shared that position with Hurrem, her new rival.

Suleiman ignored the custom. Even after the birth of Mehmed, he continued to visit the harem to spend time with Hurrem. He was com, pletely in love with her, as his many poems attest.

> My intimate companion, my one and all, sovereign of beauties,
>   my sultan,
> My life, the gift I own, my be-all, my elixir of Paradise, my Eden,
> My spring, my joy, my glittering day, my exquisite one who
>   smiles on and on.

The following year, Hurrem bore two additional children, a daughter, Mihrimah, and a son, Abdullah. No slave concubine had ever before borne a sultan more than one son. Tensions in the harem continued to rise, particularly between Hurrem and the older Mahidevran, as Suleiman continued to have affections only for his Roxolana. In 1524 she gave birth to yet another son, Selim, and then another, Bayezid, in 1525. Her last son, Cihangir, was born in 1531.

While Ayse Hafsa Sultan was alive, she was able to impose peace on the harem. But Hurrem's many children and the extraordinary favor that Suleiman showed her was an enormous strain. Mahidevran, whose son, Mustafa, was a bright young man in his teens, naturally dreaded each announcement of another son born to Hurrem. When the valide sultan died in 1534, the harem exploded in strife. Mahidevran made clear to Hurrem that she was now the mistress of the harem, for she had been with Suleiman first and was the mother of his firstborn son. Hurrem strongly disagreed. Harsh words flew, and soon a fight broke out. Screaming that Hurrem was "used meat," Mahidevran beat her rival severely and roughly scratched her face. When Suleiman next visited the harem and summoned Hurrem, he received instead a message saying that she was unworthy of the sultan's attentions for she was ugly and used, just as Mahidevran had said. It was a clever move, calculated to stir up anger in the ruler's heart. Suleiman summoned Mahidevran at once and asked if it was true that she had insulted and hurt Hurrem. Mahidevran proudly admitted it, claiming that Hurrem deserved far worse. Since Mustafa was nineteen years old, Suleiman removed the problem by sending the young man and Mahidevran to govern a province in Anatolia.

With Mahidevran out of the way, Hurrem had no rivals in Constantinople. Indeed, it appears that Suleiman had for some time been in a monogamous relationship with her, leaving the several hundred women of the harem with no hope of attracting the sultan. It was time to make it official. Stunning the people of Constantinople, a public announcement was made of the marriage of Suleiman and Hurrem Sultan. Not only did Roxolana become the legal sultana, but unlike everyone else in the Ottoman court, she was now no longer a slave. Nothing like this had happened since the dawn of the dynasty. As a wife, Hurrem was given a fabulously rich allowance, luxurious apartments, and a hundred servants. She was also, and had been for some time, Suleiman's closest confidante and most trusted adviser. It seemed there was nothing that he would not grant her. In 1536, for example, the Old Palace, which housed the harem, was badly damaged by fire. Rather than repair it, Hurrem convinced Suleiman to move the entire harem to his own palace at Topkapi. One can see readily why Suleiman would want to share a roof (albeit a very large one) with his wife. The relocation of the harem to the center of power would in time transform it into a political incubator, where intrigue and ambition bubbled along with the perfumed fountains. This marked the beginning of the Ottoman Empire's "Sultanate of Women," a period in which the harem exercised nearly complete control over the state.

It appears that Hurrem's new position brought her into conflict with the man who had initially purchased her, Ibrahim Pasha, now Suleiman's grand vizier. Some tensions were probably inevitable. For many years, Ibrahim Pasha had been the sultan's right hand. A Greek from Epirus, Ibrahim was taken from his parents, enslaved, and raised as a Janissary. By all accounts he was exceedingly good-looking, affable, and intelligent. He was given to the young Suleiman as a page, and the two became firm friends. Three years after Suleiman came to the throne, he appointed Ibrahim grand vizier. Given the history of that position under Suleiman's father, Ibrahim half-joked that he would accept it only if the sultan would be good enough to tell him when it was time to be executed. Suleiman laughed heartily, promising that he would never execute his good friend. For many years Constantinople and the empire flourished under Ibrahim Pasha's supervision. He was solely responsible for all foreign relations, which were pursued at his offices, known by Europeans as the Sublime Porte, a term that later came to mean the entire Ottoman government in Constantinople. After more than a decade of service, Ibrahim Pasha was the second-wealthiest man in the city. He built a beautiful palace on the ruins of the Hippodrome's northwestern stands. (It is today the Museum of Turkish and Islamic Arts.) He was also responsible for constructing, at his own expense, many mosques, alms kitchens, and other charitable institutions.

With the exception of a few disagreements and misunderstandings, Ibrahim Pasha's relationship with the sultan had remained very good. It is all the more surprising, then, that on the evening of March 15, 1536, while staying at Topkapi, he was murdered and buried in an unmarked grave. All his property was confiscated by the state. It is impossible to know precisely the reason for his fall, but it is hard not to see the hand of Hurrem in it. As the sultan's sons entered manhood, they naturally began to jostle against one another, watchful for the day when they would need to move quickly to gain power and avoid execution. Friends in high places could help with that. Ibrahim Pasha had for some time favored Suleiman's eldest son, Mustafa. Such a succession would be a calamity for Hurrem. Not only would her four sons be killed, but she could expect much the same when the hated Mahidevran returned to Constantinople as valide sultan.

The death of a grand vizier was hardly unusual in Ottoman Constantinople, but the secret murder of one who had enjoyed the sultan's confidence for so long was deeply troubling. Across the city there was more than a little grumbling about the bizarre goings-on at Topkapi. How had this one woman managed to ensnare Suleiman the Magnificent, win her freedom, and eliminate all her rivals? An Italian observer, Luigi Bassano, reported that "the Janissaries and the entire court hate her, and her children as well, but because the Grand Turk [Suleiman] loves her very much, no one dares to speak. Still, I have heard them speak badly of her and her children, and well of the first-born [Mustafa] and his mother [Mahidevran]." Many suspected that Hurrem employed love charms and incantations to enslave the sultan. According to Bassano, the people commonly called her *ziadi*, "witch."

Charms or not, there was no denying that Hurrem Sultan had unprecedented power for a woman. Although wealthy Ottoman women often endowed charitable organizations, they never did so in the capital. Hurrem did. Sinan built for her a complex placed, appropriately enough, next to the women's slave market at Aksaray. It consisted of a mosque, *medrese*, alms kitchen, elementary school, hospital, and fountain. He later built for her the famous Hurrem Sultan Baths, very near Hagia Sophia. Because of its location at the center of the tourist trade, the place has been restored and today offers traditional baths amid Ottoman luxury.

Hurrem Sultan's unpopularity among the military and the people of Constantinople translated likewise into a dislike for her sons, who were thought to be under her control. Little wonder, then, that Suleiman's oldest son, Mustafa, remained the favored successor among most people—but not in the palace. Hurrem positioned her eldest son, Mehmed, well, keep, ing him close at hand should anything happen to her husband. It was prob, ably at her suggestion that, in 1541, Suleiman transferred Mustafa from the nearby province of Manisa to the remote Eastern province of Amasia, making way for Hurrem's son to be close to the capital. That strategy collapsed, however, in 1543, when Mehmed died. Suleiman's extraordi, nary grief and his dedication of the Şehzade *külliye* in the heart of Constan, tinople speak clearly of the sultan's attachment to the firstborn of his beloved wife. It is hard not to believe that Suleiman favored Mehmed to succeed him.

Hurrem still had three sons (Abdullah had died as a child). Selim and Bayezid were in their late teens, with no experience in the prov, inces, and Cihangir, who was twelve, had developed a physical defor, mity, probably a hunched back. Support for Mustafa was so widespread that it was difficult to see how Hurrem's offspring might ever win the throne. The Janissaries and the army so strongly favored Mustafa that any sultan other than Suleiman might have worried that he himself would be toppled, just as Suleiman's father had done to his grandfather. Undeterred, Hurrem, in 1544, managed to convince Suleiman to ap, point Rustem Pasha as grand vizier. Kidnapped as a child in Bosnia, Rustem had served the court over many years and appears to have worked well with Hurrem. She had married her eldest daughter, Mih, rimah, to him in 1539, making him the son,in,law of the sultan. Rustem Pasha was widely seen as a pawn of the sultana. Together the two did their best to promote Bayezid and Selim, who were eventually given their own provincial governorships. Bayezid, in fact, was given the much, coveted Manisa, very close to Constantinople.

For the next ten years the uneasy situation between Suleiman's sons continued to fester. According to Europeans reporting the word on the street in Constantinople, it was rumored that Hurrem Sultan and Rustem Pasha had presented a forged letter to Suleiman exposing a con, spiracy against him by Mustafa in league with the sultan's greatest en, emy, the Shah of Persia. Whether this was true or not, something convinced Suleiman that Mustafa was a danger to him—one that had to be neutralized before it resulted in civil war. In 1552, while Suleiman was campaigning in Persia, Rustem Pasha informed him that, in his absence, the Janissaries were urging Mustafa to seize Constantinople, which would welcome him with open arms. Suleiman returned to the empire the following year, and ordered Mustafa to meet him in the Ereğli valley to give an answer to these reports. When Mustafa entered the sultan's tent, he was attacked by a group of eunuchs, who wrestled him to the ground. According to one report that claimed to be from an eyewitness, the eunuchs had difficulty subduing Mustafa. Suleiman, who was seated behind a curtain, became impatient and peeked out, scowling menacingly at the eunuchs to complete their task quickly. At last they wrapped a bowstring around the prince's neck and strangled him.

The people of Anatolia, who had come to know Mustafa well, were outraged. Some areas even revolted. The army and Janissaries were also angry—so angry, in fact, that Suleiman found it necessary to pay them a large settlement and to dismiss Rustem Pasha to appease them. Mustafa received a dignified state burial. His body was sent to Constantinople, where thousands of mourners wept over it in Hagia Sophia. It was then sent to Bursa, where it was laid to rest in a grand tomb. Suleiman's youngest son, Cihangir, was so upset about his father's part in his brother's death that he perished a few months later, either from grief or by his own hand. That left only Bayezid and Selim, who quickly squared off against each other. Unlike Mustafa, both of them were quite willing to overthrow their father if given an opportunity. It was only Hurrem Sultan who kept them in check.

In Constantinople, disgust for the situation in the palace was everywhere. European visitors often described the outrage aimed directly at Hurrem Sultan and the emotional chains with which she had enslaved her lord. It did not help matters that shortly after Suleiman returned to Hurrem, he reinstated Rustem Pasha as grand vizier. Despite the family strife, the empire continued to flourish and Constantinople continued to grow. By the 1550s there were as many as half a million people living in the greater metropolitan area, including the Asian Bosporus shore, with perhaps three hundred thousand in the walled city. Sinan's office was kept very busy as money poured in for more and more building projects. One of these was the splendid mosque of Rustem Pasha, built near the shore of the Golden Horn, down the hill and to the northeast of Süleymaniye. Its interior and colonnaded courtyard are lavishly decorated with blue İznik tiles. It is a testament to the wealth that a grand vizier, even one deeply hated by the people, could command.

In April 1558, Hurrem Sultan fell ill and died. She was in her early fifties. Suleiman was inconsolable, having lost his dearest love and clos-est friend. Together they had defied the conventions of their age. With-out her, the joy and laughter that had enriched his life were gone, replaced by grasping sons and troublesome courtiers. Sinan was given the task of constructing a mausoleum for the great lady, which was placed directly beside that of Suleiman in his *külliye*. It remains there still. It is richly embellished within by colorful İznik tiles that depict the delights of paradise—an obvious commemoration of the joys Hurrem gave to the sultan. She was the first woman in the Ottoman Empire ever to be hon-ored in this way: buried with a state ceremony in a sultan's *külliye*, before even the sultan himself.

Suleiman's crushing grief only added to his many woes. He was now in his sixties, and his health was not good. He had always had difficulty with gout, but that was now accompanied by painful arthritis and a leg sore that would not heal. Without their mother to restrain them, Bayezid and Selim began positioning themselves against each other and their father. Suleiman ordered them both to be relocated farther from Constantino-ple, probably for his own safety. Selim he sent to Konya, while Bayezid was to go to Mustafa's old province, Amasya. Suspecting that he would meet the same fate as his unhappy half-brother, Bayezid refused to go. Instead, he assembled forces to defeat Selim and thereby leave his father no choice as to an heir. Suleiman sent armies to Konya to assist Selim, who defeated Bayezid in 1559. Bayezid and his four sons then fled to Per-sia, where the shah was glad to receive this threat to his enemy. After several years of negotiation, Suleiman finally convinced the shah, in ex-change for an enormous sum of gold, to allow one Ottoman executioner to enter Bayezid's apartments to strangle him and his sons. After so much struggle and murder, Suleiman had only one son left, Selim.

Suleiman the Magnificent lived another seven joyless years. He died, appropriately enough, while on a campaign to Hungary. Under his rule, the Ottoman Empire had reached its greatest extent and posed a serious danger to what was left of the Christian world. The Constantinople of Suleiman was also a changed place, filled with new constructions of rare beauty that only a wealthy and powerful empire could afford. Much of that transformed city can still be seen in the magnificent panorama drawing of Melchior Lorck, produced from the northern shore of the Golden Horn during the Danish artist's time in Constantinople near the end of Suleiman's reign. From this stunning view, one can still see just beyond the bustling harbor the elegant *külliyes* floating on the city's hills, above houses and greater buildings all speckled with rich orchards. It portrays Constantinople at the height of its Ottoman period. Like the majestic city of Justinian, it is a place that has largely passed away.

Chapter 19

———◆———

The Sultanate of Women

Suleiman the Magnificent was the last of his kind among Ottoman sultans. Since the beginning of the dynasty, it had been the glory of the Turkish rulers to lead their warriors in battle, expanding their empire and, as pious *ghazis*, crushing the infidels. No longer. Although Suleiman had died while on campaign, he had been cutting back his absences from Constantinople with each passing year. And as long as the sultan remained in the capital, Topkapi Palace grew. The inner palace, the home of the sultan, his harem, and his personal pages and servants, expanded dramatically in the sixteenth and seventeenth centuries. Its lush gardens and luxurious apartments were already legendary. The "third courtyard," entered through the Gate of Felicity, became an earthly paradise of every delight—a fitting home for a sultan with no desire to leave his beloved Constantinople.

It suited Suleiman's son Selim II well. After taking the throne, Selim arrived at Topkapi with his concubines and children and settled in. For the most part, he left the governance of the Ottoman Empire to the grand vizier Sokollu Mehmed Pasha, who had served Suleiman in that capacity during the last year of his life. Selim was forty-two when he arrived and had plenty of experience in provincial government as well as on the battlefield. He gave all that up to devote himself full time to hunting, artistic patronage, and the pleasures of the harem. He also liked to drink. Indeed, he quickly earned the nickname "the Sot."

Selim was the first sultan since the conquest of Constantinople not to begin construction on a *külliye* in the capital. For reasons that are still not clear, he ordered Mimar Sinan to build one in Edirne (ancient Adrianople), the Ottoman Empire's former capital. Selim often visited Edirne, where the forests offered excellent hunting, but that does not adequately explain his decision. Perhaps he was simply uninterested in the construction of a *külliye*, which was chiefly a pious act. He certainly had no intention of being buried there. Instead, he ordered Sinan first to spruce up Hagia Sophia and then to design a suitable mausoleum for him next to that ancient church/mosque. Sinan obeyed. The chief architect added further buttressing to Justinian's structure and two additional minarets, bringing the total to four—the number reserved for imperial mosques. Sinan then tore down the last portions of the old Patriarchal Palace complex and constructed Selim's tomb there. It remains a magnificent structure, covered completely in marble and decorated with İznik tiles, gold, and beautiful calligraphy.

The new sultan may have co-opted Hagia Sophia as his burial mosque, but Sinan was still obsessed with besting its dome. According to his autobiography, Sinan finally succeeded in his quest with the construction of Selimiye Mosque in Edirne. As the architect himself put it, the Şehzade Mosque was his apprenticeship, the Süleymaniye Mosque his journeyman piece, and the Selimiye Mosque his masterpiece. That judgment has stood the test of time. The Selimiye Mosque is widely considered the greatest architectural achievement of the Ottoman Empire. It is a structure dominated by its dome, covering nearly half the mosque's total space. The dome's enormous weight is supported by an elegant octagonal column structure that wraps fluidly around the central prayer area. Light pours in from the dome and the hundreds of windows in archways and lower domes. It is an awe-inspiring structure, focused resolutely in its perfect symmetry on the proud display of its mighty dome. According to his biographer, Sinan boasted:

> Those who consider themselves architects among Christians say that in the realm of Islam no dome can equal that of Hagia Sophia. They claim that no Muslim architect would ever be able to build so large a dome. In this mosque, with the help of God and the support of Sultan Selim Khan, I erected a dome six cubits higher and four cubits wider than the dome of Hagia Sophia.

That is not quite true. Thanks to fifteen centuries of repairs and restorations, Hagia Sophia's dome is slightly oval. Its center diameter is about 102 feet across, precisely the diameter of the Selimiye dome. Sinan matched it but did not surpass it. The height of Justinian's dome is considerably greater than Sinan's. From the floor to the center of Hagia Sophia's dome is 182 feet, 5 inches. At Selimiye, the dome's height is 162 feet, 6 inches—almost 20 feet lower. To have raised his dome higher, Sinan would have had to increase the size and supporting framework of his structure substantially. The Selimiye Mosque beautifully presents the viewer with its stunning dome, which overwhelms the entire structure. Hagia Sophia's dome, by contrast, is dwarfed by the monumental nature of the church itself. The dome covers only 15 percent of the church's vast square footage. As a much smaller construction with a similar dome, Selimiye's had to be lower.

With the sultan preoccupied with the pleasures of the palace, power shifted to his grand vizier, Sokollu, and the valide sultan. Since Selim's mother, Hurrem, was dead, the honored position was taken up by his sister, Mihrimah. Her mother's daughter, Mihrimah exercised a great deal of authority in the palace, and thereby the empire. Her wealth was legendary. She built not one but two mosques in Constantinople, both designed by Sinan. One, Mihrimah Sultan Camii, was constructed at the crest of the Sixth Hill, near the Edirne Gate (Edirnekapı) of the Theodosian Walls. It is one of the highest points in the city, making it visible from great distances. The basic design was not innovative—a cube surrounding four columns supporting a single dome—but Sinan experimented with the use of light in this mosque: the entire structure is pierced by hundreds of windows, making it the brightest of all Sinan's mosques. Mihrimah's other mosque, often called Iskele, was constructed across the Bosporus, in Scutari, which the Turks called Üsküdar. It is a much larger structure, with flanking semidomes and two minarets.

As befitting someone focused on the pleasures of his capital, Selim did not engage in the sort of territorial expansion that characterized the tenures of his father and grandfather. He did, however, send a major Ottoman force to Cyprus to wrest it from the Republic of Venice. The fortified city of Famagusta held out for almost a year, hoping for a rescue from a war fleet that was forming at Crete. It never came. The Turkish commander at Cyprus, Lala Mustafa Pasha, negotiated an honorable surrender with the Venetian leader, Marcantonio Bragadin, not unlike the one arranged with the Knights of St. John by Suleiman. But things did not go the same way in this case. Mustafa became convinced that Bragadin was conspiring with the leaders of the relief force. After the Venetians surrendered, Mustafa ordered the massacre of most of the inhabitants of the city and the brutal torture of Bragadin, who died of his wounds. Back in Constantinople, Selim was delighted to receive not only the news of Cyprus's conquest, but also the heads of the Venetian commanders and the skin of Bragadin, which had been stripped off him while he was still alive and crying out his prayers to Jesus Christ. The skin was stuffed with straw.

News of the passion and death of Bragadin horrified and enraged Westerners. Pope Pius V had earlier called a Crusade against the Ottomans, and the events at Cyprus only intensified the urgency. More than two hundred major war vessels converged at Crete, ready to avenge the martyred Bragadin. The Crusaders aboard were from a variety of Mediterranean lands, but all their vessels flew the standard of the Crucifixion. For the moment at least, national animosities were forgotten. Catholics across Europe had been praying the Rosary for the success of the Crusade for nearly two years. The Crusaders did the same, begging God to give them victory through the intercession of the Virgin Mary. The Crusade fleet set sail and quickly encountered a Turkish armada of about equal size off Lepanto, in Greece, on October 7, 1571. What followed was one of the most famous naval engagements in history. The Christian forces were commanded by the young and charismatic Don John, the illegitimate son of Emperor Charles V. The Ottoman fleet was led by the grand admiral Sufi Ali Pasha. The Battle of Lepanto lasted about five hours, and in the end produced an amazing victory for the Christians. The Ottomans lost 113 vessels, the Christians only 12. The Crusaders captured 117 Turkish vessels, freed 15,000 Christian galley slaves, and looted an enormous haul of riches from the Pasha's ship. In one engagement, the Turks had lost the bulk of their navy. The Battle of Lepanto had an electrifying effect on Europe. It was the first time that a major attack against the Ottomans had succeeded. Church bells pealed across the West, even in Protestant countries, where Crusades were forbidden. The victory is still celebrated by the Catholic Church on October 7, the Feast of Our Lady of the Rosary.

Yet Lepanto had little lasting impact on the Ottoman Empire. The naval workshops of Constantinople were so efficient that within one year the city had completely replaced the lost fleet. It was not the naval defeat that spelled trouble for the Turks, but rather the products of those busy workshops. An unprecedented scientific revolution was taking hold in parts of Europe, particularly in France and England. Yet the vessels that fought on both sides in the Battle of Lepanto were hardly state of the art. Cannons played only a minor role in the battle, since most of the rowed galleys could not carry them. Instead, the real action took place with handguns or close-quarters fighting between galley crews. This type of warfare was not much different from that practiced in medieval naval engagements. By contrast, the warships produced in France and England were massive galleons with long rows of heavy cannons belowdecks. These powerful vessels did not engage enemies directly, but fired devastating broadsides, destroying them from afar. Constantinople lacked the expertise to produce this kind of vessel.

The growth of the sultan's palace and the unwillingness of Selim II to campaign in the field had the effect of binding Ottoman rulers much more closely to the capital. The warlords of the past had been supplanted by the pleasure-seekers of sixteenth- and seventeenth-century Constantinople. Selim accelerated this trend by declaring an end to the practice of murdering one's brothers upon taking the throne. Hoping to save his sons, he added to the Topkapi complex a large number of luxurious but highly secure apartments, known as *kafes* (cages), which were attached to the main harem and separated by a locked door called the Genie's Gate. Boys continued to be raised in the harem by their mothers, but now, when a prince reached the age of adulthood he, his mother, and a small harem of around twenty sterile women would be moved to one of the *kafes*, where they would remain indefinitely. Only Selim's eldest son, Murad, was sent to an Anatolian province to acquire the skills of governing. The intention was not only to save the lives of the princes, but also to reduce the threat to Selim. A sultan who remained shut up in the palace was deeply unpopular among the Janissaries, who relied on conquests for booty and slaves. Keeping possible coup leaders under lock and key in Constantinople was an effective way to minimize the threat.

In that, it was successful. But it did nothing to save the lives of the princes. When Murad III succeeded Selim in 1574, his first action was to order the strangulation of his five brothers. Nevertheless, Murad liked the *kafes* system so much that he improved on it. None of his sons was sent to the provinces. All remained in the lavish prison of Topkapi Palace. Like his father, Murad was hated by the Janissaries—so much so that he rarely left the palace grounds for fear that they would kill him. Part of the problem was his unwillingness to lead the armies. Also there was a general disgust at the hedonism of a royal family that had allowed the women of the harem to take over. Murad was greatly influenced by his mother, Valide Sultan Nurbanu, and his favorite slave/concubine, Safiye. The latter had borne Murad a son, Mehmed. Safiye controlled Murad so completely that he, like Suleiman before him, stopped visiting the harem, preferring to spend his time exclusively with her. Fearful for the Ottoman dynasty, Nurbanu had words with her son, insisting that he use the harem to its fullest to produce more male heirs and introducing new virgins to him regularly. He dutifully impregnated many of them. Over the twenty years of Murad's reign, he fathered more than twenty sons and even more daughters. All the sons who made it to adulthood went to the *kafes*.

The Sultanate of Women was good for the women in charge and, one assumes, pleasurable for the sultans. It was bad for the Ottoman Empire, for it almost guaranteed a low quality of ruler. With no experience outside the palace, sultans were raised by their mothers to be addicted to pleasure and utterly dependent on them. To become the valide sultan was nearly as good as becoming the sultan himself. These women naturally clashed with other advisers, such as the grand vizier, chief black eunuch, and chief white eunuch, who was the managing officer of the palace. It was widely known, even among foreign diplomats, that to get something done in Constantinople, one must go first to the sultan's mother.

Safiye became the valide sultan in 1595, when Murad died and her son, Mehmed III, assumed the throne. She kept Mehmed close to the palace complex that he knew so well. His first action, surely condoned if not suggested by Safiye, was to strangle his many half-brothers. Safiye's hold on Mehmed was so strong that she would occasionally sit behind a curtain or screen during his meetings with the Divan and principal advisers. When she had something to say, she did not hesitate to do so, interrupting the conversation and even overruling the sultan. The Janissaries and army seethed over this intrusion of a woman into the affairs of men. Although Mehmed won some support by success, fully leading the Ottoman armies against the Habsburgs at Eger in 1596, it evaporated with every word from his mother's lips.

Equally upsetting was Safiye's decision to construct her own mosque in the old Venetian Quarter, a commercial district along the shore of the Golden Horn, where the Galata Bridge today connects to the old city. To make way for this high-profile structure, wharfs were destroyed and a whole Jewish quarter relocated. The cost was, of course, enor, mous. Earlier mosque complexes in Constantinople had been funded by the spoils of a rapidly expanding empire. But those days were over. Safiye's mosque had to be paid for with regular treasury funds, which meant budget cuts for the civil and religious bureaus and for the mili, tary. This made enemies. When Mehmed III died unexpectedly at the age of thirty-seven, his thirteen-year-old son, Ahmed I, decided to rid himself of the liability. He sent Safiye to live in the Old Palace and or, dered construction on her mosque halted. Half-finished and in an in, creasing state of decay, the ruined project stood as a monument to its namesake's ambition and overreach. More than half a century later, in 1660, it was rescued by another valide sultan, Turhan, the mother of Mehmed IV, who paid to have it finished and provided for its financial upkeep by including in the complex the famous Egyptian Spice Bazaar. It is today known as Yeni Camii (New Mosque).

Having ceased operations on his grandmother's mosque, Sultan Ahmed I ordered the construction of his own shortly after he came of age. A deeply religious young man, Ahmed wanted to build a *külliye* in Constantinople that would rival all others. Yet he faced much the same problems as Safiye. Pouring money into a magnificent structure when the empire was stalled and the economy declining would not be popu, lar. Rather than fulfill his role as *ghazi* warrior against the infidel, in 1606 he signed a treaty with the Habsburg Empire that recognized the equality of the Austrian emperor with him and abolished the annual tribute the Habsburgs owed to Constantinople. The young man's dreams and the reality of his state were clearly at odds.

Ahmed spent some time searching for a suitable location for his *külliye*. His essential problem was that after a century and a half of building, all the prime locations in Constantinople had been taken. The steady rise of the population in the sixteenth century meant that the walled city was already well built up, although most of the buildings remained wooden. In a bold move, Ahmed decided to place his mosque complex at the Hippodrome (called Atmeydani by the Turks) on the site of the upper portions of the old Byzantine Great Palace. Because it had been terraced with subterranean vaulting by the Romans, the area there was reasonably flat, although certainly constrained. It was also occupied by a number of mansions of Constantinople's wealthy. These were systematically dismantled and the materials reused in the construction. Many of these stone blocks had originally come from the ruins of the Hippodrome and the Great Palace, so this was at least their second reuse. To these were added all the remaining stone blocks of the Hippodrome that were not supporting the landscape. Sultan Ahmed's mosque's courtyard was paved with the seats from the stands of the nearby racecourse. At its structural core, the Sultanahmet Mosque is a reorganization of materials that had been in the neighborhood for more than a thousand years.

Another problem with the site was its close proximity to Hagia Sophia, which would naturally invite comparisons between Ahmed's mosque and the great church of Justinian. Sinan had died back in 1588, but one of his students, Mehmed Ağa, took up the project. Unlike his teacher, Mehmed Ağa was not preoccupied with Hagia Sophia's dome. Instead, his main objective seems to have been to build a structure with sufficient architectural weight so that it would compare well from the outside with its much older neighbor. In that he was reasonably successful. The building is a conscious, and not altogether successful, attempt to mimic the triumphs of both Sinan and Justinian. The symmetrical design of the square mosque clearly derives from Sinan's Şehzade Mosque, while its dome and semidomes are in stark imitation of Hagia Sophia. Inside, the wide-open prayer area is bathed in the light of hundreds of windows and is beautifully decorated by the rich blues of its İznik tiles—thus earning it its common name in the West, the Blue Mosque. The interior, however, lacks the elegance of the structures it sought to emulate. The four enormous piers that hold up the central dome (sometimes referred to as "elephant feet") jarringly break up the smoothness of the composition, leading to the impression that it is a group of parts rather than a composite whole. Hagia Sophia's dome, by contrast, is not only much larger and higher than that of Sultanahmet, but its supports are ingeniously hidden, leading to the impression that, as Procopius long ago observed, the dome is suspended by a chain from Heaven. The Sultanahmet Mosque is beautiful, but its modern fame rests more on its location in the core of the tourist district than on its architectural achievement.

In addition to the mosque, the Sultanahmet *külliye* has a large court-yard stretching out toward Hagia Sophia, several schools, a hospital, an alms kitchen, a market, a bath, and the sultan's tomb. As an imperial mosque, it was surrounded by four minarets, but Ahmed ordered an additional two minarets to flank the corners of the courtyard, bringing the total to six—more than any other in Constantinople. This was widely interpreted as an act of arrogance, for it elevated his mosque higher than those of the Lawgiver (Suleiman) and the Conqueror (Mehmed II), and set it as the equal of the Great Mosque in Mecca. To deflect the charge of impiety at least, Ahmed ordered the construction of a seventh minaret in Mecca.

The remainder of the seventeenth century in Constantinople wit-nessed a government battered by a maelstrom of treachery, intrigue, and hedonism that rivaled even the worst days of the Byzantine Empire. Ahmed broke with tradition by allowing his mentally disturbed brother, Mustafa, to live under guard at the Old Palace. He also abandoned the principle of one son for one concubine. Although he enjoyed the many hundreds of women in his harem, Ahmed had children with only two. Mahfiruz Sultan first bore him four sons. Then, after her death, Ahmed became transfixed by Kösem Sultan, a Greek famed for her beauty, who bore him four sons as well. When Ahmed died at the age of twenty-seven, his eldest son, the child of Mahfiruz, was the thirteen-year-old

Osman. In a nest of dark intrigue impossible to penetrate, though, the Divan passed over Osman and offered the throne to Mustafa, who remained tucked away in the *kafes*. It is likely that Kösem, who had a great deal of pull in the council, was instrumental in this decision, since it edged out a child who was not her own. This was the first time that succession had gone to a brother, thus further complicating the increasingly arcane nature of royal power in Constantinople.

Mustafa's mental problems made him unfit to rule. After three months of erratic behavior, a palace faction managed to send him back to the *kafes* and replace him with his younger brother, now Osman II. Although young, Osman was well educated and seemed to have clear ideas about reforming the Ottoman Empire. A student of history, he correctly discerned that the Janissary corps had become the equivalent of Rome's Praetorian Guard, an elite military institution that exercised too much authority over the ruler. Numbering some 15,000 men, the Janissaries had a huge barracks complex in the center of the city, between the Aksaray and Fatih districts. It consisted of 368 dormitories, 130 garden pavilions, 60 meeting halls, 90 rooms for study or exercise, 158 stables, and numerous other smaller buildings clustered around a central courtyard. Their initial mission had been the protection of the sultan, but that was later expanded when the corps accompanied the conquering rulers on their campaigns. With the end of those wars, the Janissaries had taken up permanent residency in Constantinople, ostensibly protecting the people, but in reality often preying on them.

To undercut their position, Osman needed the support and approval of the regular armies, who were unhappy with the recent goings-on at Topkapi Palace. Osman decided to strengthen his position with them by taking on the role of the *ghazi*. He announced that he would lead the armies of Islam against the Christians in Poland (what is today part of Ukraine). The resulting campaign in 1621 was a disaster for the Ottomans. Nearly forty thousand men were killed. Rather than finding glory, Osman returned to Constantinople in shame. He blamed the defeat on the poor quality of the military, especially the Janissaries. He made plans to dramatically overhaul both institutions. He also announced that on the occasion of the one-thousandth anniversary of the Hegira,

Muhammad's flight from Mecca to Medina, he would be the first Ottoman sultan to make the hadj. Along the way, he planned to meet with
military leaders and begin recruiting a new Anatolian corps to replace
or eject the Janissaries in Constantinople. It never happened. To forestall his reforms, the Janissaries led an armed rebellion that captured
Osman and later strangled him. They had indeed become the Praetorian Guard.

The Janissaries capitalized on their victory by reforming their order.
Throughout their history, this slave army had been recruited through the
seizure of male infants from Christian populations. After murdering Osman, however, they declared themselves virtually free men. Henceforth,
they would have the right to marry, have children, and live outside the
barracks. Because of their connections to the corps, they could purchase
businesses and bully their competition, becoming rich in the process.
They later demanded that their sons succeed them as Janissaries. These
young men were eager to acquire the prestige and power of the corps, but
they received none of the training. As a result, over the course of the seventeenth century, the number of Janissaries in Constantinople exploded,
growing to well over fifty thousand. Naturally, their effectiveness on the
battlefield sharply declined. They became a high-status specialized force
designed only to protect their own interests in Constantinople. The Janissaries who had frightened generations of Christians had become merely
an armed political party in the capital.

Back at Topkapi, the deranged Mustafa was given another turn on
the throne. He liked it as little as those he ruled, yearning to go back to
the relative safety of the *kafes*. In the meantime, the empire descended
into turmoil. Military uprisings in Anatolia were mirrored in Constantinople by undisciplined Janissaries who treated the city as if it were
their own. To restore order, Mustafa was sent back to the Old Palace,
and the eleven-year-old Murad IV was elevated to the throne. His
mother, Valide Sultan Kösem, who had been a player in this chaos for
years, became the official regent—the first time in Ottoman history
that a woman took this position. She administered the empire and met
with the Divan, albeit always from behind a curtain.

Murad IV grew to be a physically powerful man with a cruel streak
and a talent for campaigning—something not seen in Constantinople for

more than century. He ordered the executions of several of his brothers in the *kafes*, much to the dismay of Kösem. Many officials were also killed, and many more frightened into doing his will without question. In keeping with Islamic restrictions, he declared new, draconian laws for Constantinople that forbade under penalty of death all consumption of alcohol, coffee, and tobacco. Since all three of these were popular in the cosmopolitan city, that meant a great deal of unrest and many executions. Some of these Murad saw to himself, for he would patrol the streets looking for transgressors. Oddly, Murad was himself a great lover of wine. One report has it that he died at the age of twenty-seven due to liver failure. Before then, however, he successfully defended the empire's eastern border and quelled the rebellions that had threatened Constantinople.

The only male adult in the dynasty of Osman left alive in 1640 was Murad's younger brother Ibrahim. Raised in the *kafes*, Ibrahim had managed to escape the executioner, but only just barely. While on his deathbed, Murad had given the order for his brother's strangulation, but Kösem managed to delay it until the sultan passed away. When the grand vizier and Ibrahim's mother came to him to inform him that he was the new sultan, he refused to believe it, thinking it a test of loyalty by his cruel brother. Only when they allowed him to inspect the dead sultan would he finally accept the throne.

Ibrahim's duty, Kösem informed him, was to busy himself in the harem so that the dynasty would not die out. This he did, although not always without difficulties. Ibrahim had health problems, which included severe headaches and some psychological problems. He had a fetish for furs, insisting that the harem and his apartments be filled with them. According to one source, he once became so angry with the women in his harem that he ordered them all sewn into sacks and thrown into the Bosporus. While Ibrahim rearranged the harem, Kösem tried to manage the empire, although she had competition from other officials. She was unable to stop Ibrahim from declaring war on Venice in an attempt to capture the island of Crete. That war would drag on for nearly a quarter century and cost the empire dearly. The Venetians responded by bringing their warships to the Dardanelles (Hellespont) and cutting off shipping to Constantinople. Food prices soared, and unrest in the city rose to extraordinary levels. Realizing that a coup was imminent, Kösem joined it, consenting to the arrest and execution of Ibrahim in favor of one of her grandsons, Mehmed IV. He would reign for the next four decades, completely under the control of his mother, his viziers, and the Janissaries.

Although the Venetian blockade affected the people of Constantinople, the machinations of the ruling classes generally did not. Constantinople's population had continued to grow throughout the sixteenth and seventeenth centuries. Modern estimates put it at around seven hundred thousand people. Roughly 40 percent were non-Muslims, mostly Greek Orthodox, but also many Armenian Christians and Jews. The non-Muslims were required to pay the head tax, but otherwise were usually free to live their lives as they chose. It was not unusual to find very wealthy Greeks and Jews with posh palaces in the city. Most of the real money was to be made in the Ottoman government, and Christians and Jews also found their way into those positions. Jews dominated the medical profession and often did very well serving the Turkish aristocracy. Greeks were active in commercial shipping, fishing, and the tavern trade. Non-Muslims in Constantinople generally lived along the shores of the Golden Horn and the Sea of Marmara as well as in Galata, across the harbor. There were some Italian communities in Constantinople, but they were not large. The days when Italian merchants dominated Constantinople were long past. All commerce had been declining steadily in the capital since the Portuguese established trading colonies in India. As Europeans spread out on a global scale in the seventeenth century, Constantinople was no longer at the center of the world. Like Venice, it had been left behind by the new and much more lucrative East Indies and Atlantic trade.

Muslim citizens of Constantinople had a higher status, but they were at all economic levels. Many lived in ramshackle wooden structures, while others lived in rich masonry houses. Only Muslims could own slaves—and there were many of those. Some twenty thousand or more slaves were sold in Constantinople's markets every year in the sixteenth and seventeenth centuries. We have seen the women's market in Aksaray, where virgins were paraded naked before potential buyers. Not all the women were purchased solely for sexual pleasure, though; many were slated for housekeeping duties—although most would end up doing both jobs. The male slaves were purchased for their strength or skill; many were tailors, carpenters, or cobblers. Since it was forbidden to enslave a Muslim, virtually all the slaves were Christians, captured in raids across the Mediterranean and Central Europe. Black slaves from Africa were rare and always eunuchs, purchased for duty in a harem.

Muslim men were allowed by law four wives, although in practice only the wealthy could afford that many. An average Muslim man in Constantinople would have one or two wives, and several concubines who doubled as housekeepers. Wealthy men, of course, would have multiple houses and hundreds of slaves. Muslim women in Constantinople were kept strictly confined to their homes. On the crowded streets, one would generally see only non-Muslim women. When a Muslim woman was forced to travel, such as to the baths or a wedding, she was covered from head to foot or shielded all around by heavy curtains carried by slaves. Although Muslim women largely controlled Constantinople during this period, they were nonetheless forbidden to have anything to do with the world outside their home. Even there they were segregated from the males of the household. A wife, who would have a separate apartment for herself, her children, and her slaves, would entertain her husband but would not share the same living space with him.

Aside from the *külliye* of the elites, major mosques, and mansions of the wealthy, the rest of Constantinople was built in wood. That meant fires—and there were many in the sixteenth and seventeenth centuries. Most began in the dense markets or warehouses at the wharfs. Depending on the winds, these fires could be devastating, leveling whole sections of the city. The fire of 1633, for example, destroyed nearly one-third of the houses in the city. In 1660 a massive blaze that skirted the shores of the city on all sides leveled 120 palaces and mansions, 40 baths, 360 mosques, and numerous churches, warehouses, shops, and homes. It killed approximately 4,000 people. The government decreed several times that new constructions had to be in brick or masonry, but with little effect. Wood was cheap and readily available. It was the job of the Janissaries to fight the fires, but they were also often their cause. Frequently a Janissary rebellion would begin with a fire, or occasionally the Janissaries would simply burn down the properties of their enemies and loot the charred ruins. With each new fire, the map of the city was re-formed, for new wooden buildings went up quickly, creating new winding dirt streets to snake their way among them.

Constantinople in the seventeenth century had much in common with its former self in the seventh century. In both cases the imperial capital faced down a changing world, gloriously beautifying itself while its empire gradually declined. For the Byzantine emperors, it was the rise of Islam that threatened their ancient city. For the sultans, it was the disturbing rumors of modernity amid the improbable rise of the West.

Chapter 20

———◆———

Return of the West

In 1717 the Byzantine emperor Constantine XI returned to Constantinople.

He had been expected for some time. After the conquest of the city
in 1453, a story circulated among the surviving Greeks that at the moment the Turks breached the walls, their beloved leader was lifted up
by angels and deposited in a subterranean cave near the Golden Gate.
There he was placed in a deep sleep and turned to stone. The report
seemed to be well confirmed by a collection of medieval prophetic
drawings, known as the Oracles of Leo the Wise. Oracle 13 depicts a
sleeping man bound from head to foot in bandages and attended by
angels. Since the conquered Greeks believed that they had lost Constantinople as punishment for their sins, they were certain they would
one day have it returned, when they had paid sufficiently for their iniq-
uities. On that blessed day, God would awaken Constantine, restore to
him his sword, and open the Golden Gate. Then, after a great deal of
bloodshed, the Turks would scatter and the Byzantine Empire would be
reborn.

The story of the "petrified emperor" was immensely popular, with
many permutations. Yet, in all of them, the Turks were on the losing
side. Since the Turks were just as superstitious as their Greek neighbors
in Constantinople, they took the prophecy seriously. Mehmed II had
surrounded the walled-up Golden Gate with additional walls and towers, making up the Fortress of the Seven Towers (Yedikule), perhaps as
a defense against an emperor reborn. Travelers to Constantinople in
subsequent centuries were regularly told the story of the sleeping
avenger. The Englishman Peter Mundy, for example, reported in the
early seventeenth century that "there is a Prophecy among the turcks
that it [Constantinople] shall bee lost againe by the said gate."

Mundy's contemporary Sir Thomas Roe had direct experience with this prophecy. A special envoy of the English Crown, Roe was in Constantinople in 1626 to conduct business for his government and for various English noblemen. By the sixteenth century, European science had invaded the study of history. Wealthy Europeans were eager to obtain relics of antiquity for their growing collections, and a great many of those artifacts could be found in the Ottoman Empire. Fortunately, the Turks did not value the objects for their historical worth and were therefore more than willing to sell them. The museums of the world are filled with the product of that trade. During his time in Constantinople, Thomas Roe was acting on behalf of the Earl of Arundel and the Duke of Buckingham in an attempt to acquire the life-size stone reliefs of the labors of Hercules still affixed to the entryway of Constantinople's Golden Gate. After bribing the necessary officials, he finally made the sale. On a pleasant day in May, he rode out to Yedikule with the great treasurer of the Ottoman Empire and the surveyor of the city walls. The Turkish officials told Roe to wait for them at a nearby dock. They would then go to the Golden Gate, have the reliefs removed, and transport them back so that they could be loaded aboard a vessel bound for England.

When the surveyor and treasurer ordered workmen to remove the ancient sculptures, the governor of Yedikule refused to allow it. Word quickly spread among the local population that an infidel from the West was tampering with the Golden Gate. Hundreds, perhaps thousands, of people rushed to the area. From the distance of the port, Roe could see and hear an angry mob gathering, yelling and pushing against the guards; they seemed on the verge of killing the officials. When the treasurer finally returned to the dock, he brought no ancient sculptures, but he was visibly upset. He demanded to know if Roe had an "old booke of prophesy" that told of the mystical power of the Golden Gate. When the bewildered Englishman protested that he did not, the treasurer accused him of knowing "that those statues were enchanted, and that we knew, when they should be taken downe so great an alteration should befall this citty. He spake of a vault underground, that I understand not; which . . . filled them with superstition and suspition of me." At last Roe was able to convince the treasurer that he truly had no idea what he was talking about. Nonetheless, the treasurer ordered Roe never again to speak or even to think about the Golden Gate, lest it cost both their lives. When the envoy returned to his lodging that night, he wrote to the earl and duke, informing them that the reliefs would not be coming to England. Indeed, they "are like to stand, till they fall with tyme." "And it is true," he continued, "although I could not get the stones, yet I almost raised an insurrection in that part of the citty." Roe was quite right about the ancient reliefs. They were never preserved, and are today lost.

The strong determination on the part of the Turks in Constantino‑ ple to forestall the return of the Byzantine Empire had not waned when the emperor returned in 1717. It was in that year that an Egyptian mummy was transported through Constantinople on its way to Europe. The mummy had been purchased a few years earlier by King Louis XIV of France, who wished to make a present of it to King Charles XII of Sweden. Charles, who had lived in Constantinople for a short time, had a passion for antiquities. The ancient corpse traveled across the eastern Mediterranean and arrived at Constantinople, where it would begin the last leg of its long journey west. At Edirnekapı (Edirne Gate), Ottoman officials stopped the mummy's transporters and insisted on inspecting the crate in which it was packed. After prying open the ornate sarcoph‑ agus, they discovered to their astonishment an ancient, seemingly petri‑ fied man bound in bandages from head to foot. The same suspicion that scuttled Roe's attempt to take the reliefs from the Golden Gate led these inspectors to conclude that they had before them the body of the last Christian emperor. Obviously, these infidels were attempting to spirit it out of Constantinople so that the ruler could be revived. They confiscated the mummy and sent it to Yedikule—back to Golden Gate from whence it must have come. When the mummy arrived, the Turks appear to have treated it with the respect due to a conquered Christian leader. First, he was decapitated. Then, to make doubly certain that he would not restore his empire, the mummy was cut in two at the torso. The three parts were then carefully placed back into the sarcophagus and locked into one of the towers.

This Turkish response to Greek superstitions sheds stark light on the dramatically different perspectives that were emerging between Constantinople and the West. Back in the twelfth century, an envoy from the king of France wrote to his master advising him to launch an immediate attack on the city because "it is written on the Golden Gate, which has not been opened for the past two hundred years, 'When comes a blonde king from the West, I will open myself to him.'" By the eighteenth century, however, Europe had undergone such extraordinary changes that the whole concept of magic was considered unscientifically absurd. When word of the Egyptian mummy's arrest in 1717 spread among Constantinople's European expatriates, it elicited a chorus of chortles and shaking heads. Lady Mary Wortley Montagu, the wife of the English ambassador to the Sublime Porte, wrote:

> The Turks fancied it the body of God knows who; and that the state of the [Ottoman] Empire depended on the conservation of it. Some old prophecies were remembered on this occasion, and the mummy was committed to the Seven Towers.

Yet the mummy's career was not yet over. A little more than eighty years later, it remained a prisoner at Yedikule. At that time, it shared its prison with François Pouqueville, a French doctor incarcerated because France had invaded Egypt. Pouqueville made friends with his jailors, who would often allow him to roam the grounds. One day he managed to get into the mummy's tower and discovered there the decorated sarcophagus. When he opened the lid, he found the would-be conqueror still resting there in three pieces. Pouqueville relieved the mummy of its head, squir-reling it away under his cloak. He knew that the Turks considered the corpse to be a threat to the Ottoman Empire, although he was uninter-ested in the details. For Pouqueville, it was nothing more than a merry joke. As he wrote in his memoirs, by taking the mummy's head, "I have broken the charm, and accelerated the downfall of a great empire."

It was this sharp division between Eastern and Western attitudes and perceptions that would drive much of the remainder of Constantinople's history. In the modern world, we tend to think of history as a straight line of technological and cultural progress. When someone is accused of "turning back the clock," it is never a compliment. Yet this sort of linear development is in truth a unique product of the post-sixteenth-century West. It is by no means humanity's norm. The whole world would at one point or another have to come to terms with the unprecedented advances occurring in western Europe. Constantinople, which stood as the mem, brane of East and West, would be shaken to its core. The seventeenth century had seen European technology soar, fueled by the printing press, banking, and vessels that could circumnavigate the planet. The eigh, teenth century brought the Enlightenment, with its strict focus on a secular reason devoid of or even hostile to religion. As Europeans stretched their reach across the globe, the economies of Europe skyrock, eted, dwarfing all others. Their cities and populations boomed. Western Europe left behind the Middle Ages and was building the modern world.

For Muslims, and especially the Turks, this was difficult to accept. For centuries they had known almost nothing about western Europe, save that it was filled with infidels. They did not bother to learn about its people or kingdoms, referring to all of it as Frangistan, the "land of the Franks." More important, Europe was the Abode of War, where good Muslims must go to expand the Abode of Islam and subjugate the infi, dels. The Ottoman Empire had been built on these mainstream Muslim ideas. As time went on, however, those concepts no longer fit reality. Su, leiman's sieges of Vienna were the last serious opportunities to expand Islam into the heart of the West. After that, the rapid changes in Eu, rope, coupled with imperial dysfunction in Constantinople, led to the rise of the former and the decline of the latter. We have seen how in 1606 the Ottomans were forced to make a treaty with the Holy Roman emperor that recognized him as an equal to the sultan. In an attempt to reverse the trends of the previous century, grand viziers from the Köprülü family later prepared and then launched a bold attack on Vi, enna in 1683. It failed badly, and when the Austrians counterattacked, they managed to capture areas of Hungary, Greece, and the Black Sea coast. In 1699 the sultan was forced to accept the peace treaty of Karlo, witz. For the Turks it ushered in a new, most uncomfortable era. It was the first time that the Ottoman Empire concluded an agreement with a victorious infidel; the first time that lands in the Abode of Islam were returned to the Abode of War. History was marching backward.

It might not have been so disastrous had the Ottomans kept up with the military advances of the West. Mehmed II had been willing to hire Europeans to make the cannons with which he pounded the walls of Con, stantinople. During the next several decades, Ottoman forces adopted handguns, muskets, and more advanced cannons. They copied new galley designs from Venice, although these were already behind the vessels of the Atlantic powers. By the eighteenth century, Ottoman naval ships and local privateers from North Africa were capable of piracy but not sustained warfare against the Europeans. Attempts to implement long-range artillery and other innovations in weaponry were suppressed by the Janissaries, who saw the rise of the new technologies and their trained specialists as a threat to their traditional position and power.

The same was true with the single most important device of early modern Europe, the printing press. In the West, it revolutionized religion, culture, economics, and politics. In Constantinople it was banned. Near the end of the fifteenth century, Jews from Spain petitioned the sultan to open a printing press in the capital. The religious authorities ruled that it was sacrilege to render Arabic in print, although they were willing to allow the printing of Greek, Hebrew, and Armenian. Religious concerns aside, the powerful scribal and calligraphy guilds in Constantinople were determined in their opposition to the press. As a result, literacy remained an attribute of the wealthy, and new ideas moved slowly in seventeenth-century Constantinople.

The capital's medieval guilds were also behind rulings that forbade any modernization to the production of goods. This came at a particularly bad time. The Turkish economy was based on silver coinage, which was experiencing serious debasement as a result of the flood of New World silver pouring into Europe. The export market for Turkish goods quickly dried up, while Europeans began purchasing their raw materials at bargain prices. These were then turned into finished goods in Europe's nascent Industrial Revolution and sold back to the Turks, thereby undercutting local production. The result was a relentless drain on wealth and resources, sapping the already strained Ottoman economy. What was needed was a new economic policy that focused on entrepreneurism backed by new banking mechanisms. Yet commercial activity was heavily restricted in the Muslim world, and left largely to the infidels. The government in Constantinople lacked the tools and the know-how to reverse the situation. The sultans simply expanded the government, spending more on lavish palaces and rich stipends for officials and Janissaries. Just as Constantinople had once safeguarded antiquity amid the waves of the Middle Ages, it now preserved the medieval in the face of the modern.

The streets, houses, and city services of seventeenth-century Constantinople had not changed much since the fifteenth century. Sewage was still dumped into the street or thrown into the sea. Streets at night were lit only by the moon. Packs of wild dogs roamed the darkened backways, preying on the unwary. There were no fire codes or brigades (save the Janissaries, who often set the fires). Constantinople had not changed, but the Europeans who visited the city had changed a great deal. Their expectations for urban environments were now starkly different. One can see it readily enough in the countless travelers' accounts that complain of the filthiness of Constantinople's streets, the stench of its waters, and the ignorance of its people. Back in the thirteenth century the French knight Robert of Clari rhapsodized on the marvels of Constantinople. In the seventeenth century, Westerners still admitted of the beauty of the city when seen from a distance—but were much less impressed once they entered it. In 1610 the English traveler George Sandys wrote of Constantinople, "I think there is not in the world any object that promiseth so much afar off; and entered, that so deceiveth the expectation." His countryman William Lithgow agreed, poetically describing the city as:

A painted Whoore, the maske of deadly sin,
Sweet faire without, and stinking foule within.

Nothing had changed by the nineteenth century, when the American author Mark Twain reported:

Seen from the anchorage or from a mile or so up the Bosporus [Constantinople] is by far the handsomest city we have seen. . . . But its attractiveness begins and ends with its picturesqueness. From the time one starts ashore till he gets back again he execrates it. . . . A street in Constantinople is a picture one ought to see once—not oftener.

The people of Constantinople noticed the change in the Europeans, of course. The wide-eyed gawkers and groveling petitioners of the medieval past had been transformed into haughty visitors with as many sneers as complaints. Perhaps the grossest example of Europeans behaving badly was the vandalism of the Serpent Column of Delphi in 1700. This extraordinary bronze artifact, forged by the ancient Greeks from the armor of the defeated Persian armies, had been on public display for more than 2,100 years. Placed by Constantine at the center of the Hippodrome, it was later repurposed as a fountain, with water gushing forth from the mouths of its three intertwined snakes. Despite the ruinous condition of the Hippodrome, the Ottomans had carefully preserved the bronze column, for they believed it to be a talisman keeping poisonous snakes from entering Constantinople. Nevertheless, the practice of Ottoman soldiers playing *jereed* in the area posed a danger both to people and to monuments. At some point in the mid-sixteenth century, one of the bronze serpent heads lost a lower jaw. Then, during the seventeenth century, a whole head was knocked off. (It is today on display in the Istanbul Archaeological Museums.) The final destruction of the Serpent Column occurred on the night of October 20–21, 1700, in an event that speaks volumes about the changing relationship between the Ottoman Empire and Christian Europe.

Several months before, a delegation from Poland led by Stanislaus Lesinski arrived in Constantinople to exchange ratifications with the sultan for the humiliating Peace of Karlowitz. During his formal entry into the city on April 18, Lesinski was accompanied by a train of six hundred Austrian soldiers. Each of them wore the mail armor of a fallen Turkish warrior from the siege of Vienna in 1683. Many of the Turkish men forced to greet this display of bad taste recognized the armor as belonging to their lost friends. As one French observer noted, they responded only by whispering, "See, see these proud infidels." Lesinski and his entourage were treated by the Porte with every courtesy and lodged in the splendid palace of Ibrahim Pasha, at the Hippodrome. They immediately treated it and the wide-open area outside as their private playground. Indeed, on one occasion a European resident of Constantinople who had converted to Islam came to the palace to attend one of the nightly parties. Lesinski ordered him decapitated and thrown out into the Hippodrome. The Turks quietly buried him, just as they cleaned up the debris from the evening bacchanalias that spread across the area. After months of this behavior, the peace treaty was at last signed. In mid-October Lesinski departed. His entourage, however, still had one last day of pleasure in the palace. That night, locals reported hearing a loud noise "as if a powerful man were chopping down trees." In the morning, the top half of the Serpent Column was missing, leaving only the stump that survives today. Not wishing to anger the delegation, no accusations were made. What happened to the top half of the monument is still a mystery. Perhaps it is packed away somewhere in Ukraine or Austria, but it has never come to light.

Despite these difficulties, Constantinople, more than any other Muslim city, was in a position to learn from and exploit the successes of the West. After all, it was a European city. And it remained the most cosmopolitan city in the world. Lady Mary Wortley Montagu wrote to one of her friends:

> I live in a place, that very well represents the Tower of Babel; in Pera they speak Turkish, Greek, Hebrew, Armenian, Arabic, Persian, Russian, Sclavonian, Walachian, German, Dutch, French, English, Italian, Hungarian; and what is worse, there are ten of these languages spoken in my own family. My grooms are Arabs, my footmen French, English, and Germans; my nurse an Armenian; my house maids Russians; half a dozen other servants Greeks; my steward an Italian; my janizaries Turks, so that I live in the perpetual hearing of this medley of sounds, which produces a very extraordinary effect upon the people who are born here; for they learn all these languages at the same time, and without knowing any of them well enough to write or read in it. . . . I know, myself, several infants of three or four years old, that speak Italian, French, Greek, Turkish, and Russian, which last they learn of their nurses, who are generally of that country.

This diversity was not something confined to the servants of the great or the streets of the city. It was in the highest circles. Although non-Muslims were forbidden to hold government positions, many performed services that made them just as integral. Besides, most of the highest officials of the Ottoman government as well as the wives of the sultans were slaves from western Europe. As the Ottoman Empire declined in the face of European ascendancy there were an increasing number of voices in Constantinople calling for reform along Western lines.

The first attempt at this sort of Westernization came under the grand vizier Damad Ibrahim Pasha, who served Sultan Ahmed III between 1718 and 1730. In 1720 he did something unprecedented for the Porte, sending an ambassador to a foreign head of state. The days when a sultan could lounge in his palace and await the world to seek his favor were decidedly over. Yirmisekiz Mehmed Efendi was sent to Paris with instructions to "make a thorough study of the means of civilization and education, and report on those capable of application," in Constantinople. Mehmed Efendi was warmly welcomed by King Louis XV, taken to Versailles, and given a tour of much of the country. France was the most powerful kingdom in Europe, and its culture dominated the West. The ambassador returned to Constantinople in 1721 and not only delivered his report, but wrote the first Turkish account of a journey to Europe. It was a sensation, the beginning of a current of Westernization that would ebb and flow in the city to this day. His stories of the magnificence of Versailles, with its precise gardens, beautiful pools, dancing fountains, and stunning architecture, led to a frenzied decade of French-inspired building in and around Constantinople known as the Tulip Period. The sultan and his highest officials, including Mehmed Efendi, built palace complexes on the upper Golden Horn and later on the Bosporus that allowed elites to take in the air and "promenade," as was the custom in France. Even the harem women were allowed out into the new palace gardens to smell the hundreds of varieties of tulips and take part in late-night festivities lit by candles mounted on hundreds of turtles wandering through the gardens.

These lavish new palaces did nothing for the modernization of the empire or Constantinople, but Mehmed Efendi's report did have an impact in that regard. Shortly after his return, the sultan gave permission for the opening of one Turkish- and one Arabic-language printing press restricted to nonreligious books. Mehmed Efendi's book was one of the first to come off the press. Fierce opposition by the scribal guilds, however, caused them to be closed, and printing did not return to the city until later in the century. Ahmed III and his successors also attempted to introduce their own versions of urban structures found in Paris. They were not about to straighten the streets, but Ahmed did construct the beautiful fountain that bears his name, near the Imperial Gate of Topkapi. A square, marble-clad kiosk with drinking fountains and places for those inside to offer cups and other free refreshments, the fountain was like nothing ever seen in Ottoman Constantinople, the city's first truly public building, constructed for the welfare of the citizens without religious affiliation. Other such fountains became a routine construction throughout the city. Although there were frequent reactions to this Westernization, even the harshest critics adopted the French rococo style of the late Baroque period when building new structures. Something had changed.

While the sultan was enjoying his gardens, the Persians attacked his frontiers, dealing a harsh blow to the East. A revolt in Constantinople sparked by the Janissaries but supported by an angry mob demanded the execution of Ibrahim Pasha and the resignation of Ahmed III in 1730. Ahmed acquiesced, allowing his nephew Mahmud I to succeed him. But Mahmud was just as enamored of French ways, and within a year he executed the leaders of the revolt and continued his uncle's program of reform and modernization. It was slow work. At its core was a group of French engineers and military men who had traveled to Constantinople and converted to Islam, and who now received huge stipends for their guidance. New barracks and military education buildings popped up in the areas outside old Constantinople, all built in the European style. There Mahmud and his successor, Mustafa III, tried to organize a modern Ottoman army, one that could hold its own against the West and Russia, now a dangerous enemy to the north. Yet these efforts were strongly opposed by the Janissaries, and for the same reason the scribes had shut down the printing presses: it threatened their position.

Despite the rapid increase in seaside palaces and the addition of public fountains, eighteenth-century Constantinople remained largely unchanged. Few roads were paved. Carts were unknown, since even the old Mese was too narrow for them to pass. A few donkeys could be found carrying items on their backs, although horses were reserved only for the highest elites. Goods and materials were moved about

Constantinople on the backs of human porters, who could be found on every street.

The capital city now consisted of four main areas: the ancient walled city, commonly known as "Stamboul," with a mixed population and the seat of government and commerce; Galata, on the north shore of the Golden Horn, inhabited by Westerners and their embassies as well as sizeable populations of Greeks, Jews, and Armenians; Üsküdar, across the Bosporus on the Asian side, a mainly residential area populated by Turks; and Eyüp, to the west of the land walls, with a variety of residences, military buildings, and palaces along the shore. The continued and regular devastation of the urban core in Stamboul by fire in the eighteenth century led much of the population to move outside the old city. The waterways of Constantinople, therefore, became the essential avenues of the expanded city. Without bridges, thousands of ferries and other vessels traveled across the Golden Horn and Bosporus night and day. The skilled boatmen who toiled over the waves were largely Greeks and Armenians; their powerful frames and self-assured swagger made them Constantinople's most notorious playboys.

Although the modernization of Constantinople was excruciatingly slow, it was entirely French. France in the eighteenth century was producing the most efficient and largest armies in the world, and the French monarchy occasionally sent military advisers to the Porte to assist with the development of a modern army. Their help was by no means an act of altruism. The Ottoman Empire remained quite large, and it was in France's interest to support a distant and powerful state that could menace its enemies in Austria and Russia. It was slow work.

The pace picked up considerably in 1789. It was in that year that a new reform-minded sultan, Selim III, came to the throne in Constantinople. It was also in that year that the French Revolution began. At first the event went unnoticed by the Turks. The new government in Paris continued to send advisers to Constantinople to assist with the modernization of the military, but now they also came with a missionary zeal to spread the principles of revolution. With their help, Selim III created the Nizam-i Cedid, "New Order." Originally it was a comprehensive reform of provincial governorship, taxation, and trade controls. Mostly, though, it was a military reform. It produced a new military corps, recruited from young Anatolian Turks schooled and trained by French officers. It included a new artillery corps, engineer corps, and regular forces that wore Western-style uniforms. The corps took on the name of the reform itself. The Janissaries, naturally, hated the Nizam-i Cedid. They refused to fight with the upstarts and instead began to contem-plate fighting against them.

Selim also adopted a Western style of diplomacy, sending Ottoman ambassadors to the capitals of Europe to create permanent embassies there. The ambassadors themselves were members of the old guard, and therefore found nothing of interest in the infidel West, not bothering even to learn the languages of their hosts. It was their embassy staffs, made up of eager young men, who learned the Western tongues, talked to their people, and read their books with zeal. These first "Young Turks" brought Western ideas back home, which would later be filtered into the sultan's court and finally throughout Constantinople's society.

At first the French Revolution made Ottoman participation with the West more palatable. It was Europe's first secular revolution, carrying no baggage of the Christian faith. In time, the revolution would become posi-tively hostile to Christianity. This allowed the Muslim empire to accept the military support of a nation that seemed to be rebelling against its faith. Many believed, in fact, that by engaging the French, they would in time convert to Islam. In reality, revolutionary France was in constant flux. It had unleashed a raw power of reform that blindly lashed out at a world unwilling to convert to its new secularism. France's powerful armies in-vaded their neighbors, bringing liberty, equality, and fraternity along with military garrisons and French governors. From the distance of Constanti-nople, the targets of the French seemed to be well chosen. In 1797, French armies led by General Napoleon Bonaparte conquered the longtime cru-sading Republic of Venice. The following year, they captured Malta and ejected the crusading order of the Knights Hospitaller. Habsburg Austria, Russia, the papacy in Italy, and the rest of western Europe were their other targets. All had been enemies of the Ottoman Empire.

It was only a matter of time, though, before the erratic expansionism of the French armies touched Constantinople. Already the Balkans had been shaken with the introduction of French forces at former Venetian territories in Corfu and Albania. In 1798, however, Napoleon led some thirty thousand French soldiers directly into Egypt. The region had been in more or less open revolt from Constantinople for some time, but it was still technically part of the empire. With relative ease, Napoleon conquered Alexandria and Cairo and prepared for an invasion of Syria. Perhaps he even meant to continue on to Constantinople. As he did with all his conquests, Napoleon assured the people of Egypt that he was no conqueror, but their liberator.

> The French are also true Muslims. The proof is that they have gone to Rome and overthrown the government of the pope, who always urged Christians to make war on Muslims. They then went to Malta and destroyed the knights, who pretended that God ordained them to make war on Muslims. By long tradition, the French are the true friends of the Ottoman Sultan (may God preserve his empire), and the enemies of his enemies.

The message was meant for Egyptians. It obviously did not play well in Constantinople. The Ottoman government responded by declaring war on France and printing a response to Napoleon in Arabic to distribute in Egypt and Syria. It read in part:

> O you who believe in the unity of God, community of Muslims, know that the French nation (may God devastate their dwellings and abase their banner, for they are tyrannical infidels and dissident evildoers) do not believe in the unity of the Lord of Heaven and Earth, nor in the mission of the intercessor on the Day of Judgment, but have abandoned all religions, and denied the afterworld and its penalties. . . . They assert that the books which the prophets brought are clear error, and that the Koran, the Torah and the Gospels are nothing but fakes and idle talk. . . . They are wholly given up to villainy and debauchery, and ride the steed of perfidy and presumption, and dive in the sea of delusion and oppression and are united under the banner of Satan.

For the next three years the French firmly held Egypt and continued moving north into Syria—the first time a French army had come to the region since the expulsion of the Crusaders. Ironically, they were stopped at Acre, the last stand of the Crusader Kingdom. There Ottoman forces supplied by the British navy repulsed Napoleon. Critical were the Nizam-i Cedid, who used the techniques they had learned against their old teachers. The war ended with a French withdrawal in 1801, precipitated by continued losses and Napoleon's desire to return to Paris to seize power for himself. He was elected first consul in 1799 and crowned emperor in 1804. He continued to wage war in Europe, seeking to topple all kingdoms and bring everything under his imperial rule. Although he lost his navy to the English in 1805, he was determined to consolidate power on the Continent and defeat the English with trade embargoes. In Constantinople, Napoleon's defeat of Habsburg Austria and continued hostility toward Russia brought France and the Ottomans back together. In August 1806 a French ambassador, Horace Sébastiani, came to Constantinople. He had orders to convince the sultan to join with France in a war against Russia. He quickly became one of the sultan's most trusted advisers.

Selim now enthusiastically supported the French cause. The Ottomans had been fighting the Russians for more than a century and had already lost valuable territories in the Crimea. The Russians, for their part, claimed to be the special protectors of the Orthodox Christians in the Ottoman Empire—a useful excuse to attack whenever the opportunity presented itself. The English ambassador in Constantinople warned the sultan that if he backed Napoleon, the Royal Navy would descend on the capital. Rebuffed, the English left Constantinople, and a small fleet stationed itself at the Dardanelles in preparation for an attack. It would be the first attack on the city by a foreign power in more than three centuries. Sébastiani and his French engineers got to work upgrading and manning the shore batteries in the Sea of Marmara and Constantinople. The Ottoman navy played no part in the defense, since its vessels were technically far inferior to those of the English. On February 19 the small British fleet of a little more than a dozen vessels approached Constantinople. It had already done significant damage to the fortifications of the Dardanelles and the Marmara shore. Still, Sébastiani's command of Constantinople's defensive fire won the day, forcing the English to retreat.

Sébastiani was celebrated in the palace, but not among the people of Constantinople. Years of Westernizing reforms had become unpopular.

Everyday Muslims naturally worried about this headlong rush to emulate the French, a people who had made war on the empire and had now provoked war with England and Russia. What good had come to Constantinople or its empire by these fawning overtures to the infidel West? The people were less safe and their economy still in a ruinous state, while the sultan and his government continued to build pleasure villas mimicking those they admired in France. Christian residents of Constantinople were also unhappy with the new state of affairs. Following its revolution, France had made war on the Catholic Church, dissolving the monasteries of Europe, despoiling the sanctuaries, scattering the precious relics, and persecuting the pope. They had no wish to see those elements of liberty employed in Constantinople. The Janissaries, who saw themselves as the repository of past Ottoman glories, reviled the Westerners and their military modernization.

In 1806 a revolt of Janissary and other elements of the army broke out in Greece. Selim sent the Nizami Cedid forces from Anatolia to suppress it, but they failed. With Constantinople fuming and the Janissaries on the march, Selim agreed to send the Nizami Cedid forces back to Anatolia; dismiss his proWestern advisers, including Sébastiani; and confirm any grand vizier whom the leader of the Janissaries in Constantinople appointed. However, once the suppressed antiWestern sentiments had been unleashed, there was no way to stop the momentum. In May 1807 a regiment of auxiliaries known as Yamaks mutinied when they were ordered to wear Western uniforms. Their leader, Kabakçioğlu Mustafa, made common cause with the Janissaries and other religious officials in Constantinople and marched on the capital. He pitched his tents in the Hippodrome and formed a junta of sorts with the new grand vizier and the chief mufti. Making lists of reformers in Constantinople, they then set about killing them all, many in their homes. Finally, on May 29, the anniversary of the conquest, they published a ruling from the chief mufti that Selim was an enemy to Islam and should be deposed. Accepting the decision—he had no choice—Selim abdicated the throne to his cousin Mustafa IV. He attempted suicide, but the new sultan snatched the cup of poison from his hands. Selim instead was sent to the *kafes*.

The reactionaries had won. Under the chief mufti and the Janissaries, most of the painstaking reforms implemented during the past century were undone: the printing presses were smashed, the Nizam-i Cedid disbanded, the military schools closed, and all the empire's foreign ambassadors recalled. Constantinople withdrew again from the world—or at least made the attempt. In truth, the forces unleashed by Western technologies and ideologies were too great for any city to avoid, let alone one so firmly attached to both West and East. It was one thing to kill today's reformers. A generation of tomorrow's watched and waited.

Chapter 21

━━━◆━━━

Sick Man of Europe

Smoke billowed and curled around the ancient seawalls, rushing past the Sea of Marmara and up the Bosporus like a genie pouring forth from its lamp. Pressing through the heavy air of a warm June afternoon in 1889, the trailing plume of steam finally came to rest on the southern shore of the Golden Horn, where the first inhabitants of the city had centuries earlier docked their triremes. The harbor was gone, covered over with soil and crowned with a barnlike wooden structure designed to house the belching monster. Suddenly the air was filled with whistles and the clatter of steel as the new iron visitor ground to a halt. Applause and cheers arose, accompanied by a small brass band to welcome the first arrival of this modern marvel. And it was a marvel. For, just sixty-eight hours earlier, this train had lurched out of Paris's Gare de l'Est, sped across Europe, and now deposited its passengers in Constantinople's newly built Sirkeçi station. Not since the Romans connected Byzantion to the Via Egnatia had the city been so clearly attached to the West. At long last, the Orient Express had arrived.

It was not the first train to make its noisy way into the city of crossroads, but it was the first to have come so far. And Constantinople had come far to meet it. The European elites who stepped off the train in their morning coats and top hats were greeted by a city transformed by a century that began with a rebellion against the modern and ended with its firm embrace.

Nothing like this could have been imagined in 1807, when the deposition of Selim III shattered Constantinople's hopes for reform along with its printing presses. It was not the practice of the Janissaries to be gracious in victory. Having deposed one sultan, set up another, and expelled their military rivals, they then had their way with Constantinople. For months, chaos reigned. The famed Janissaries who had once forged the empire had become little more than armed gangs, killing their enemies and bullying and extorting everyone else. Whatever support they had among the people quickly evaporated under the yoke of their old-style oppression. Little wonder, then, that when word spread of a counterrevolt led by a pro-reform governor in Bulgaria, Bayraktar Mustafa, a wellspring of sympathy flowed in the streets.

With fifteen thousand Western-trained troops, Bayraktar Mustafa easily captured Constantinople, executed the main ringleaders of the rebellion against Selim, and occupied the palace grounds. His demand was simple and expected: he wanted Selim III restored to power. Realizing the danger, the new sultan, Mustafa IV, had ordered both Selim and his own brother, Mahmud, put to death. This would leave Mustafa the only male descendant of Osman, and therefore the only possible sultan. Selim fought bravely for his life, but was overpowered and strangled. Young Mahmud, however, somehow managed to avoid his executioners, hiding out on the palace grounds. When the victorious Bayraktar Mustafa made his demands, Mustafa IV replied with the mangled body of his former lord. The general broke down, shedding tears over Selim's lifeless corpse and cursing the ruthless sultan whose rule he must now accept. It was at that moment that Mahmud appeared, offering his services as sultan. With joy he was accepted.

Mahmud II was a strong reformer who believed that Constantinople and its empire could never be repaired without implementation of the best that western Europe had to offer. Like Selim, he began recruiting a new Western-style army, although he gave it a different name so as not to upset the Janissaries. He encouraged Western styles of dress and even wore them himself. He launched investigations into the worst abuses of the Janissaries, although in this he was often constrained by the fear of riots and unrest in the capital. Nevertheless, under Mahmud II and his successors in the nineteenth century, Constantinople would begin its transformation into a modern city.

The West had much to offer the city of Constantinople, but also much to threaten its empire. In Europe, the days of multiethnic empires were passing away. Born of the French Revolution and fueled by new technologies such as the railroad and the telegraph, the ideology of nationalism had set fire to the West. It was all the more potent because it was not an invented philosophy, but had grown organically from the new circumstances of the modern world. In premodern societies, the average person would live his entire life without leaving the locality of his birth. Thus, he identified with his local clans, associations, and cults. The only thing binding him to the wider world was his religion, and even that was practiced locally. The development of railroads and other means of instant communication changed that. As common people began to travel, or spoke to those who had, they discovered that there were people in the world who were not like them—people with very different customs and languages. And some of those people were their rulers. The French, bound together in their great national experiment after 1789, were the first to burn with the zeal of nationalism. They unwittingly brought those flames to other national groups along with their conquering armies. There was, as it happened, no better way to teach Italians about what they had in common than to garrison their cities with French troops.

Nationalism became the most powerful dynamic in the course of modern Western history, and remains so today. It is, however, toxic to old-style multiethnic empires. Habsburg Austria (the medieval Holy Roman Empire) would be shattered by it. Vienna, though, had a strong economy, and modern armies with which to fight back. Constantinople did not. For the Ottoman Empire, nationalism first took root in the western Balkans, where French soldiers had come after their extermination of the Republic of Venice. The Serbs were the first to band together in a determined effort to win independence from their Turkish overlords. Between 1804 and 1815, Serbian fighters with Russian support managed to neutralize the Ottoman provincial government and form their own autonomous principality based in Belgrade.

The success of the Serbs and the weakness of the Turks inspired others living under Ottoman rule to seek their own independence. A secret group of Greek intellectuals and businessmen known as the Friendly Society began working quietly to prepare for a rebellion. The time came in 1821. Greek militias in Moldavia, Wallachia, Central Greece, and the Peloponnese revolted, killing many Turkish soldiers and others friendly to the empire. The Ottomans managed to quell most of the rebellions, but were unable to do so in the Peloponnese, where the

Greeks had taken control over rural areas. The Greek revolt posed a serious problem for the government in Constantinople, for unlike the localized Serbs, the Greeks were scattered across the empire, particularly in Thrace, Anatolia, and Constantinople. Since this was a nationalist revolt, Mahmud's initial reaction was to punish all Greeks. The patriarch of Constantinople, Gregory V, was summoned to Topkapi Palace, where he assured the sultan that he and the Greeks of the capital had had nothing to do with the rebellion. Mahmud ordered Gregory to excommunicate the revolutionaries, which he did. One week later, on Easter Sunday, Gregory was snatched from the patriarchal church and hanged over its gateway. It was not safe to be a Greek in Constantinople during the next several months. Numerous bishops and priests were hanged or decapitated. Shops were ransacked and people disappeared. The bloodshed became so great that the Russian and English ambassadors protested, threatening military action if the violence did not stop. When news of the killings reached the Greek militias, they of course retaliated by executing local Turks.

Nationalism was not the only driving force behind Greek independence. From the beginning, the Friendly Society envisioned more than the creation of a Greek state; it sought the restoration of the Byzantine Empire. Constantinople, which Greeks still revered as the City, was integral to that dream. Dreams alone were insufficient to win them success. The assistance they needed came from western Europe. In the Middle Ages the West had sent Crusades to help the Greeks defend themselves against the Turks. In the nineteenth century it was the new ideology of Romanticism that came to their rescue. A reaction to the strict rationalism of the Enlightenment, Romanticism extolled the natural, the heroic, and the chivalric. As reports filtered into Europe of the Greek people throwing off the yoke of their Oriental despots, they were clasped to the breasts of the Romantics. Here were the descendants of the Ancient Greeks, who had given the world democracy and Western philosophy, struggling to live free or die. The Greek rebellion became the cause célèbre in all the smart circles in France, England, and the United States. Enormous amounts of money were raised by philanthropic societies and sent to Greece to help with the effort. The famous English poet Lord Byron left his dalliances in Italy to join the war effort in Greece, dying there in 1824. The French artist Eugène Delacroix publicized the oppression of the Greeks in numerous paintings. Philhellenism grew to such extremes in Europe that Britain, France, and Russia sent military support to defeat the Ottomans and bestow on the Greeks their independent state. Faced with the realities on the ground, the sultan had no choice but to ratify Greek secession in 1832. Appropriately enough, Athens became the capital of the new Greek state. Whatever the Romantics believed, though, the newly independent Greeks did not seek a return to the days of Plato, but of Justinian. Their eyes would remain on Constantinople.

The initial success of the Greeks in the Peloponnese was itself a reflection of the poor quality of the Ottoman troops there. Much of the blame fell on the Janissaries. Mahmud II had a remedy for that, one that eluded his predecessors. His new Western-style corps had been growing in size and ability since he took the throne. He carefully disassociated it from Selim's Nizam-i Cedid, but it was much the same sort of military force, only bigger. To the chief mufti and other religious authorities, Mahmud cast the corps as a return to the days of Suleiman the Magnificent and promised that it would be trained only by Muslims familiar with modern warfare. On June 5, 1826, the chief mufti ruled that the modern Ottoman force was justified as a tool of jihad to be used against the infidels. To celebrate the approval of the new corps, many of them were brought to Constantinople to drill for the people. Predictably, the Janissaries revolted. On June 15, five battalions of Janissaries assembled at their main barracks in Aksaray and began the rebellion, preparing to start fires in the city and storm the palace. This time, however, the people would not support them. Instead, the Janissaries were forced to fight the new corps alone. The whole engagement lasted less than an hour. Modern cannons fired grapeshot into the packed square where the Janissaries began their riot, ripping apart the flesh of the rebels. When thousands of them lay dead, the sultan's men set fire to the barracks, killing everyone inside. In the weeks and months that followed, the remainder of the Janissaries were hunted down and executed or exiled. Mahmud's masterly stroke against them was later referred to by the reformers as the Vak'a-i Hayriye, the "Auspicious Incident." It was indeed auspicious: it brought to an end the long history of Constantinople's medieval warriors and paved the way for the modernization of the city and the empire.

Without the Janissaries to check his reforms, Mahmud moved swiftly to concentrate in Constantinople all power in the empire. He began by abolishing decentralized medieval practices. Tax farming, for example, was scrapped for a Western method of tax collection by government officials answerable to a bureaucracy. To that end, Mahmud ordered the empire's first census in 1831. He also abolished all remnants of feudalism, which was still widely practiced. *Timars* were the equivalent of medieval fiefs, plots of land for which the holder owed military service. These lands were confiscated and leased back to their holders for cash payments, which were in turn used for specialized modern armies. The entire central government in Constantinople was overhauled along Western lines. The religious authorities, known as the ulema, were organized as a bureau of state. To these were added Ministries of Justice, Education, State, War, Interior, Foreign Affairs, and Civil Affairs. The office of the grand vizier was replaced with that of prime minister. New office buildings were constructed in classical styles, and the officials who worked there sat behind Western desks on Western chairs and donned Western clothes.

Indeed, clothing became a major component in Mahmud's reform of Constantinople. In traditional Muslim societies, clothing varied widely between people of different social classes. This was especially true in the Ottoman Empire. The history of Islam is filled with admonitions that Muslims are not to dress like infidels and especially never to abandon their turbans. Turkish society starkly differentiated a man's position based on what he wore on his head. It so defined him that his headwear even appeared on his tombstone. Mahmud ended all this. In 1828 he noticed a new headgear that had become fashionable in North Africa: the fez. In his clothing decree of 1829 he outlawed the use of the turban by anyone save the members of the ulema. All other men, including the sultan, were to wear the fez. There were strict penalties for violations. Men were also henceforth to wear Western-style trousers, jackets, and boots. Beards were to be trimmed to Western standards. Mahmud himself not only wore Western clothing, but entertained officials and foreign dignitaries in Western-style receptions, where he mingled with the crowd and was even seen to be deferential to Western ladies.

Many of these reforms were, of course, purely cosmetic. The sultan might dress like a Western monarch, but he still had a harem of concu‑ bines and fathered nearly fifty children with them. By the same token, although Mahmud outlawed slavery of white races in 1830, the edict was not enforced. Many Westerners complained that the sultan had simply given new names to the same despotic state and its officials. Yet behind these outward changes were substantial reforms that did dra‑ matically alter the character of life in Constantinople.

And more reforms were coming. Abdülmecid I, who succeeded Mahmud in 1839, continued the program. Among his first acts was the issuance of the "Rescript of the Rose Chamber," a comprehensive pro‑ gram for reform that would be reissued and expanded upon in subse‑ quent years. The entire strategy begun by the rescript is usually referred to as the Tanzimat, or "Reorganization." The most controversial provi‑ sion, and therefore the most difficult to implement, was the equality of all Ottoman subjects before the law. Islamic law, the sharia, carefully sepa‑ rated orthodox believers in Islam from non‑Muslim infidels. The Tanzi‑ mat sought to undo that separation. In time, it would abolish the head tax paid by non‑Muslims and even open positions to them in the military and government. The ulema opposed these reforms—indeed all reforms that sought to replace sharia with Western legal codes—yet by the end of the nineteenth century, they were firmly in place.

Education was another focus of reform in Constantinople. Western‑ style schools in which Muslims and non‑Muslims sat side by side opened for the first time. This was a gross abrogation of the prerogatives of the religious authorities, who had always controlled education in Constanti‑ nople. These new schools did not teach the Koran or Persian poetry, but math, science, and French—three things necessary for the Ottoman Empire to survive in a rapidly changing world. The numbers of these public schools were small, in part because the government lacked the will to fund them, and in part because of a lack of interest among the population. Also, although grand plans to build a University of Con‑ stantinople were unveiled, the building itself was abandoned shortly after construction began. Across the Golden Horn, in the European

section of the city, the American Roberts College (today Boğaziçi Uni/
versity) was founded in 1869, offering English-language instruction to
Turks from a variety of backgrounds. It was in these schools and the
many military schools sprouting up across the cityscape that a new gen/
eration of elites would be educated in Western modes before working
for the imperial government at home or heading off to Europe to serve
in foreign embassies.

The Tanzimat reformers also implemented an overhaul of the finan/
cial system in Constantinople, even forming the first imperial bank and
issuing paper money. In this, however, they were less successful. During
the Crimean War (1853–56), the Ottoman Empire, at great expense,
fought off a Russian attack with the help of the French and English. The
sultan frequently turned to his allies for loans, which he was never able
to repay fully. The problem was that, appearances notwithstanding,
Constantinople was not a modern city. After free-trade agreements
signed in the 1850s, smokestacks of industrial factories sprang up along
the Golden Horn, pushing out the pleasure palaces of the empire's
golden age and bringing new jobs and new wealth. But the owners of
those factories and many of their workers were European. The Otto/
man Empire lacked a wealthy middle class, the engine that had driven
innovation and reform in the West. Without it, the Ottoman economy
continued to slide further into debt.

Halting the reforms was no longer a choice. Now a debtor, the sultan
had to appease his Western creditors. And it was not just the economic
situation that focused Turkish attention on the West. European powers
had achieved so great a level of prosperity and raw military might that
their only rivals were one another. Russia, which continued to see itself
as the protector of Orthodox Christianity, was eager to use its increas/
ing military to get its hands on the Ottoman Empire. As it had since
the city's founding, Constantinople's strategic position galvanized the
attention of mighty empires. The Bosporus and the Dardanelles, both
under Ottoman control, remained the keys to the Black Sea, and thereby
Russia's commercial shipping. France and England, of course, recog/
nized this. That is why they were determined to keep Russia from mak/
ing significant gains against the Ottoman Empire. These were the days
of the Concert of Europe, when statesmen of the Great Powers worked

to maintain the balance of power and preserve the status quo. It was a delicate task, one that would ultimately fail. Still, it was preferable, they believed, to enduring another Napoleon.

By keeping Constantinople under the control of the sultan, the status quo was maintained. It was not an ideal solution, for Europeans still considered the Ottoman government to be cruel and despotic. At dinner parties across Europe, people debated the "Eastern Question," which could be stated as simply "What is to be done with the Ottomans?" By the 1860s it was common to refer to Constantinople's empire as "the Sick Man of Europe." Death seemed imminent, but the sick man was given medicines and treatments, kept alive only because the alternative seemed worse. The medicines were not voluntary. Reform was the price of continued life support. The Tanzimat, therefore, offered tangible evidence that the Ottoman Empire could become a civilized member of the community of European nations.

All this had a profound impact on Constantinople. Free-trade agreements led thousands of Europeans to relocate to the city, invariably settling in the Galata/Pera areas that had been home to expatriates since the days of the Genoese merchants. Throughout the second half of the nineteenth century, 15 percent of Constantinople's population was expatriate. They brought their customs with them and plenty of their money. Foreign-language newspapers in Constantinople found their echo with the first Turkish newspapers from the 1860s onward. European-style theaters in Pera were copied with the opening of the first Turkish-language theater in the old city (Stamboul) in 1869. The First Turkish Industrial Exhibition was held in the Hippodrome in 1863 in imitation of the London exhibition of the previous year. When news of the construction of the Paris Métro came to Constantinople, Turkish planners got to work building their own, although it would be a much smaller affair.

As we saw in the last chapter, despite these improvements, Westerners continued to report on the filthy, chaotic conditions of Constantinople in the nineteenth century. Thousands of English soldiers had firsthand experience with that during the Crimean War. Florence Nightingale took over a Turkish hospital in Üsküdar that had been commandeered by the British Army. The conditions there were appalling. The hospital's roof leaked, the halls and rooms were infested with rats, the drinking water was polluted with raw sewage, and the entire building was covered in dirt. Nightingale and her nurses got busy cleaning it up, but they lost many hundreds of patients, which she blamed on the pitiful condition of the institution and the city in general.

For many Europeans, the Tanzimat was much like Constantinople itself. Although it consisted of impressive decorations, the underlying rot remained. After the war, the reform government made some attempts at introducing urban planning and municipal zoning to a city that had seen neither for almost a thousand years. It was a difficult task. A new Commission for City Order was established in 1856 that established norms for street widths, house sizes, and garbage collection. Responsibility for adhering to these norms was left to local district municipalities that corresponded to specific regions of greater Constantinople. In the old city there were three: Fatih, Aksaray, and Hagia Sophia (today Sultanahmet). Others included Eyüp, Üsküdar, Kadıköy (Chalcedon), Pera, and Kasımpaşa. Of these, it was Pera that most emulated the West, even as it still does today. This was no accident, of course, since its inhabitants were overwhelmingly Western. In 1845 the first wide wooden bridge across the Golden Horn connected Pera/Karaköy with the Eminönü district of the old city, directly before Yeni Camii. In Pera they built the Karaköy Square, outfitted with cafés and theaters, to greet the bridge. In 1869 the inhabitants of Pera built a Western-style boulevard, the Grand Rue de Pera (today the pedestrian street İstiklal Caddesi). Flanked by shade trees, this wide road with promenade-worthy sidewalks made its way up the hill to the military school at Taksim. There at the end of the road they built the first French-style park, today Taksim Gezi Park. The Grand Rue became the Main Street of Western culture in Constantinople. Bars, salons, shops, and high-end hotels jostled for space along it and near it. Many of those who alighted from the Orient Express were shuttled to the rich velvets and deep wood paneling of the Pera Palace, owned by the train's French firm, Wagons-Lits. But it had competitors, such as the Hôtel de Londres and the Tokatlian, both gone today. The sumptuously restored Pera Palace still accepts visitors.

The Galata Bridge that stretched from Pera to Stamboul in the late nineteenth century connected two remarkably different cities. While Westerners strolled along the Grand Rue exchanging pleasantries in the park to the north, in the old city most neighborhoods remained unchanged. The problem was one of culture. Old Constantinople was a collection of neighborhoods and quarters that were accustomed to a fair amount of autonomy in construction (Illustration 15). Central planning was incomprehensible. The government could go into a district and tear down buildings to widen the streets, but the locals would simply build them again. Almost overnight, new wooden structures would appear, crowding every open space. Front doors opened directly onto hopelessly narrow walkways that curled around the structures in bewildering patterns. Space was at such a premium that second and third stories jutted out over the streets, blotting out all but the noonday sun. The only reliable ally that the reformers had were the fires that continued to plague the cheaply made timber neighborhoods. "Yangın var!" ("There's a fire!") was the old city's daily chorus, accompanied by a brigade of volunteers carrying water through the snarled backways. Small fires they could quench, but anything greater they tried to isolate by tearing down everything around it. These routine fires scoured the cityscape, keeping it always in flux. When fire cleared an area, the authorities would come in and attempt to rebuild the streets and regulate the new constructions, but often without success. The fires did, however, allow for the digging of a municipal sewer system.

Sultan Abdülaziz (1861–76) was responsible for many of these city improvements, including the arrival of the railroad. It was rumored that he had said that he would run tracks through his own body if necessary to bring trains to Constantinople. In the end, he only had to run them through the Topkapi Palace grounds. They entered the old city at the far southern end of the Theodosian Walls, just south of the ancient Golden Gate. Then they hugged the shoreline of the Sea of Marmara and the Bosporus before rounding Seraglio Point and pulling into the station at Sirkeci, on the Golden Horn, the former site of the pleasure gardens of Topkapi Palace. Abdülaziz did not miss them, for by then the sultans had moved their permanent residence to the modern and more lavish Dolmabahçe Palace, north on the Bosporus. To match the character of the luxurious Orient Express, the temporary wooden train

station was replaced in 1890 with a splendid Orientalist-themed masonry structure designed by the German architect August Jasmund. It
was also during these years that modern wharfs were installed in the
Golden Horn to accommodate the growing number of steamships con-
necting the various parts of the city and the train station. The waters of
Constantinople, for centuries a hive of activity, now churned with the
turbines and propellers of a new era.

The population of Constantinople saw a dramatic increase in the
second half of the nineteenth century, largely a result of refugees from
the capital's ever-shrinking empire. In the Balkans, Bulgaria, Romania,
Serbia, Montenegro, and Bosnia-Herzegovina broke away, becoming either autonomous or fully independent. Russia gnawed at the Ottoman
borders, annexing southern Bessarabia and the Kars region. Britain assumed control over Cyprus and Egypt, in both cases to subdue revolts
that the Ottoman military was powerless to stop. The Suez Canal,
which opened in 1869, was too important to the administration of the
British Empire to leave it to the sultan or his disgruntled subjects. Empire building closer to home, France had previously colonized Algeria,
and in 1881 captured Tunisia.

All these losses drove the Turks living in the territories to relocate
to Constantinople or Anatolia. By 1900 the population of Constantinople stood at just over a million people, a level not seen since the twelfth
century, when it was the largest city in the Western world. That was no
longer the case, dwarfed by cities such as London (with 6.5 million
souls) and New York (with 4.2 million). Constantinople's population nonetheless remained diverse. A little less than three-quarters were Muslim,
with the remaining people mostly Greek and Armenian Christians;
there was also a sizeable Jewish minority. Most of the population gain
occurred outside the old city, most notably in the north. Although Stamboul remained the commercial and government center, the expansion
of industry along the Golden Horn and the sultan's abandonment of
Topkapi Palace signaled a clear shift to the more Westernized portions
of greater Constantinople. This, in turn, mirrored the sentiments of
many of the city's inhabitants.

The Tanzimat reforms had dramatically changed the character of
Constantinople. Indeed, with the assistance of regular fires, the city was

completely rebuilt along Western lines during the course of the nine-teenth century. Only the great mosque complexes and ancient antiquities survived from the Constantinople of the previous century. Architectural, financial, and military reforms were one thing, but many in the empire began to seek more profound changes in the Ottoman government. For all the innovations they brought, the Tanzimat reforms actually increased the authority of the sultan, since he no longer had any check on his power from the Janissaries, the ulema, or even the harem. An extreme centralization allowed for impressive reforms, but it sparked a desire among educated Ottomans for a Western-style democracy or constitutional monarchy. Many of the young, well-schooled members of the military and civil service began to form secret societies and publish journals spreading their ideas far and wide. Known collectively as the Young Turks, they drew liberally from European philosophies of government, proclaiming that the Ottoman Empire would not survive in the modern world with a medieval despotism. Without a large, wealthy middle class to demand reforms, however, the Young Turks had no well of self-interested support from which to draw—only ideas and promises that they would make the empire stronger.

Their opportunity came in 1876, when a fresh batch of bad news hit the streets of Constantinople. Already the people were upset over losses in the Balkans. Added to this were crop failures in Anatolia that dramatically increased food costs, continued increases in taxation, and massive public debt. Also of concern was the sharp rise in the number of imperial palaces built along the Bosporus. Making common cause with members of the Young Turks, imperial officials deposed Sultan Abdülaziz I on May 30, 1876, and installed a new sultan who would enact a constitution and call a parliament. Unfortunately, the new sultan, Murad V, was mentally unstable, and unable (or unwilling) to move the Young Turks' agenda forward. Returning to Abdülaziz was not a possibility, since he had committed suicide a few days after his deposition. On August 31, therefore, Murad was deposed and replaced with his brother Abdülhamid, known to be favorable to the reform agenda. He agreed to declare a constitutional monarchy.

The circus of sultans in Constantinople only confirmed Western assessments of the Ottoman government as pitifully byzantine. A few months after the installation of Abdülhamid, delegates from the Great Powers arrived in Constantinople for an international conference to deal with the situation in the Balkans. The Ottomans had ruthlessly put down rebellions in Bulgaria and Serbia with shocking massacres. The Russians were determined to declare war, and England was just as determined to keep the Ottoman Empire from becoming an appendage of Russia. As the delegates convened their opening ceremonies on December 23, they were interrupted by the roar of cannon fire. When they asked its meaning, they were told that the Ottoman people had just that moment adopted a constitution. A new bicameral parliament was to be elected, and a new age had dawned. Since it was now a constitutional monarchy much like England or France, there was no longer any need for the Great Powers to concern themselves with the Balkans. The new, enlightened Ottoman government would see to the situation there.

The delegates rejected this idea. Indeed, most of them seem to have been justly suspicious of the whole Constitution. Nonetheless, the Ottomans continued to insist that the conference was unnecessary. When the delegates proposed the creation of autonomous Bulgarian principalities, the Ottomans rejected it outright. Although the Constitution had not forestalled European meddling, its reforms nevertheless went forward. In 1877 the Ottomans conducted the first general election in Islamic history. The parliament members met twice, in 1877 and 1878. Without a culture of representative assemblies, though, most of the elected delegates who arrived in Constantinople had little idea how to conduct themselves. Many gave banal speeches, which were rudely cut short when they went on too long. They legislated nothing, but complained a great deal about corruption and mismanagement in the provinces. After their second assembly, the sultan dissolved the body and suspended the Constitution. The parliament would not reconvene for thirty years.

Considered from the perspective of the previous thirteen centuries, matters in Constantinople had returned to normal: one man ruled the city and its empire. Abdülhamid managed to hold on to power by exiling those whom he or his police suspected of planning revolution. A new generation of Young Turks formed societies in places such as Paris,

Geneva, and Cairo, where they held meetings and wrote journals that were smuggled back to Constantinople. Abdülhamid knew well that they were conspiring against him. He managed to hold off the Young Turks by making separate deals with some of their leaders to return to Constantinople and accept well-paid jobs in the government. This sowed enough discord among the intellectual wing of the reformers that they were unlikely to be a threat.

Commanders in the Ottoman military, however, were another matter. Many of them had been sympathetic to the Young Turks when they were themselves in school, but the commanders were now less interested in political philosophies than in the health of the Ottoman Empire. Fiercely distrustful of the military, Abdülhamid had severely cut back its funding. Many units were no longer paid and had to forage for supplies.

It was among the military men that a new revolution was brewing. In 1908 several units began marching toward Constantinople. Among their list of demands was the restoration of the Constitution, the release of political prisoners, and the full funding of the military. Abdülhamid complied, opening the new parliament on December 17, 1908.

Within a year the sultan was deposed.

Chapter 22

Empire's End, Again

Abdülhamid, the last sultan to rule Constantinople, waved good-bye from the city's train station on April 24, 1909. He took with him some of his children, all his wives, and a few select concubines. He also brought four eunuchs, fourteen servants, several Angora cats, and his beloved Saint Bernard. His destination was a comfortable exile in Thessalonica, a city that in a stark sign of the times would be lost to the empire in just a few years. Abdülhamid and his family would then live out their days in comfortable confinement in Constantinople's Beylerbeyi Palace, on the Bosporus.

The new sultan, Mehmed V, was an obese man in his sixties who had rarely been out of the harem—perfect for a city that yearned for a constitutional monarchy. The voting for the new parliament had been conducted across what was left of the empire, and the first assembly was opened in Hagia Sophia with much fanfare and hope. One problem that no one seems to have noticed was that the Young Turks' party, the Committee of Union and Progress (CUP), won all but one of the seats in the Chamber of Deputies. In practice, this meant that all the power in Constantinople was shared by the CUP and the military leaders who had toppled Abdülhamid.

In 1912 the newly independent states of the Balkans (Greece, Bulgaria, Serbia, and Montenegro) made an alliance whose sole purpose was to carve out more territory from the Ottoman Empire. They did so with ease. The Greek navy dominated the Aegean, capturing most of the islands there. The Bulgarian army crashed into Thrace, defeating the Ottoman forces and capturing Adrianople (Edirne), the old Ottoman capital. It then pressed eastward toward Constantinople. The city, which was already convulsing under repeated political assassinations, went into a panic. Refugees from Thrace poured into the capital, forcing the government to open mosques and other religious buildings as temporary housing. Food became a major problem. Sanitation, which was never good, became worse. A cholera outbreak killed some twenty thousand people.

Meanwhile, the Orthodox Bulgarians, with their own ideas about the restoration of the Byzantine Empire, continued their conquests eastward, despite a warning from their friends the Russians that Russia would declare war if the Bulgarians took the great seat of Orthodoxy on the Bosporus. As it happened, though, the Ottoman forces were able to halt the Bulgarian advance themselves, just twentyfive miles from Constantinople. As Bulgaria's territorial gains stalled, a peace was finally hammered out in 1913. However, in Ancient Greek fashion, the Balkans allies soon attacked one another over the spoils. The Ottomans took advantage of the disruption by recapturing Edirne, thus pushing the Thracian border farther west. It was all that was left of the empire's European possessions.

The unrest in Constantinople in the wake of these defeats led to a brutal coup d'état by the CUP. It consisted of its leaders rallying a mob and marching on the Sublime Porte government buildings. Once there, they calmly shot the minister of war. The grand vizier, Kämil Pasha, was forced to resign at gunpoint. The whole affair shocked Europeans, only confirming their suspicions that the Turks were incapable of democratic government. Shortly after the coup, the Ottoman government was taken over by a triumvirate of Young Turks known as the Three Pashas. They were Enver Pasha, who became minister of war, Talaat Pasha, the minister of the interior, and Djemal Pasha, the new minister of the navy. Until 1918 these three would rule Constantinople as despotically as any sultan.

Despotism, however, can be good for city modernization. During those years, the Young Turks expanded sewage and drainage programs in Constantinople, reorganized the police services, brought in electricity, provided running water for more districts, and built new, modern apartment buildings and shops in the recently burnedout areas of Aksaray and Beyazit. The packs of wild dogs that had long terrorized Constantinople's residents and shocked visitors were rounded up, placed aboard ships, and dumped into the middle of the Sea of Marmara or left to starve on small islands. The CUP also gave to Constantinople its first municipal parks. The old lower Topkapi Palace gardens were opened up as Gülhane Park. The area between Hagia Sophia and the Sultanahmet mosques (including the old Byzantine Augusteion) was cleared of buildings and turned into Sultanahmet Park. Fatih Park was opened between the Şehzade and Fatih mosques, and Doğancılar Park appeared in Üsküdar. Transportation in the city was modernized by the paving of many dirt roads, the widening of streets between Hagia Sophia and the train station, and the extension of electric tram cars into the old city.

In the meantime, Europe, and the world, was preparing for war. Even as the troubles that would lead to World War I were brewing, the government in Constantinople made overtures to Germany, believing that France and England would no longer protect the empire against the Russians. On August 2, 1914, the day after Germany declared war on Russia, the Ottoman government made a secret treaty of support with Germany. After some preparations at home, on November 11, 1914, Sultan Mehmed V, who remained the caliph of Islam, dutifully declared jihad on the Allied Powers. It was the last of many blunders by an empire that had been drowning in a sea of missteps for years.

By late 1914, the Great Powers had reached a military stalemate and dug their trench lines across Europe. There, a generation of young men would go to die. Russia, now cut off from Britain and France, asked its allies to capture the Dardanelles and Constantinople, thus allowing Russian cargo and battleships to navigate freely from the Black Sea into the Mediterranean. The attack came in April 1915, when Allied forces stormed Gallipoli in an attempt to capture the southern straits. The battle would continue for the next eight months and, in the end, would claim nearly one hundred thousand lives. Once again, when Constantinople was at stake, the Ottomans managed to rally and fight off their attackers. One of their commanders, Lt. Col. Mustafa Kemal, would become a hero for his brave defense of the straits and Constantinople. He would have much to say about the future of the city.

The Ottoman victory at Gallipoli was not the norm during the Great War. In the Persian Gulf, Syria, and Palestine, Ottoman forces suffered heavy losses. British troops in Egypt stirred up Arab nationalist revolts and waged war against Turkish forces across what was left of the empire in the Middle East. An Arab government separated itself from Constantinople in Arabia. Damascus, where Mustafa Kemal commanded the defenses, fell to the British on October 1, 1918. Throughout the war, Enver Pasha continued to be optimistic, and attempted to impart that optimism to the military and the people. Although the Ottomans might have had the worst of their battles with the Allies, they had nonetheless held the straits and thereby seriously harmed the Allies' ability to coordinate their attacks against the Central Powers. When in 1917 catastrophic losses in Russia led to troop mutinies and the overthrow of the tsar by the Bolshevik Revolution, the Ottomans could claim some credit for isolating their old enemy. The Communists immediately removed Russia from the war. In addition, the Ottoman theater drew precious resources and men from the Allies that they would otherwise have devoted to the Western Front against Germany and Austro-Hungary.

Ultimately, though, it was the Western Front that decided the war. The years of bloody stalemate ended when the United States declared war on Germany in April 1917 and began sending hundreds of thousands of fresh soldiers to the trenches soon after. In September 1918, Grand Vizier Talaat Pasha visited Berlin, where he learned that the Germans were actively seeking a separate peace, having come to the conclusion that military victory was impossible. Back in Constantinople, the leaders of the ruling party moved quickly. Their only hope of saving the Ottoman Empire, they believed, was to make their own separate peace. They were at first attracted to Woodrow Wilson's Fourteen Points, which laid out his aims in sending U.S. forces into war. These included national self-determination, which would guarantee "the Turkish portion of the present Ottoman Empire . . . a secure sovereignty." The Turkish leaders sent an offer of surrender to Washington, but received no reply, probably because the United States was not at war with the empire. As an "associated power," the United States had declared war only on Germany.

Faced with the grim realities of a brutal defeat that had already left the Ottoman Empire impoverished, demoralized, and depopulated, the Three Pashas, Talaat, Enver, and Djemal, boarded a German gunboat and fled Constantinople. Sultan Mehmed V had died of heart failure in

July and was succeeded by his brother Mehmed VI. With the departure of the triumvirate, the new sultan appointed a new grand vizier, Ahmed Izzet Pasha, and ordered him to make peace with the Allies under any terms. On board the HMS *Agamemnon*, off the coast of the island of Lesbos, the vizier signed an armistice on October 30, 1918. The war for the Ottoman Empire was over.

In early November a large fleet of British, French, Italian, and Greek war vessels steamed into the Sea of Marmara, anchored off Constanti, nople, and took possession of the city. It was the first time that the city had changed hands since 1453—a fact not lost on the victors. The French officers were especially steeped in the medieval precedents of their actions in the now-prostrate Ottoman Empire. Romantic colonial, ism in France was strong, leading these men to turn their thoughts to the days of their ancestors' great Crusades. In Damascus, where the French general Henri Gouraud entered triumphantly, he boldly proclaimed, "Saladin, we have returned." Similarly, in Constantinople, French general Franchet d'Espérey entered through the Theodosian Walls on a white horse, evoking the memory of Sultan Mehmed II's conquest of the city and its modern undoing. The Christian populations of the city joyously celebrated, while the Muslims looked on in disbelief as their empire crumbled around them. The Allies garrisoned Constantinople, establish, ing strict control over the Golden Horn port, the transportation system, the police, and of course the artillery guns. In 1919, control of Constanti, nople was split into three zones. The French took Stamboul, the British Pera, and the Italians the suburbs across the Bosporus (Illustration 16).

Sultan Mehmed VI obligingly dissolved the Chamber of Deputies, blaming all his empire's troubles on the CUP. Enver and Djemal were tried in absentia, but many other leaders and supporters of the CUP were arrested and later convicted of various crimes. In January 1919 the victor nations assembled at Paris to dictate the terms of peace and, in the process, redraw the maps of Europe and the Middle East. The Turks of Constantinople and Anatolia watched it all with a feeling of inevitabil, ity. There was no doubt that the last remnants of the empire would be parceled out to the Great Powers to administer as mandates until new independent nations could be formed. One proposal had Constantinople and the straits transferred to international control, while Asia Minor would be under an American mandate for the immediate future. Many in Constantinople favored that plan as the least objectionable.

The Paris Conference, though, was beset by the contradictions of earlier promises and grand visions. Although U.S. president Woodrow Wilson wanted a "peace without victors" that would set borders along national lines, many of the other participants had entered the war with assurances concerning the spoils. One such participant was Greece, whose prime minister, Eleftherios Venizelos, had championed the Allied cause in his own country and now wanted his due. One of the strongest proponents of the Great Idea (that is, the restoration of the Byzantine Empire), Venizelos insisted that the Allies support a Greek occupation of western Asia Minor starting with an invasion of Smyrna (İzmir). Since the city and the region had a large, and in some places majority, Greek population, it was acceptable to most participants at Paris. Protected by Allied warships, a Greek invasion force landed at Smyrna on May 15, 1919. The Greeks quickly occupied the city and began consolidating control over the coast. The following year, they moved eastward, pushing deep into Anatolia.

In occupied Constantinople, the Greek victories were the hardest lash of defeat to endure. To have the Greeks, who had been the subject people of the Turks for five centuries, now winning victory after victory in an attempt to undo the holy wars of the sultans was nearly intolerable. There was little doubt where the Greek forces would end up. Anatolia was nothing to them compared to the holy city of Constantinople. Given all that had happened in recent years, it was hardly a stretch to imagine Hagia Sophia soon filled with the smell of incense and the chanting of Greek Orthodox priests. Anti-Greek demonstrations broke out all over the city.

The day after Smyrna fell to the Greeks, Mustafa Kemal boarded a steamship bound for the Black Sea. He was on a mission from the sultan to dismantle the Ottoman army. It was a job poorly suited to a charismatic war hero who had led his men through the horrors of Gallipoli, only to see the empire's capital handed to those he had fought. Born in the early 1880s, Mustafa Kemal was schooled in the modern war colleges, where he and his generation of officers absorbed the religion of reform preached there. He had taken part in the military coup

of 1908 that restored the parliamentary assembly and ultimately deposed the sultan. In 1909 he personally commanded the forces in Constantinople that crushed a military countercoup, the last gasp of the
conservative Ottomans. With the end of World War I, he joined the
many Ottoman officers and bureaucrats who rushed to occupied Constantinople seeking a place in the new order—whatever that was. When
the Allies showed no interest in him, Mustafa Kemal courted various
underground resistance groups, none of which had open positions or
particularly good plans. After six months of searching, he finally managed to land the job of inspector of the Ottoman army in Eastern Anatolia. He would undertake it in ways that no one, least of all the sultan
who sent him, could have imagined.

Had any other nation invaded Anatolia, it is unlikely that the defeated Turks would have responded. Indeed, Italy had already occupied
the city of Antalya without objection. It was not so with the Greeks.
These two peoples had lived together for centuries and knew each other
too well. The Greek success sparked in the Turks a determination to
resist. In Anatolia, Mustafa Kemal began organizing and recruiting
Turkish forces to defend against further Greek incursions. Things
moved quickly after that. Resigning his position in the military, Kemal
organized several congresses, which ultimately resulted in the conven-
ing of a Grand National Assembly in Ankara in April 1920. The delegates insisted that they were loyal to the sultan, and committed to
rescuing him and his empire from their foreign invaders.

In Constantinople, Turkish nationalist groups continued to make
trouble as Kemal and his forces grew. Disgusted with the sultan, who
seemed to serve only the Europeans, they protested in the streets and
raided Allied military depots, sending to Ankara what they could sal-
vage. The British responded by arresting and deporting nationalists
when they could find them, but it was difficult work. Mehmed VI
greeted the creation of the Grand National Assembly with a fatwa, issued in his role as caliph of Sunni Islam. It strongly denounced Kemal
and his supporters and even declared that the murder of the nationalists was the duty of all Muslims. Mustafa Kemal and his associates were
tried in absentia in Constantinople and sentenced to death. In Ankara,
the Assembly responded by collecting more than a hundred muftis,

who declared the caliph's fatwa invalid because of foreign duress and reiterated the call to rescue the sultan.

The situation in Constantinople changed radically with the events in Anatolia. During the Greek military victories in 1919 and 1920, Westernized Pera became a place of jubilation and perpetual parties. Waving their blue-and-white flags in the streets, the Greeks of Constantinople threw off their fezzes and celebrated the resurgence of their people. Many began to plan their recovery of the City. Indeed, there was so much talk of the reconsecration of Hagia Sophia as a Christian church that the Ottoman authorities stationed armed soldiers around it. Turks complained about the proud bareheaded Greeks whose broad smiles seemed to promise doom. In London, Prime Minister David Lloyd George made clear that he wished to see Constantinople either internationalized or returned to the Greeks.

On August 10, 1920, the sultan's government signed the Treaty of Sèvres, which dictated the final peace settlement for the Ottoman government. Greece was to be given Adrianople and most of Thrace as well as its captured territory in Asia Minor. The Dardanelles and the entire shore of the Sea of Marmara would be demilitarized and placed under international control, while Constantinople would remain nominally in Ottoman hands although administered by a coalition of Western nations. The rest of Asia Minor would either be Turkish controlled or under mandates by Italy or France. The sultan ordered Turkish forces everywhere to stand down and prepare for implementation of the treaty.

Constantinople's fate was decided in the war between Kemal's nationalist army and the Greek forces. That war continued in Anatolia through 1921, when the Turkish nationalists won a great victory at Sakarya. Foreign governments, tired of the ineptitude of Constantinople, began to recognize Mustafa Kemal and his nationalists as a legitimate state. The Soviets made a treaty with them in March 1921, and the French did the same in October. Meanwhile, a disastrous change in government in Athens led to the replacement of the Greek field commanders at the worst possible time. The Turkish nationalist forces took advantage of the situation and began driving the Greeks back in August 1922. The Greeks had to retreat from all their gains, leaving the continent at Smyrna (İzmir) in September. With them went hundreds of thousands of Greek refugees, who fled before the Turkish nationalist forces. The Great Idea in Asia Minor was firmly at an end.

Mustafa Kemal's next objective was to drive Greece out of Thrace, restoring Turkish control of Edirne. To that end, he needed to cross at the Dardanelles, which were controlled by the British. Lloyd George was determined to go to war to keep Mustafa Kemal and his armies out of the straits and away from Constantinople. But the British people and the Conservative Party disagreed. The British prime minister fell from power, and negotiations began. Peace was finalized among the nationalists, the empire, and the Allies in the Treaty of Lausanne, signed on July 24, 1923, although largely put into place before that. The treaty removed all foreign forces from Thrace, Constantinople, and Asia Minor, although it still insisted on the demilitarization of the Dardanelles. Edirne was restored to the empire. It was a stunning victory. Recognized by international treaty, the nationalist government had managed to do what had eluded all the other defeated powers in World War I. It had rejected the terms dictated to it, issued a new framework for peace, and emerged stronger than before the war.

The genius of Mustafa Kemal was that he could move effortlessly from military commander to political leader. Despite fatwas against him, he had determinedly not condemned the sultan, always insisting that he was defending the empire and the Muslim faith from outsiders. Mustafa Kemal knew that the outsiders were willing to allow him his victory because it fit well with their passion for national self-determination, and his Assembly seemed more reasonable than the chaotic situation in Constantinople. Had he decided to extend his military victories to the lost territories in Syria, Palestine, or Macedonia, Mustafa Kemal would have shown himself to be not only untrustworthy, but a holy warrior bent on rebuilding a medieval empire. The general and his supporters were instead determined to build up the Turkish nation, not necessarily the Ottoman Empire.

That, of course, was the problem. The sultan remained the legitimate head of state and was a signatory to the Treaty of Lausanne. He was also the caliph, supported by the religious authorities, revered and respected by most Turks. Even among the nationalist leaders, there was a strong feeling that the reform of the country must be grounded on the sultanate and caliphate. Mustafa Kemal disagreed. In October he put before the Assembly in Ankara a proposal to end the sultanate. There was a heated debate, although, in the end, Mustafa Kemal won the day. His argument was simple and succinct: The house of Osman, he said, held the sultanate not because it had been given to that line by nature, but because the house had seized it six centuries earlier. Now the Turkish people had taken the government back. It was only right, then, that the sultanate come to an end, for its purpose had also ended. The final resolution, passed on November 1, 1922, declared the end of the office of sultan. It did not end the caliphate, but it asserted that it was the right of the Turkish state to give that holy office to whichever of the sons of Osman best deserved it.

Two weeks later, Sultan Mehmed VI sent a note to the British commander of forces in Constantinople, General Charles Harington, asking for asylum. Given the popular support for Mustafa Kemal and the Assembly in Constantinople, he feared that he would be shot during one of his ceremonial Friday processions to prayer. Harington obliged, spiriting the monarch onto an awaiting British warship, which deposited him on the island of Malta—the former home of the last crusading order, but now controlled by Great Britain. The departure of Mehmed VI ended a period of Constantinople's history that had begun with Mehmed II in 1453. The sultanate was finished. In Ankara, the Assembly later elected Mehmed's cousin as the new caliph of Islam. He would hold the position for only two years before the Assembly abolished the caliphate as well.

For the first time in sixteen centuries, Constantinople no longer ruled an empire. It remained a city of palaces and monuments, but had no government or ruler to fill them. It was also becoming less cosmopolitan. The victory of the nationalists led the triumphant Greeks of Constantinople to pack away their flags and hastily don their fezzes. The Treaty of Lausanne included the largest forced repatriation of people in modern history. Greece was to send some 500,000 Turks to Turkey and accept 1.5 million Greeks, mostly from Anatolia. This "ethnic cleansing," as it is known today, was brutally efficient, as both countries were strongly committed to it. Hundreds of thousands of Greeks, whose ancestors had settled in Asia Minor in 1000 BC, were sent "home," leaving their villages, businesses, and lands empty. According to the treaty, the Greeks of Constantinople were alone exempted from the forced transfer. The Greek government in Athens claimed that they did not have the resources to resettle those in Constantinople, but there was also a strong reluctance to allow the city to lose its Christian population. Not surprisingly, the Greeks who remained found life in the city increasingly difficult. Many thousands of them fled with the departure of the British. Thousands more would flee in the years following. The Greek population of Constantinople plummeted from around 350,000 in 1919 to fewer than 100,000 in 1925. The same was true for Constantinople's other minorities, particularly the Armenians and Jews. Turkey was a nation-state for Turks. Others were no longer so welcome.

What came next was even more surprising. On October 2, 1923, the last Allied troops evacuated Constantinople. Four days later, nationalist forces entered the city to cheers from the Turkish majority. Then, on October 13, the Assembly decreed that henceforth Ankara would be the seat of government of the Turkish state. Just like that, the great city on the Bosporus was a capital no more.

In retrospect, the decision to move the capital from Constantinople was the right one for the formation of a modern state. It indicated a clear break with the past and the birth of something genuinely new. The city of Constantinople, with its imposing *külliye*, grand mosques, and sprawling palaces, was a constant reminder of the sultans, the ulema, and the empire. The new Turkish state, according to an Assembly decree of October 29, 1923, was a constitutional republic—the first in the Muslim world. Constantinople, though, had not been associated with a republic for nearly two millennia. It was the city of caesars and sultans. It was the cosmopolitan metropolis at the crossroads of the premodern world—the ideal capital for a multiethnic empire. Ankara, on the other hand, was a small hillside town in central Anatolia. Situated in the Turkish heartland, it could be built to order as the center of a new Turkish nation. Constantinople was of the old world; Ankara was the way forward.

And there was one more change. In the decree establishing the Republic of Turkey, Constantinople was officially renamed Istanbul.

PART IV

ISTANBUL

1923–2016

Istanbul located at the junction of two great worlds, the ornament of the Turkish nation, the treasure of Turkish history, the dearest object of the Turkish nation, has a place in the heart of every Turk.

Mustafa Kemal

Chapter 23

＊

Becoming Modern

There was nothing new about the name "Istanbul." Arab and European writers had used it since at least the tenth century. It was, as
we have seen, a version of the Greek στην Πόλη or εις την Πόλιν, meaning "in/to the city." Constantinople was the greatest of all cities, so people across the eastern Roman Empire referred to it as simply "the City."
Foreigners heard that and gave their best approximations in their own
tongues. It was, after all, just a place name, the origins of which are usually irrelevant. Few know or care, for example, that "Chicago" is an An-
glicized version of a French hearing of the Miami-Illinois Native
American word *shikaakwa*, meaning "leeks." The same principle applies.

The Turks, too, had long referred to Constantinople by its Greek
nickname. In Turkish usage, it is common to precede a name contain-
ing hard consonants with an *i* or *is* sound. This was true with other
Greek cities, such as Smyrna, which became İzmir, and Nicaea, which
became İznik. In the case of Constantinople, στην Πόλη became "Istanbul." It was in such common usage during the Ottoman Empire that in
the seventeenth century some writers claimed that it should be "Islam-
bol," meaning "full of Islam." It did not take. Instead, the city continued
to have two common names. Constantinople was the formal version,
and Istanbul (or Stamboul, as the Europeans phrased it) was the informal. In that sense, it is not unlike "Los Angeles" and "LA," or "Philadelphia" and "Philly."

Yet if the city had managed with two names for centuries, why did
the nationalists insist on using only the informal "Istanbul" after 1923?
And why, in 1930, did they pass a law forbidding the Turkish postal
service from delivering mail addressed to "Constantinople"? Many in
the West suspected that stamping the city firmly with a new Turkish
name was an attempt to de-Westernize or de-Christianize it. But it was

a Greek name. Indeed, Greeks still call it η Πόλη, "the City." As with the change in the capital, the answer probably lies with the city's identi, fication with the sultanate. Versions of "Istanbul" may have been in use for centuries, but in the formal ceremonies and documents of the sul, tans, it was always referred to as "Kostantiniyye." In the Ottoman mili, tary, from which the various reform and nationalist movements drew breath, the less formal "Istanbul" was universally used. Constantinople was the city of the sultans. Istanbul was the city of reform.

Foreigners were slow to adopt the name change in 1923. Maps, books, and newspapers published in the West stuck with "Constantinople." The National Geographic Society did not add it to their map of Europe until the end of 1929. The *New York Times* and *Chicago Tribune* began using "Istanbul" in late 1929, and dropped "Constantinople" entirely shortly thereafter. After the 1930 law was passed, "Istanbul" did begin to acquire wider acceptance in Anglophone countries; the U.S. State Department officially changed its usage on May 27, 1930. But "Constan, tinople" remained the norm in works of fiction and common parlance until World War II. The new name was certainly well established in 1953, when the hit song "Istanbul (Not Constantinople)," by the Four Lads, reached No. 10 on the *Billboard* charts.

Still more profound changes were coming to the city and people of Istanbul. With the abolition of the caliphate in 1924, Constantinople was no longer the center of the Muslim world. Shortly thereafter, Mus, tafa Kemal and the National Assembly moved against all the religious institutions in the country, since they not only posed a danger to the revolution but had begun actively preaching against it. A series of de, crees dramatically changed the religious and legal framework of the country. The ulema was abolished, the Ministry of Sharia shuttered, and hundreds of religious schools and colleges closed down. The entire structure of family law and basic education that flowed from the reli, gious authorities in Constantinople was upended. Henceforth, law was to be administered by independent courts in a Western, secular style. There were, of course, strong objections and even uprisings. But Mus, tafa Kemal put them down efficiently and brutally.

Mustafa Kemal's approach to reform became increasingly clear. When the Young Turks ruled Constantinople, they had sought to reform Ottoman civilization so that it would be compatible with Western civilization yet still retain its Muslim character. Mustafa Kemal argued that there was only one civilization and those who did not join it would be buried by it. "Uncivilized people," he said, "are doomed to remain under the feet of those who are civilized." Abolishing medieval Islamic law was a first, major step. The next was equally profound though, from a Western perspective, almost trivial. A century earlier, the reformers had sought to level Muslim society by banishing the elaborately diverse turbans and other headgear that characterized a man's status. Their answer was the fez. Since then, the fez had become the ubiquitous symbol of an Ottoman citizen, a defiant and proud refusal to become entirely like the infidels. Mustafa Kemal saw it as a pitiful badge of backwardness. In 1925 the Assembly outlawed its use. As Mustafa Kemal later explained, "[I]t was necessary to abolish the fez, which sat on the heads of our nation as an emblem of ignorance, negligence, fanaticism, and hatred of progress and civilization, and to accept in its place the hat, the headgear used by the whole civilized world."

Women's dress was another matter. As in all Muslim countries, Turkish women traditionally covered themselves from head to toe on the rare occasion that they left their homes. That had started to change among elite Turkish women under the CUP, who began to uncover their faces at least. During the period of the Allied occupation, more elites in Constantinople began dressing in a Western fashion, but this still included only a small number of Turkish women. Mustafa Kemal strongly urged the women of Turkey to cast off their veils. He condemned the idea that a woman must cower and cover her head simply because a man walked by. "Can the mothers and daughters of a civilized nation adopt this strange manner, this barbarous posture?" he asked. "It is a spectacle that makes the nation an object of ridicule." He passed no law banning the veil, but continued to preach against it. In time, the adoption of Western, yet modest, modes of dress for Turkish women became a symbol of patriotism and devotion to the revolution. The veil, though, never went the way of the turban or the fez, and remains a potent symbol in Istanbul today.

Even as fedoras populated the crowded streets of Istanbul, more changes in everyday life were on the way. In 1925 the Muslim calendar was dropped and replaced with the Gregorian calendar, a reckoning based on the birth of Jesus Christ and established by the pope in Rome. Yet it was the calendar of the modern world, so the Turks would adopt it. The same was true with Western clocks, which went up all over Istanbul. In 1928 the Assembly deleted from the Constitution the phrase "the religion of the Turkish state is Islam," thus making it a secular state more thoroughly than most European states that still had established religions.

On the evening of August 9, 1928, Mustafa Kemal, now the president of the Republic of Turkey, held a joyous, Western-style party in the Gulhane Park of Istanbul's Seraglio Point. When the time came for the president to speak, he announced the completion of a new project. Throughout the country, written Turkish would be converted from Arabic script to Roman letters. Then, with a blackboard and chalk, he was transformed from party host to schoolroom teacher, demonstrating to the assembled this new way of writing their language. It would be, he said, instituted immediately:

> We must free ourselves from these incomprehensible signs that for centuries have held our minds in an iron vise. You must learn the new Turkish letters quickly. Teach them to your compatriots, to women and to men, to porters and to boatmen. Regard it as a patriotic and national duty.

Arabic letters had always been ill-suited for the Turkish language. They were difficult to learn and expensive to print. The shift to Roman letters, Mustafa Kemal believed, would expand literacy, which even in Istanbul was still less than 30 percent, and further integrate Turkey into the company of advanced nations. The experiment was an unqualified success. Following the president's example, Turkish elites fanned out into the schools and meeting rooms of the nation to teach this new literacy. Within a year it had been adopted by all governments in Turkey.

Daily life in Istanbul was rocked again in 1935, when the government required all citizens to adopt legal surnames. It also decreed that

Sunday would henceforth be a day of rest on which the government and the workplace would be closed. The concept of a weekly day off is not a Muslim one. Friday is the day of prayer but not rest. During the reforms of the Young Turks, some businesses and government offices had closed on Friday, but this latest reform changed that to the Christian day of rest. Once again, the initiative was meant to put Turkey in sync with the West.

In Istanbul, Mustafa Kemal's Westernization had a profound effect on attitudes toward the city's antiquities. Traditionally, medieval Ottoman structures in the city, such as mosques and *külliye*, were maintained by the religious foundations created when the structures were built. Byzantine and Roman antiquities, where they survived, were not maintained at all. Wooden houses were commonly built against and even inside the Theodosian towers and land walls and against the sphendone of the Hippodrome. The Column of Constantine had been stabilized in 1779 by covering up its Roman base with masonry and later strapping it with giant iron bands. This was judged less expensive than tearing it down and hauling off the massive drums. In the 1920s and '30s, a number of new urban plans were enacted that widened streets, exposing more antiquities. Beyazit Square was completely cleared of wooden structures, restoring the open space of the original Forum of Theodosius in front of the thriving University of Istanbul. Houses that clustered around Hagia Sophia were also pulled down.

Rather than shipping off Turkey's antiquities, the new Turkish government sought to uncover and preserve them in museums. Istanbul's Archaeological Museum was opened before the war, followed by others, such as the Museum of Turkish and Islamic Arts, the Naval Museum, and the Military Museum. The Turkish government actively supported archaeological digs in Istanbul and brought in specialists from Europe and the United States to uncover some of the lost layers of the ancient metropolis. Excavations in the Hippodrome uncovered the bases of the three surviving monuments, while digs in the Great Palace area revealed gorgeous floor mosaics of the Byzantine imperial residence.

Nothing could compare, though, with what was found in the mosque of Hagia Sophia. Thomas Whittemore, an American socialite and fundraiser, had come to Istanbul after the First World War to organize schools for the Russian refugees who landed there in the wake of the Bolshevik Revolution. He had gone on to become one of the best-known foreigners in the city. Well traveled, well dressed, and very well connected, Whittemore became enamored of Byzantine art and embarked on a mission to recover it. Establishing the Byzantine Institute in Boston and partnering with the wealthy collectors Mildred and Robert Woods Bliss of Dumbarton Oaks (in Washington, DC), Whittemore decided to take advantage of the reform spirit in Istanbul and seek permission to uncover the mosaic decorations of the city's most famous building. To a certain extent, he knew what he would find. Nearly a century earlier, in 1847, Sultan Abdülmecid had hired Giuseppe and Gaspare Fossati, Italian Swiss architects, to renovate Hagia Sophia. Over the next two years the brothers oversaw the repair of buttressing, columns, and ceilings. While overhauling the mosque's walls, they removed centuries of soot, paint, and plaster, revealing the Byzantine mosaics hidden beneath. Given the constraints of time, the Fossatis did their best to record sketches of the lost images, but then covered them over again in preparation for the mosque's reopening. As far as the main structure was concerned, their primary job was restoration and repair.

With persistence and charm, Thomas Whittemore obtained from Ankara the extraordinary permission to again uncover the mosaic decorations in Hagia Sophia mosque. He started working in 1931, painstakingly peeling back the wall layers to release the hidden art, some of which had not seen daylight since the time of the conquest. Slowly and surely, armed with cameras and a good head for publicity, Whittemore brought the images of forgotten Constantinople to an astonished world.

President Mustafa Kemal was fascinated by the discoveries in Hagia Sophia. He was not slow to see that they offered another means of closing the door on the country's imperial past. Hagia Sophia had for centuries been the sultan's official mosque. Mustafa Kemal had already opened Topkapi Palace to tourists as a museum. Why not the mosque as well? Each new emperor or saint who peeked out from behind his plaster prison made the building less suited as a Muslim house of worship. Mustafa Kemal met with Whittemore several times, including once at the president's residence in Ankara. He urged him to continue his good work and discussed with him the possibility of turning Hagia

Sophia into a museum. This was strictly against Muslim law, but that was no longer the law of Turkey. Whittemore was enthusiastic about the possibility. After a perfunctory study of the matter, the Turkish Council of Ministers declared on November 24, 1934, that Hagia Sophia was no longer a mosque, but "a unique architectural monument of art," that would henceforth serve as a museum. Although its minarets would continue to sound the call to prayer, the prayers themselves would no longer echo in the cavernous interior of Justinian's great church. On February 1, 1935, Hagia Sophia Museum opened its doors to tourists. Mustafa Kemal, proclaimed "Atatürk" (Father of the Turks) on the same day as Hagia Sophia's secularization, visited the rare and beautiful place a few months later.

On November 10, 1938, Mustafa Kemal Atatürk died of cirrhosis of the liver in the sultan's palace of Dolmabahçe. His political party and the movement he started lived on. In Europe, fascist governments were sprouting across the landscape and marching anew toward a terrible world war. This time, though, the Turks would stay out. The government in Ankara declared its neutrality early on and stuck to it. Naturally a good deal of military and matériel shipping came through the Bosporus during those years, yet no favoritism was shown to one or another side. Monitoring the vessels was useful intelligence, so a great many countries sent spies to Istanbul during the war. This was the romantic heyday of international espionage, when spies clustered in the cafés and bars of luxury hotels in Pera, such as the famous Park Hotel, next door to the German consulate, or the Pera Palace, down the street from the American mission. All the major governments had agents in the city, each willing to buy information about the enemy or pass a bribe to harm one. The problem was that there was too much money and not enough intelligence, which led to a vibrant market in bad reports fed by double agents. This unique period in the city's history would provide rich fodder for novelists and screenwriters for generations. Writers such as Ian Fleming and John le Carré fixed in the Western imagination a picture of Istanbul as an exotic and decadent home of treachery and subterfuge. And indeed it was.

The effects of the war fell hardest on Constantinople's minorities. In order to raise funds for the Turkish military in preparation for a possible attack, the government in Ankara levied a special tax in 1942. Although theoretically applied to all Turkish citizens, the rates for Muslims were so low as to be negligible. The rates for non-Muslims were beyond confiscatory. Armenians were assessed 232 percent of their real property, Jews 159 percent, and Greeks 156 percent. Turkish Muslims paid a little under 5 percent. Since non-Muslims lived almost exclusively in Istanbul, this had a dramatic effect on the city. Many could not pay the taxes, even after they had sold all they owned. More than a thousand of those unlucky individuals were shipped to labor camps in Eastern Anatolia. These enormous taxes followed on the heels of a law the previous decade that forbade non-Muslims from engaging in thirty professions, including real estate, medicine, and law. Not surprisingly, many of Istanbul's minorities fled—particularly Greeks, who had a welcoming state close by. Some Armenians immigrated to New Zealand or Australia. Istanbul's Jews resented the impoverishing taxation, but their plight in neutral Turkey was infinitely better than that of Jews in many European cities.

The first free multiparty elections were held in Turkey in 1946, the same year that the punitive taxes were rescinded. It was not until the elections of 1950, though, that Atatürk's Republican Party lost control of the government and was replaced by the Democratic Party, led by Adnan Menderes. Dominating Turkey for the next decade, the Menderes government had a profound effect on Istanbul. This was in part a reaction to Atatürk's fixation on building his capital at Ankara. Menderes, who cautiously sought a new way, was determined to put resources into the modernization of the old Ottoman capital.

Part of modernization in the postwar world meant choosing sides in the Cold War. Turkey had already joined the United Nations, headquartered in New York, in 1945. Under Menderes, it would also join NATO, in 1952. American culture reigned supreme in Istanbul as the country moved into the Western alliance. Blue jeans, T-shirts, Hollywood movies, skyscrapers, and most of all cars were symbols of progress that the new superpower projected to the world. Menderes and his city planners expanded Istanbul to include large new areas to the west and north of the city. Practicing a more liberal approach to economics, Menderes opened Turkey up for increased immigration in the East, which led many of the Anatolian Turks to move into Istanbul in the hope of obtaining cheap housing and good jobs. High-rise apartment buildings shot up across the urban landscape. The city of wood and marble was quickly becoming the city of asphalt and concrete.

The new government, flush with U.S. aid from the Marshall Plan and the Truman Doctrine, spent liberally on Istanbul's infrastructure. The greatest change came with the introduction of motorways. Ottoman Istanbul was a densely packed pedestrian city. Horses were rare, and carts almost unknown. Now bulldozers plowed up the ancient roadways, expanding and paving them into broad boulevards. The ancient way of the Byzantine Mese was replaced with modern motorways between Sultanahmet and Aksaray (Ordu Caddesi). At Aksaray, the site of the old Forum of Theodosius, a massive interchange was built, directing automobile traffic in several directions. The northern Mese route was covered by another motorway (now Adnan Menderes Boulevard) stretching all the way to Edirnekapı. At the Aksaray interchange, the city was also bisected by a north–south motorway (Atatürk Boulevard). Additional motorways were added along the shoreline of the old city, necessitating the destruction of many of the Byzantine seawalls and the expansion of land into the sea. These motorways were connected to the expanded Galata Bridge and to other bridges crossing the Golden Horn. Additional motorways were added to the north and west. To compensate for the destruction of open-air markets, new pedestrian underpasses were built that provided commercial space beneath the rumbling traffic overhead. This dramatic increase in Istanbul's capacity for cars came at a time when inhabitants could finally afford them. An economic boom and doubling of the city's population occurred in the 1950s. The number of cars in Istanbul went from around three thousand in 1945 to thirty-five thousand in 1960 to more than one hundred thousand in 1970. In 1973 the two halves of modern Istanbul were joined by the Bosporus Bridge, which elegantly stretches across two continents. By 1980, even the historical core had become a smoggy, sooty traffic jam of honking cars, buses, taxis, and *dolmuşes* (minibuses).

The rapid expansion of the city within and without the old walls brought extraordinary changes to every aspect of life in Istanbul. The

sea, which had always been at the center of commerce and transporta﹐
tion, became merely a scenic backdrop. New industries were built along
the Golden Horn that further polluted the water and complicated the
ancient practice of fishing there. By the 1970s the smell of the Golden
Horn was so foul that it was advisable to hold one's nose while crossing
it. This was bad news for businesses nearby and for the many seafood
restaurants that had opened beneath the new modern Galata Bridge.

The ethnic character of Istanbul continued to change in the 1950s.
The tensions of the previous decade only increased, particularly after
the fight over Cyprus between the Greek and Turkish governments.
Greeks in Istanbul felt increasingly unsafe in their own city. The worst
of it came on September 6, 1955, when the Menderes government
staged a massive riot against the Greeks in Istanbul. After setting off a
bomb in the Turkish consulate in Thessalonica (the birthplace of
Atatürk) to rile the mobs, government operatives distributed hammers
and shovels and urged the crowd to go after the homes and business of
their Greek neighbors. The police watched approvingly. The riots be﹐
gan at Taksim and spread out across Pera (Beyoğlu). Particularly hard
hit were the rows of Greek shops on İstiklal Caddesi, the old Grande
Rue de Pera. The destruction was near total: 5,600 homes, churches, or
businesses were damaged. Many Greeks and some Armenians were
beaten and about a dozen were killed. Eventually the government im﹐
posed martial law on Istanbul. With their livelihoods in shambles and
the hatred of their Turkish neighbors starkly evident, the Greeks of the
city, whose ancestors had founded it twenty﹐six centuries earlier, began
leaving for good. By 1964 there were fewer than fifty thousand Greeks
in Istanbul. A decade later, there would be only a few thousand. Today
the aged Greek population in Istanbul continues to decline to extinc﹐
tion. The city, like the nation, has become Turkish.

The remainder of the history of Constantinople in the twentieth
century can be summed up in one word: expansion. Beginning with the
Menderes government and continuing during the military coups and
subsequent governments, Istanbul was promoted as the country's great
economic engine—a massive megalopolis in a country of small towns.
Consistently during the second half of the twentieth century, Istanbul
has produced 40 percent or more of the economic output of the entire

country. This has led to the dramatic growth of the city's physical space and the explosion in its population. In 2015 the metropolitan area of Istanbul was more than twenty times larger than the great walled city of the caesars and sultans. In 1950 the population of Istanbul was roughly 1 million people. By 1960 it had grown to 1.8 million. In 1980 the total was 5 million. Sometime around 1995, Istanbul reclaimed its distinction of being the most populated city in Europe, surpassing London's 8 million. In 2015 it became the fifth-largest city in the world, with a population approaching 15 million.

This extraordinary growth is driven by two main factors: the city's ever-closer integration into the world economy, and the abysmal state of Turkey's rural peasants, particularly in the eastern provinces. For decades these dynamics have drawn poorly educated rural peasants to the big city with the promise of good jobs and modern living. That in itself, however, would not be enough to account for the rapidity of the growth. That comes from a unique structure: the *gecekondu*.

Literally "built in one night," the *gecekondu* was a one- or two-room dwelling illegally constructed on the outskirts of Istanbul after World War II. These were not shanties of the sort one might find in South America. The squatters built regular wooden houses, though of poor quality. Since many of the squatters came from the same rural villages, they would often build their houses near to one another, thus creating a sea of *gecekondu* villages to the west of Istanbul. Since there were jobs for them in the city's growing industries, the government would periodically help improve the villages, and on several occasions offered amnesty, incorporating the *gecekondu* districts directly into the city. This led to additional squatter villages as more rural people rushed to Istanbul to take advantage of the situation. *Gecekondular* even sprang up in posh areas of the city, although those were eventually torn down. The *gecekondu* villages lacked running water, electricity, and sewers. Even so, they were still better than rural peasant life. And income in Istanbul was two to three times greater than the national average. Soon a regular pattern set in, which still largely continues: a *gecekondu* district would grow in size; the government, responding to health concerns and recognizing the inhabitants as potential voters, would eventually bring utilities and streets and amnesty. The pattern became so regular that real estate speculators would invest in the process, transforming the one-room *gecekondu* into the four-story apartment block, illegally built and ready for immediate occupancy. Today approximately 60 percent of Istanbul's population lives in *gecekondu* districts.

How the city's population moved around was another problem. Tramways and subways were built haphazardly while the roadways clogged amid a torrent of cars and buses. The greatest bottleneck was the Bosporus itself, as the growing city brought greater pressure on the waterway that runs through it. Another bridge farther up the straits and increased ferries were insufficient. By 2013, more than two million people were crossing the Bosporus daily. A major plan to build a high-speed rail tunnel under the Bosporus and connect it to the subway at Yenikapı began in 2004, but immediately hit a snag. The problem with subways in the old city is that virtually anywhere one digs, relics of antiquity will appear. Since the entire old city was designated a UNESCO World Heritage site in 1985, coming across a buried building means delays. That is why the planners chose Yenikapı as the new subway node. It is a new area of Istanbul, created by the modern filling in of the Byzantine Port of Theodosius—a place where there could be no ruins. As the digging began, though, the engineers were surprised to find something after all: shipwrecks. Between 2005 and 2013, excavations at Yenikapı discovered thirty-seven perfectly preserved vessels dating from the fifth to the eleventh centuries. These were studied and preserved, and many of them can now be seen in the Archaeological Museums. Below the Byzantine seabed, the archaeologists then found something even more surprising: During the Ice Age, the sea level was lower at Istanbul, making the Byzantine harbor dry land. Human settlements dating back to around 6000 BC were uncovered, the earliest ever found in the region. The delay was irritating, but worth it for the discoveries it allowed. The new tunnel opened in 2014, transporting passengers from one side of the Bosporus to the other in four minutes.

Conditions in the ever-expanding urban sprawl are at stark variance with the extraordinary wealth and sophistication of a few districts of the city. Taksim and its nearby areas, with their European feel and green parks, were quickly enhanced by the skyscrapers of luxury hotels and international businesses. Tourism was always a source of income in

Istanbul, but during the first decade of the twenty-first century much more was done to attract well-heeled visitors from the United States and Asia. The closing of Golden Horn industries banished the stink, and new parks along the shoreline beautified the ancient harbor. The historical core was spruced up with green spaces and fountains in Sultanahmet Park. The greatest change in the older parts of the city was the selective closing of streets near Hagia Sophia and Sultanahmet. This had the effect of banishing the noise and smell of the traffic and restoring some measure of serenity, particularly in the evenings. Likewise, across the Golden Horn, İstiklal Caddesi was turned into a pedestrian walkway serviced by chic restaurants, noisy bars, and cafés/bookshops. The "French Quarter" in Cezayir Sokaği opened in 2004, with its winding streets packed with trendy establishments offering the feel of a Pera that disappeared more than a century earlier.

All these modern amusements were supported by an astonishingly large and still growing contemporary art scene in Istanbul. Copying the Venetians who once called Constantinople home, the Istanbul Foundation for Culture and Arts opened the first Biennial art fair in 1987. It was later succeeded by the Contemporary Istanbul festival, which brought artists from around the world to display their creations. Another event, the Istanbul Art Fair, draws more than four hundred thousand visitors yearly. There are today more than two hundred commercial galleries in Istanbul, almost all of them in the old European areas of Galata/Pera.

This sharp turn toward the West in the older parts of Istanbul was balanced politically in Turkey by the rural dwellers moving into the suburbs, and by those they left behind in the Anatolian heartland. In the countryside, Istanbul tends to be seen as one giant Gomorrah. This was the view of the Justice and Development (AK) Party, which took over the government in Ankara in 2002. Its leader, Recep Tayyip Erdoğan, had been mayor of Istanbul in the 1990s and came to national power when his party took over parliament in 2002. Erdoğan grew up in the Kasımpaşa area of Istanbul, a conservative, working-class section of Beyoğlu, north of the Golden Horn. His rise to power would in many ways challenge the Kemalist model that had long ago cast Istanbul as a symbol of a backward Ottoman past. Erdoğan embraced not only

Istanbul, but also the past. In little more than a decade, he would be, come the most powerful prime minister in Turkish history. He had plans for Istanbul.

Like many in his neighborhood, young Erdoğan attended a religious school before becoming active in an Islamist movement called Millî Görüş. While it was no Muslim Brotherhood, Millî Görüş did advocate for closer ties between Islam and the government of Turkey. It chafed at Atatürk's strict secularism and was generally suspicious of Western governments. As Istanbul attracted ever-greater numbers of provincials, a man with Erdoğan's convictions and political skills was in a position to rise. In 1994 he was elected mayor of the city, which sounds more powerful than it is. Because of Atatürk's reforms, virtually all real authority resides in Ankara. Still, Erdoğan and his supporters began paving the way for future victories, supporting Istanbul's immigrants and building additional *gecekondu* districts. Naturally there were tensions with the central government. In the late 1990s, Erdoğan was briefly jailed for re, citing an Islamist poem in public. That experience seems to have led him to change his political strategy. He began giving speeches more in line with Turkey's strong desire to win acceptance into the European Union. He outlined a pro-business policy that he claimed would dra, matically boost the country's economy, making it not a supplicant but an equal partner with the West. As for his Islamist cultural agenda, he reframed it as a question of religious liberty and basic tolerance.

It was a winning combination. Erdoğan's new message won the approval of revered imam Fethullah Gülen, whose vast international network of schools and supporters boosted Erdoğan to national prominence. His followers, known as Gulenists, embrace a cultural Islam that seeks engagement with the West. They are strictly nonviolent, unfailingly pro-business, and strongly patriotic. Gulenists had been establishing themselves in Istanbul's police force and in the prosecuting offices for years before they partnered with Erdoğan and his new AK Party. After his election, Erdoğan began a widespread reform of Turkish law, bring, ing it into conformance with the European Union, but also increasing the opportunities for foreign investment. The result was a massive in, flux of foreign wealth, which Erdoğan augmented with extensive infra, structure projects and other constructions across the country. The new skyscrapers, malls, bridges, and luxury apartments that sprang up across Istanbul became a visible symbol of Erdoğan's economic policy. Between 2002 and 2015, more than $600 billion was spent on government-supported construction projects, with one-third of that coming directly from the treasury. These structures literally changed the skyline of Istanbul, weaving ultramodern spires into a panorama of minarets.

But these were only the more mundane of Erdoğan's plans for Istanbul. Also on the drawing board were a variety of megaconstructions that Erdoğan believed would place the city once more at the crossroads of the world. These were, in his own words, the "crazy projects." In 2010 he announced the construction of a third suspension bridge accommodating a motorway and railroad line across the Bosporus about an hour's drive north of Istanbul. The impressive structure, which opened in 2015, is the largest road/rail suspension bridge in the world. Like Erdoğan himself, however, it was controversial from the start. Its construction required the elimination of forests the size of Manhattan, which not only were important habitats but also formed part of the city's aquifer. When he was mayor, Erdoğan had called plans for a third bridge the "murder" of Istanbul. Now they were its salvation. Erdoğan provocatively named the bridge after Sultan Selim I "the Grim," the terror of the West and the first Ottoman caliph of Islam.

The bridge's real purpose is understandable when considered alongside the other two "crazy projects," which at this writing are still under development. The first is the construction of a third international airport about twenty miles northwest of Istanbul. After its completion, the new airport will have six runways stretching across thirty square miles and could service 150 million passengers per year. In terms of size and activity, it would therefore become the largest airport in the world, dwarfing London's Heathrow and Atlanta's Hartsfield-Jackson. Construction has, however, experienced a number of delays, chief of which is related to the third project of craziness: the Istanbul Canal. This last endeavor is in every way the largest. The plan is to dig a quarter-mile-wide canal on the European side (west) of Istanbul stretching twenty-seven miles from the Black Sea to the Sea of Marmara, thus effectively turning much of the Istanbul area into an island. The canal, which would provide quicker transportation than the Bosporus for those willing to pay, would be lined with parks, villas, high-end residences, and businesses. Funds to begin the project have been slow in coming, however. And because the soil from the canal excavation was slated to be used as landfill for the nearby airport construction, both projects have stalled.

Environmentalists have sharply criticized the projects for the widespread deforestation they require. It is also not clear that there is any need for another airport in Istanbul, particularly one so large. As for the canal, which some are calling a "second Bosporus," scientists have warned that it would lower the water levels of the Black Sea and starve the Sea of Marmara of oxygen, leading to a massive die-off of sea creatures and a degradation of the environment.

Erdoğan's pro-Istanbul approach won him many supporters in the city, despite his poorly hidden Islamist agenda. Although secularists often criticized him for selling out the legacy of Atatürk, the extraordinary boom in Turkey's economy made it difficult to argue with his policies. With prosperity, Erdoğan brought Islam further into the mainstream of city life. It is seldom overt, though. A number of Byzantine church ruins in Istanbul were reconstructed as mosques. New mega-mosques were planned in Istanbul's suburbs. Stricter regulations on the sale of alcohol at streetside restaurants were instituted. The ban on headscarves for women at the University of Istanbul was revoked. Members of the AK Party have repeatedly discussed turning Hagia Sophia back into a mosque. Indeed, demonstrations calling for the restoration erupted outside the ancient structure in 2014 and 2015, and are likely to continue.

In 2013, Erdoğan announced that in Taksim Square, at the center of the Westernized areas of cosmopolitan Istanbul, a new mall would be built in the style of an Ottoman military barracks that once stood there. This latest reference to the Ottoman past seemed an affront to a neighborhood that did not vote for the AK Party and generally opposed Erdoğan. Even worse, it would mean the destruction of the French-style Gezi Park. Spontaneous protests erupted, which were brutally put down by the police. The violence, in turn, captured international attention, which fed the fire of anger even more. For the next nineteen days, thousands of protestors occupied the park, while riots and marches continued throughout the summer of 2013.

The international fallout from the Taksim protests led to a break between Erdoğan and his Gulenist supporters. The Gulenists had already been worried about the increasingly dictatorial power Erdoğan wielded, fearing that it would raise the ire of the West. Gulenists seek to win hearts and minds through patient service. Erdoğan was clearly interested in a more direct approach. The breach soon became evident. Erdoğan began closing Gulenist schools in Istanbul, which were a major source of recruitment for the movement. Gulenist prosecutors then announced widespread corruption charges at high levels of Erdoğan's government, most regarding kickbacks and bribes in construction bids and contracts. Erdoğan's son was among those accused. Erdoğan retaliated by declaring the Gulenists to be a "parallel state," and began purging thousands of them from the police forces and replacing them as corruption prosecutors. After accusing the Gulenists of treason, Erdoğan's government in October 2015 began seizing media outlets and banks with ties to the group. In March 2016, government police in Istanbul stormed the offices of Zaman, the publisher of the largest newspaper in Turkey, which had reported on the corruption investigations, which Erdoğan characterized as a coup attempt. A real coup was launched on July 15, 2016, when portions of the military seized roads, bridges, and other locations in Istanbul and Ankara. Erdoğan called on the Turkish people to defend the government, and they did. With its large Islamist population, Istanbul erupted in angry protests against the rebels. But the Islamists were joined by many of Istanbul's secularists, who opposed the use of violence in a political struggle. Erdoğan, of course, blamed the failed coup on the Gulenists and ordered the arrests of thousands of them. He declared July 15 to be a national holiday, for it was, he said, the founding of a "New Turkey," one that embraced its modern democracy as closely as its Islamic, Ottoman past.

As of this writing, tensions and uncertainties continue, but they do not seem to be slowing down Erdoğan or his projects. Although he was elected president of Turkey in 2014, in many ways he remains the mayor of Istanbul.

The feuds and unrest that ripple across modern Istanbul find endless echoes across the city's centuries. Commerce, too, has been at the city's core since the first Megaran merchants sailed into the Golden Horn hoping to capitalize on the Black Sea trade. Set as it is between worlds, Istanbul has been a meeting place and a battlefield for cultures since the Persian general Megabazus first joked about its blind neighbors. That is what makes it as compelling today as it was across the millennia. Too important to abandon, too strategic to avoid, too beautiful to resist, Istanbul long drew to it the peoples of the Mediterranean, muddled them together in its streets and markets, and produced a community that is ever changing. Its strength was never solely in its mighty walls or its well-trained militaries, but in the determination of its inhabitants to hold firm to it no matter the cost. It is hardly surprising, then, that its two world-spanning empires ended their days on the Bosporus, still clinging to the City until that, too, was taken from them.

Modern Istanbul no longer rules an empire, although it still towers over all other cities in Europe and the Middle East. Yet it has never been sheer size that has placed it apart. Since its founding on a water-way coursing between two seas and two continents, Istanbul has been suspended between diverse peoples, languages, religions, and ideas. It has been, and remains, a membrane stretched across horizons, balancing opposing forces outside while drawing liberally from them to remake itself again and again. Istanbul remains fascinating not just because it is old, or big, or rich, but because it is exquisitely unique, embracing the future while holding lovingly on to the past. Founded on the frontiers of its age, it remains there today—still a city at the crossroads of the world.

ACKNOWLEDGMENTS

It was my fascination with Istanbul that led to my career as a profes‧ sional historian, and enriched it at every turn. It is difficult, then, to thank all of those who deserve it, who have helped make possible a project stretching across more than two decades. Legions of teachers, colleagues, archivists, and curators have aided my historical research and communities of friends and family have supported me along the way. But a few of those most directly involved in this book really should be thanked.

I am eternally grateful to my old mentor, the late Donald E. Queller, who took a chance on a doctoral student with passion for his subject, but little else. It was his work on the Fourth Crusade that introduced me to medieval Constantinople, and it was under his guidance that I learned to love it and Venice. The late Ronald C. Jennings, a specialist in Ottoman history who was another of my graduate school teachers, introduced me to the study of the topography of the medieval city and made it possible for me to return to Istanbul to conduct my studies. The eminent historian of Byzantine architecture Robert Ousterhout, now at the University of Pennsylvania, helped me both in my early days as a professor and also in Istanbul. The opportunity he afforded me to climb onto the domed roof of the monastery church of Pantocrator and gaze across the City had a profound effect on my understanding of space in Constantinople's long history. I must also thank the distin‧ guished historians of medieval Islam Carole Hillenbrand and Robert Hillenbrand, both of the University of Edinburgh and St Andrews Uni‧ versity, for their extremely generous help over the years. They are the clearest example one can find of the maxim that the best scholars are also the kindest people.

I am thankful to my financial benefactors. Research in Istanbul,

Acknowledgments

Venice, and elsewhere in Turkey that contributed to this project was supported by the John Simon Guggenheim Memorial Foundation, the American Council of Learned Societies, the Gladys Krieble Delmas Foundation, and the Mellon Faculty Development Fund at Saint Louis University. I must also thank my editor at Viking, Melanie Tortoroli, who with a light touch but boundless enthusiasm helped to enliven the prose and quicken the pace of a manuscript often a bit too enamored with its subject. And as always, I am grateful to my agent, John Thornton, ever in my corner.

I could never forget to thank my wife, Page, and my daughters, Helena and Melinda. Over the past twenty-some years they have traveled to so many faraway locations, not because they were exotic, or beautiful, or even very interesting (at least, to them), but simply because my work was in the local archives, libraries, field sites, or institutes. Nevertheless, with a joyful demeanor they made each place their own. It was a delicious pleasure to introduce them to Istanbul, which quickly captivated them just as it has generations before. It is difficult not to love historical research when accompanied by such extraordinary women.

NOTES

xv: "inhabit it or rebuild it": Pierre Gilles, *The Antiquities of Constantinople*, trans. John Ball, ed. Ronald G. Musto (New York: Italica, 1988), xiv.

1: "merchant-captains drunk": Menander, *The Flute Girl* (fragments), in *The Fragments of Attic Comedy*, ed. and trans. J. M. Edmonds (Leiden: Brill, 1957), 2:567.

27: "her sweet leaves": Moero of Byzantion, in *The Greek Anthology*, vol. 1, trans. W. R. Paton (Cambridge, Mass.: Harvard University Press, 1916): 6:119.

38: "under their own laws": Livy, *History of Rome*, vol. 9, trans. Evan T. Sage (Cambridge, Mass.: Harvard University Press, 1935), 32:33. Translation mine.

38: "law might prevail": Ibid. 32:33.

45: "transport of supplies": Tacitus, *Annals*, vol. 4, trans. John Jackson (Cambridge, Mass.: Harvard University Press, 1937), 62.

47: "passed it on": Dio Cassius, *Roman History*, trans. Earnest Cary (Cambridge, Mass.: Harvard University Press, 1927), Epitome of Book 75.

50: "embarrassing to enemies": Ibid.

52: "than it was in fact": Ibid.

59: "throughout the world": Robert of Clari, *The Conquest of Constantinople*, trans. Edgar Holmes McNeal (New York: Columbia University Press, 1936), 101.

59: "Health it brings!": Edwin A. Grosvenor, *The Hippodrome of Constantinople and Its Still Existing Monuments* (London: Sir Joseph Causton and Sons, 1889), 34.

92: "seductive tunes": John Chrysostom, *Sermon on the Hippodrome and Theatre*, in David M. Gwynn, *Christianity in the Later Roman Empire: A Sourcebook* (London: Bloomsbury, 2014), 91.

110: "'glorious death shroud'": Procopius, *History of the Wars*, 1:24. Translation mine.

115: "He has chosen": Procopius, *The Buildings*, in William Richard Lethaby and Harold Swainson, *The Church of Sancta Sophia* (New York: Macmillan, 1894), 27.

172: "extravagant preparations": Nicetas Choniates, *O City of Byzantium: Annals of Niketas Choniates*, trans. Harry J. Magoulias (Detroit: Wayne State University Press, 1984), 177.

173: "even by Byzantine standards": Donald M. Nicol, *Byzantium and Venice: A Study in Diplomatic and Cultural Relations* (Cambridge: Cambridge University Press, 1988), 110.

174: "whose cut was deeper": Nicetas Choniates, *O City of Byzantium*, 193.

185: "would not believe it": Robert de Clari, *The Conquest of Constantinople*, 101.

190: "ponder over it": Ibid., 102–14.

191: "before those flames": Nicetas Choniates, *O City of Byzantium*, 303.

192: "they could do nothing": Geoffrey de Villehardouin, *La Conquête de Constantinople*, ed. E. Faral (Paris: Société d'édition "les Belles lettres"), sec. 203. Translation mine.

198: "medicine of salvation": Ibid., 313.

203: "dinner or dessert": Ibid., 314.

204: "imperial guard": Ibid.

205: "beginning with their carts": Ibid.

205: "murderous men?": Ibid.

207: "sacred sacrilege": Gunther of Pairis, *The Capture of Constantinople*, ed. and trans., Alfred J. Andrea (Philadelphia: University of Pennsylvania Press, 1997), 109–11.

211: "their adoring mother": Nicetas Choniates, *O City of Byzantium*, 323–25.

237: "but Escomboli": Ruy González de Clavijo, *Narrative of the Embassy*, trans. Clements R. Markham (London: Hakluyt Society, 1859), 46.

237: "magnificence of the bases": Manuel Chrysolorus, *Epist. 1*, in Cyril Mango, *The Art of the Byzantine Empire, 312–1453* (New York: Prentice Hall, 1972), 250–51.

249: "capital of the world": *The Turkish Letters of Ogier Ghiselin de Busbecq*, trans. Edward Seymour Forster (Baton Rouge: Louisiana State University Press, 2005), 34.

249: "empire of the world!": M. Adolphe Thiers, *History of the Consulate and the Empire of France Under Napoleon*, trans. D. F. Campbell and H. W. Herbert (Philadelphia: Claxton, Remsen, and Haffelfinger, 1879), 2:326.

272: "who smiles on and on": *Nightingales and Pleasure Gardens: Turkish Love Poems*, ed. and trans. Talat S. Halman (Syracuse: Syracuse University Press, 2005), 46.

275: "called her *ziadi*, 'witch'": Luigi Bassano, *I costume et i modi particolari della vita de' Turchi*, ed. Franz Babinger (Munich: Hueber, 1963), 44. Translation mine.

281: "dome of Hagia Sophia": Sheila S. Blair and Jonathan M. Bloom, *The Art and Architecture of Islam, 1250–1800* (New Haven: Yale University Press, 1994), 226.

295: "by the said gate": *The Travels of Peter Mundy in Europe and Asia, 1608–1667*, ed. and trans. R. C. Temple (London: Hakluyt Society, 1907), 32.

297: "that part of the citty": *The Negotiations of Sir Thomas Roe*, ed. S. Richardson (London: Richardson, 1740), 512.

298: "open myself to him": *Gesta Regis Henrici Secundi*, ed. W. Stubbs (London: Rolls Series, 1857), 2:52. Translation mine.

298: "to the Seven Towers": Lady Mary Wortley Montagu, *Complete Letters* (Cambridge: Clarendon, 1965), 1:365.

298: "downfall of a great empire": F. C. H. L. Pouqueville, *Travels in Greece and Turkey* (London: Richard Phillips, 1820), 119.

301: "deceiveth the expectation": George Sandys, *Travailles* (London: np, 1658), 27.

Notes

301: "stinking foule within": William Lithgow, *The Totall Discourse of the Rare Adventures and Painefull Peregrinations* (Glasgow: James MacLehose, 1906), 124.

301: "not oftener": Mark Twain, *The Innocents Abroad* (Hartford: American Publishing, 1875), 358.

303: "chopping down trees": Thomas F. Madden, "The Serpent Column of Delphi in Constantinople: Placement, Purposes, and Mutilations," *Byzantine and Modern Greek Studies* 16 (1992): 111–45.

303: "generally of that country": Lady Mary Wortley Montagu, *Letter 41*, in *The London Magazine*, January 1763, 415.

308: "enemies of his enemies": Gerard Chailiand and Sophie Mouseset, *L'héritage occidental* (Paris: Odile Jacob, 2002), 973.

308: "banner of Satan": Bernard Lewis, *A Middle East Mosaic* (New York: Random House, 2000), 40–41.

339: "heart of every Turk": Mustafa Kemal, in *Constantinople: City of the World's Desire, 1453–1924* (London: St. Martin's, 1996).

FURTHER READING

The number of historical studies on Byzantion/Constantinople/Istanbul is vast, yet nearly all are fairly technical scholarly works. This list includes complete books written in Western languages that could be of interest to those seeking to know more about some aspect of the city's history. For more specialized studies, see the notes and bibliographies in the books listed here.

GENERAL HISTORIES

Freely, John. *Istanbul: The Imperial City.* New York: Viking, 1996.

Grosvenor, Edwin A. *Constantinople.* Boston: Roberts Brothers, 1895.

Kuban, Doğan. *Istanbul: An Urban History.* Istanbul: Türkiye Bankası, 2010.

Rice, David Talbot. *Constantinople: From Byzantium to Istanbul.* New York: Stein and Day, 1965.

Yerasimos, Stéphane. *Constantinople: Istanbul's Historical Heritage.* Trans. by Sally M. Schreiber, Uta Hoffmann, Ellen Loeffler. Potsdam: H. F. Ullmann, 2012.

BYZANTINE CONSTANTINOPLE

Angold, Michael. *The Fourth Crusade: Event and Context.* London: Longman, 2003.

Bassett, Sarah. *The Urban Image of Late Antique Constantinople.* Cambridge: Cambridge University Press, 2004.

Cameron, Alan. *Circus Factions: Blues and Greens at Rome and Byzantium.* Cambridge: Clarendon Press, 1976.

——. *Porphyrius the Charioteer.* Oxford: Oxford University Press, 1973.

Dagron, Gilbert. *Constantinople imaginaire.* Paris: Presses Universitaires de France, 1984.

——. *L'hippodrome de Constantinople: Jeux, people et politique.* Paris: Gallimard, 2011.

——. *Naissance d'une capitale: Constantinople et ses institutions de 330 à 451.* Paris: Presses Universitaires de France, 1974.

Downey, Glanville. *Constantinople in the Age of Justinian.* Norman: University of Oklahoma Press, 1960.

Further Reading

Ducellier, Alain, and Michel Balard, eds. *Constantinople, 1054–1261*. Paris: Éditions Autrement, 1996.

Grig, Lucy, and Gavin Kelly, eds. *Two Romes: Rome and Constantinople in Late Antiquity*. Oxford: Oxford University Press, 2012.

Haldon, John F. *Byzantium in the Seventh Century: The Transformation of a Culture*. Cambridge: Cambridge University Press, 1990.

Harris, Jonathan. *Constantinople: Capital of Byzantium*. London: Continuum, 2007.

Hatlie, Peter. *The Monks and Monasteries of Constantinople, ca. 350–850*. Cambridge: Cambridge University Press, 2007.

Jenkins, Romilly. *Byzantium: The Imperial Centuries, AD 610–1071*. London: Weidenfeld and Nicholson, 1966.

Laiou, Angeliki E. *Constantinople and the Latins*. Cambridge, Mass.: Harvard University Press, 1972.

Mango, Cyril. *Le développement urbain de Constantinople (IVe–VIIe siècles)*. Paris: De Boccard, 1985.

Mango, Cyril, and Gilbert Dagron, eds. *Constantinople and Its Hinterland*. Aldershot: Variorum, 1993.

Miller, Dean A. *Imperial Constantinople*. New York: John Wiley and Sons, 1969.

Necipoğlu, Nevra, ed. *Byzantine Constantinople: Monuments, Topography and Everyday Life*. Leiden: Brill, 2001.

Nicol, Donald M. *The Immortal Emperor: The Life and Legend of Constantine Palaiologos, Last Emperor of the Romans*. Cambridge: Cambridge University Press, 1992.

Ousterhout, Robert. *Master Builders of Byzantium*. 2nd ed. Philadelphia: University of Pennsylvania Museum Publications, 2008.

Philippides, Marios, and Walter K. Hanak. *The Siege and the Fall of Constantinople in 1453*. Aldershot: Ashgate, 2011.

Queller, Donald E., and Thomas F. Madden. *The Fourth Crusade: The Conquest of Constantinople*. 2nd ed. Philadelphia: University of Pennsylvania Press, 1997.

Runciman, Steven. *The Fall of Constantinople, 1453*. Cambridge: Cambridge University Press, 1965.

Treadgold, Warren. *A History of the Byzantine State and Society*. Palo Alto: Stanford University Press, 1997.

Ottoman Constantinople

And, Metin. *Istanbul in the Sixteenth Century*. Istanbul: Akbank, 1994.

Babinger, Franz. *Mehmed the Conqueror and His Time*. Princeton: Princeton University Press, 1978.

Boyar, Ebru, and Kate Fleet. *A Social History of Ottoman Istanbul*. Cambridge: Cambridge University Press, 2010.

Çelik, Zeynep. *The Remaking of Istanbul: Portrait of an Ottoman City in the Nineteenth Century*. Seattle: University of Washington Press, 1986.

Criss, Nur Bilge. *Istanbul Under Allied Occupation, 1918–1923*. Leiden: Brill, 1999.

Eldem, Edhem. *French Trade in Istanbul in the Eighteenth Century*. Leiden: Brill, 1999.

Further Reading

Eldem, Edhem, Daniel Goffman, and Bruce Alan Masters. *The Ottoman City Between East and West: Aleppo, Izmir, and Istanbul*. Cambridge: Cambridge University Press, 1999.

Hamadeh, Shirine. *The City's Pleasures: Istanbul in the Eighteenth Century*. Seattle: University of Washington Press, 2007.

Kafescioğlu, Çiğdem. *Constantinopolis/Istanbul: Cultural Encounter, Imperial Vision, and the Construction of the Ottoman Capital*. College Park: Pennsylvania State University Press, 2009.

Lewis, Bernard. *Istanbul and the Civilization of the Ottoman Empire*. Norman: University of Oklahoma, 1963.

Mansel, Philip. *Constantinople: City of the World's Desire, 1453–1924*. London: St. Martin's Press, 1996.

Necipoğlu, Gülru. *Architecture, Ceremonial, and Power: The Topkapi Palace in the Fifteenth and Sixteenth Centuries*. Cambridge, Mass.: MIT Press, 1991.

Rogan, Eugene. *The Fall of the Ottomans: The Great War in the Middle East*. New York: Basic Books, 2015.

Rozen, Minna. *A History of the Jewish Community in Istanbul: The Formative Years, 1453–1566*. Leiden: Brill, 2002.

Runciman, Steven. *The Great Church in Captivity*. Cambridge: Cambridge University Press, 1968.

Zarinebaf, Fariba. *Crime and Punishment in Istanbul, 1700–1800*. Berkeley: University of California Press, 2010.

Modern Istanbul

Göktürk, Deniz, Levent Soysal, and İpek Türeli. *Orienting Istanbul: Cultural Capital of Europe?* New York: Routledge, 2010.

Gül, Murat. *The Emergence of Modern Istanbul: Transformation and Modernisation of a City*. New York: I. B. Taurus, 2009.

Keyder, Çaglar, ed. *Istanbul: Between the Global and the Local*. Lanham: Rowman and Littlefield, 1999.

King, Charles. *Midnight at the Pera Palace: The Birth of Modern Istanbul*. New York: W. W. Norton and Co., 2014.

Lewis, Bernard. *The Emergence of Modern Turkey*. 2nd ed. Oxford: Oxford University Press, 1968.

Nelson, Robert S. *Hagia Sophia, 1850–1950: Holy Wisdom, Modern Monument*. Chicago: University of Chicago Press, 2004.

Neuwirth, Robert. *Shadow Cities: A Billion Squatters—A New Urban World*. New York: Routledge, 2005.

Rutz, Henry J., and Erol M. Balkan. *Reproducing Class: Education, Neoliberalism, and the Rise of the New Middle Class in Istanbul*. New York: Berghahn Books, 2009.

Vryonis, Speros. *The Mechanism of Catastrophe: The Turkish Pogrom of September 6–7, 1955, and the Destruction of the Greek Community of Istanbul*. New York: Greekworks, 2005.

White, Jenny B. *Islamist Mobilization in Turkey: A Study in Vernacular Politics*. Seattle: University of Washington Press, 2002.

Further Reading

Architecture and Archaeology

Barillari, Diana, and Ezio Godoli. *Istanbul 1900: Art Nouveau Architecture and Interiors.* New York: Rizzoli, 1996.

Casson, Stanley, et al. *Preliminary Report upon the Excavations Carried Out in the Hippodrome of Constantinople in 1927.* London: British Academy, 1928.

————. *Second Report upon the Excavations Carried Out in the Hippodrome of Constantinople in 1928.* London: British Academy, 1929.

Dark, Ken, and Ferudun Özgümüş. *Constantinople: Archaeology of a Byzantine Megapolis.* Oxford: Oxbow Books, 2013.

Ebersolt, Jean. *Le grand palais de Constantinople.* Paris: Ernest Leroux, 1910.

Freely, John, and Ahmet S. Çakmak. *Byzantine Monuments of Istanbul.* Cambridge: Cambridge University Press, 2004.

Goodwin, Godfrey. *A History of Ottoman Architecture.* Baltimore: Johns Hopkins University Press, 1971.

Guilland, Rodolphe. *Études de topographie de Constantinople byzantine.* Berlin-Amsterdam: Adolf Hakkert, 1969.

Harrison, Martin. *A Temple for Byzantium: The Discovery and Excavation of Anicia Juliana's Palace Church in Istanbul.* Austin: University of Texas Press, 1989.

Janin, Raymond. *Constantinople byzantine: Développement urbain et répertoire topographique.* 2nd ed. Paris: Institut Français d'Études Byzantines, 1964.

Mainstone, Rowland J. *Hagia Sophia: Architecture, Structure, and Liturgy of Justinian's Great Church.* London: Thames and Hudson, 1988.

Mango, Cyril. *The Brazen House: A Study of the Vestibule of the Imperial Palace of Constantinople.* Copenhagen: Munksgaard, 1959.

Marinis, Vasileios. *Architecture and Ritual in the Churches of Constantinople, Ninth to Fifteenth Centuries.* Cambridge: Cambridge University Press, 2014.

Mark, Robert, and Ahmet S. Çakmak, eds. *The Hagia Sophia: From the Age of Justinian to the Present.* Cambridge: Cambridge University Press, 1992.

Matthews, Henry. *Mosques of Istanbul.* New York: Scala, 2010.

Matthews, Thomas F. *The Early Churches of Constantinople.* College Park: Pennsylvania State University Press, 1971–77.

Müller-Wiener, Wolfgang. *Bildlexikon zur Topographie Istanbuls.* Tübingen: Ernst Wasmuth, 1977.

Ousterhout, Robert G. *The Architecture of the Kariye Camii in Istanbul.* Washington, D.C.: Dumbarton Oaks, 1987.

Striker, Cecil L. *The Myrelaion (Bodrum Camii) in Istanbul.* Princeton: Princeton University Press, 1981.

Tsangadas, Byron C. P. *The Fortifications and Defense of Constantinople.* New York: Columbia University Press, 1980.

Van Millingen, Alexander. *Byzantine Churches in Constantinople: Their History and Architecture.* New York: Macmillan and Co., 1912.

————. *Byzantine Constantinople: The Walls of the City and Adjoining Historical Sites.* London: John Murray, 1899.

Yeomans, Richard. *The Art and Architecture of Ottoman Istanbul.* Reading: Garnet, 2012.

INDEX

Index

Index

Index

Index

Index

Index

Index